Law, Politics, and Birth Control

by
C. THOMAS DIENES

University of Illinois Press
URBANA   CHICAGO   LONDON

To

My Mother and My Wife

© 1972 by The Board of Trustees of the University of Illinois
Manufactured in the United States of America
Library of Congress Catalog Card No. 71-182195
ISBN 0-252-00200-8

Law, Politics, and Birth Control

Acknowledgments

Acknowledgments afford an author the opportunity to express his appreciation to the numerous individuals who assisted in the completion of his work. In this instance it would be impossible to express my gratitude to the great number of persons who gave willingly of their time and capabilities in Chicago, Evanston, New York, Albany, Boston, New Haven, Hartford, Houston, and Washington. There are, however, certain individuals and organizations who are deserving of special recognition in making the present book possible.

Because this study was originally undertaken while I was a Russell Sage Fellow in Law and the Social Sciences in the graduate political-science program at Northwestern University, my gratitude must first be directed to the Russell Sage Foundation. The foundation's activities in stimulating inquiry into the intersection of law and society and the relationship of law and the social sciences has permitted numerous scholars and students to pursue their commitment through research, study, and teaching; the present manuscript is one more product of that contribution.

The challenge to undertake this study as well as continual guidance during its early development is due to the efforts of my three mentors at Northwestern University: John E. Coons, now professor of law at the University of California, Berkeley, Victor A. Rosenblum, who has recently returned to Northwestern, and Richard D. Schwartz, now dean of the law school at the State University of New York at Buffalo. I want to take this opportunity to express my appreciation to Professor Rosenblum, who not only served as my graduate advisor but as a source of inspiration and as personal confidant during those trying years; to Professor Coons, who introduced me to the Russell Sage program and assisted me in so many ways during law school, graduate school, and professional career; and to Dean Schwartz, for the ingenuity and inspiration which contributed so vitally to the formative stages of the study, and for his continued interest and support. Behind them stood the other fellows of the Russell Sage program at Northwestern and the numerous members of the political-science faculty, whose assistance was so readily available.

The present study has been substantially revised and enlarged from the original graduate school product. And again, the assistance of others in reading and criticizing the resulting manuscript has proven invaluable. I want especially to express my gratitude to Michael Barkun, Herbert Jacob, Leonard Kaplan, Stuart Nagel, Harriet Pilpel, and Herbert Tillema for their special effort in this regard. The valuable editorial criticism and constant encouragement of Kerry Hoover, formerly of the University of Illinois Press, also deserves recognition. In the process of completing this manuscript I came to appreciate him not only as an editor but as a friend.

Data for the study had to be gathered from all of the cities mentioned above. Members and staff of the U.S. Congress and the state legislatures of Illinois, New York, and Massachusetts not only provided valuable material but gave of their extremely limited time to answer questions and supply insights that can be obtained only from those intimately involved in the action. Planned Parenthood—World Population and its local affiliates promptly responded to my requests for data, and its officers in many cities submitted to extensive interviews. Representatives of various religions (especially the Roman Catholic Church), physicians, the American Medical Association, officers of welfare agencies, and attorneys made their background knowledge available in spite of the fact that extremely sensitive matters were involved. I cannot list all of them here, but they are mentioned frequently throughout the footnotes where their contributions are recognized.

I also want to express my appreciation to faculty, students, and staff at American University and the University of Houston. On the numerous occasions when I have had to tap their resources, I have always received full cooperation. Valuable research assistance was provided in the case of Chapter Eight, dealing with late-breaking litigation, by Judy Catterton and Norman Sirak, students at American University, Washington College of Law. The agonizing task of completing the final manuscript was made far easier by the highly competent secretarial assistance of Mrs. Renate Long and Miss Kathleen Enzler of the American University law school staff.

Although I have dedicated this book in part to my mother, Florence

Dienes, that is a most inadequate expression of my feelings. Her love, encouragement, and assistance, not only in the completion of the book but through the years, deserve far more than a dedication. Anything that I do today is in large part a product of her very special efforts. Similarly, my brother Bob, my sister Florence, and my mother-in-law Elfrieda Clements know, I am sure, of my gratitude for their support and assistance.

Finally, and most important, I want to express my gratitude to my wonderful wife Peggy. It would be impossible to put into words the extent of her contribution to this book and to all my work. Not only has she served as editor-in-chief and typist, but she readily put aside her own work to assist in the successful completion of mine. Most important, she gave completely of herself—her love, support, and encouragement—and that cannot be expressed in words. But in the difficult months of research and writing, it provided the most valuable contribution to the successful completion of this study.

Contents

	Introduction	3
One:	The Origins of Comstockery	20
Two:	Early Reactions to Comstockery	49
Three:	Organization for Change: Origins of the Birth-Control Movement	74
Four:	Defeat and Victory in the Federal Forum	103
Five:	Repression and Defeat: Massachusetts and Connecticut	116
Six:	Modern Revisionist Efforts: Judicial Abstention and Response	148
Seven:	Modern Revisionist Efforts: Legislative Abstention and Response	184
Eight:	Modern Revisionist Efforts: A Judicial Epilogue	210
Nine:	The Dynamics of Change: Publicly Supported Birth Control	253
	Conclusion	304
	Appendixes	311
	Bibliography	335
	Index	367

Law, Politics, and Birth Control

Social change and changes in the law are constant and interacting processes, present to a considerable extent in all contemporary societies. . . . the study of these phenomena can contribute much to our understanding of the relationships between law and society and to the policy approach to law and law making.

Yehezkel Dror, "Law and Social Change," *Tulane Law Review*, XXXIII (June, 1959), 802.

Introduction

Through the centuries, men have grappled with the problems posed by their changing environment. In modern society this task takes on a new sense of urgency, as scientific and technological advances seem to occur in geometric progression. Recognized values become antiquated, archaic relics of a past that was recently the present; established institutions and social roles are rendered dysfunctional in the changed order and must adjust or be replaced. Society generally must face the task of providing mechanisms consistent with the social changes wrought by expanding technology or suffer the danger of a chaotic social order. But institutions arguably tend to change at a slower rate than their societal constituency—a phenomenon sociologists have termed "cultural lag."[1] Institutions, by the very fact that they embody established recognized modes of conduct, are conservators of the old order tending to resist change.

This same picture has been drawn for legal institutions. Law is seen as an impediment, a conservative force, which protects the established order against new interests demanding recognition. Like all social institutions, legal institutions are said to lag behind the changing social environment.[2] But is this a completely accurate evaluation of the function

---

[1] See, e.g., William F. Ogburn, *Social Change* (New York, 1966). See generally Derek J. D. Price, "Disease of Science," *Readings on Social Change*, ed. Wilbert E. Moore and Robert M. Cook (Englewood Cliffs, 1967), 49–68.

[2] Yehezkel Dror, "Law and Social Change," *Tulane Law Review*, XXXIII (June, 1959), 794, suggests that a lag between law and the social situation occurs "when there is more than a certain tension, when the law does not in fact answer the needs arising from major social changes or when social behavior and the sense of obligation generally felt towards legal norms significantly differs from the behavior required by law. In other words, while a certain difference between actual behavior and legally required behavior can be found in all societies, the concept of lag applies to law and social change in dynamic situations after either social change or changes in the law occur and no parallel changes and adjustment processes take place in law or society respectively." Dror adds that social change refers to changes

of law in our changing society? Is law necessarily an impediment to social change or can it be a mechanism for a regulated creative adjustment—can it assist in producing a changed environment that is not merely a facade for chaos and anarchy?

The present study probes these questions and the more general subject of the dynamics through which the legal system and, more particularly, courts and legislatures respond to the demands of a changing society. In this Introduction an attempt will be made to set forth the general outline of a framework for use in analyzing: (1) the process through which institutions interact in producing legal change; (2) the tools or capabilities available to these institutions in making their responses; and (3) the motivations and influences affecting not only decisions to act, but also the form that the action will take. In the chapters following the Introduction, the framework is more fully developed as it is applied to the general formulation of public policy regarding birth control.

While the substantive area of birth control was selected primarily because of the author's personal interest, it does provide an excellent example of a social problem which has severely challenged the ability of legal institutions to respond creatively to social change. Although we tend to think of birth control as a relatively modern practice, in reality its history dates back to primitive times. But only in the nineteenth century did its spread occasion a deliberate public policy making contraception per se a crime. Since then, the legal problems posed by the dissemination of artificial birth-control devices and information has produced a constant interplay of social pressures and legal policy-making at both the national and state levels.[3]

Courts and legislatures in the national jurisdiction and in New York, Connecticut, and Massachusetts have been constantly called upon to interact in fashioning legal policy, and their experience should provide an adequate basis for at least an initial evaluation of the usefulness of the framework. Developments in other states will be considered, but only as tangential to the primary inquiry. The major exception will occur

---

in the society as such, including the various social institutions, roles and status definitions, accepted ideologies, value patterns, pattern variables, and value profiles. In other words, the concept of social change refers to changes in social structure or in culture. *Ibid.*, 788.

[3] On the history of contraception see generally Norman E. Himes, *Medical History of Contraception* (Baltimore, 1936); Norman St. John-Stevas, *Birth Control and Public Policy* (Washington, 1964), 5-12; Peter Fryer, *The Birth Controllers* (New York, 1966).

in Chapter Nine, where the controversy in Illinois and Pennsylvania regarding publicly supported birth control will be of prime importance.

The study will encompass a time span of over a hundred years, stretching from the emergence of birth control as a social and legal problem in the early nineteenth century to the present fashioning of a policy for publicly supported fertility control. The focus will be on the activities of Anthony Comstock and his Puritan vice hunters in the Society for the Suppression of Vice as they waged their holy crusade against obscenity; the judicial martyrdom and legislative travails of the feminist reformer Margaret Sanger as she fought to tear down the legal and social barriers impeding the dissemination of family-planning services; the fervid resistance of the Roman Catholic Church to the birth-control movement and the changes within the Catholic "monolith"; and the gradual emasculation and eradication of the legal prohibitions against birth control in response to changing social needs and values. We will then turn to the modern family-planning movement designed to assure to the poverty sector the availability of fertility control; to the increasing concern over the consequences of population growth, especially environmental quality; and to the harbingers of a new period of turmoil involving population control.

The subject area, then, is well developed and developing; the courts and legislators have been, and continue to be, actively involved in adapting legal norms to changing social conditions. But before turning to the dynamics of birth-control policy-making, it is necessary that there be an initial understanding of the conceptual framework governing the inquiry.

INITIAL LEGAL RESPONSE

The Recommending Function:[4] *Promotion of Policy Alternatives*

It can be argued that there is recourse to the public forum only when a conflict generated by social change cannot be settled by private social devices, or when an interest seeks public recognition of a private

[4] The decision-making scheme used in this study is primarily that of Harold Lasswell, "The Decision-Process: Seven Categories of Functional Analysis," *Politics and Social Life*, ed. Nelson W. Polsby, Robert A. Dentler, and Paul A. Smith (Boston, 1963), 93–105, and Richard C. Snyder, "A Decision-Making Approach to the Study of Political Phenomena," *Approaches to the Study of Politics*, ed. Roland Young (Evanston, 1958), 3–38.

settlement in its favor.[5] Under these circumstances, the demand for action may be addressed to any of the legal forums—legislature, judiciary, executive, administrative agencies. However, we actually know very little about the decision to seek legal redress. There is need for both theory and data on the multiple input sources to the legal forums, on the conditions increasing the saliency of a particular institution, and on the strategies available for gaining access. Essentially this is the "communications" problem: how are needs produced by changing social conditions communicated to a particular legal decision-maker? Why is this particular forum chosen—out of necessity, for perceived political advantage, or for some other reason? What types of resources are needed and what types of disputes are deemed suitable to initiate intervention by one legal institution rather than another? These are only suggestive of the questions that must be answered for an evaluation of the recommending process; they are not so much concerned with whether a favorable decision will be secured as with who initiates action, how the action is initiated, and why a particular forum is chosen.

It can be suggested, for example, that in a change situation, legal response tends initially to be a product of judicial rather than legislative action.[6] *Legislative* response designed to meet a societal problem through a change in legal norms tends to occur

[5] See Henry M. Hart, Jr., and Albert M. Sacks, *The Legal Process: Basic Problems in the Making and Application of Law* (Cambridge, 1958), 43. Carl Auerbach also approaches law as being a forum for unresolved disputes and recognition of private settlement: "The recognition of a private sphere implies that many of the conflicting claims which different individuals and groups seek to satisfy will be adjusted privately. But an individual or group which is dissatisfied with the adjustment-decision reached privately must be able to resort to law for relief, just as the private decision-makers must be able to resort to law to enforce their decisions against non-conforming individuals and groups." "Law and Social Change in the United States," *University of California at Los Angeles Law Review*, VI (July, 1959), 517. See Philip Selznick, "Legal Institutions and Social Controls," *Vanderbilt Law Review*, XVII (Dec., 1963), 83.

[6] Hart and Sacks, *The Legal Process*, 185–86, suggest that "emerging problems of social maladjustment tend always to be submitted first to the courts." They explain this conclusion in the following manner: "In the development of Anglo-American legal systems, courts have functioned characteristically as the place of initial resort for the settlement of problems which failed of private solution. . . . All these systems include the immensely significant institution of courts of *general* jurisdiction. Courts are regularly open for the settlement of disputes as legislatures are not. They function ordinarily, as legislatures do not, under the obligation of deciding one way or the other the disputes which are submitted to them. Disputants with a sense of wrong are likely to seek first of all not a change in the law but a declaration that the existing law is in accordance with their position. Legislatures, with far more comprehensive responsibilities than any other official institution, are unlikely to stop to listen to demands for a change in the law unless it is plain that such a change is

(1) when there is an organized and articulate interest group seeking change;
(2) when substantial harm is resulting from inaction and the proposed solution appears the most practical;
(3) when the perceived political consequences favor taking action;
(4) when the personal value system of the legislator is favorable to action;
(5) when institutional variables, e.g. rules and personal relationships, favor taking action.

An analysis of these factors affecting access to the legislature suggests that unorganized, inarticulate interests (i.e., individuals in either unorganized or weakly organized groups, or individuals not fully aware of their needs) can provide little impetus for legislative response. Similarly, legislative institutional response to rapid social change arguably tends to lag behind social change partially because the organization needed to obtain even a hearing takes time to develop.

The courts, on the other hand, unlike the legislature, arguably cannot refuse to hear a dispute "because the job is hard, or dubious, or dangerous."[7] The judiciary generally lacks the legislative prerogative of deciding that a matter has not developed to a point of justifying action—that it must be given a lower priority, that it is politically too hot to handle, or that another branch must act first. In referring a matter to another branch, it denies a claim; refusal to take action *is* action regarding the claim, thereafter serving as precedent. Nor can a judge, like the legislator, initiate a policy decision on his own volition; he lacks a self-starter. Further, it is considered bad form for him to define the issues to be adjudicated; it is for the parties to delineate the matter in dispute. Judicial policy action, therefore, is dependent on the ability and willingness of adverse social interests to press their claims in the judicial forum.

As has frequently been noted, however, the courts are particularly attractive to change interests (e.g. civil-rights and anti-poverty interests), since access is more readily available. Although organized groups

---

needed. This is unlikely to be plain unless a court has spoken." Carl A. Auerbach et al., *The Legal Process: An Introduction to Decision-Making by Judicial, Legislative, Executive and Administrative Agencies* (San Francisco, 1961), vi, also suggests that the interaction process begins with judicial decision-making: "Initial decision by the courts; followed by legislative intervention; and finally, the choice of a solution which required creation of administrative agencies and continuing efforts of courts, legislatures, administrative agencies, and executive agencies in manifold relationships."

[7] Karl N. Llewellyn, *The Bramble Bush* (New York, 1930), 35.

play a vital part in the judicial process, any individual litigant has standing to press his claim to the courts. But while the judiciary is available to the individual litigant, this does little good if he lacks the means to initiate and press a claim.[8] Court litigation is often a long, drawn-out process and an individual, or even a group, frequently lacks the means or inclination to suffer through the requisite ordeal. The increased emphasis being placed on assuring legal representation for the poor can be perceived as an attempt to assure more adequate lines of communication to the legal system for otherwise inarticulate interests.

The Intelligence Function: Informing the Policy-Maker

Assuming that the demand has been pressed on the legal system, the question arises as to the capacity of the particular legal actor to process the data necessary for effective policy-making. Social change posits a relatively new social situation for which adequate data might well be quite scarce, suggesting the danger of an information gap. If law-making is to be creative, it must be an informed activity.

Some students of decision-making have approached the process as a rational means-end type of action through which needs are established, alternative modes of meeting the problem are defined, a particular goal is selected, and appropriate means prescribed. In the logical method, "action follows upon a decision and the decision is the outcome of an inquiry, comparison of alternatives, weighing of facts; deliberating or thinking has intervened."[9] Others picture the decisional process in in-

---

[8] Herbert Jacob, *Justice in America* (Boston, 1965), 6–8, suggests five requisites before such a claim is initiated: (1) a potential plaintiff must have the resources necessary to hire a lawyer and engage in protracted litigation; (2) the courts must assume jurisdiction over the controversy; (3) if parties are to seek relief, there must be adequate remedies available; (4) social interests must perceive the court as an available forum; (5) the petitioners must believe there is a chance of winning. He notes that all of these factors circumscribe the willingness of people to use the courts and hence limit the institution's policy-making potential.

[9] John Dewey, "Logical Method and the Law," *Cornell Law Quarterly*, X (Dec., 1924), 17. Julius Cohen suggests that the essence of a legislative proposal lies in an assessment of a fact situation, a means-end hypothesis that a certain means would be appropriate to the desired end and an instrumental value judgment that the intermediate ends would be conducive to more general goals. "Hearings on a Bill: Legislative Folklore?," *Minnesota Law Review*, XXXVII (Dec., 1952), 34. See Kenneth S. Carlston, *Law and Structures of Social Action* (New York, 1956), 13; Irwin D. J. Bross, *Design for Decision* (New York, 1953); C. West Churchman, *Prediction and Optimal Decision* (Englewood Cliffs, 1961); Yehezkel Dror, *Public Policymaking Reexamined* (San Francisco, 1968), especially chap. 12; Carl J. Friedrich, ed., *Rational Decision* (New York, 1964).

cremental terms, a more haphazard form of action under "conditions of bounded rationality." There are at best only "successive limited comparisons" of alternative policies, a gradual approximation by the decision-maker toward some ill-defined objectives.[10] Given the pressures produced by a change situation, it seems likely that the incrementalist approach is a more accurate description of policy formation. But whatever the actual mode of decision-making, a purposive approach assumes an attempt to process those facts upon which decisions can be made. It is necessary, therefore, to consider further the fact-gathering capabilities of the individual legal actors.

Legislative inertia or apathy in the face of social change reflects the failure of the legislative process to react to a felt need in the social system. The legislator is like a doctor: "his job is to cure ills."[11] The adequate performance of this function demands institutionalized mechanisms whereby legislators can be informed on the nature and extent of social needs and the alternative lines of satisfaction available. Even if legislative behavior does not conform to the logical model, this should not negate the possibility of more closely approximating such rationality. Further, although the legislature may not in reality act because of an informed determination of a need for action, it is essential that its actions or inactions be framed in terms of necessity. The legislature has functions other than merely legislating. It also acts as a safety valve for societal pressures. Men must be assured that their demands and problems are being adequately perceived and acted upon by public authorities. They require at least symbolic reassurance that the legislative process provides a mechanism for the reasoned settlement of disputes.[12]

A judicial counterpart of the legislative hearing is the trial. Unlike the legislative inquiry, however, court proceedings are governed by far more formalized rules and procedures. It is a particular strength of the judicial process that the decision is rendered concerning a concrete case. Unlike the legislature, which must often determine policy in the abstract, the court can observe how the rule of law has actually functioned. The dispute has a reality not present in the legislative forum. However, this same factor accounts for one of the vital weaknesses

---

[10] Charles E. Lindblom, "The Science of Muddling Through," *Public Administration Review*, XIX (Spring, 1959), 79–88; David Braybrooke and Charles E. Lindblom, *A Strategy of Decision* (New York, 1963).

[11] John C. Wahlke et al., *The Legislative System* (New York, 1962), 255.

[12] Roscoe Pound, *Social Control through Law* (New Haven, 1942), 79, 80. See generally Murray Edelman, *The Symbolic Uses of Politics* (Urbana, Ill., 1964); Edwin W. Patterson, *Law in a Scientific Age* (New York, 1963), 31.

of the court as a creative law-maker. Because it deals with the concrete case, its scope of inquiry is severely restricted. The task of gathering and presenting information is charged to the adversary parties themselves, reflecting the belief that through their desire for success, the requisite data will emerge. The judge cannot freely inquire into any problem that may interest him; the litigants define the general lines of battle—"judicial policy action flows not from a broad-ranging inquiry into the problems and prospective solutions, but from a narrow-gauged encounter."[13]

Indeed, it is questionable whether the greater social interests involved in social change can be adequately represented in such a proceeding. Courts, in handling extremely complex socio-legal problems, can usually only deal with specific facets of the problems as they are presented. Of course, the language of an opinion can anticipate questions and provide rather substantial cues as to their future disposition, but these are tangential to the inquiry and fall under that nebulous classification of dictum. Even if the courts over time could, through case-by-case decision, fashion a comprehensive policy, the rate of change in modern society challenges the adequacy of this process. This alleged informational preeminence of the legislature has frequently led judges to advocate deference to legislative judgment[14] and is often cited as the primary obstacle to effective, creative, judicial policy action.[15]

[13] Richard S. Wells and Joel B. Grossman, "The Concept of Judicial Policy-Making: A Critique," *Journal of Public Law*, XV, no. 2 (1966), 306. See Benjamin N. Cardozo, *The Growth of the Law* (New Haven, 1924), 5. Oliver Wendell Holmes expressed much the same thought in Southern Pacific Co. v. Jensen, 244 U.S. 205, 221 (1917), when he commented that while judges necessarily legislate, "they can do so only interstitially; they are confined from molar to molecular motions."

[14] See, e.g., South Carolina State Highway Dep't v. Barnwell Bros., 303 U.S. 177 (1938); International News Services v. Associated Press, 248 U.S. 214, 264–67 (1918) (Brandeis, J., dissenting); Aero Spark Plug Co. v. B. G. Corp., 130 F.2d 290, 296 (2d Cir. 1942) (Frank, J., concurring); Cheney Bros. v. Doris Silk Corp., 35 F.2d 279 (2d Cir. 1929); Molitor v. Kaneland Community Unit Dist., 18 Ill.2d 11, 40, 163 N.E.2d 89, 103 (1959) (Davis, J., dissenting); Reisman v. Monmouth Consolidated Water Co., 9 N.J. 134, 87 A.2d 325 (1952).

[15] Arthur Lenhoff, "Extra-Legislational Process of Law—the Place of the Judiciary in Shaping New Law," *Nebraska Law Review*, XXVIII (May, 1949), 567, for example, notes: "With all allowance made for judicial inventiveness and with all insight in the mechanism of judicial thinking, it still remains true that the factual information of a court is relatively slight compared with the large material which might be brought to light through legislative investigations and hearings, through research done by a legislative staff and through a process enabling the examiners to obtain an all-around picture of social and economic facts." Charles G. Howard and Robert S. Summers, *Law: Its Nature, Function and Limits* (Englewood Cliffs,

The Prescriptive Function: Enacting Legal Norms

Finally, in considering the character of the initial legal response to a change situation, it is necessary to consider those factors which influence the final prescriptive behavior of the particular legal institution. Even if it is decided that social change has made action necessary, the task of decision-making has only begun. Need is only one of the factors bidding for the decision-maker's favor; it must compete with other influences, sometimes supportive but often pulling in different directions. Like all individuals, legal policy-makers are subject to a variety of cross pressures in their orientation to a situation, and decision arises from some resolution of these lines of force. Perception of the situation, the competing interests, and their saliency are crucial considerations.

The legislator, for example, must assess the perceived political consequences of a particular action (including constituency pressures, party demands, and interest-group activities); he is subjected to the influence of his own personal value system; and he must operate under a set of institutional rules of the game.[16] In many instances the "need" for legislative response pales in comparison to other motivations. In fact, it might be argued that generally "need" must reach crisis proportions before the legislature will act, especially if there are powerful vested interests supporting the status quo. Witness the examples of pollution control and the elimination of racial injustice.

Studies of judicial behavior suggest that similar *external* forces also operate on the judicial actor, but that their salience may be markedly different. Whereas the legislator is openly subjected to an array of political pressures, judges tend to be more insulated from direct pressure; external forces tend to operate more indirectly and subliminally.

1965), 371, also make this claim for legislative preeminence in fact-finding: "Further, courts do not have the techniques for the investigation of a social problem that legislatures have, and, under the strict rules of evidence, courts cannot take into account data that might be significant. Legislatures, however, can conduct extensive investigations. Also, the techniques available to a court for dealing with a problem are much more limited than the techniques available to a legislature." See generally Bernard Botein and Murray A. Gordon, *The Trial of the Future* (New York, 1963), 10-11; Morris Cohen, *American Thought: A Critical Sketch* (Glencoe, Ill., 1954), quoted in Henry J. Friendly, "The Gap in Lawmaking—Judges Who Can't and Legislatures Who Won't," *Columbia Law Review*, LXIII (May, 1963), 791n32.

[16] Cleo Cherryholmes and Michael Shapiro, *Representatives and Roll Calls* (Indianapolis, 1969), Malcom E. Jewell and Samuel C. Patterson, *The Legislative Process in the United States* (New York, 1966), and Wahlke et al., *The Legislative System*, provide excellent compilations of the studies of factors affecting legislative behavior.

The judicial system, like the legislature, is an institution, with all the structural influences, formalized procedures and norms, and role orientations that the term implies.[17] While bargaining may be common in collegial courts, it tends to be more discreet and invisible than in the legislative process.[18] There is also a tendency at times to forget that a judicial decision is not the product of an isolated mind but the result of the judge's interaction with a complement of other actors within the judicial subsystem. To understand judicial behavior it is essential to view it through the behavior and expectations of the multiplicity of actors at work (e.g. lawyers, clerks) and the rules governing that behavior. Jeremy Bentham once noted: "Law is not made by judge alone but by judge and company."[19]

The salience of external forces may be affected not only by the character of the court's working environment but also by the circumstances of the decision. When a new legal problem generated by social change arises, the court is required to act without the traditional guidance supplied by precedent or statute. This is the case of first instance, or unprovided case, which maximizes the strain on the capabilities of the courts while affording an excellent opportunity for judicial creativity. Three options would appear to be available to a court operating under such conditions: (1) apply traditional legal categories to a new situation; (2) deny the claim, often with deference to the legislative prerogative; (3) fashion a new rule for the changed circumstances either directly or through modification of established categories. The choice of the judicial policy-maker from among these alternatives will have a vital bearing on the character and quality of subsequent policy action.

The options available in confronting change demands also have a vital

[17] There are numerous compilations of behavioral studies dealing generally with motivations behind judicial policy-making. See, e.g., Joel Grossman and Joseph Tanenhaus, eds., *Frontiers of Judicial Research* (New York, 1969); Glendon Schubert, ed., *Judicial Behavior* (Chicago, 1964). For discussions of the work product of the judicial behavioralist school see Stuart S. Nagel, *The Legal Process from a Behavioral Perspective* (Homewood, Ill., 1969); Glendon Schubert, *Judicial Policy-Making* (Chicago, 1965); Theodore Becker, *Political Behavioralism and Modern Jurisprudence* (Chicago, 1964); Symposium, "Social Science Approaches to the Judicial Process," *Harvard Law Review*, LXXIX (June, 1966), 1551–1628; Wells and Grossman, "The Concept of Judicial Policy-Making."

[18] See Walter Murphy, *The Elements of Judicial Strategy* (Chicago, 1964).

[19] Jeremy Bentham, quoted in Glendon Schubert, ed., *Constitutional Politics: The Political Behavior of Supreme Court Justices and the Constitutional Policies That They Make* (New York, 1960), 82. See Samuel Krislov, *The Supreme Court in the Political Process* (New York, 1965), 55.

impact on the character of the prescriptive function. Legislation, for example, can be permissive, prohibitory, or regulatory. It can carry affirmative or negative sanctions or can merely be an expression of policy. Through the use of licensing, taxing, and report requirements, the legislature may not only make an immediate determination on a policy issue but can seek to provide for subsequent implementation. Special agencies can be created to maintain continuing surveillance (e.g. fair employment practices commissions). A statute may provide for the government itself to perform a desired task or it may seek to induce others to perform it by persuasion or by offer of reward or assistance (e.g. construction of public housing or FHA mortgage guarantees). Policy can be formulated in such a manner as to accommodate contending parties—negotiation and compromise are hallmarks of the legislative process. When the legal system deals with complex social or economic change presenting a wide range of legal issues, legislative rather than judicial resources can assume a vital importance.

An initial judicial decision might act as a catalyst for legislative intervention, a possibility to be discussed below. If the legislature fails to act, however, judicial policy formulation continues, constantly subject to a legislative decision to intervene. This is the common-law method—a case-by-case fashioning of the applicable legal policy; a process of inclusion and exclusion of factual situations under legal categories which are constantly reconsidered and reworked in response to further social change. But as the policy is fashioned, the judge is subject to an influence that was absent in the case of first instance, i.e. precedent, the reasoning and decision of a prior court on a like question.

REACTIVE LEGAL ACTION

As suggested above, the decision by a legal policy-maker in response to a change demand is only the first stage in the interactive process through which legal policy is formulated. Even if an initial response tends to lack the comprehensiveness and expertise desirable, it arguably can serve as an impetus to further policy formation. Perhaps it is the limitation of our institutional actors in fashioning a "complete" policy that best explains the importance of the interactive behavior. None of the actors is really equipped to handle the task on its own.

Indeed, a basic thesis of this analysis is that the behavior of one element of the legal system can have a vital bearing on the subsequent behavior of other legal policy-makers.[20] The original decision and its social ramifications, if any, become part of the total environment to which other policy-makers are asked to respond. Any adequate appreciation of subsequent policy formation, therefore, must consider the effect of prior decisional behavior taken by other components of the system. The fact of past decision and its impact are "fed back" not only to the original decision-maker, but also to the other institutions constituting the legal system.

Legislative Action Following Initial Judicial Policy-Making

In the sections above we were concerned with the behavior of either the legislature or the judiciary in a change situation *prior* to action by any other legal institution. The present proposition deals with legislative action taken *after* the judiciary has intervened—the judicial action becomes a factor altering the situation confronting the legislator. In such a case, the legislature resembles an appellate court to which an aggrieved party can appeal. As has been noted, this appears to be the normal role of the legislative actor—"an intermittently-intervening, trouble-shooting, back-stopping agency."[21]

[20] Schubert, *Judicial Policy-Making*, 3-4, defines "system" as a structure or pattern of interaction among the actors. Jay A. Sigler, *An Introduction to the Legal System* (Homewood, Ill., 1968), 2, in an effort to stress the boundaries of the legal system, refers to it as "a self-contained unit of analysis, whose components are linked by interconnecting processes of communications." See Talcott Parsons, *The Social System* (New York, 1964).

The systems perspective adopted in this analysis is derived essentially from the works of David Easton, especially *A Framework for Political Analysis* (Englewood Cliffs, 1964) and *A Systems Analysis of Political Life* (New York, 1965).

The action perspective (see Snyder, "A Decision-Making Approach," 11) seems to have received its early baptism in the writings of Arthur F. Bentley. He described the raw material of politics as "first, last and always activity, action, 'something doing,' and shunting by some men of other men's conduct along changed lines, and gathering of forces to overcome resistance to such altercations, or the dispersal of one grouping of forces by another grouping." *The Process of Government* (Cambridge, Mass., 1967), 176. It is doubtful whether political life could ever be described in the purely activist terms suggested by Bentley, but it does suggest the dynamic character of the policy-making process.

More recent formulations of action theory can be found in the writings of sociologists. See, e.g., Talcott Parsons, *The Structure of Social Action* (Glencoe, Ill., 1951); Talcott Parsons and Edward Shils, eds., *Toward a General Theory of Action* (Cambridge, Mass., 1951). It is the "problems inherent in or arising from social interaction of a plurality of individual actors" defining a system that occupies the action frame of reference. *Ibid.*, 7.

[21] Hart and Sacks, *The Legal Process*, 186. The authors suggest instances for such legislative intervention: (1) where corrective judicial action would dis-

It may be suggested that initial judicial policy formation tends to produce either of the following consequences: (1) the creation of a legislative acquiescence or apathy, resulting in legislative inaction, or (2) acceleration of the change process by producing greater awareness of the problem, thereby stimulating interest aggregation and articulation, thus generally adding impetus for legislative action. Legislative response may seek to implement, modify, extend, or reverse the judicially fashioned policy; or it may (although not likely at this early stage) be directed against the court itself. The form and extent of legislative response will tend to reflect the same motivational factors suggested earlier, although the changed situation may alter their salience.[22] The initial choice to be faced by the legislature, however, is whether to act at all.

In many cases, judicial decision appears to be an element which can restructure the situation and perhaps affect the legislative orientation. In fact, the judiciary may try directly or indirectly to influence legislative behavior by communicating the need for action.[23] The impact of the judicially fashioned policy on society might itself become an impetus for legislative intervention. It is essential that increased attention be given to the influence of the process itself on policy formation, to the ability of legal institutions to influence each other formally or informally and to communicate their needs, to provide relevant information, and to express policy preferences to the other actors in the legal system.

Judicial Policy-Making Following Legislative Action

It is unlikely that either initial legislative activity or reactive legislative action as described above would terminate the process of legal change. Even if the legislature were intermittently to review its actions in light of changed social conditions, disappointed parties in society would

---

appoint the reasonable expectations of the parties; (2) where complex rules have to be formulated—"cast in terms of arbitrary, fixed quantities or involving form requirements beyond the capacity of judicial innovation." *Ibid.*, 817. See Walter Gelhorn, "The Legislative and Administrative Response," *Vanderbilt Law Review*, XVII (Dec., 1963), 6.

[22] See note 16 *supra*.

[23] Murphy, *The Elements of Judicial Strategy*, suggests that Supreme Court communications to other legal policy-makers may be formal, e.g. via a judicial case opinion, or informal, e.g. speeches, personal contacts. See Dillon v. Legg, 69 Cal. Rptr. 72, 88, 441 P.2d 912, 928 (1968) (Burke, J., dissenting), for an example of a formal appeal.

probably seek judicial interpretation of the legislative enactment or a determination regarding its constitutionality. And it is at this stage of the process that the two legal institutions are most likely to come into direct confrontation. The judiciary has the option of determining the nature of legislative policy or passing on the propriety of the legislative action. With the increasing number of court decisions involving action taken under legislative mandate, there is a greater opportunity for hostility within the legal system. Excessive hostility could imperil the efficacy of the interactive process while controlled interactions could maximize the capabilities of both legal institutions for managing problems created by social change.

The manner in which the courts exercise their prerogative in the areas of statutory interpretation, constitutional determination, and procedural abstention will have a vital effect on the character of the legal response to social-change situations, influencing not only the role of the judiciary in the process but also that of the legislature. A literalist approach to the interpretative function, a limited perspective on the role of the courts in constitutional decision-making, or an active use of techniques to avoid decision will act to place a greater burden on the legislature. Alternatively, emphasis on the purpose of the statute, greater acceptance of the political role of the courts in constitutional decision-making, and an emphasis on the need for greater access to the courts will tend to expand the role of the judiciary as a coordinate branch in the policy-making process. It arguably would permit the courts to apply their special attributes and capacities to the task of creative social engineering, while serving to stimulate responsive behavior from other legal actors.

Again, inquiry into the motivations for choosing among these alternatives at this stage of the process is essential. But we should also reiterate that, although the same factors discussed above may be operative, their direction and effect might be altered—legislative action has intervened. For example, deference to legislative action will be a more vital consideration than in the case of first instance or in the fashioning of common law. Concepts of judicial restraint or judicial activism, in spite of their nebulous meanings, will tend to be operative.[24]

An activist model of judicial behavior at this stage of the process again

[24] Schubert, *Judicial Policy-Making*, 154, defines "activism" as a conflict between the policies of the court and those of other decision-makers and "restraint" as a case when they are compatible. It would seem preferable, however, to consider the problem in terms of the values of the individual justices toward the judicial function. See, e.g., Wallace Mendelson, ed., *The Supreme Court: Law and Discretion* (Indianapolis, 1967).

suggests the vital importance of intelligence-gathering for effective policy formation. The judiciary would require extensive data on the social consequences of legislatively fashioned policy, the possible social impact of suggested policy revisions, and the possible reactions of other legal institutions which might produce a response directed at the court itself. It is questionable, however, whether the social sciences are presently capable of providing the required data, and it is equally questionable that the courts would generally be willing to receive it even if available.

Legislative Policy-Making Following Judicial Reaction

Even judicial reaction to a legislatively fashioned policy does not necessarily mark an end to the policy-making process. In fact, legislative response to such judicial reaction may be fundamentally different from the legislative reaction to a case of initial judicial policy-making. The courts have not merely acted in virgin territory; their activity in this instance has intruded into a matter on which the legislature had spoken.

The tendency to view the Supreme Court as a court of last resort, the final arbiter from which there is no recourse, ignores the fact that this court, like all legal institutions, represents only another stage in the adjustment of legal disputes. Whether making constitutional or interpretative decisions, it can expect to have its determinations reviewed internally by the lower courts, by the administration in the extent to which the decision is implemented, by the public in the character of their compliance, or by Congress in the form of a reaction through constitutional amendment or legislation directed against a particular decision or against the court itself.[25]

Further, the tendency of behavioral studies done thus far to limit their inquiry to negative legislative response[26] has tended to ignore the

[25] See Harry Stumpf, "Congressional Response to Supreme Court Rulings," *Journal of Public Law*, XIV, no. 2 (1965), 383; Robert A. Dahl, "Decision-Making in a Democracy: The Supreme Court as a National Policy-Maker," *Journal of Public Law*, VI (Fall, 1957), 285; Note, "Congressional Reversal of Supreme Court Decision, 1945-1957," *Harvard Law Review*, LXXI (May, 1958), 1336-37; Note, "Evasion of Supreme Court Mandates in Cases Remanded to State Courts since 1941," *Harvard Law Review*, LXVII (May, 1954), 1251-59; Walter F. Murphy, "Lower Court Checks on Supreme Court Power," *A.P.S.R.*, LIII (Dec., 1959), 1017-31; "Five Ways of Nullifying a Supreme Court Decision," *Constitutional Politics*, ed. Schubert, 257-59.

[26] See Walter Murphy, *Congress and the Court* (Chicago, 1962), 257; C. Herman Pritchett, *Congress versus the Supreme Court, 1957-1960* (Minneapolis, 1961).

fact that judicial action may serve as an impetus to positive legislative action designed to implement the court's policy decision. Consideration must also be given to the possibility of legislative non-action as a viable alternative, especially where the judicial actor has accepted the legislative policy in its reactive behavior or where the legislature acquiesces in a judicially fashioned policy. Alternatively, non-action may be the consequence of apathy or negative motivational factors. In any case, there is a real need to inquire into the considerations that influence the particular form of legislative response, into the actual communication patterns, both within the court and the legislature and between these legal institutions when policy differences occur, into court and legislative policy action under stress, and into the effect that an alteration of course may have on subsequent behavior at this late stage of the legal-change process.

THE DYNAMICS OF CHANGE

While the analysis presented thus far has sought to delineate the sequence of activities that constitutes the process of legal adjustment to social change, the present section stresses the dynamic character of the process; not a circular development, but rather a linear progression through time. The legal process is in a continuous state of adjustment because the social system "bears within itself the seeds of incessant change, which mark every action and reaction even in a fixed environment."[27] Even if law were approached solely as a response mechanism rather than also as a lead device, it would still be in a state of constant change. Thus we must come to accept the lack of certainty and a continual process of challenge and response as social change poses new problems for legal adjustment. A willingness to accept the reality of

[27] Pitirim A. Sorokin, "Reasons for Sociocultural Change and Variably Recurrent Processes," *Readings on Social Change*, 69. Fred V. Cahill, *Judicial Legislation* (New York, 1952), 151, notes this increased emphasis on change: "When combined with the ideal of a dynamic society, the conception of law as a social technique implies an acceptance of the impermanence of any particular set of legal relationships.... In modern juristic theory, therefore, the legal system ceases to be a social adjustment and becomes a process by which social adjustment is secured. However social adjustment is defined, the task of law is to define the relations between variable points, and, it is important to note, these points are always socially defined." See Symposium (Stuart S. Nagel, ed.), "Law and Social Change," *American Behavioral Scientist*, XIII (Mar.–Apr., 1970), 483–593.

flux appears to be the primary requisite in achieving a stable legal order; one that accepts constant social change and seeks to adjust creatively for the alterations that it produces.

This does not mean, however, that there is a constantly increasing uncontrolled stress on the system. The very function of law as a social institution demands that change be managed. Law has been approached as a purposive, goal-oriented system; the behavior of the legal actors is designed to achieve a settlement of social disputes, to achieve effective social engineering. Hence, the interactive process is assumed to result in a point of new stability (homeostasis) as the dispute is resolved; a heightened sense of order is achieved as the interests are compromised. The legislature and judiciary come together at some point in the give-and-take on a mutually satisfactory policy in the given situation.

Any legal settlement, however, also alters the social situation, thereby generating new problems. The "settlement" of a legal dispute is merely a temporary refuge as new interests are aggregated and new demands articulated. "In one sense, in a successful political process all decisions are interim. We live in a perpetual state of unresolved conflict. It should never be a complete resolution. The majority does not rule; a majority decision is simply a setting of the terms under which the minority continues the discussion—a discussion which presumably goes on forever or at least for the lifetime of the organization."[28]

CONCLUSION

The legal system, then, will be approached as a dynamic process of recommending, intelligence, and prescribing activity by each legal institution and the interaction among the forums themselves and with social forces in fashioning legal policy responsive to changing social conditions. It is an attempt to achieve greater understanding of the processes of legal change through an enhanced ability to describe and analyze the workings of the legal system in terms of time and process. This is the perspective governing the conceptual framework that will now be used to identify, organize, and analyze the behavior of the courts and legislatures of New York, Connecticut, Massachusetts, and the federal forum as they grappled with the task of birth-control policy formation.

[28] Kenneth E. Boulding, *The Image* (Ann Arbor, 1956), 103.

One

The Origins of Comstockery

> *Social Vice and National Decay stand to each other as parent to child, cause to consequence, fountain to stream, the one begetting, the other begotten. That Social Vice, by which we broadly mean fornication, prostitution, a defiance of the Divine Law of continence, is the only or even primary cause of National Decay would be too much to assume, but to affirm that the prevalence and increase of the Social Evil among a people is a sure sign and symptom of national degeneracy which it greatly promotes and accelerates, is only to utter an obvious and terrible truth, which history, reason, and experience alike set beyond dispute.*[1]

These words may appear somewhat strange to many modern readers, but for nineteenth-century America they merely expressed accepted basic truths. Morality, religion, and laws were necessarily intertwined; each was essential to the well-being of the other. Distinctions between crime and sin were blurred and ignored. Legal norms were perceived as weapons by which the dominant morality sought to root out deviation destructive of society. Such was the thinking that inspired Anthony Comstock to lobby Congress in 1873 for reform in the postal laws. New weapons in the struggle against evil had to be forged and Congress was to respond with sweeping laws reaching a broad range of human behavior.

But as is generally the case, the new laws were to contain strong linkages with prior legal policy-making. Old legal concepts are often

[1] William T. Sabine, "Social Vice and National Decay," *The National Purity Congress*, ed. Aaron M. Powell (New York, 1896).

merely redrawn or expanded to encompass new problem areas; existing interest groups frequently shift their attention to include newly emerging areas of controversy; the reality of legal change can pass unnoticed as old ways of doing things are adjusted under the guise of continuity. Except in instances of dramatic legal response to technological innovation or discovery, legal norms often, like Topsy, "jes growed."

This problem is especially evident in developing an appreciation of the formation of birth-control policy given its close historical association with the law of obscenity. Consequently, a discussion might begin with the common-law and statutory fashioning of obscenity policy. In England, for example, even prior to the passage of the landmark obscene-publications legislation, Lord Campbell's Act, in 1857,[2] there was judicial precedent for treating dissemination of obscene material as criminal.[3] And in this country there had been early legislative and judicial acceptance of the ambivalent common-law principle that dissemination of obscene and indecent materials constituted a criminal offense against public morals.[4] The courts, as *custos morum*, custodians of the public morals, were charged with suppression of whatever was found to be destructive of social morality. As Judge Yeates explained the underlying principle in *Commonwealth v. Sharpless*, in 1815: "The destruction of morality renders the powers of the government invalid, for government is no more than the public order; it weakens the bonds by which society is kept together. The corruption of the public mind, in general . . . must necessarily be attended with the most injurious

---

[2] 20 & 21 Victoria C. 83 (1875). For an account of the passage of Lord Campbell's Act, see vols. CXLV–CXLIX of Hansard's *Parliamentary Debates*. See generally James C. Paul and Murray L. Schwartz, *Federal Censorship: Obscenity in the Mail* (New York, 1961), 12–15; Norman St. John–Stevas, *Obscenity and the Law* (London, 1956).

[3] See Rex v. Curl, 2 Str. 788, 93 Eng. Rep. 849 (1727), establishing the distribution of an obscene book as a common-law crime, an offense against morality. *Contra*: Queen v. Read, 11 Mod. 142, 88 Eng. Rep. 953 (1708). See generally Alec Craig, *Suppressed Books* (New York, 1963), 17–39.

[4] The early American cases include Commonwealth v. Holmes, 17 Mass. 336 (1821); Commonwealth v. Sharpless, 2 S. & R. (Pa.) 91 (1815); Knowles v. State, 3 Day (Conn.) 103 (1808).

Congress had enacted obscenity legislation in 1842, 1865, 1872. State statutory condemnations of obscenity in this early period include an Act Concerning Crimes and Punishments, sec. 69 (1821), Stat. Laws of Conn. 109 (1824); Rev. Stat. of 1842, chap. 113, sec. 2, Rev. Stat. of N.H. 221 (1843); Act for Suppressing Vice and Immorality, sec. XII (1798), N.J. Rev. Laws 329, 331 (1800); Rev. Stats. of Mass., chap. 130, sec. 10 (1836). For a historical treatment of obscenity policy, see Paul and Schwartz, *Federal Censorship*; St. John–Stevas, *Obscenity and the Law*.

consequences and in such instances, courts of justice are, or ought to be, the schools of morals."[5]

Establishing that common-law courts could deal criminally with matters of obscenity did not, however, provide guidelines for determining what was obscene. More particularly, dissemination of contraceptives or contraceptive information was not necessarily encompassed by the criminal proscription. In the early 1830s, therefore, when Dr. Charles Knowlton, an early American exponent of birth control, was tried by three Massachusetts courts on charges of obscenity for publication of his treatise *Fruits of Philosophy* (1832), which not only presented the arguments for birth limitation but also discussed the methods for birth prevention (especially chemical devices and douching),[6] the case was essentially a matter of first impression.

As indicated in the Introduction, such cases tend to maximize the strain on the resources of the courts, while affording an excellent opportunity for judicial creativity.[7] To consider them only occasional oddities, or merely to reduce all cases to existing precedent, whether applicable or not, reflects a refusal to accept the unique situations many cases pose. The "gaps" in precedent or statute to which Cardozo refers as instances for judicial law-making are frequently instances of the unprovided case.

> Although it is possible in a strictly formal sense to postulate the complete inclusiveness of a legal system in as much as any given conduct is either legal or illegal, it is clear that from a social viewpoint there are actually many gaps in the law. Cases arise which the legislators and judges did not in the least consider. The whole movement of social change, including major shifts in public opinion, often renders the existing law completely silent on many issues. New meanings emerge which, guided by a more

---

[5] Commonwealth v. Sharpless, 2 S. & R. (Pa.) 91, 103 (1815).

[6] Charles Knowlton, *Fruits of Philosophy, or the Private Companion of Young Married People* (3rd ed., London, 1841), reissued as *Fruits of Philosophy, or The Private Companion of Adult People*, ed. Norman E. Himes (New York, 1937). For biographical treatment of Charles Knowlton see Fryer, *The Birth Controllers*, 99–106; Robert E. Riegel, "The American Father of Birth Control," *New England Quarterly*, VI (Sept., 1933), 470–90; Norman E. Himes, "Note on the Early History of Contraception in America," *New England Journal of Medicine*, CCV (Aug. 27, 1931), 438–40.

[7] See text following Introduction, note 19 *supra*. James F. Davis et al., *Society and the Law* (New York, 1962), 122, suggests that such cases "may engender an atmosphere that precludes the normal weighing and balancing of interests and their compromise and reconciliation that mark the judicial process and lean to an extreme or absolute and unqualified position that only time will erode."

pertinent sense of justice, override logic, and legal redress is allowed. These conditions imply a degree of unavoidable uncertainty as a constant factor in every legal order.[8]

Nevertheless, courts continue to treat the unprovided case as though it had been provided, using the language of precedent as if a regular case were under consideration. Basically, this reflects a view that "it is the province of the judge to expound the law—not to speculate upon what is best in his opinion for the advantage of the community"; "judges are more to be trusted as interpreters of the law than as expounders of what is called public policy";[9] courts exist only to give effect "to the will of the law."[10] There is assumed to be a "logical completeness" to the law which does not admit of an unprovided case.

> The theory is thus that it is not necessary to go outside the boundaries of existing law to find the ground of decision of new cases; that the law, being complete, is necessarily self-contained, and that the ground of decision of new cases is to be sought not in something outside the precedents, like natural justice or a common sense opinion of right or wrong, but within the body of technical law itself as expressed in the precedent.[11]

Concepts embodied in rules are "treated as real existences and developed with merciless disregard of consequences to the limit of their logic."[12] Their beguiling simplicity permits them to be manipulated for the purposes of the interpreter and extended to encompass situations for which they were never intended. The judge in this instance is making policy, but it is hardly creative. He ignores the novel aspects of the case and employs legal concepts ill suited to the modern problem.

---

[8] Jerome Hall, *Living Law of a Democratic Society* (Indianapolis, 1949), 43. See Benjamin N. Cardozo, *The Nature of the Judicial Process* (New Haven, 1921), 14–23; Morris Cohen, *Law and the Social Order* (New York, 1933), 122–23.

[9] Judicial statements quoted in Lord Radcliffe, *The Law and Its Compass* (Evanston, 1960), 46, 49.

[10] Chief Justice John Marshall in Osborn v. Bank of the United States, 9 Wheaton 738, 866 (1824), claimed that "the judiciary has no will in any case.... Judicial power is never exercised for the purpose of giving effect to the will of the judge; always for the purpose of giving effect to... the will of the law."

[11] John Dickinson, "The Problem of the Unprovided Case," *University of Pennsylvania Law Review*, LXXXI (Dec., 1932), 118.

[12] Benjamin N. Cardozo, *The Paradoxes of Legal Science* (New York, 1928), 61. George Gurvich, *Sociology of Law* (New York, 1942), 13, is extremely critical of the "intense constructive element" in law, "the particularly thick conceptual crust" which "leads to a 'mumification' of categories and formulas with consequent slowness and serious difficulty in adapting jurisprudence... to the new living reality of law, a perpetual dynamism, always in motion, always in flux."

An alternative approach to the case of first instance, which, if prevalent, would also raise doubts as to the creative abilities of the judiciary, arises from deference to other actors in the legal system: the court dismisses the claim with references to the availability of appeal to the legislative forum.[13] In spite of the fact that the court is denying its capacity to decide, its dismissal of the claim is a form of action. The social interest seeking judicial recognition may lack the organization requisite to press a claim through the legislature, or the balance of political, ideological, or institutional variables may not be favorable. For a court to dismiss a claim under these circumstances may well deny the parties any hearing on the merits of their claims.

A third alternative, which is endorsed in this analysis, is recognition by the judge of the novel aspects of the case and a policy approach to its solution—"innovate, however, to some extent, he must, for with new conditions there must be new rules."[14] The court fashions a new rule for the changed circumstances either directly or through modification of established categories. "But implicit or open, an appeal to public policy is frequently made when constitution, statute and former decision are silent. It is here that the courts extend, limit or modify some old principle, or recognize some new principle."[15]

This has been the traditional mode of growth in the common law. Great judges have been willing to take a bold new step when circumstances demanded such action. The policy-oriented judge realizes the potential impact of his decision, the wide discretion that the case of first instance affords, and will accept the responsibility for initiating action. The judge does not, however, ignore precedent and statute, but rather uses them, not as directly applicable and binding, but as analogies to reveal possible lines of reasoning; he makes a conscious choice based on social considerations from among competing premises fashioned for the new situation. Indeed, such a use of analogies appears to be a pri-

[13] This approach seems to be especially common when the case is part of a complex legal problem requiring extensive fact-finding. See Lenhoff, "Extra-Legislational Process of Law," 524; United States v. Standard Oil Co., 332 U.S. 301, 314 (1947); Introduction, note 23 *supra*.

[14] Cardozo, *The Nature of the Judicial Process*, 137.

[15] Leon Green, "The Study and Teaching of Tort Law," *Texas Law Review*, XXXIV (Nov., 1956), 15. See Wells and Grossman, "The Concept of Judicial Policy-Making," 263, 267–68.

During the formative period of the common law, judges frequently had recourse to a sense of equity embodied in the concepts of "natural justice." See Karl N. Llewellyn, *The Common Law Tradition: Deciding Appeals* (Boston, 1960); Dickinson, "The Problem of the Unprovided Case," 117; Stephans and Co. v. Albers, 81 Colo. 488, 256 Pac. 15 (1927).

mary mode of decision-making in such cases. Admittedly an experiment, the decision often will prove unworkable. Subsequent action will probably be necessary to rework the policy to encompass additional dimensions of the problem. But the initial case can act as an impetus to further action, as the first step in the creative fashioning of legal policy.

Through the criminal prosecution of Charles Knowlton, the novel problem of contraception had come initially to the judicial rather than the legislative actor. And a creative option for policy formation was available. Given the fact that earlier judicial suppression of sex obscenity had tended to be limited to instances of rather extreme writings or practices and dealt generally with individuals who might be deemed smut peddlers,[16] the Massachusetts courts could have distinguished the Knowlton case on the basis of the character of the treatment and/or the intent of the writer. While the technical discussion in Knowlton's treatise reflected the somewhat primitive state of birth-control knowledge, it is difficult to conceive of any basis on which it could be branded as obscene. But the sweeping judicial decisions of the period regarding "obscenity" made such a refined approach to policy formation highly unlikely. Terms like "indecency," "scandalous," "wicked," "lascivious" served as gross substitutes for any real attempt to delineate the boundaries of the evils being denounced.[17]

Unfortunately, little information is available concerning the handling of the cases, but their disposition is known. In Taunton, Massachusetts, where Knowlton was fined $50, in Cambridge, where he was forced to serve three months of hard labor in the house of correction, in East Cambridge, where he was again sentenced to a jail term, the courts applied the traditional legal category of obscenity to the problem of birth control apparently with little concern for the unique dimensions of the subject. While there was some public outcry from free-thought elements, there was little organized support at this time for serious consideration of public policy toward contraception.[18] The Knowlton

---

[16] See Craig, *Suppressed Books*, 35. The author makes the point that during the eighteenth century obscenity was generally a make-weight for seditious and blasphemous libel. *Ibid.*, 34.

[17] The terms are derived from Commonwealth v. Sharpless, 2 S. & R. (Pa.) 91 (1815).

[18] Charles Knowlton, *A History of the Recent Excitement in Ashfield Part I* (Ashfield, Mass., 1834); Knowlton, letter in *Boston Investigator*, Sept. 25, 1835, p. 1, cols. 2, 3. See Fryer, *The Birth Controllers*, 105.

A small group of Free Enquirers in Pittsburgh did organize a protest (*Boston Investigator*, Apr. 19, 1833), and a newspaper criticized the "monopoly of knowledge" reflected in the convictions. Knowlton, *History of the Recent Excitement*, 20.

trials appear to be isolated instances of criminal prosecution (probably because there were few individuals actively proselytizing the subject). Nevertheless, there now existed at least ad hoc precedent for treating any discussion of birth control as obscene. It is difficult, however, to say that there was yet any coherent public policy regarding birth control per se. But such an expression of policy was forthcoming.

FEDERAL LEGISLATIVE ACTION

The Recommending Function

America in the mid-nineteenth century provided an ideal breeding ground for revision of this ad hoc treatment of obscenity policy. Technological innovations, primarily the vulcanization of rubber, offered the possibility of mass-producing cheap, fairly effective birth-control devices. Although, as noted below, many of these prophylactics were somewhat deficient in safety and effectiveness, most of the control devices presently in use originated in the nineteenth century.[19]

Further, it was during this period that the movement for socialization and democratization of birth control took root. Francis Place, England's counterpart to Charles Knowlton, published tracts not only imparting knowledge to the masses on "how to do it" but also laying the groundwork for a thesis on the economic and social desirability of contraceptive practices. Birth control was perceived not solely as a medical technique, but also as a vehicle of reform. The working class was told that they need not produce children that they could not properly care for; that they might increase wage rates by limiting the numbers in the working force; that early marriages did not necessarily mean large families; and, generally, that the control of births was a vital tool in fighting the extreme poverty of the industrializing and urbanizing society. This was the message which the disciples of Place, in England, and Knowlton, in the United States, were to carry to an ever-expanding part of the populace.[20] As the historian of contraception, Norman Himes, indicates: "Stress upon the social and economic desirability of birth control is a characteristic of the nineteenth century, and hardly antedates it."[21]

[19] Himes, *Medical History of Contraception*, 20, 210; Alan F. Guttmacher, *Babies by Choice or by Chance* (New York, 1959), 94.
[20] Himes, *Medical History of Contraception*, 224–310. See Graham Wallas, *The Life of Frances Place* (London, 1898). Especially important in laying the foundations of the American birth-control movement was the work of Robert Dale Owen.
[21] Himes, *Medical History of Contraception*, 211.

And the expanding channels of communication through which the message of these early "birth controllers" was transmitted to the populace also served the purpose of a wide array of groups challenging the dominant morality; neo-Malthusians, free lovers, free thinkers, joined under that nondescript label of "liberals," preached a new code of sexual ethics and a new morality.[22] In journals such as *The Word*, published by Ezra Hervey Heywood, *Woodhull and Claflin's Weekly*, the voice of the wild and uninhibited sisters, Victoria Woodhull and Tennessee Claflin, the free-thought *Truth Seeker*, the *Boston Investigator*, and *The Index*, as well as through books published by independent liberal houses, they devoted themselves "to assist in delivering woman from degradation to which the ignorance, stupidity, lust and avarice of men have consigned her."[23] For some elements of the liberal movement, female emancipation in turn mandated the weakening and ultimate demise of the monogamous marital union—"our whole marital system is the house of bondage and the slaughter-house of the female sex."[24] Even among those liberals who did not accept the radical faction's extreme rejection of extant moral norms, there was an insistence on free pursuit of knowledge.[25] It is not very surprising that such premises would make these sexual revolutionaries a frequent ally, although often of questionable value, in the pursuit of wider dissemination of birth-control information and promotion of its social and economic theory.

[22] The term "liberal" was apparently preferred by these elements rather than the term "infidels" applied by the pro-Christian forces. The *Free Religious Index* (Boston), Aug. 25, 1881, defined "liberal" as "one who does not acknowledge the authority of the Bible or admit the supernatural character of the Christian system."
 Malthus is frequently cited as the father of the modern birth-control movement because of the reaction to his thesis that while population increases geometrically, the resources available for maintaining it increase only arithmetically. However, Malthus personally opposed the use of contraceptives. See Garrett Hardin, ed., *Population, Evolution and Birth Control* (San Francisco, n.d.), 192–93. Also the early American movement, blessed with a wealth of lands, never needed to emphasize population to the extent of the English neo-Malthusian movement.

[23] Ezra Heywood, quoted in Sidney Ditzion, *Marriage, Morals and Sex in America: A History of Ideas* (New York, 1953), 179. See Sidney Warren, *American Freethought, 1860–1914* (New York, 1943), 22–23, for a listing of the primary liberal journals.

[24] Quoted in Ditzion, *Marriage, Morals and Sex*, 166. Chap. 5 of Ditzion's treatise, entitled "Free Land, Free Labor, Free Love," provides an excellent account of the philosophy and activities of the radical element of the liberal movement.

[25] "Free thought" has been defined as "the contrary of thought, research, science and philosophy fettered by the dogmas and principles of religion.... [It] recognizes no restriction but that imposed upon its progress by the rules of logic, scientific methodology, and epistemology." *Encyclopedia of Social Sciences*, VI (New York, 1931), 465. See Stow Persons, *Free Religion: An American Faith* (New Haven, 1947); Warren, *American Freethought*.

In the realm of science, new discoveries and theories also challenged the tenets of fundamentalist religion. Darwin's evolutionary theories questioned simplistic versions of the origin of man based on a literal reading of the Bible, although a number of religionists believed that evolution was not necessarily inconsistent with basic religious beliefs. Lister, Pasteur, Koch, and others produced serious problems for the devout Christian who saw God's will as the basic explanation for all human ills.[26] It was an age of skepticism, pragmatism, discovery, and change. Although the Puritan morality reigned supreme, there were impending aspirants to the throne.

Indeed, the dominant morality was being undermined throughout society in a variety of ways. The post–Civil War era, properly labeled by Mark Twain and Charles Dudley Warner as "The Gilded Age," was an era in which vast fortunes were won and lost with little concern for the moralities of life or the constraints of legal norms. Speculation was rampant; the *nouveaux riches* offered living proof of easy money for those willing to gamble. But public officials were too engrossed in securing their share of the pork barrel to concern themselves with the social well-being. The robber barons, Jim Fisk, Jay Gould, Cornelius Vanderbilt, Jay Cooke, Daniel Drew, battled for wealth and power, and bought the guardians of the public interest as tools. Legislators willingly sold themselves and their votes to the business interests; court decrees were freely purchased. As a journalist of the period noted: "There is hardly a legislature in the country which is not suspected of corruption; there is hardly a court over which the same suspicion does not hang."[27]

[26] See, e.g., Charles A. Briggs, *Whither?* (New York, 1889); Washington Gladden, *Who Wrote the Bible?* (Boston, 1891). On Darwinism see Merle Curti, *The Growth of American Thought* (2nd ed., New York, 1951), 548–54; Charles Hodge, *What Is Darwinism?* (New York, 1874); Bert J. Loewenberg, "Darwinism Comes to America, 1858–1900," *Mississippi Valley Historical Review*, XXVIII (Dec., 1941), 339–68; "Evolution and Theology," *Nation*, Jan. 15, 1874, pp. 44–46; "What Is Darwinism?," *Nation*, May 28, 1874, pp. 348–50. See generally Andrew D. White, *A History of the Warfare of Science with Theology* (New York, 1941).

[27] The decline in business ethics during the period is treated generally by John D. Hicks, *The American Nation* (3rd ed., Cambridge, Mass., 1955), 79–84; Vernon L. Parrington, *The Beginnings of Critical Realism in America, 1860–1920* (New York, 1930), chap. 1; Allan Nevins, *The Emergence of Modern America, 1865–1878* (New York, 1927), 191–201. More detailed accounts of the business dealings of the "robber barons" can be found in Dennis T. Lynch, *The Wild Seventies* (New York, 1941); Don C. Seitz, *The Dreadful Decade, 1869–1879* (Indianapolis, 1926), chap. 2; Matthew Josephson, *The Robber Barons* (New York, 1935); "New Field for Fanatics," *Nation*, May 14, 1868, p. 386. Corruption in state politics is discussed in Samuel E. Morison and Henry S. Commager, *The Growth of the*

In the growing cities, politics was in the hands of groups such as the Tweed ring in New York, which, operating through Tammany Hall, freely took from the public coffers. Having purchased a city charter from the Albany legislature giving them the means to milk the city, Boss Tweed and his associates sold contracts, franchises, and municipal jobs, issued fraudulent bonds, inflated construction costs, until at the height of power they were draining off 85 percent of all city and county expenditures. What the Tweed ring was doing to New York, other rings were doing to cities across the country. Minneapolis had its Doc Alonzo Ames, San Francisco its "Blind Boss" Buckley, and in Philadelphia the Gas ring increased the municipal debt at the rate of $3 million annually.[28]

At the national level the situation was very much the same. The Grant administration had produced a level of public corruption unparalleled in our history. Senators, congressmen, and even Vice-President Schuyler Colfax were tainted by their involvement in the Credit Mobilier scandal of the late 1860s. Nepotism, graft in the Indian service, fraud by Internal Revenue agents, contract manipulation in the Treasury and Navy departments, a "salary grab" by the Forty-second Congress produced scandals that rocked the republic.[29]

And the moral breakdown was not limited only to the political, legal, and business sector. Looting and killing were rampant in the West as the returning soldiers practiced the trade learned so well during the war years. In the cities gambling, prostitution, and drinking had reached new levels of prominence as the slums and unemployment grew. New York City was reputed to have 2,000 gambling houses; the Louisiana Lottery flourished; gangs roamed the streets of the major cities while

---

American Republic, II (4th ed., New York, 1950), 74; Nevins, *The Emergence of Modern America*, 178–82.

[28] For an account of the activities of the Tweed ring see Gustavus Myers, *The History of Tammany Hall* (New York, 1917); Dennis T. Lynch, *"Boss" Tweed: The Story of a Grim Generation* (New York, 1927); Lynch, *The Wild Seventies*; Seitz, *The Dreadful Decade*, 159–99. On municipal corruption during the period see generally Arthur M. Schlesinger, *The Rise of Modern America, 1865–1951* (4th ed., New York, 1951), 48–49; C. W. Patton, *The Battle for Municipal Reform* (Washington, 1940); H. Zink, *City Bosses in the United States* (Durham, 1930); Hicks, *The American Nation*, 84–85; Nevins, *The Emergence of Modern America*, 182–87.

[29] See Matthew Josephson, *The Politicos, 1865–1900* (New York, 1938); J. B. Crawford, *The Credit Mobilier in America* (Boston, 1880); Seitz, *The Dreadful Decade*, chap. 8; Lynch, *The Wild Seventies*; Hicks, *The American Nation*, 47–51; Morison and Commager, *The Growth of the American Republic*, 71–74; Nevins, *The Emergence of Modern America*, 187–90; "Our Better Politicians," *Nation*, July 10, 1873, pp. 21–22.

one-fifth of Boston's population lived in tenements and 20,000 of New York's 100,000 slum dwellers spent their lives housed in cellars.[30]

But lest this be a distorted picture of America in the mid-nineteenth century, it must be emphasized that the masses generally remained true to their Puritan heritage, and religion continued to play a dominant role in community life. James Bryce, in his classic work on *The American Commonwealth*, observed that even in the waning years of the nineteenth century, religion and the clergy had a more prestigious place here than anywhere in western continental Europe, and equal to that of Victorian England.[31] Churches were everywhere; the number of communicants mounted steadily; the Sabbath was generally diligently observed; and even denominational differences did not stand in the way of a fairly close working relationship. The American of the period in culture and tastes displayed the Victorian morality that today we so readily associate with the nineteenth century. His values were still industry, morality, and temperance, and he freely accepted the teachings of the Bible and institutional religion as the guides for his life and that of his children—"religion and conscience have been a constantly active force in the American Commonwealth. . . ."[32] Not that he always lived according to these moral preachments, but he did espouse, accept, and support them. Both at home and in the schools the child was taught a strongly fundamentalist Christianity, for, after all, as a prominent geography text of the period explained: "Christianity is the only system which elevates man to a true sense of moral relations and adds to his importance."[33] Within this milieu the movement launched by the National Reform Association to have an amendment inserted into the Constitution declaring this to be a Christian nation seemed most natural.

[30] Hicks, *The American Nation*, 79–80; Nevins, *The Emergence of Modern America*, 201–2; Lynch, *The Wild Seventies*.

[31] James Bryce, *The American Commonwealth*, II (rev. ed., New York, 1927). In 1850 there were 38,183 church edifices, but by 1890 the number had increased to 142,521—an increase of 272 percent. Similarly, the increase in the number of communicants, even in light of the rising population, was phenomenal. Warren, *American Freethought*, 25–26. The *New York Daily Tribune*, Dec. 26, 1897, commented that "Christianity in this country has lost none of its vitality and little, if any, of its power over the heart and conscience of the Nation."

[32] Bryce, *The American Commonwealth*, 794. Excellent analyses of the latter-nineteenth-century American's values, attitudes, and tastes is provided by Henry S. Commager's *The American Mind* (New Haven, 1950), 3–40; Parrington, *The Beginnings of Critical Realism*; Curti, *The Growth of American Thought*, pt. VI.

[33] Quoted in Winfred E. Garrison, *The March of Faith: The Story of Religion in America since 1865* (New York, 1933), 66–67. Further examples of the moralistic flavor of the school texts of the period are provided in Curti, *The Growth of American Thought*, 533–38.

The ethical standard of the average man is of course the Christian standard, modified to some slight extent by the circumstances of American life, which have been different from those of Protestant Europe. The average man has not thought of any other standard, and religious teaching, though it has become less definite and less dogmatic, is still to him the source whence he believed himself to have drawn his ideas of duty and conduct.[34]

But the America of the latter nineteenth century was hardly consistent with the "holy state" of Puritan teachings. As the evangelist Dwight L. Moody predicated: "I do not know of anything that America needs more today than men and women on fire with the fire of heaven."[35] And the cause of Puritanism was not without ardent crusaders. Religious revivalism spread across the country ignoring denominational lines. As Ira D. Sankey sang the praise of God, Dwight L. Moody, proudly trumpeting that every ounce of his 280 pounds "belonged to God," spoke to thousands on the need for religious renewal. Henry Ward Beecher, John B. Gough, and DeWitt Talmage all used their pulpits to preach the need for moral regeneration. In 1870 some 407 religious periodicals used the printed word to carry the message of revival,[36] and even political reformers manifested the moralistic orientation.

But the message for moral regeneration was not only for believers. Puritanism was essentially a militant creed—"its aim is not to lift up saints, but to knock down sinners."[37]

> The Puritan hated the Flesh in himself and he hated even more fiercely that Flesh appearing as the vices of others. . . . It is useless to tell such a man to love his neighbor as himself; he hates so

---

[34] Bryce, *The American Commonwealth*, 791. On the proposed amendment see Warren, *American Freethought*, 176–77.

[35] Dwight L. Moody, *Short Talks* (Chicago, 1900), 100. See Rev. B. B. Hotchkiss, *Infidelity against Itself* (Philadelphia, 1850), 7–10, on the concern felt by religious elements over the challenge to organized religion and to religious belief generally; Warren, *American Freethought*, 211. On the thought and influence of Dwight L. Moody see Moody, *Gospel Awakening* (16th ed., Chicago, 1883); Gamaliel Bradford, *D. L. Moody: A Worker in Souls* (Garden City, 1928); W. R. Moody, *D. L. Moody* (New York, 1930). The emphasis given revivalism and moral regeneration during the period is discussed in B. D. Loud, *Evangelized America* (New York, 1923); S. G. Cole, *The History of Fundamentalism* (New York, 1931); Curti, *The Growth of American Thought*, 533–38; Garrison, *The March of Faith*.

[36] Garrison, *The March of Faith*, 10.

[37] Henry L. Mencken, "Puritanism as a Literary Force," quoted in Heywood Broun and Margaret Leech, *Anthony Comstock: Roundsman of the Lord* (New York, 1927), 75–76. See Ralph B. Perry, *Puritanism and Democracy* (New York, 1944), 321–22, on the evangelistic character of Puritanism.

much of himself. His hate, reservoired within him, gets its drainage in raids on vice, in the persecutions and suppressions carried on by anti-vice societies and in campaigns of reform that call for the punishment of all evil-doers.[38]

Across the country religious societies were formed to take the teachings of Christianity out of the churches and into the streets. Magdalen Homes, Reserve Midnight Missions, Christian Industrial Clubs, the American Purity Alliance, the Women's Christian Temperance Union were the order of the day. Women's crusades, with banners flowing and bands playing, were the harbingers of the Salvation Army. And the YMCA and YWCA constituted prestigious organizations for directing the evangelistic fervor. Anti-vice societies, law-enforcement leagues, temperance unions were zealous expressions of the crusading spirit of Puritanism.[39] After all, when one has a message of salvation, it cannot be confined inside walls and limited to the few. Morality was considered the rockbed of the republic, and religious societies, in doing the work of God, were saving the nation.

It is in this context that the work of Anthony J. Comstock and his associates must be understood. For Comstock, "religion and morality are the only safe foundations for a nation's future prosperity and security." These were the restraining forces that kept the ship of state from being "dashed to pieces upon the boulders and quicksands of immorality."[40] Law was to be used in support of public morality—"the courts of justice are, or ought to be, the schools of public morals."[41] Indeed, Comstock's personal definition of "Comstockery" was "the applying of the noblest principles of law . . . in the interests of Public Morals, especially those of the young."[42] Too often the cause of public morality was inadequately served because of the absence of strong and effective laws for the suppression of vice.

Comstock's cause was framed primarily in terms of the need to protect youth from the forces of organized vice. Newspapers, cheap

[38] Harvey O'Higgins and E. H. Reede, *The American Mind in Action*, quoted in Broun and Leech, *Anthony Comstock*, 24.
[39] See Leonard W. Bacon, *A History of American Christianity*, XIII (New York, 1893), 366–67.
[40] Anthony Comstock, "Vampire Literature," *North American Review*, CLIII (Aug., 1891), 162, 171.
[41] Anthony Comstock, "Lotteries and Gambling," *North American Review*, CLIV (Feb., 1892), 217.
[42] Quoted in "How Came 'Comstockery,'" *Literary Digest*, XCIII (Apr. 2, 1927), 52.

books, and magazines became instruments of Satan—"Satan lays the snares and children are his victims. His traps, like all others, are baited to lure the human soul."[43]

> What follows? The susceptible mind of the boy receives impressions that set on fire his whole nature. His imagination is perverted. A black stain is fixed indelibly upon it, and conscience, once a faithful monitor, is now seared and silenced. The will, which once raised a strong barrier against solicitations to evil, no longer asserts itself, and our bright noble boy often becomes a wreck of his former self.[44]

It was this message on the vital need for legal reform to bolster public morality, especially among the young, which Comstock sought to convey to the Congress when he came to Washington in 1873. He portrayed a moral crisis, and crisis is, perhaps, one of the factors that best motivates a legislature to act. But, as was suggested in the Introduction, legislation is seldom the function of the discrete individual. Alone it is unlikely that Comstock could have attracted the support necessary even to gain access to the legislature, much less overcome the pressure of conflicting demands for the limited legislative time and effort. Comstock, however, did not stand alone. Behind him was the influential New York Young Men's Christian Association and, more particularly, its Committee for the Suppression of Vice, a counterpart of the prototype English anti-vice society.[45] Yet even this does not suffice to explain the impetus for legislative consideration of Comstock's demands. Behind the reformer and his group stood the aforementioned forces of Puritanism and the dominant moral opinion of the period, the churches, the anti-vice societies, the purity and temperance leagues. Although we tend to glamorize the role of an individual, "Comstockery" did represent the prevailing orientation of the period toward sexual matters. Contraception, abortion, sterilization, obscenity, vice were blended in the Puritan mentality and unequivocally condemned. Since social change posed a threat to this established morality, Comstock's activities in securing legal action can best be understood as the reaction of vested interests. Societal and interest-group support gave Comstock both his

---

[43] Anthony Comstock, *Traps for the Young* (New York, 1884), 9.
[44] New York Society for the Suppression of Vice, *Sixth Annual Report* (New York, 1880), 11. See Comstock, *Traps for the Young*, especially chap. 8.
[45] On the activities of the anti-vice societies see Paul S. Boyer, *Purity in Print: The Vice-Society Movement and Book Censorship in America* (New York, 1968).

access to the legislature and eventually his legislative triumph. As Comstock's biographers, Heywood Broun and Margaret Leech, indicated:

> Anthony Comstock was adapted to the folkways of his time and place. Often in the fight against obscenity he stood alone. Always he was in the van. But somewhere behind him an army of Puritans was solidly massed. For this reason, he was feared and hated—because he was so strong. Had his crusade run counter to the mores of his people, he would have been a pitiful picture, a martyr to his lonely ideal. But in him people cursed the spirit of enforced righteousness made palpable—fleshly and menacing, with ginger colored whiskers and a warrant and a Post Office badge. He was the apotheosis, the fine flower of Puritanism.[46]

The decision to seek legislative action appears to have been made in 1872. Comstock convinced the YMCA committee of the need for more effective postal laws to prevent interstate transmission of vile articles and literature, more encompassing laws which could be used to suppress all questionable materials. The committee's prestige, lines of communication, and influence were dramatized by the willingness of Supreme Court Justice William Strong to assist in drafting the bill and in serving as liaison with friendly congressional elements. Comstock was also warmly received by his legislative contacts. Vice-President Henry Wilson permitted him to use his office as a base of operations and prominent legislators were most receptive to his appeal for new tools to fight vice. He was assured that he could "have any law he might ask for, if it was only within the bounds of the Constitution."[47] Representative Merriam of New York was selected to shepherd the bill through the House, and Senator Windham of Minnesota agreed to serve as Senate sponsor.

This short account of the recommending function does suggest the parity between the primary elements suggested in the Introduction and those present in the recommendation of the Comstock legislation: external pressures from public opinion and an influential interest group having access; available legislators who agreed to act as group spokesmen; and even a Supreme Court justice, acting informally, instrumental in communicating group demands to the legislative actor. If Comstock had acted only as a citizen, it is doubtful that he would have received

---

[46] Broun and Leech, *Anthony Comstock*, 88–89.
[47] Quoted from the diary of Anthony Comstock by Broun and Leech, *Anthony Comstock*, 131. The ability of reform interests of the period to influence Congress is criticized in "The Intimidation of Congress," *Nation*, Feb. 12, 1874, pp. 103–4.

such legislative empathy. But Anthony Comstock could, with credibility, claim to speak for the mothers and fathers across the country concerned for the virtue of their children; he could speak for the churches and religious societies shocked at the immorality that had become so rampant in postwar America; and he could purport to represent those myriad interests identified with the maintenance of "traditional morality" shaken by the new ideas and practices gradually gaining acceptance. Given such a constituency, Comstock was indeed a force to be reckoned with.

This account also suggests a possible motivation for pursuing change through the legislative forum. Although Comstock had worked under existing obscenity laws through the courts in fighting vice, the judiciary could not provide him with the comprehensive sweeping tools that would permit full freedom to fight the enemy. The courts might have been willing, on occasion, to expand the reach of existing legislation or even to use the common-law concept of an offense against the public morals, but such a policy was far too indefinite and haphazard for the vice fighter. As he noted in a 1915 interview: "If you open the door to anything, the filth will all pour in and the degradation of youth will follow."[48] The legislative institution, capable of providing the all-encompassing prohibitive tools, was indeed the proper forum to pursue such an objective; the politics of the recommending function had made its achievement possible.

The Intelligence Function

The primary formal institutional mechanisms through which the legislature seeks to consider "rationally" the need for action are legislative hearings and floor debates. There is, however, a wide divergence of opinion as to their efficacy for providing the requisite data. The following two evaluations present very different accounts of what may be expected of legislative hearings.

> Committee responsibility usually results in more complete and competent information than the judicial method of brief and argument. The appellate tribunal must depend upon a lawyer's evaluation of a proposed decision. The committee, in addition to its lawyers, enjoys the counsel of economists, public administrators, and business men. And bi-party committee representa-

[48] Mary A. Hopkins, "Birth Control and Public Morals," *Harpers*, May 22, 1915, p. 490.

tion insures additional divergent viewpoints. Practical evaluation of proposed legislation is ever available in the committee room.[49]

Despite much gospel to the contrary, a legislature is not a fact-finding body. There is no mechanism as there is with a court, to require the legislature to sift facts and to make a decision about specific situations. There need be no agreement about what the situation is. The members of the legislative body will be talking about different things; they cannot force each other to accept even a hypothetical set of facts. The result is that even in a non-controversial atmosphere just exactly what has been decided will not be clear.[50]

It has been suggested that the fact-gathering functions of the committee hearings are probably the least important. More often, the hearings provide a forum for competing interests to relieve their frustration as well as a propaganda channel to reach the public, to expand the scope of the conflict, and to enable the legislator to discover the interest alignments. Unless a member of the committee has a special interest, much testimony goes unchallenged; the hearing becomes a pro forma ritual. If a committeeman is interested, there is a good possibility that he is a partisan more determined to further a particular point of view than to seek an accurate evaluation of the facts. Exceptions occur in which the hearings function according to the ideal model where all evidence is screened, analyzed, briefed, and communicated to the legislature, but "as an institution for informing the entire legislative body about the content of proposed legislation and the problems with which it deals, a legislative committee leaves much to be desired."[51]

Such a judgment certainly seems accurate in the instance of the hearings and debates associated with the 1873 passage of an "Act for the Suppression of Trade in, and Circulation of Obscene Literature and Articles of Immoral Use."[52] After accommodating the desires of other anti-vice elements seeking legislation, the proposed bill consisted of five

---

[49] Frank E. Horack, Jr., "The Common Law of Legislation," *Readings in Jurisprudence and Legal Philosophy*, ed. Morris R. and Felix S. Cohen (New York, 1951), 496.

[50] Edward H. Levi, *An Introduction to Legal Reasoning* (Chicago, 1948), 31.

[51] Cornelius J. Peck, "The Role of Courts and Legislatures in the Reform of Tort Law," *Minnesota Law Review*, XLVIII (Dec., 1963), 276. The analysis of the legislative fact-finding process is based on Jewell and Patterson, *The Legislative Process*, 455, quoting Congressman Clem Miller; David Truman, *The Governmental Process* (New York, 1951), 372; James W. Hurst, *The Growth of American Law* (Boston, 1950), 36, 60–61; Cohen, "Hearings on a Bill," 39.

[52] 18 U.S.C. 1461–62 (1964); 19 U.S.C. 1305 (1964).

sections; (1) prohibition on distribution of obscene materials or articles for the prevention of conception in the District of Columbia; (2) prohibitions on usage of the mails for transmitting such materials; (3) a prohibition on the importation of contraceptive devices with provisions for seizure; (4) sanctions for officials knowingly aiding the violation of the law; and (5) authorization for the issuance of writs for search and seizure. The early ad hoc judicial approach of utilizing the established legal category of "obscenity" to birth control was now to receive legislative sanction. (See Appendix A for the text of the federal legislation.)

At the postal committee hearings on the proposed legislation, in the hallways of Congress, and whenever possible, Comstock displayed a mass of pornographic literature and postcards, contraceptive and abortifacient devices, and a variety of other "vile" materials. Coupled with an unsubstantiated argument on the relationship between such literature, the increasing availability of "rubber articles for masturbation or for the professed prevention of conception," and social decay, this served as the primary data through which the legislature was "informed." *After* the vote had been taken, Representative Merriam inserted correspondence between himself and Comstock into the record which indicated his concern with the effect of pornography and indecent articles on the morality of youth and the extent of organized vice. Even if the letter had been available for legislative consideration, however, it only suggested causal lines without establishing any empirical linkage.

But presumed causality sufficed without the need for logical discussion in an atmosphere of moralism born of a Puritan mind that closely linked purity with national well-being.

> Purity is fundamental in its importance to the individual, to the home and to the nation. There can be no true manhood, no true womanhood except as based upon the law of Purity. There can be no security for the home, there can be no home-life in its best sense, except as it is based upon the law of Purity. There can be no true prosperity, there can be no perpetuation of a nation except as its life is based upon the law of Purity. Impurity is destructive alike to the individual character, of the home, and of the nation.[53]

Further, the relation of moral well-being to political development was accepted as an a priori principle requiring no proof.

---

[53] Aaron M. Powell, "The President's Opening Address," *The National Purity Congress*, ed. Aaron M. Powell (New York, 1896), 1.

I can only say, in a word that Social Purity is indispensable to Political Purity; and that free institutions cannot endure without a high standard of Social Purity among people. The lofty Puritan spirit to which we in America owe so much, was perhaps the most important factor in the formation of that free government on which the hopes, not only of America, but of the whole world so largely rest.[54]

Such bland reliance on moralistic assertions would hardly fulfill the criteria for a rational, informed, goal-oriented mode of decision-making. No attempt was made to demonstrate empirically the corruption of youth by the availability of contraceptive knowledge or the negative effects of contraceptives on society generally; no apparent consideration was given to the consequences of a restrictive policy or its potential social efficacy. Why was prohibitive legislation enacted when regulation would apparently have sufficed for the needs set forth? Where was any consideration of alternative values such as individual freedom, the needs that birth control might satisfy, or the possibility of a future change in the dominant moral beliefs? While it might have been possible to justify legislation in terms of nineteenth-century society, e.g. on health grounds, because of the poor quality of many extant contraceptives,[55] no such justification was provided. There is no indication that the legislature seriously considered whether contraception really conformed to the class of evils sought to be encompassed in obscenity legislation. Like the courts in the Knowlton cases, the legislature turned to established legal concepts without serious consideration of the peculiar problems generated by the social development involving birth control. Given the absence of any semblance of creativity in this legislative response to social change, the comments of Senator Conkling at the time seem quite appropriate: "And if I were to be questioned now as to what the bill contains, I could not aver anything certain in regard to it. The indignation and disgust which everybody feels in reference to the acts which are here aimed at may possibly lead us to do something which, when we come to see it in print, will not be the thing we would have done if we had understood it and were more deliberate about it."[56]

The rapidity of passage also suggests the legislature's lack of concern

---

[54] Letter from Charles C. Bonney to Aaron M. Powell, *ibid.*, 20.
[55] See Fryer, *The Birth Controllers*, 120–21; text accompanying note 18 *supra*.
[56] U.S., *Congressional Globe*, 42nd Cong., 3rd Sess., 1873, II, 1525.

with fashioning creative policy. In fact, the frequently vague and rambling style of the language reflects the quality of the inquiry that accompanied its passage. Although Comstock felt that legislative policymaking was unnecessarily delayed, it is questionable that any appropriate action could have been achieved in the short time that the bill was under consideration. Introduced in the latter part of the session (February 11, 1873), it had become law in less than a month (March 1, 1873). Only about fifteen minutes of debate had been devoted to the matter; no roll-call vote was taken; it was passed without any real opposition. While two legislators expressed perfunctory concern with the "hot haste" of passage, it was consistent with the last-minute rush that generally characterizes the end of legislative sessions.[57] The provisions regarding contraception were not even mentioned in the debate.

The Prescriptive Function

It is quite easy for a modern-day analyst to shake his head sadly at legislative bodies that would enact such a sweeping change on such a vital subject with hardly a modicum of debate and a lack of in-depth inquiry. But when motivational circumstances are considered, the legislative behavior, although not justified, becomes far more understandable.

The militant attitude of interests favoring the proposed legal change appears to have been a primary element influencing the legislative actor. As David Truman noted in his work *The Governmental Process*: "Organized interest groups . . . from their very nature bulk large in the political process. Collections of individuals interacting on the basis of shared attitudes and exerting claims upon other groups in the society usually find in the institutions of government an important means of

---

[57] See "The Way Congress Does Business," *Nation*, Feb. 27, 1873, pp. 145-46. Morris E. Ernst suggests that such haste is common when a legislature ignores facts or is ignorant of science. Symposium, "What Should Be the Relation of Morals to Law?," *Journal of Public Law*, I (Fall, 1952), 304.

For a detailed account of the legislative deliberations on the Comstock legislation see Mary Ware Dennet, *Birth Control Laws* (New York, 1926), 19-45; Alvah Sulloway, *Birth Control and Catholic Doctrine* (Boston, 1959), 170-72; Paul and Schwartz, *Federal Censorship*, 18-24. In fact, one of the primary changes in the bill, an amendment introduced by Senator Buckingham removing an exemption for licensed physicians, was destined to become a major source of dispute. Although Senator Conkling claimed that "no Senator is able to get any intelligent idea of the substance of the amendment as contrasted with what it is to take the place of," Senator Buckingham claimed that it made "no material alteration in the section." U.S., *Congressional Globe*, 42nd Cong., 3rd Sess., 1873, II, 1525.

achieving their objectives. That is, most interest groups become politicized on a continuing or intermittent basis."[58] In this instance, the various religions were united in their condemnation of contraception and all other forms of obscenity. Represented by anti-vice, temperance, and purity groups, and especially the prestigious YMCA, the vested interests supporting the moral consensus not only obtained an audience for reformers like Comstock, but also used their power to secure passage of "reform" legislation—"reform" here meaning legal support for moral taboos under social attack. A possible example of the exercise of this influence occurred when delays hampering the quick passage of the Comstock bill provoked influential members of the Committee for the Suppression of Vice to send protest telegrams to House Speaker James G. Blaine. He, in turn, promptly assured Comstock that the bill would be called; it was voted upon at the next day's session. An equally vivid demonstration of the committee's influence took place when it was incorporated as the New York Society for the Suppression of Vice. The committee's new charter instructed police to assist agents of the society in implementing the state vice laws, thereby establishing its position as a quasi-governmental body. Its agents frequently arrested and prosecuted violators of the laws and Comstock himself became a special agent of the Post Office Department, a role he played with great enthusiasm.

Nor can we ignore the fact that the efficacy of group action is generally determined by its status vis-à-vis competing interests. In comparison to the prestigious Puritan vested interests supporting the demands made by Comstock, elements opposed to Comstockery were seriously deficient. They were primarily liberal, free-thought, free-love exponents who could claim little influence in a society dominated by Victorian morality. The birth-control movement was still in a nascent stage. Medical, scientific, and sociological opinion was generally hostile.[59]

In order for a group to achieve a desired position, it must be able to

[58] Truman, *The Governmental Process*, 502. He compares the legislature to a court to which petitioners come seeking indulgences and a redress of grievances: "As a seat of power it is one of many points to which appeals can lie from disturbances in the society at large or from acts of judicial courts and administrative agencies. Especially in a loosely integrated system like that in the United States, the legislative process offers an interest group alternative means of effectively asserting its claim. This process has long since outclassed that of the common-law courts as a means of declaring the law." *Ibid.*, 394.

[59] John T. Noonan, *Contraception: A History of Its Treatment by the Catholic Theologians and Canonists* (Cambridge, Mass., 1965), 394.

demonstrate public support; constituents' response to interest-group stimuli can be a vital criterion by which legislators judge group activity. While legislators may differ widely in their role orientations to group pressures, seldom can they afford to ignore the political consequences of the proposed action. In this instance, any legislative balancing of political interests in terms of power left little doubt as to the result. Vested interests worked through the legislature to ward off threats to the dominant morality; legal change was employed as an impediment to social change.

In addition, it appears that legislative cleavages based on party affiliation were inoperative. Reform and Puritanism were the temper of the times and it would have taken a brave or foolish legislator, or party, to resist the demands of its exponents. When Comstock arrived in Washington, Congress was suffering the aftermath of the Credit Mobilier and other scandals; reform was in the wind and it was hardly the time for a legislator to challenge the pervasive morality. Love of God, motherhood, and country, hatred of sin, vice, and impurity were politically safe.[60] Representative Merriam warned his colleagues that "the masses of their people . . . will not wonder that their representatives have consented to enter upon an investigation of a most disagreeable and sickening nature; nor would they pardon us should we fail to put an end to this nefarious and diabolical tariff."[61] When a senator suggested revising the Comstock bill to make it more specific, he was told: "Let the Senate take the bill as it has been reported and pass it. *The country demands it.*"[62] The national consensus on morality thus became embodied in legal policy. In a trial for violation of the act, an assistant district attorney summarized this societal consensus for the

[60] See Carol F. Brooks, "The Early History of the Anti-Contraceptive Laws in Massachusetts and Connecticut," *American Quarterly*, XVIII (Spring, 1966), 22. The *New York Times*, Mar. 8, 1873, p. 7, col. 2, reprinting an article from the *New York Journal of Commerce*, declared that Congress could now be forgiven its improprieties, since it had now "powerfully sustained the cause of morality. . . . Those wretches who are debauching the youth of the country and murdering women and unborn babes, will soon be in the strong grip of the government."

[61] *New York Times*, Mar. 15, 1873, p. 3, col. 3. Merriam also accepted the recurring theme that public morality and national well-being were inseparably intertwined: "The outraged manhood of our age will place, in the strongest possible manner, its seal of condemnation upon the low brutality which threatened to destroy the future of this Republic by making merchandise of the morals of our youth." In fact, the dissemination of obscenity was compared to "war, pestilence or famine." *Ibid.*

[62] U.S., *Congressional Globe*, 42nd Cong., 3rd Sess., 1873, II, 1525.

jury. "Now, gentlemen, this case is not entitled 'Anthony Comstock against D. M. Bennett'; this case is not entitled 'The Society for the Suppression of Vice against D. M. Bennett.' Yes, it is. It is the United States against D. M. Bennett, and the United States is one great society for the suppression of vice."[63]

We should not, however, blithely assume that the legislators acted as automatons responding to pressure-group tactics. While no scientific data can be presented on their moral and ideological values, it would be extraordinary were they incompatible with the pervasive moral orientation. Selling out to a business interest on occasion did not necessarily negate the possibility of a strong moralistic response to sexual matters consistent with the Puritan environment. The specific evils condemned by Comstock were probably also personally abhorrent to most of the legislators.

A final question might be raised concerning the character of the legislative response: why was total prohibition rather than regulation employed? Although again no data appear to be available, a suggestion might be offered. The Puritan mind seems to have identified regulatory legislation with a tacit endorsement of the subject. Indeed, shortly after passage of the Comstock legislation, a national purity alliance was formed to oppose governmental *regulation* of vice.[64] The only way to express the appropriate degree of abhorrence of the subject would be total prohibition. Given the militancy of the anti-vice societies, the regulatory approach may not have been a realistic alternative. As suggested in the Introduction, the choice of devices for legislative action, like the decision to act itself, is a function of social, political, personal, and institutional variables. And all of these elements called for legal change to condemn the threat to the dominant morality.

STATE LEGISLATIVE ACTION

In advocating passage of the Comstock legislation, Representative Merriam had made a comment that was to prove highly prophetic. "I believe the calling of the attention of the country to this monstrous crime, and

---

[63] Broun and Leech, *Anthony Comstock*, 89. See Morris L. Ernst and William Seagle, *To the Pure . . . : A Study of Obscenity and the Censor* (New York, 1928).
[64] Antoinette B. Blackwell, "Immorality of the Regulation System," *The National Purity Congress*, ed. Powell, 21.

the determination of the representatives of the people in Congress to go to the furthest constitutional point, within their power of legislation for its annihilation, will incite every State Legislature to enact similar laws for its final destruction."[65] While the new act might be used to curtail interstate dissemination of obscene materials, it was still necessary to move against the vice trade within the states. As will be noted frequently below, the policy formulated at one governmental level in our federal system often forms a vital part of the environment influencing the behavior of policy-makers at other governmental levels. In this instance, the militancy of the anti-vice forces, coupled with the favorable moral climate, practically assured that the national victory would be translated into legislative action at other governmental levels.

Following passage of the Comstock Act, then, a general campaign was launched to obtain similar legislation in the states which would not only allow anti-vice forces to attack the intrastate dissemination of contraceptive information and services, but also provide greater flexibility in forum selection. As a result of this campaign, over half of the states enacted obscenity legislation specifically dealing with contraceptives, while all but two of the remaining states already had obscenity laws which could be interpreted to encompass birth control.[66] (See Appendix B for a compilation of the statutory situation as of 1960 and an indication of subsequent developments.)

As in most instances of state legislative activity, there is a serious deficiency in the information available (records of state legislative proceedings, for example, are generally not available). Nevertheless, even the limited data available does suggest that the enactment of legislation in New York, Connecticut, and Massachusetts, the three states on which the present study focuses, followed the general pattern of the national action. In each case the impetus for action came from Anthony Comstock and his anti-vice associates,[67] the proposed bills received only perfunctory review and limited attention to draftsmanship, and the legislation was passed with minimal debate.

New York had actually dealt with contraception summarily in an 1868 obscenity law passed at the behest of the New York YMCA. However, it was hardly mentioned in the statute; the ban was apparently

[65] *New York Times*, Mar. 15, 1873, p. 3, col. 3.
[66] See Dennett, *Birth Control Laws*, 3-45.
[67] Comstock claimed credit for the passage of the legislation. See New York Society for the Suppression of Vice, *Sixth Annual Report*, 6; Brooks, "The Early History," 8.

never enforced; and the whole provision was finally dropped in an 1872 revision. But one year later, Comstock and his New York society secured a more sweeping provision modeled on the federal act.[68] The bill was introduced by Hon. George Clark, who later became a member of the anti-vice society, and probably was written by Comstock himself. There is no doubt that the reformer and his society in this, their home state, were instrumental in its passage. Comstock frequently appeared in Albany displaying his wares of vile materials corrupting the youth and exhorting the assemblymen to do their duty. Only one assemblyman apparently opposed Comstock's entreaties. But when Anthony threatened to expose the fact that among the items included in the assemblyman's import business were obscene rubber goods, he also joined the crusade.[69] In 1887, upon request of the anti-vice elements, the prohibition was extended to advertising and representations concerning the preventive capabilities of contraceptive devices. Even though subsequent interpretation would prove otherwise, the act, as amended, appeared to be as sweeping as its federal counterpart, with little concern for clarity of language or limitation of scope. (See Appendix C for the text of the New York statute.)

The origins of the Massachusetts policy against contraceptives can also be traced to the activities of Comstock's legion. In May, 1878, Anthony attended a meeting in Boston which resulted in the formation of the New England Society for the Suppression of Vice, later to become the Watch and Ward Society. Although the new group was to center most of its activities in Boston, it included prestigious representatives from all of the other New England states. There was Rev. Noah Porter, president of Yale (Connecticut), Rev. E. G. Robinson, president of Brown (Rhode Island), Rev. Matt H. Buckham, president of the University of Vermont, Rev. S. C. Bartlett, president of Dartmouth (New Hampshire), Rev. Henry E. Robins, president of Colby (Maine). Massachusetts was represented by Rev. Philip Brooks, Rev. Edward E. Hale, Rev. A. J. Gordon, Rev. Julius H. Seelye, president of Amherst, and Hon. Edward S. Tobey. The group elected as president Col. Homer B. Sprague, principal of a girls' high and normal school, who appears to have accepted completely the Comstock philosophy regarding law, morality, and vice. Given the outstanding luminaries founding the society, it should not be surprising that the group exerted considerable

---

[68] William J. McWilliams, "Laws of New York and Birth Control: A Survey," *Birth Control Review*, XIV (Feb., 1930), 46–47, 61–63.
[69] Broun and Leech, *Anthony Comstock*, 148.

influence. Comstock himself credited the organization with the passage of the Connecticut and Massachusetts legislation.[70]

The Massachusetts legislation, "An Act Concerning Offenses against Chastity, Morality and Decency," was enacted in 1879, apparently without any discussion and probably without any dissent. (See Appendix D for the text of the Massachusetts law.) Like its federal counterpart, it was sweeping in character and passed with maximum dispatch. Introduced by Representative Hamilton A. Hill of Boston on February 5, it was sent to the Judiciary Committee; reported out on February 28; passed; sent to the Senate on March 12; concurred in on March 20; signed by Governor Talbot on March 26.[71]

There was apparently some opposition by liberal forces in Boston. The free thought–free love advocate, Ezra Heywood, led a protest meeting which resolved that the recently enacted law, "ostensibly for the purpose of punishing all attempts at the regulation of the increase of families, but really for the purpose of suppressing heterodoxy in medicine, is the latest development of the contemptible conspiracy to deprive the people of their liberties." Heywood saw the fine work of Comstock in the legislation: "No citizen of Massachusetts asked for the passage of the 'law'; it was slyly worked through by Comstock himself. . . . What do the Republican Party and Governor Talbot mean by importing this pious scamp from Brooklyn to 'regulate' morality in Massachusetts."[72] However, there seems little doubt that Comstock did not stand alone in urging legal change on the Massachusetts legislature, and it is equally unlikely that Heywood's attacks, the liberals' resolutions, or a similar resolve of the New England Free Love League had any great impact on the legislative policy-makers. Massachusetts was the home of the Puritan theocracy; it was the birthplace of the New England Society for the Suppression of Vice; it was a bastion of the old order resisting the

---

[70] New York Society for the Suppression of Vice, *Sixth Annual Report*, 6. See generally Brooks, "The Early History," 149.

[71] Massachusetts, *Journal of the House, 1879*, 178, 311, 320, 348; Massachusetts, *Journal of the Senate, 1879*, 239, 256. On the origins of the Massachusetts law see Birth Control League of Massachusetts, *Contraceptive Advice and the Massachusetts Law* (Boston, 1930); Stephen D. Howard, "The Birth Control Law Conflict in Massachusetts" (unpublished B.A. thesis, Harvard College, 1959), 1–7 (from the files of the Planned Parenthood League of Massachusetts, PPLM); Brooks, "The Early History," 8–9.

In 1905 the law was amended to include contraceptive literature, although the groups seeking a revision of the laws apparently had not contemplated this change. Birth Control League of Massachusetts, *Contraceptive Advice and the Mass. Law*, 21–30.

[72] *The Word*, May, 1879, p. 3.

tides of social change. It was, simply, most amenable to demands for entrenchment.

The Connecticut assault on the birth controllers originated on February 7, 1879, when Senate Bill 43, "An Act to Amend an Act Concerning Offenses against Decency, Morality and Humanity," was introduced by Senator Carlos Smith of New Haven.[73] The likelihood that Comstock contributed to its passage is again highly probable, even though an important role seems to have been played by the reformer-performer Phineas T. Barnum, chairman of the Joint Standing Committee on Temperance, who shared Comstock's general orientation to the proper role of morality in fashioning laws. Further, although there is no solid evidence that the New England Society for the Suppression of Vice contributed concretely to the passage of the legislation, it should be noted that Connecticut was represented at the founding of the society by Rev. Noah Porter, president of Yale, and Hon. B. G. Northrup, secretary of the Connecticut Board of Education.

Unlike the previous instances of birth-control policy-making, some discussion, revision, and dissent occurred within the legislature—not that it was very extensive, but at least it was present. Moral exhortations that the bill was "in the interest of the highest morality and against crimes of the worst sort; no more righteous bill has been presented here"[74] suggest the flavor of the argument. In fact, one of the most important legislative changes was the inclusion of a unique prohibition against the *use* of contraceptives. Apparently the total unenforceability of such a provision was not even considered. Of course, even if it had been discussed, there seems to be no reason to believe that the legislative behavior would have been altered. The Protestant community demanded legal policy expressive of the dominant morality as well as condemnation of threats to the established order—this moral orientation appears to have been the primary motivation for all the legislative action under discussion.

The final legislation, signed into law March 28, 1879, appears as vague and sweeping as its federal counterpart, linking contraception, abortion, and obscenity indiscriminately, with no attention to the peculiarities of each.

[73] On the origin of the Connecticut law see Brooks, "The Early History," 9–13; Comment, "The History and Future of the Legal Battle over Birth Control," *Cornell Law Quarterly*, XLII (Winter, 1964), 279.

[74] Brooks, "The Early History," 10, quoting the *Hartford Courant*, Mar. 20, 1879. See Connecticut, *Journal of the Senate, 1879*, 236, 294, 317, 339, 414, 449, 586; Connecticut, *Journal of the House, 1879*, 271, 333, 488, 548, 576, 594.

The Origins of Comstockery : 47

Every person who shall sell, or lend, or introduce into any family, college, academy or school, or shall have in their possession, for any unlawful purpose or purposes, any obscene, lewd, or lascivious book, pamphlet, paper, picture, print, drawing, figure, or image, or other publication of an indecent nature, or who shall manufacture, sell, advertise for sale, or have in their possession, for any such unlawful purpose or purposes, any article, thing, or instrument designed, intended and adapted for, any indecent or immoral use, purpose, nature, or use any drug, medicine, article, or instrument whatsoever for the purpose of preventing conception, or causing unlawful abortion, shall be fined not less than fifty dollars nor more than three hundred dollars or imprisoned not less than sixty days nor more than one year or both.[75]

CONCLUSION

Social changes producing new interests challenging the vested morality had generated a demand for legal change. But the demand in this instance originated with the status quo forces for legal reinforcement of moral norms; interest groups having "access" pressed their claims in the legislative forum. The legislative action raises provocative questions concerning the use of legal norms to enforce moral beliefs, but for our purposes it is the responsive character of the legal actor that is most important.

In all cases the character of legislative inquiry was hardly consistent with the ideal model of the intelligence function. Debate was perfunctory; hearings were meaningless occasions for moral exhortations; and no real attempt was made to secure nonlegal assistance. It was hasty and ill-considered policy-making in which traditional legal categories were revised and expanded to encompass a new social problem. This is not to pass judgment on the objectives of the legislators responding to change but only to criticize the lack of care with which it was done. Vague and rambling language, indiscriminately treating disparate subjects alike with little concern for future needs and problems, characterized the legislative activity.

[75] Connecticut, *Public Acts Passed by the General Assembly of the State of Connecticut, 1879*, chap. 78, p. 428. In 1886 a revision of the Connecticut statutes resulted in removal of the contraceptive provision from the obscenity statutes and the drafting of a single statute.

Although party and institutional variables do not appear to have played any major role at the prescriptive stage, considerations of constituency attitudes and interest-group strength, as well as the legislator's personal value system, do seem to have been vital. All were component elements of the moral consensus; all pulled the legislator in the same direction. The legislative reaction, although perhaps disappointing to many, is not really surprising. While compromise and bargaining might have effectuated a less restrictive form of legal change, such a reaction was most improbable, given the social milieu and the demands of the militant interests supporting the legislative revision. Social change relating to birth control was still in a nascent stage and the legal bulwarks erected in the 1870s were to prove a source of frustration in its future development.

Two

Early Reactions to Comstockery

Passage of the Comstock laws had introduced a new chapter into America's experience in the legal control of "obscenity." But the efficacy of a legal norm can be evaluated only after the law in the books is transformed into the law in action. In the implementation of the law, the legal norm attains meaning; it becomes socially relevant. Similarly, it is the social application of the law that usually generates the motivation for subsequent legal action. As noted in the Introduction, neither the initial legislative nor judicial response to a problem generated by social change is likely to be a terminal point in the process. One of the primary characteristics of the American legal system is its multiple points of access. Parties disappointed in one forum can press their demands to one of the other legal policy-makers and through this process of action and reaction legal policy is molded. The present chapter will focus on this interactive process in the period between the passage of the Comstock Act in 1873 and the early part of the twentieth century.

EARLY JUDICIAL REACTION

In the years following passage of the Comstock provisions, the courts were afforded numerous opportunities to respond to the legislatively fashioned birth-control policy. At the local level, the societies for the suppression of vice became quasi-legal organs,[1] diligently pursuing im-

[1] The YMCA committee was reorganized in 1873 as an independent organization. Its charter from the New York legislature clearly recognized its quasi-legal status, even to the point of providing for a sharing of the fines resulting from the society's activities. See Boyer, *Purity in Print*, 5; C. H. Hopkins, *The Rise of the Social Gos-*

plementation of the new enactments. By 1882 some 442 persons had been arrested by the New York society alone for prosecution under that state's laws[2]—a worthy model to inspire its cohorts in other states. And the purveyors of contraceptive devices, whom Comstock labeled as abortionists, were accorded his most passionate zeal.

In enforcing the state laws, agents provocateurs of the societies, masquerading as potential purchasers of the forbidden materials, would visit distributors, buy articles, arrest the sellers, and then use the purchased materials in the subsequent prosecution. The case of Ann Lohman, popularly known as Madame Restell, is illustrative of the tactics employed. Living in an elegant New York mansion, the sixty-seven-year-old woman had amassed a large fortune in the abortion-contraception trade, and apparently was planning to abandon her business in an effort to move into social circles. But Comstock had marked her for retribution. Assuming a fictitious name, he approached her with an impassioned plea to provide the means for preventing further births in his impoverished family. When she supplied the requested contraceptives, Comstock revealed his true identity and placed her under arrest. In this instance, however, the vice hunter was denied a court victory—Madame Restell slit her throat with a carving knife. Comstock's epitaph was simple, if somewhat indelicate: "a bloody ending to a bloody life."[3]

Following the passage of the 1873 legislation, Comstock had been appointed special agent of the Post Office Department to enforce the new federal laws. Financial backing from the independently chartered Society for the Suppression of Vice compensated somewhat for his adamant refusal of any salary from the government. Again the tactics of agent provocateur served as his basic means for suppressing the interstate trade in obscene articles. A decoy letter would be sent through the mails by an agent acting under a fictitious name to a suspected offender, pleading for assistance from child-bearing. The reply,

---

pel in American Protestantism (New Haven, 1940), 107, 384; Broun and Leech, *Anthony Comstock*, 149, 152; "Anthony Comstock's Work," *New York Times*, Jan. 19, 1887, p. 8, col. 4 (Comstock commentary on the close association between his agents and the police). In addition to the New York and New England societies, there were groups in St. Louis, Chicago, Louisville, Cincinnati, and San Francisco. Boyer, *Purity in Print*, 5; New England Watch and Ward Society, *Annual Report, 1887–88* (Boston, 1888), 25–26.

[2] Comstock, *Traps for the Young*, 137. See Broun and Leech, *Anthony Comstock*, 148, regarding Comstock's prosecution of dealers in contraceptives.

[3] Broun and Leech, *Anthony Comstock*, 156. See generally chap. 11, discussing the Restell incident.

giving further information on how and where to secure assistance and/ or actual contraceptive devices, would then be used to prosecute the offender in the federal courts. Care was taken to assure not only the successful prosecution of the offender, but also the seizure and destruction of the offensive materials. Between 1873 and 1882 Comstock and his associates had been involved in the arrest of over 700 persons (258 under the federal laws); 311 of the cases resulted in convictions and imprisonment; 27,586 pounds of "obscene books" and 64,836 "articles for immoral use" were seized.[4] Comstock would later boast of having convicted "enough persons to fill a passenger train of sixty-one coaches containing sixty passengers each and the sixty-first almost full."[5]

Of course there was ample criticism of the vice hunters' methods (especially of Comstock's, who clearly was *primus inter pares*), and occasionally this took the form of physical violence.[6] Not only the free-thought organs but newspapers and journals generally favorable to the objectives of the anti-vice crusade frequently expressed concern with the tactics employed. Following the Restell incident, for example, the *Herald Presbyter* commented:

> It is a nice question how far Christian people may go in "skillfully playing" a part of this sort.... We are well aware that "strategy"—often the very essence of deception—is regarded as essential in war, and that employing "detectives" is often deemed necessary to ferret out crime, where deceit is the most potent weapon a detective can use; but are these to be employed in the category of Christian methods and work, in intercepting the unworthy and carrying on our schemes of philanthropy? Does an enlightened Christian community sanction such proceedings?[7]

---

[4] Comstock, *Traps for the Young*, 137.
[5] *Ibid.*, 15–16, quoting the 1913 *New York Evening World*.
[6] See "The Suppression of Vice," *New York Times*, Jan. 1, 1876, p. 2, col. 3, indicating a few of the numerous physical attacks on Comstock. By 1876 he had been assaulted five times. "Annual Meeting of Society for the Suppression of Vice," *New York Herald Tribune*, Jan. 28, 1876, p. 5, col. 4.
[7] *Cincinnati Herald Presbyter*, quoted in Broun and Leech, *Anthony Comstock*, 156–57. See generally Boyer, *Purity in Print*, 12–15. The *New York Herald Tribune*, Nov. 16, 1887, p. 4, col. 5, referred to Comstock as "one of our least judicious censors of the public morals." See the critical "Editorial on Anthony Comstock," *New York Herald Tribune*, June 24, 1878, p. 4, col. 3, and "Letters in Rebuttal," *ibid.*, June 29, 1878, p. 2, col. 2, July 13, 1878, p. 2, col. 3. Another *Tribune* denunciation of Comstock and his tactics was printed Sept. 10, 1878, p. 4, col. 3. But see the *Tribune* editorial of Mar. 28, 1883, p. 4, col. 5, which is generally favorable to the society. The *New York Times* was generally favorable to Comstock and the society's work, although it occasionally criticized the tactics used and became increasingly hostile as time passed. See, e.g., the editorial of Jan. 21, 1885, p. 4, col. 2.

But Comstock and his cadres firmly rejected such criticism as "mere mawkish pity for wrongdoers" which undermined "the recognized standards of justice and right."[8] The severity of the threat posed to the national well-being justified the use of extreme tactics—the crusaders for moral purity were merely "fighting the devil with his own weapons."[9]

> The Society for the Suppression of Vice and that noble band of White Ribbon women—the National Woman's Christian Temperance Union—represent a work similar to the advance guard and the pioneer or sappers and miners corps of the army. We are locating worse than masked batteries, sunken mines and ambuscades. We are contending against dangers and foes worse, a thousand fold worse, than any foe that simply destroys life or blows the body into fragments. We are assailing foes more to be dreaded and shunned than any contagion that ever arose from sewer pipe or stagnant pool. We are camped upon the trail of an insidious and deadly foe; one that not only wrecks the physical but infects the moral nature, opening the door to spiritual degradation and death. Corrupt publications are pestilential blasts from the infernal region that wither and sere holy aspirations in the soul. They are precursors of evil, and only evil. They are practically the devil's kindling wood with which he lights the fires of remorseless hell in the soul.[10]

And there were many quite willing to defend the cause and methods of their champion.

> People will not so seriously consider or so implicitly accept the truth about the inexorable working of the moral law, when it is a question of maxims in a book, as they will when it is a living example. To show that God is not mocked today, any more than in Bible times, and that whatever a man soweth that shall he also reap, is a part of the justification of criminal trial, and of the uncovering by the legal process of the foul lives of fair seeming men.[11]

> They had to be treated like rats, without mercy. It was the duty of the society to enforce upon the civilized world the feeling that

---

[8] Anthony Comstock, "The Reign of Vice," *New York Times*, July 16, 1873, p. 4, col. 6.

[9] "Anti-Criminal Societies," *New York Times*, Jan. 30, 1881, p. 6, col. 4. Comstock attributed the criticism to the "ignorance of magnitudes of the evils which the Society seeks to eradicate." *New York Times*, Feb. 16, 1881, p. 2, col. 5.

[10] Anthony Comstock, "Demoralizing Literature," *The National Purity Congress*, ed. Powell, 420.

[11] "The Exposure of Vice," *Nation*, Feb. 21, 1907, p. 169.

men who made vice their business should be caught and caged like wild beasts.[12]

Let a righteous, self-respecting and patriotic people, without regard to party, ostracize and brand as traitors those who have sacrificed public morals, peace, order and future welfare. . . . Let no mawkish sentiment condone the treasonable capitulation to the dishonest and lawless class. . . . To bargain away public morals is to stab the State in its most vital parts.[13]

It must be admitted that the general caliber of the persons under attack probably would not have inspired the courts to strike out in new directions. The defendants were frequently purveyors of nostrums and quack remedies. As long as the impetus for change rested in the claims of a few disreputable advocates, there was little real hope for revision. There were, however, exceptions. In a number of instances, the vendetta was directed against reputable book dealers, merchants, medical practitioners, literary figures, and even an art school. Some of the leading luminaries of the liberal movement, D. M. Bennett, editor of *The Truth Seeker*, Ezra Heywood, editor of *The Word* and author of *Cupid's Yokes*, Moses Harman, editor of *Lucifer, the Light Bearer*, and later the *American Journal of Eugenics*, were subjected to Comstock's wrath in the federal and state courts, although in at least one instance presidential clemency impaired the completion of Comstock's justice.[14]

Equally as important as the prosecution of medical practitioners for disseminating contraceptives or birth-control information was the in-

---

[12] New York Lieutenant Governor Stewart L. Woodford, quoted in "The Suppression of Vice," *New York Times*, Jan. 28, 1876, p. 8, col. 3. An equally violent approach was expressed by Dr. H. S. Patterson, keynote speaker at the annual meeting of the society, reported in the *New York Times*, Jan. 20, 1880, p. 2, col. 7: "We want even more stringent laws. We want a revival of the whipping post. We want these fiends in human form who deal in vile literature lashed on the back in the public streets. . . ."

[13] Rev. Dr. Kempshall, president of the Law and Order League, quoted in Anthony Comstock, "Pool Rooms and Pool Selling," *North American Review*, CLVII (Nov., 1893), 610.

[14] See note 52 *infra*; Warren, *American Freethought*, 196; Fryer, *The Birth Controllers*, 194-96; Ditzion, *Marriage, Morals and Sex*, 172-74; Broun and Leech, *Anthony Comstock*, 170-77. Further possible exceptions would appear to include the defendants in United States v. Whittier, 28 Fed. Cas. 591 (no. 16,688) (E.D. Mo. 1878), and Ackley v. United States, 200 Fed. 217 (8th Cir. 1912), which involved physicians; United States v. Kelly, 26 Fed. Cas. 695 (no. 15,514) (D. Nev. 1876), and Tresca v. United States, 3 F.2d 556 (2d Cir. 1918), involving newspaper publishers who had printed advertisements on birth-control devices; and United States v. Foote, 25 Fed. Cas. 1140 (no. 15,128) (S.D. N.Y. 1876), involving an author with considerable medical experience.

hibiting effect of the law. Edward B. Foote, Sidney Barrington Eliot, William Josephus Robinson were all required to delete sections dealing with birth-control methods from their medical treatises because of potential criminal prosecution. Robinson, in his book *Fewer and Better Babies* (1915), left two chapters of blank pages with the comment:

> The further discussion of this subject has been completely eliminated by our censorship, which . . . is . . . as real and as terrifying as any that ever existed in darkest Russia. . . . Our censorship hangs like a Damocles' sword over the head of every honest radical writer. . . . Not only are we not permitted to mention the safe and harmless means, we cannot even discuss the unsafe and injurious means and methods. And this we call Freedom of the Press![15]

Perhaps the most potent societal impact of the Comstock Act and its state counterparts, then, was not their sensational enforcement, which Comstock himself frequently sought to avoid because of the publicity, but their terrorizing effect on free expression concerning, and experimentation on, devices for family limitation.[16] Fear of prosecution and the natural inhibiting effect of legal prohibitions introduced impediments to the development and dissemination of birth-control knowledge that only gradually were emasculated. While much material of questionable value was probably terrorized off the market, much legitimate information was never disseminated. But in Comstock's perspective: "Decaying matter breeds disease, whether confined in costly receptacles or ash barrells. . . . The smooth flow of genius and talent thus prostituted more easily deludes and captivates the fancy and engages attention"[17]— "the genius has no more right to be nasty than the common mind. . . ."[18] But whatever the inhibiting effect of the Comstock Act, the prosecution of the disseminators of birth-control information and devices had afforded the courts an opportunity to respond to the legislative action.

Although there is little data available, the intelligence activity in these

---

[15] William J. Robinson, *Fewer and Better Babies; or The Limitation of Offspring by the Prevention of Conception* (New York, 1915), noted in Fryer, *The Birth Controllers*, 197-98.

[16] Comstock preferred to "secretly strike a blow at the fountain-head by seizing the publication and plates and [then] arresting the publisher and author." Comstock, "Vampire Literature," 161. William E. Dodge, a founder of the New York society, explained that they tried to "frown and drive away" the evils. Quoted in Boyer, *Purity in Print*, 10.

[17] Comstock, "Pool Rooms and Pool Selling," 166.

[18] Quoted in "Work of the Society for the Suppression of Vice Reviewed by A. Comstock," *New York Times*, Jan. 23, 1884, p. 3, col. 3.

early cases apparently was limited almost entirely to typical legal arguments regarding the appropriate rules of statutory construction, the validity of the methods employed in administering the laws, and the scope of the power to regulate morality. The activities of the Society for the Suppression of Vice had given birth to a National Defense Association, charged with providing assistance to those accused under the Comstock laws.[19] There is, however, no indication that this organized interest pursued any coherent strategy for legal change through judicial activity. Rather, it provided defense counsel on a case-by-case basis, employing standard legal challenges. The courts apparently were not asked to process nonlegal data, although, given the time period under analysis, it is questionable that such an attempt would have met with any notable success.

At the prescriptive stage, courts were afforded an opportunity to mitigate the impact of the act and to achieve an individualized justice through the use of their interpretative capabilities. As suggested in the Introduction, a prime factor in assessing the willingness of the judicial actor to accommodate change is the manner in which it gives meaning to the legislative judgment. One approach that might be taken in performing this task is to limit inquiry solely to what the legislature said, utilizing the "plain meaning" or the "literal meaning" of the words as the governing standard. For the courts to go beyond the words into legislative "intent" or "purpose" would be deemed by the literalist to be a violation of the judicial function, a facade hiding judicial policymaking. This approach manifests the same distrust of unfettered judicial discretion that characterizes mechanistic jurisprudence generally. The judicial role is to be circumscribed by narrowing the confines within which judicial discretion operates. If an injustice is done by the literal interpretation of statutory words, recourse can be had only to the legislature.[20]

[19] National Defense Association, *Words of Warning to Those Who Aid and Abet in the Suppression of Free Speech and Free Press* (New York, 1879). See Warren, *American Freethought*, 183; Broun and Leech, *Anthony Comstock*, 179.

[20] See text accompanying Chapter One, notes 9–12 *supra*; Roscoe Pound, *The Task of Law* (Lancaster, Pa., 1944), 44–45; Davis et al., *Society and the Law*, 162, discussing the literalist approach to statutory interpretation. The comments of Eli Root are illustrative of this negative approach. "It is not the duty of our courts to be leaders in reform, or to espouse, or to enforce economic social theories, or, except in very narrow limits to readjust our laws to new social conditions. The judge is always confined within the narrow limits of reasonable interpretation. It is not his function or within his power to enlarge or improve the law. His duty is to maintain it, to enforce it, whether it be good or bad, wise or foolish, accordant with sound or unsound economic policy." Quoted in Cahill, *Judicial Legislation*, 14.

The initial objection to this literalist approach is its assumption that words have a "plain meaning." Words, concepts, rules have a beguiling simplicity. They can be manipulated to the purpose of their interpreter and seldom convey a necessary meaning—"if individual words are inexact symbols, with shifting variables, their configuration can hardly achieve invariant meaning or assured definiteness."[21] What is the "plain meaning," for example, of words like "obscene," "lewd," "lascivious," "indecent," "immoral," "vile." Even when these words are read in the entire context of the Comstock Act, without more information, it is not clear exactly what evils the legislature intended to attack.

Occasionally such legislative vagueness may be purposeful—a device to "throw the ball" to the courts to implement and refine the very general legislative policy. Indeed, the legislature is capable of making its language more or less general depending on the extent of leeway it chooses to leave the judicial actor. A statute can be drawn in a highly mechanical fashion setting forth exceptions and seeking to encompass a wide variety of situations. Alternatively it can provide only general guidelines, thereby inviting extensive judicial interpretation. Ambiguity in language can also be the natural result of the legislative process. Compromises must be reached; vague, indefinite language may be the only mechanism for achieving consensus. Obscure language can also be employed to limit the political repercussions that might follow a clear expression of legislative policy by depending on the safer independent judiciary to clarify the policy. The ambiguity and vagueness of the Comstock Act, on the other hand, was probably not purposeful, but was rather the product of the lack of legislative craftsmanship attributable to inadequate review and the hot haste of its passage.

A final impediment to a literalist approach to statutory language lies in the dynamics of change.

> Not only do new situations arise, but in addition people want change. The categories used in the legal process must be left ambiguous in order to permit the infusion of new ideas. And this is true even where legislation or constitution is involved. The words used by the legislature or the constitutional convention must come to have new meanings. Furthermore, agreement on any other basis would be impossible. In this manner the laws come to express the ideas of the community and even when writ-

[21] Felix Frankfurter, "Some Reflections on the Reading of Statutes," *The Record of the Association of the Bar of the City of New York*, II (June, 1947), 214. See Jerome Frank, "Words and Music: Some Remarks on Statutory Interpretation," *Columbia Law Review*, XLVII (Dec., 1946), 1259–78.

ten in general terms, in statute or constitution, are molded for the specific case.[22]

Statutes have never kept up with the variety and subtlety of social change. They cannot at the very best avoid some ambiguity, which is due not only to carelessness but also to the intrinsic impossibility of foreseeing all possible circumstances, since without such foresight, definitions must be vague and classifications indeterminate.[23]

The reality of social change belies simplistic reliance on the literalist words of the statutory instrument in judicial interpretation—often the legislature never considered the applicability of its language to new social contexts. The legislature lacks the omniscience too often assumed in a literalist approach to the interpretative function. While the existence of the statute inhibits "free decision" by judges, a realistic appraisal of the complexities of statutory interpretation suggests that courts necessarily retain a wide ambit of discretion furnishing occasions for the fashioning of policy.

Interpretation emerges then as an art challenging the capability of the judicial actor. Courts must go beyond the literal words of the statute to the purpose of the legislation. In order that this purposive approach to the interpretative function be performed adequately, the courts must be informed not only of the legislative history essential to determining the statutory purpose, but also of the present social situation which gave rise to the case under consideration. If the inquiry reveals a legislative policy which is reasonably applicable to the present controversy, it generally should be applied regardless of whether the judge believes it to be the *wisest* policy.

The manner in which the judge approaches this task of interpretation can have a decisive effect on the character of the interaction between legal institutions. If the court behaves in an overly simplistic, literalist fashion, there is an excellent possibility that the legislature, assuming motivational impediments can be overcome, will be forced to react on a continuous basis to avoid excessive lag between law and society. A purposive approach, on the other hand, seems to relieve the legislative policy-maker of some of the excessive pressures for change. Equally as important, it constitutes a recognition of the cooperative character of the law-making process. Should the judiciary err, the legislature can (although often not without difficulty) intervene to correct the error.

[22] Levi, *Legal Reasoning*, 4.
[23] Dewey, "Logical Method and the Law," 26.

58 : Law, Politics, and Birth Control

By accepting its role in the policy-formation process, courts can assist in mitigating legal lag and seek to employ law for creative change.

In the cases brought under the Comstock provisions during this period, questions arose regarding the requisite specificity of the indictment (primarily whether it must state with specificity the objectionable character of the material),[24] the extent of knowledge and intent required of an offender,[25] and the necessity that the article be an effective preventive.[26] Although the judicial response does not appear to have taken any clear trend toward either a literalist or a purposive approach to the interpretative function, one decision is worthy of note.

Edward Bliss Foote, a free-thought journalist who frequently collaborated with medical authorities in writing treatises, was convicted of disseminating a birth-control tract and required to pay a fine of $3,000. In his defense he sought to limit the contraceptive prohibition to "obscene" activity and read in an exemption for physicians. While the court might have employed the broad definition of "obscene" typically used by courts of that period[27] or disposed of the defense simply on grounds that Foote was not a licensed practitioner, it chose instead to rely on the sweeping language of the legislative prohibition.

> It is plain that an attempt to exclude information given by medical men from the operation of the statute would afford any easy way of nullifying the law. If the intention had been to exclude the communications of physicians from the operation of the act, it was certainly easy to say so. In the absence of any words of limitations, the language used must be given its full and natural

---

[24] Compare United States v. Kelly, 26 Fed. Cas. 695 (no. 15,514) (D. Nev. 1876), United States v. Foote, 25 Fed. Cas. 1140 (no. 15,128) (S.D. N.Y. 1876), Pilson v. United States, 249 Fed. 328 (2d Cir. 1918), Ackley v. United States, 200 Fed. 217 (8th Cir. 1912), and United States v. Currey, 206 Fed. 322 (D. Ore. 1913), with United States v. Kaltmeyer, 16 Fed. 760 (E.D. Mo. 1883), United States v. Pupke, 133 Fed. 243 (E.D. Mo. 1900), and Winters v. United States, 201 Fed. 845 (8th Cir. 1912).

[25] United States v. Bott, 24 Fed. Cas. 1204 (no. 14,626) (S.D. N.Y. 1873); United States v. Whitehead, 24 Fed. Cas. 1204 (no. 14,626) (S.D. N.Y. 1873); United States v. Currey, 206 Fed. 322 (D. Ore. 1913); Tresca v. United States, 3 F.2d 556 (2d Cir. 1918).

[26] United States v. Bott, 24 Fed. Cas. 1204 (no. 14,626) (S.D. N.Y. 1873); Bates v. United States, 10 Fed. 92 (N.D. Ill. 1881).

[27] The primary standard for obscenity utilized by the courts in the nineteenth century was derived from Lord Cockburn's opinion in Queen v. Hicklin, L.R. 3 Q.B. 360 (1868): "whether the tendency of the matter charged as obscenity [i.e., the excerpted passages of the work] is to deprave and corrupt those whose minds are open to immoral influences, and into whose hands a publication of this sort may fall."

significance, and held to exclude from the mails every form of notice whereby the prohibited information is conveyed.[28]

Sixty years later this interpretation was to be rejected.[29]

The court in the *Foote* case could have distinguished between the "reputable" and the "disreputable" disseminators of birth-control information and materials on the theory that the legislative purpose was only to ferret out those elements that sought to corrupt the morals of youth. Scientific and medical activity relating to contraceptives would arguably be neither available to youth nor a stimulant to immoral thoughts and activity any more than any material relating to sex. But at the time the court spoke, the rejection of such an approach would appear to have been fully consistent with the legislative intent. There is every reason to believe, in light of the statutory history described above (especially in light of Congress's removal of an exemption for physicians from the final act), that Congress intended its proscription to be definitive and all-encompassing.[30] There does not appear to have been any desire to delineate permissible and impermissible activity in this field; the prohibition was intended to be absolute. Similarly, as will be noted below,[31] the social context in which the courts were making their judgment was not significantly different from that which existed when the act was passed. If the literal words admitted of no exceptions, neither did the congressional purpose or social environment.

At this prescriptive stage, challenges to the entrapment tactics of the vice hunters also provided ample opportunity for the judicial actor to mitigate the harshness of the Comstock provisions. By exercising control over administration of the act, the courts might have limited the social impact of the legal norms. The cases that were presented did not challenge the constitutionality of these administrative practices, but instead argued that the statutory offense was never consummated, since there was no real person to whom the prohibited material was being sent. Apparently one judge, while expressing his moral indignation at dealings in birth-control information and materials, did accept the

---

[28] United States v. Foote, 25 Fed. Cas. 1140, 1141 (no. 15,128) (S.D. N.Y. 1876). See Fryer, *The Birth Controllers*, 117–18.

[29] United States v. One Package, 13 F. Supp. 334 (E.D. N.Y. 1936), aff'd 86 F.2d 737 (2d Cir. 1936). See text accompanying Chapter Four, note 26 *infra*; Peter W. Kilborn, "Birth Control Statutes: Constitutionality and Other Aspects" (unpublished manuscript, 1960), 4–6 (from the files of PPLM).

[30] On Congress's decision *not* to include an exemption for physicians, see text accompanying Chapter One, note 57 *supra*.

[31] See text accompanying notes 42–46 *infra*.

principle that the defendants' "clear *moral* guilt" did not constitute *legal* criminality.[32] Even in this single instance, the court went to great pains to limit its opinion to cases where the sealed letter or package was removed from the mail by the agent provocateur prior to reaching its destination. Decoy letters sent by real persons acting under fictitious names were fully accepted as permissible detective practices.[33] It should be noted, however, that all of these cases involved individuals who were clearly involved in the "criminal" trade; they were, generally, not instances of innocent people being duped into criminal activity, as is usually required for an entrapment defense.

The courts were also afforded an opportunity to review the constitutionality of the legislative prohibition. Few decisions in our legal system afford as great an opportunity for institutional conflict as the exercise of the judicial power to declare a legislative act unconstitutional. The legislature is charged with the primary role in formulating legal policy and then a small group of unelected men, appointed for life (subject to impeachment), is permitted to negate that policy. Unlike the instance of statutory interpretation, a declaration of unconstitutionality usually cannot be overcome by a mere legislative clarification of intent.

On the other hand, the alternative for the court is either to abstain from decision completely, which will be discussed later, or to legitimize the legislative policy. Charles P. Curtis once argued that "to call a statute constitutional is no more of a compliment than it is to say that it is not intolerable."[34] Such an evaluation, however, seems to denigrate erroneously the importance of a judicial finding of constitutionality. Any political system requires legitimacy if it is to operate effectively. The populace must generally recognize the authority of governmental officials to make and implement decisions, although the decisions themselves may be unpopular. Most acts of government appear to be obeyed, not because a negative sanction will be visited on a violator (although this may be an important consideration), but because they are accepted as authoritative. A "crisis in legitimacy" is basically a breakdown in these authority relationships. In a period of extremely rapid social

[32] United States v. Whittier, 28 Fed. Cas. 591, 593 (no. 16,688) (E.D. Mo. 1878).
[33] Compare Bates v. United States, 10 Fed. 92 (N.D. Ill. 1881), and Ackley v. United States, 200 Fed. 217 (8th Cir. 1912), with United States v. Whittier, 28 Fed. Cas. 591 (no. 16,688) (E.D. Mo. 1878), and United States v. Adams, 58 Fed. 674 (D. Ore. 1894).
[34] Charles P. Curtis, "A Modern Supreme Court in a Modern World," *Vanderbilt Law Review*, IV (Apr., 1951), 433.

change, an even greater degree of legitimacy may be required if government is to function effectively.

In the American political system, a vital component of this legitimization is the judicial sanction of legislative acts. A court finding that a governmental action does not violate the Constitution assists in legitimizing the action by evoking from the populace a greater acceptance of public authority and more willing acquiescence to its demands.

> But a case can be made for believing that the prime and most necessary function of the Court has been that of validation, not that of invalidation. What a government of limited powers needs, at the beginning and forever, is some means of satisfying the people that it has taken all steps humanly possible to stay within its powers. That is the condition of its legitimacy, and its legitimacy, in the long run, is the condition of its life. And the Court, through its history, has acted as the legitimator of the government. In a very real sense, the Government of the United States is based on the opinions of the Supreme Court.[35]

In addition to this legitimization of governmental authority, the "affirmative" use of judicial review would also seem to serve the more practical political ends of the legislator. A judicial imprimatur can be used to justify questionable legislative action to unhappy constituents. Often politically powerful interest groups will have engaged in intense combat prior to the passage of the statute. A judicial legitimization lends the support of another powerful legal actor to the legislative decision.

The judicial determination does not end merely with the legitimization of legislative behavior. Its decision becomes part of our constitutional heritage available for use by other courts in subsequent policy formation. The use of precedent pervades the judicial decision-making process whether the action involves the common law, statutory interpretation, or constitutional determination. The principle fashioned by the court "lies about like a loaded weapon ready for the hand of any authority that can bring forward a plausible claim of an urgent need. Every repetition embeds that principle more deeply in our law and thinking expands it to new purposes."[36]

The question arises as as to why the decisional behavior of the courts,

---

[35] Charles L. Black, Jr., *The People and the Court* (New York, 1960), 52. See Frederick K. Buetel, "Pressure of Organized Interests in Shaping Legislation," *University of Southern California Law Review*, III (Oct., 1929), 52.

[36] Korematsu v. United States, 323 U.S. 214, 242 (1944).

and especially the Supreme Court, should have this ability to legitimize legislative acts. After all, the legislature is the representative body whose institutional structure conforms more closely to democratic values. The best answer offered thus far appears to be the symbolic reinforcing roles of the court and the Constitution. Men react constantly to the emotive force of symbols. The flag, a patriotic song, the cross, all have meanings beyond their mere structure—so it is with court and Constitution. They represent stability and continuity with the past and a commitment to fundamental values of the system whatever the merits of this evaluation. In an era of rapid change, this quest for security would seem even more pervasive; there should be an even greater tendency to perceive the court and Constitution in terms of symbolic reassurance and long-term value commitments.

> The support of the judicial power lies largely in the psychological realm; its roots are in the minds of the people. Historically the judicial power must be seen as an instrument of the few; psychologically it is the symbol of the many. We live by symbols, wrote Mr. Justice Holmes. It is to the Supreme Court and the Constitution as symbols that we must turn.[37]
>
> Every tribe needs its totem and its fetish, and the Constitution is ours.[38]

It is this symbolic strength of the judicial imprimatur that the courts lent to the 1873 legislative behavior by legitimizing its action.

Although the literature of the period suggests that a number of individuals, including many of Comstock's victims, believed that the act violated constitutional guarantees of free speech and press, the author has been unable to locate any reported cases in which this claim was considered and answered in the federal courts. Indeed, the primary constitutional challenge to which the courts responded was directed at the power of Congress.

The defendant in the 1899 federal district court case, *United States v. Popper*,[39] had been arrested for sending an article for the prevention of conception through Wells Fargo Express to a resident of Nevada in violation of the 1897 amendment to the Comstock Act covering transit of obscene material by express companies. In his defense, Popper

---

[37] Max Lerner, "Constitution and Court as Symbols," *Yale Law Journal*, XLVI (June, 1937), 1292. See Jerome Frank, *Law and the Modern Mind* (New York, 1949).

[38] Lerner, "Constitution and Court," 1294.

[39] 98 Fed. 423 (N.D. Cal. 1899).

argued that control over such articles was properly part of the police power of the state and that Congress therefore lacked constitutional power to legislate. But, as the U.S. Supreme Court had indicated in the 1877 case, *Ex parte Jackson*, legitimizing Congress's power in the 1873 act to prohibit the interstate transmission of lottery materials: "All that Congress meant by this act was, that the mail should not be used to transport such corrupting publications and articles, and that anyone who attempted to use it for that purpose should be punished.... The only question for our determination relates to the constitutionality of the Act, and of that we have no doubt."[40]

What Congress was able to do regarding the mails under its power over post offices and post roads it could do in relation to express transit through its power over interstate commerce. The commerce power, over which Congress has plenary authority, included the power to define the permissible articles of commerce. Although it may be difficult for some to understand how the interstate transmission of contraceptive articles impairs interstate commerce, the courts have generally been consistent in upholding the power of Congress to prevent the channels of commerce from being used to transmit articles deemed socially dangerous, a capability akin to state police power. In *Popper* the court merely accepted the basic proposition that the power to regulate commerce encompasses the power to exclude items which Congress might reasonably conclude to be injurious to the public morals, including contraceptive materials. And in 1899 the "public morals" was still essentially the morality of 1873.

These early cases, then, in no way diminished the efficacy of the act. Federal courts generally manifested a deferential attitude toward the legislative policy by giving it a broad effect. Although there do not appear to be any reports of state appellate decisions, secondary sources suggest that this assessment would be equally true for state court judges.[41] Statutory provisions remained all-encompassing and legitimate; Comstockery had been provided with a judicial sanction. The time for change had not yet occurred.

But this judicial behavior should not be too surprising. As indicated

[40] 96 U.S. 727, 736–37 (1877). For other cases involving the power to exclude "immoral" matter for interstate commerce, see Lottery Case, 188 U.S. 321 (1903) (lottery tickets); Hipolite Egg Co. v. United States, 220 U.S. 45 (1911) (adulterated eggs); Hoke v. United States, 227 U.S. 308 (1913) (white-slave traffic). See generally Notes, "Contraceptives and the Law," *University of Chicago Law Review*, VI (Feb., 1939), 260–62.

[41] See Broun and Leech, *Anthony Comstock*, and the annual reports of the New York Society for the Suppression of Vice.

in the Introduction, judges tend to respond to many of the same factors influencing the legislative actor. The social orientation of judicial decision-making, the reality of the courts' weighing considerations of social advantage and needs, will be a recurrent theme in this study. And this, in essence, is the function of policy formation. The judge looks to the needs and aspirations of society and seeks to maximize their realization—"the true grounds of decisions are consideration of policy and social advantage."[42]

> A truly realistic theory of judicial decisions must conceive every decision as something more than an expression of individual personality, as concomitantly and even more importantly a function of social forces, that is to say, as a product of social determinants and an index of social consequences. A judicial decision is a social event.... Behind the decisions are social forces that play upon it to give it a resultant momentum and direction; beyond the decision are human activities affected by it. The decision is without significant social dimensions when it is reviewed simply at the moment in which it is rendered. Only by probing behind the decision to the forces it reflects, or projecting beyond the decision the lines of its force upon the future do we come to an understanding of the meaning of the decision itself.[43]

The courts in the late nineteenth century were operating within the same social milieu which had spawned the act. There were the anti-vice forces pressing for protection of the dominant morality; there was the weak conglomerate of interests, often espousing radical social and political doctrines in addition to their challenge to the contraceptive prohibitions of the Comstock Act; and there was the sweeping and explicit denunciation of a liberal birth-control policy provided by the authoritative policy-making institution in 1873. Given these influences, it is perhaps more amazing that any courts employed their capabilities to release offenders.

Not only did external societal factors press for negative reaction to the change demands, but the personal values of judges were probably also consistent with the dominant moral alliance. There has been a pronounced tendency in recent years to pay increased attention to the person making the judicial decision, rather than just to the opinion

[42] Vegelahn v. Gutner, 169 Mass. 92, 105-6 (1896) (Holmes, J., dissenting). See Oliver Wendell Holmes, *The Common Law* (Boston, 1963), 31-32; Wells and Grossman, "The Concept of Judicial Policy-Making."
[43] Felix Cohen, "Transcendental Nonsense and the Functional Approach," *Columbia Law Review*, XXXV (June, 1935), 843.

which results from that decision. An individual not only retains his values, beliefs, attitudes on moving to the Olympian heights of the bench, he also acquires additional values which he associates with his new role. We are increasingly recognizing that a judicial decision is, at least in part, a product of the propensities of the decider. "All their lives, forces which they do not recognize and cannot name have been tugging at them—inherited instincts, traditional beliefs, acquired convictions; and the resultant is an outlook on life, a conception of social needs, a sense in James' phrase of 'the total push and pressure of the cosmos'; which, when reasons are nicely balanced, must determine where choice shall fall."[44]

As Comstock's biographers noted: "his success in court would have been altogether impossible but for the fact that many men upon the bench were almost wholly of his mind in matters relating to obscenity."[45] The following charge to a jury is indicative of the temper prevailing on the bench: "There is in the popular conception and heart such a thing as modesty. It was born in the Garden of Eden. After Adam and Eve ate of the fruit of the tree of knowledge, they passed from that condition of perfectability, which some people nowadays aspire to, and, their eyes being opened, they discerned that there were both good and evil; and they knew that they were naked; and they sewed fig leaves."[46] Like the legislators who had enacted the restrictive policy, the bench reflected the dominant moral orientation. Personal value systems and social influences were most likely complementary forces influencing the decisional process. Nor does it appear that the institutional role perspectives of the judges presented any cross pressures. Established norms for judicial behavior would seem to have supported a broad and sweeping interpretation of the state and federal legislative policy and a deferential attitude toward congressional power over interstate commerce. The principal variables suggested in the Introduction all tended to produce the same judicial product.

[44] Cardozo, *The Nature of the Judicial Process*, 12. See the sources cited in the Introduction, note 26 *supra*.

[45] Broun and Leech, *Anthony Comstock*, 273–74. Robert C. Cook, *The Population Awakening*, Victor Fund for the International Planned Parenthood Fund, rpt. 4 (New York, 1966), 24, notes that "in his heyday between 1873 and 1882, Comstock was involved in the arrest of 700 persons; 333 were convicted and sent to prison. Many of these convictions involved contraception, and the penalties were sometimes heavy." The *Annual Reports* of the Society for the Suppression of Vice provide an annual accounting of the conviction rate.

[46] Judge Phillips in United States v. Harmon, 45 F. 414, 423 (D. Kan. 1891), quoted in Broun and Leech, *Anthony Comstock*, 274. See *ibid.*, 87.

Although courts, because of their greater independence of vested interests,[47] are often perceived as the primary forum for legal change, the above analysis suggests that this proposition could prove to be misleading. In fact, David Truman presents a somewhat different hypothesis: "In periods of rapid change in technology and in similar human relationships with attendant shifts in interests and their relative strength in the society as a whole, defensive groups will be likely to enjoy a privileged access to the courts."[48] This would suggest the thesis that courts are an inherently conservative institution in relation to social change, protectors of the status quo. Much of the early history of the judicial response to Comstockery would appear to support this thesis. On the other hand, none of the legal actors at that time were immune to these motivational influences.

Legislative Reaction to Judicial Implementation

In the Introduction it was suggested that judicial action may serve as an impetus for further legislative action. While the courts might directly or indirectly seek a reaction, a more common influence is likely to be the impact of the enforcement of the norm on individuals and groups in society. In such cases the legislature resembles an appellate court to which aggrieved parties can appeal. It becomes "an intermittently-intervening, trouble-shooting, back-stopping agency."[49]

The suggestion that the legislature might react because of the effect

[47] While groups are active in seeking to influence judicially fashioned policy, the ideal of an independent judiciary arguably restricts their behavior. Direct influence on a judge, while not unknown, has not appeared to be a common tactic of influence. Judicial canons stress that the "court exists to promote justice" and that the judge "should not be swayed by partisan demands, public clamor or consideration or personal popularity or notoriety, nor be apprehensive of unjust criticism." Canons of Judicial Ethics 2 and 14. But see Clement Vose, *Caucasians Only: The Supreme Court, the NAACP, and the Restrictive Covenant Cases* (Berkeley, 1959); Jack W. Peltason, *Fifty-eight Lonely Men* (New York, 1961); Fowler V. Harper and Edwin D. Etherington, "Lobbyists before the Court," *University of Pennsylvania Law Review*, CI (June, 1953), 1172-77.

[48] Truman, *The Governmental Process*, 487. Felix Cohen, "Transcendental Nonsense," 845, claims that it is recognized that courts are a conservative social force—"more like a brake than a motor in the social mechanism"—but he admits "we have no scientific factual comparison of judicial, legislative, and executive organs of government."

[49] Hart and Sacks, *The Legal Process*, 186. The authors suggest instances for such legislative intervention (1) where corrective judicial action would disappoint the reasonable expectations of the parties; (2) where complex rules have to be formulated—"cast in terms of arbitrary, fixed quantities or involving form requirements beyond the capacity of judicial innovation." *Ibid.*, 817.

of the judicial policy on society or on groups having access to the legislature presupposes that a judicial policy can have an impact on society and social groups. Levi, for example, suggests that "an ideal adopted by a court is in a superior position to influence conduct and opinion in the community; judges, after all, are rulers. And the adoption of an idea by a court reflects the power structure in the community."[50] We must note, however, the nascent stage of systematic impact analysis. Given the fact that one of the most vital claims of sociological jurisprudence is that law does affect societal behavior, there certainly seems to be a need for increased attention to the impact of differential forms of legislative and judicial behavior.

The legislature, for example, may act because needs extant within the community but previously unrecognized or ignored may be given increased visibility and importance by judicial attempts to implement the legislative mandate. Judicial action may well have revealed consequences not intended or anticipated in the original legislation. As mentioned above, the complexity of the legal issues appears to be correlated with the pressure on the legislature to assume responsibility for subsequent fashioning of legal policy; the courts simply are not equipped to do the job. Alternatively, judicial application of antiquated court-fashioned policies long after their raison d'etre has ceased and conditions have changed (often because of a failure to employ a creative approach to *stare decisis*, the rule of precedent) may itself create a social problem demanding legislative attention. The possibility also exists that judicial action may affect interest groups which have legislative access, or enforcement of the legislatively fashioned norm may unite formerly disparate interests who might now perceive a common cause. These groups may well work through legislative channels to mitigate or reverse the judicial policy.

Vigorous and successful implementation of the 1873 federal obscenity statute by Comstock and his anti-vice agents in the courts was to provide

[50] Levi, *Legal Reasoning*, 6. See generally Lawrence M. Friedman and Stewart Macaulay, eds., *Law and the Behavioral Sciences* (Indianapolis, 1969), chap. 3; Richard Schwartz and Jerome Skolnick, eds., *Society and the Legal Order* (New York, 1970), pt. IV, and the sources cited therein; Theodore Becker, ed., *The Impact of Supreme Court Decisions* (New York, 1969); Stephen L. Wasby, *The Impact of the United States Supreme Court: Some Perspectives* (Homewood, Ill., 1970).
    The lack of empirical investigation of the impact of common-law decision-making reflects our preoccupation with the Supreme Court and our myopic concentration on constitutional policy. Perhaps the best material we have on common-law decision-making and social change is provided in the historical analyses of James Willard Hurst and John R. Commons.

just such an impetus for further legislative action in 1878. As the convictions began to mount, the resentment against the laws and the manner of their enforcement grew. One of Comstock's prime targets was DeRobigne M. Bennett, the outspoken liberal editor of the free-thought weekly *The Truth Seeker*.[51] Constantly hounded by Comstock for his "obscene" publications and smarting under the vice hunter's attacks on other liberal spokesmen,[52] Bennett responded with flaming assaults on Comstock, his activities, and the sweeping laws that made them possible. Joined by the other organs of the liberal press, he charged that the laws employing the vague, blanket term "obscenity" had been used to place excessive fetters on freedom of religion, speech, and press. As in 1873, the call to arms had been sounded, but in this instance against the prohibitive public policy on obscenity.[53]

The National Liberal League (later to be renamed the American Secular Union), formed in 1876 to promote secularism in the United States, became the focal point for agitation against the Comstock laws; a defense committee was formed to provide legal assistance to those

[51] *The Truth Seeker* was an attempt to unite the disparate liberal forces. Its masthead declared its devotion to "Science, Morals, Free Thought, Free Discussion, Liberalism, Sexual Equality, Labor Reform, Progression, Free Education, and Whatever Tends to Emancipate and Elevate the Human Race. Opposed to Priestcraft, Ecclesiasticism, Dogmas, Creeds, False Theology, Superstition, Bigotry, Ignorance, Monopolies, Aristocracies, Privileged Classes, Tyranny, Oppression and Everything that Degrades or Burdens Mankind, Mentally or Physically." *The Truth Seeker*, Sept., 1873.

[52] Bennett had originally been arrested in 1877 for writing and distributing "An Open Letter to Jesus Christ" and H. B. Bradford's "How Do Marsupials Propagate?" But the case was dismissed. Comstock continually tried to get Bennett's printers to stop printing *The Truth Seeker* and the American News Company to stop selling it. In December, 1878, Bennett, masquerading under the name "G. Brackett," was to be again caught by Comstock and convicted for mailing Heywood's *Cupid's Yokes*. President Hayes refused to pardon Bennett, primarily because of the tremendous amount of pressure generated by the anti-vice interests. Bennett went to the penitentiary for thirteen months. See Orvin Larson, *American Infidel: Robert G. Ingersoll* (New York, 1962), 144–49; Paul and Schwartz, *Federal Censorship*, 25–27; Broun and Leech, *Anthony Comstock*, 175–83.

Another favorite target of Comstock that generated resentment from the liberal community was Ezra Heywood, author of *Cupid's Yokes*, publisher of the liberal journal *The Word*, and an advocate of free love. In June, 1878, Heywood was convicted for mailing his book and Trall's *Sexual Physiology*, but was pardoned by President Hayes. Comstock, however, was to continue his harassment of Heywood. See Ditzion, *Marriage, Morals and Sex*, 169–81; Broun and Leech, *Anthony Comstock*, 170–84.

[53] See *The Works of Robert G. Ingersoll*, XII (New York, 1908), 216–17; Comstock, *Traps for the Young*, 212–14, citing the argument of Courtland Palmer, treasurer of the National Liberal League, for repeal of the laws; Warren, *American Freethought*, 34–37.

liberal spokesmen charged under the laws;[54] and a massive campaign for legislative revision or repeal was initiated, with over 50,000 signatures on the following petition.

> To the Senate and House of Representatives of the United States of America in Congress assembled.
>
> The petition of the undersigned citizens of the United States residing at and near the places set opposite their names respectfully shows:
>
> 1. That they are loyal and devoted supporters of the Constitution of the United States and of the republican form of government, and that they are so principally from the conviction that under them personal liberty, freedom of conscience, of the press, and of the expression of opinion, together with equality before the law and the department of government had been for the first time substantially secured among men; and your petitioners rejoiced in the belief that the rights thus guaranteed had in our own country forever abrogated every form of political, moral, and religious persecution and inquisition;
>
> [2.] That without the knowledge of your petitioners, and, they believe, without the knowledge of any great number of the citizens of the United States, certain acts were procured to be passed by Congress in 1873 (since incorporated into the U.S. Revised Statutes, as §§1785, 3878, 3893, 5389, 2491), for the ostensible purpose of suppressing "obscene literature," etc., which reversed the policy and practice of our government since its foundation;
>
> 3. That in the belief of your petitioners the government of the United States was established under the Declaration of Independence and the Constitution for the more general purposes of government only, and for the protection, and not for the limitation, of the rights aforesaid. That to that end, i.e., "to secure the blessings of liberty to ourselves and our posterity" Congress was prohibited from making laws affecting religion or conscience, or "abridging the freedom of the press, or of speech," or the right of petition; and the people were "to be secure in their persons, houses, papers, and effects," etc.; That the true construction and meaning of these great charters of liberty were declared by their authors, the founders of our government, to be, that all persons were, and of right ought to be, equal in their

---

[54] See note 19 *supra* and *The Works of Robert G. Ingersoll*, XII, 222–23, where Ingersoll argues that the committee should not defend everyone charged under the Comstock laws but only those whose works were determined by a committee of the league to be free of obscenity.

protection and privileges before the law, the courts, and all departments of the government, without discrimination or question as to their social, moral, political, or religious character. That the statutes aforesaid are, in the opinion of your petitioners, plain violations of the letter and spirit of these fundamental principles of our government; and that they are capable of, and are, in fact, being used for the purposes of moral and religious persecution, whereby the dearest and most precious rights of the people are being grievously violated under the forms of legal inquisition, fines, forfeitures, and imprisonment;

4. And your petitioners further show that they are convinced that all attempts of evil government, whether State or national, to enforce or to favor particular religious, social, moral, or medical opinions, or schools of thought or practice, are not only unconstitutional but ill-advised, contrary to the spirit and progress of our age, and almost certain in the end to defeat any beneficial objects intended. That mental, moral, and physical health and safety are better secured and preserved by virtue resting upon liberty and knowledge, than upon ignorance enforced by governmental supervision. That even error may be safely left free, where truth is free to combat it. That the greatest danger to a republic is the insidious repression of the liberties of the people. That whenever publications, pictures, articles, acts, or exhibitions directly tending to produce crime or pauperism are wantonly exposed to the public, or obtruded upon individuals, the several States and Territories have provided, or may be safely left to provide, suitable remedies.

Wherefore your petitioners pray that the *statutes aforesaid may be repealed*, or materially modified, so that they cannot be used to abridge the freedom of the press or of conscience, or to destroy the liberty and equality of the people before the law and departments of the government, on account of any religious, moral, political, medical, or commercial grounds or pretexts whatsoever.

And your petitioners will ever pray. . . .

Rob't G. Ingersoll, Chairman	Illinois
Charles Case	Indiana
Darius Lyman	Ohio
J. C. Smith	Massachusetts
Jno. B. Wolff	New York City
J. Weed Corey, ex-officio, Secretary	Penn Yan, N.Y.
W. W. Jackson, ex-officio	Washington, D.C.

Committee

and fifty thousand others attached to petition 2100 feet long, filed with House Com. on Revision of the Laws.[55]

The Committee of Seven, as the guiding force for the pro-change interests was called, secured the services of Gen. Ben Butler to introduce the petition in the House, although with the understanding that he did not necessarily support the resolution. Liberal forces, however, were at least given the psychological satisfaction of expressing their grievances before the House Committee on the Revision of the Laws. Pamphlets detailing Comstock's "persecution" of Bennett and other liberals, his "dastardly and villainous conduct" in enforcing the laws, and arguments that the laws "have been and are being enforced to destroy the liberty of conscience in matters of religion, against the freedom of the press, and to the great hurt of the learned professions,"[56] were transmitted to the Congress.

But Comstock, accompanied by the prestigious Samuel Colgate, was also present at the hearings. In his work *Frauds Exposed*, he recorded his perhaps somewhat exaggerated impressions:

> Everything looked black. I was alone. As I strolled through the vestibule and rotunda of the Capitol, the Senate Chamber, and Representatives Hall, I found on each Congressman's desk a copy of the vile paper, of which eight pages were devoted to a pretended account of the "Life and Crimes of Anthony Comstock." [This was the work of Dr. Selden, whom Comstock had arrested in 1872.] These papers were scattered everywhere. The Committee room was filled with them. As I entered the Committee room, I found it crowded with long-haired men and short-haired women, there to defend obscene publications, abortion implements, and other incentives to crime by repealing the laws. I heard their hiss and curse as I passed through them. I saw their sneers and their looks of derision and contempt. But one man, he a member of this committee, in all that audience, had the moral courage to rise up and in the face of this tremendous opposition speak to me, and greet me pleasantly. It was a brave act, and I shall always honor the memory of Hon. Rush Clark of

[55] Quoted in Comstock's *Traps for the Young*, 187-90. In chap. 13 of this work Comstock attempts to answer each of the liberals' charges against the unconstitutionality of the 1873 legislation.
[56] Letter from J. Weed Corey, secretary for the Committee of Seven, to the Senate Committee on the Revision of the Laws, quoted in Comstock, *Traps for the Young*, 191-92.

Iowa, for daring to speak a kind word to me in the darkest hour of my experience.[57]

His argument was basically the same that had proved successful in 1873. Again he displayed his wares—the mass of pornographic photographs, the dime and half-dime novels, the contraceptives and abortifacients; again the plea was cast in terms of protecting innocent children. He told of the vice peddlers' use of lists of student names compiled by the schools as a mailing list for their wares, and of the disastrous effect of evil reading on children's receptive minds. And again the committee responded appropriately.

REPORT

The Committee on the Revision of the Laws, to whom was referred the petition of Robert G. Ingersoll and others, praying for the repeal or modification of §§1785, 3878, 3893, 5389, and 2491, of the Revised Statutes, have had the same under consideration, and have heard the petitioners at length.

In the opinion of your committee, the Post-Office was not established to carry instruments of vice, or obscene writings, indecent pictures, or lewd books. Your committee believe that the statutes in question do not violate the Constitution of the United States, and ought not to be changed; they recommend, therefore, that the prayer of the said petition be denied.[58]

The Senate committee never even acted on the petition for change.

The impact of the 1873 laws achieved through their implementation by the courts had generated a demand for change and at least a pro forma legislative review of the obscenity–birth control policy. Sufficient impetus for an effective challenge, however, seems not to have even been approximated—the balance of power among the competing interests had not really altered. In fact, the National Liberal League was not a cohesive union; the very doctrine of free thought on which it was founded negated an authoritative, tightly knit interest-group organization. Nor were the change forces united on whether they wanted revision or repeal, an issue which was to produce a split in the liberal ranks and a walkout of delegates at the National Liberal League convention.[59] But even if they had been united in purpose, it is doubtful

[57] Anthony Comstock, *Frauds Exposed* (Montclair, N.J., 1969), 424–25 (originally published in 1880).
[58] Report of the House Committee on the Revision of the Laws, quoted in Comstock, *Traps for the Young*, 195.
[59] *New York Times*, Oct. 28, 1878, p. 5, col. 3, Oct. 31, 1878, p. 2, col. 7, Sept.

that they could have succeeded. While the pro-change interests included some prestigious figures as suggested by the signatories constituting the Committee of Seven (such as the free thinker Robert Ingersoll), they generally lacked the influence possessed by the anti-vice forces, e.g. Samuel Colgate, William Dodge, Jr., Morris E. Jessup, J. Pierpont Morgan. Their ranks included not only liberals seeking to further free-speech and free-press interests, but also the free thinkers and free lovers opposing the established morality. While some of the victims of Comstock's attacks were "vice peddlers" only in the most extreme Puritan interpretation of that term, others were engaged in activities which aroused even many of the liberal members of the community.

Nor had the years since the passage of the Comstock legislation produced any significant change in the moral temper of society; at least not sufficient to induce favorable congressional action. Liberal "free thought" still represented only a minority opinion in a highly moralistic environment. "If the American freethinkers had possessed sufficient strength, the consequences for the religious world might have been serious. But such was not the case. Infidelity was a weak adversary, pitting itself against a mighty citadel that could be captured only if the minds of millions of people were to undergo a revolutionary transformation."[60]

The hurried and unanimous dispatch of the demand for revision or repeal of the Comstock laws suggests that the motivations of 1873 were still operative. Judicial action had only supported the earlier legislative action, and the 1878 legislature responded accordingly. Courts and Congress were united on a sweeping obscenity policy which caught contraception in its wake. Although there would be continued agitation for modification or repeal of the Comstock laws during the remainder of the nineteenth century, at least for the present the laws remained firmly entrenched.

20, 1880, p. 5, col. 5; Warren, *American Freethought*, 165–69; *The Works of Robert G. Ingersoll*, 215–30; Broun and Leech, *Anthony Comstock*, 179.

[60] Warren, *American Freethought*, 206.

Three

Organization for Change: Origins of the Birth-Control Movement

A fundamental alteration in the character of the change demands, as well as in the manner in which they were pressed and processed, occurred in the early twentieth century through the organization of a movement specifically designed to secure revision in legal policy regarding contraception. Whereas the earlier efforts of the National Liberal League had been directed at the negative impact of the vague prohibitions against obscenity on free speech, press, and thought and had only incidentally involved birth-control policy, the new demands were pitched to the peculiar interests and values furthered by a liberalized policy regarding contraception. While the attempts for legal change of the free-thought interests had gone down to a rather ignominious defeat, time had passed and the possibility for effectuating change appeared brighter.

In the first place, it was a period of rigorous reform activity. Rampant industrialization and urbanization had continued the massive concentrations of wealth experienced in the post–Civil War era, and the political system was as susceptible as ever to the suasion of monied interests. A vast majority of the nation's wealth had been concentrated in the hands of a few and the names of Morgan, Carnegie, and Rockefeller now occupied the economic spotlight as they battled for wealth and power, often in combination against the public interest.[1] By 1904 some

---

[1] See C. B. Spahr, *The Present Distribution of Wealth in the United States* (New York, 1896), 5; Louis Hacker, *The Shaping of the American Tradition*, II (New

5,300 distinct plants had been merged under industrial trusts with a capitalization of over $7 billion.[2] United States Steel Corporation, formed in 1901, became the first billion-dollar amalgamation, combining 228 companies in 127 towns and cities in 18 states, controlling approximately 70 percent of iron and steel production.[3]

This concentration of wealth and the abuses it created again generated a demand for reform. It was the Progressive era and a mighty ax was wielded by the muckrakers, Lincoln Steffens, Charles Edward Russell, Ida Tarbell, Gustavus Myers, and Upton Sinclair.[4] In journals like *McClure's* (especially Ida Tarbell's "History of the Standard Oil Company"), *Everybody's*, *Munsey's*, *Cosmopolitan*, *Hampton's*, and *Pearsons*, the need for control of wealth and politics was consistently urged. Theodore Roosevelt, and then William Howard Taft, aggressively pressed the case against the trusts and secured legislation designed to limit their size and power. Political figures like Robert La Follette sought new devices such as the referendum, initiative, and direct primary to enhance democratic participation and hopefully to produce increased visability in the decision-making of government.[5]

Nor was the Progressive movement limited to the political and eco-

---

York, 1947), 930–41; Morison and Commager, *The Growth of the American Republic*, 362.

On economic concentration during the era of the trusts see generally T. C. Cochran and William Miller, *The Age of Enterprise* (New York, 1942); G. W. Edwards, *The Evolution of Finance Capitalism* (New York, 1938); Joseph Dorfman, *The Economic Mind in American Civilization* (New York, 1946–49); John Moody, *Masters of Capital* (New Haven, 1919); B. J. Hendrick, *The Age of Big Business* (New Haven, 1919); E. A. Ross, *Sin and Society* (Boston, 1907); Gustavus Myers, *History of Great American Fortunes* (rev. ed., New York, 1937).

[2] Moody, *Masters of Capital*, 486. See Harold V. Faulkner, *The Quest for Social Justice, 1898–1914* (New York, 1931).

[3] Schlesinger, *The Rise of Modern America*, 91. See Ida M. Tarbell, *The History of the Standard Oil Company* (New York, 1904).

[4] Herbert Croly, *The Promise of American Life* (New York, 1909), and W. E. Weyl, *The New Democracy* (New York, 1912), exemplify the ideology of the movement. See E. Mowry, *Theodore Roosevelt and the Progressive Movement* (Madison, 1946); B. P. Dewitt, *The Progressive Movement* (New York, 1915); Frederick Haynes, *Social Politics in the United States* (Boston, 1924), chap. 8; C. C. Regler, *The Era of the Muckrakers* (Chapel Hill, 1932); Parrington, *The Beginnings of Critical Realism*, 404–8; Faulkner, *The Quest for Social Justice*, 112–29; Morison and Commager, *The Growth of the American Republic*, 366–71.

[5] See Robert La Follette, *Autobiography* (Madison, 1913); E. P. Oberholtzer, *The Referendum in America* (New York, 1915); Thomas H. Greer, *American Social Reform Movements* (New York, 1949), 97–113; Hicks, *The American Nation*, chap. 18; Faulkner, *The Quest for Social Justice*, 112–29.

nomic spheres. Increasingly there was concern for the social conditions engendered by urbanization and industrialization. The new humanitarianism pictured the extensive poverty in the cities, the miserable conditions of working life, the consequences of child labor, the absence of effective relief for the poor, the inadequate provision of health services, the prevalence of alcohol, prostitution, and gambling, and sought a remedy.[6] By 1905 over 2 million copies of Henry George's *Progress and Poverty* (1879) had been sold and its indictment of the human condition was widely repeated. And in looking at the problem of poverty, there was also a deepening recognition that the poor, who had a diminished financial capacity to care for children, tended to produce larger families.

Neither the status of women nor the character of family life had remained constant. The independence of women was being recognized both in law and fact. Legally, the laws that had treated her as an appendage of her husband were revised and the suffragette movement won new rights to assure her greater political participation. Women were also increasingly rejecting the role of custodian of the home and seeking a place in the working world. Between 1870 and 1900, the number of women in jobs outside the home rose from 1,800,000 to 5,300,000.[7] Women who did not seek employment often participated in women's clubs and other social activity. Further, women with the financial capability apparently were able to secure the means of family limitation and the birth rate in the higher socioeconomic (SES) classes tended to be substantially less than that in the lower SES classes. Control of childbearing, at least for a segment of the populace, provided still another impetus toward emancipating the woman from the home. Concomi-

---

[6] Jane Addams, *Forty Years at Hull House* (New York, 1910); Jacob A. Riis, *How the Other Half Lives* (New York, 1932); Riis, *The Battle with the Slum* (New York, 1902); Riis, *The Children of the Poor* (New York, 1892); R. W. De Forest and Lawrence Veiller, *The Tenement House Problem* (New York, 1903). On the humanitarian aspects of the Progressive movement see Schlesinger, *The Rise of Modern America*, 107-26; Morison and Commager, *The Growth of the American Republic*, 369, 371-79.

[7] Schlesinger, *The Rise of Modern America*, 113. See Edith Abbott, *Women in Industry* (New York, 1910). On the legal status of women see G. J. Bayles, *Women and the Law* (New York, 1907); Jeanie L. Wilson, *The Legal and Political Status of Women in the United States* (Cedar Rapids, 1912); Elizabeth C. Stanton et al., *History of Woman Suffrage* (New York, 1881-1922); Bertha A. Rembaugh, *The Political Status of Women in the United States* (New York, 1911). Inez H. Ireven, *Angels and Amazons* (Garden City, 1933), Arthur M. Schlesinger, *The Rise of the City, 1878-1898* (New York, 1933), 121-59, and Faulkner, *The Quest for Social Justice*, 153-76, discuss generally the changing role of women.

tantly, the family was being displaced as the center of all social life. Children were increasingly perceived as economic burdens rather than financial assets. Familial responsibility for religious, economic, educative, protective, and recreational functions was greatly modified through the encroachment of other social institutions on the performance of these "family" activities.[8]

In religion also the tides of change were being felt. Church attendance continued to flourish and Americans tended to adhere rigidly to the faith of their fathers as Billy Sunday poured on the fire and brimstone. But the peremptory hold of Puritanism was more clearly on the wane than ever before. Pragmatism and skepticism challenged dogmatic responses to the basic problems of social living. Scientific discoveries continued to challenge facile explanations of events as manifestations of God's will, and the spread and enhancement of education assured the communication of the new learning. As Henry Steele Commager suggested: "In a general way it could be said that the two generations after 1890 witnessed a transition from certainty to uncertainty, from faith to doubt, from security to insecurity, from seeming order to ostentatious disorder...."[9]

Biblical criticism within Protestantism and an increased interest in comparative religion rejected the assumption that Christianity possessed all truth and that this truth was not subject to question. The social-gospel movement of the latter part of the nineteenth century continued unabated into the twentieth—religion was being removed from its institutional confines in an effort to enhance its social relevancy. And perhaps, in confronting the exigencies of social living, the clergy itself

[8] See Lydia Commander, "Has the Small Family Become an American Ideal?," *Independent*, LVI (Apr. 14, 1904), 836–40; Commander, "Why Do Americans Prefer Small Families?," *Independent*, LVII (Oct. 13, 1904), 847–50; Faulkner, *The Quest for Social Justice*, 162–67; and the works of Margaret Sanger and Mary Ware Dennett cited *infra*. A. W. Calhoun, *A Social History of the American Family* (Cleveland, 1919), William F. Ogburn and M. Nimkoff, *Technology and the Changing Family* (Boston, 1955), and Charlotte P. Gilman, "The Passing of the Home in Great American Cities," *Cosmopolitan*, XXXVIII (Dec., 1904), 139, discuss the changing character of family life.

[9] Commager, *The American Mind*, 407. The changing character of religion is discussed in H. K. Carroll, *The Religious Forces of the United States* (rev. ed., New York, 1912); Faulkner, *The Quest for Social Justice*, chap. 9; Schlesinger, *The Rise of the City*, chap. 10; Garrison, *The March of Faith*, 146 et seq. These sources provide extensive bibliographic material. Billy Sunday's influence is the subject of Lindsay Denison, "The Rev. Billy Sunday and His War on the Devil," *American Mercury*, LXIV (Sept., 1907), 451–68; and Schlesinger, *The Rise of the City*, chaps. 6–8, and Morison and Commager, *The Growth of the American Republic*, chap. 12, deal with the effects of changing science and communications.

began to question simplistic, absolutist responses. If flexibility in religious doctrine had not yet permeated the belief of the American people generally, it was having a profound impact among their spiritual advisors and on the doctrinal tenets of their churches.[10]

The Progressive movement, then, was more a frame of mind than a coherent creed. It was widely accepted that the great democratic experiment was in need of reform and the revitalization and response encompassed all sectors of American life. Moderate reform elements vied with exponents of radical change. In the labor movement especially, anarchists, syndicalists, and socialists challenged those unions that were more temperate in their reactions to the evils of capitalism.[11] While many sought to utilize the institutionalized mechanisms for change, others called for rejection of the system itself—a situation very much like the present.

It was in this context of agitation and reform that the new demand for change in the public policy regarding contraception arose. Like Comstockery, its orientation to the task of effectuating change reflected greatly the social environment that gave it birth. And like Comstockery, it had its high priest, or, in this instance, high priestess.

MARGARET SANGER: JUDICIAL MARTYRDOM AS A TECHNIQUE FOR CHANGE

In many ways Margaret Sanger was as much a product of her environment as was Anthony Comstock. Whereas the latter was raised in a highly institutionalized religious family, Margaret Sanger was constantly subject to the free-thought and socialist influence of her father. He would espouse the virtues of Robert Ingersoll, the famous free thinker and agnostic, read passages from Henry George's *Progress and Poverty* (1879), and question simplistic approaches to religious belief. Her husband, William Sanger, was also a socialist, and her home became a meeting place for some of the leading radicals of the period: William

[10] See Hopkins, *The Rise of the Social Gospel*; G. B. Smith, ed., *Religious Thought in the Last Quarter Century* (Chicago, 1927); Shailer Matthews, *The Church and the Changing Order* (New York, 1909); Garrison, *The March of Faith*, chap. 10; George Harris, *A Century's Change in Religion* (Boston, 1914); Schlesinger, *The Rise of the City*, 323–25; C. W. Schields, "Does the Bible Contain Scientific Errors?," *Century*, XLV (1892–93), 126–34.

[11] See Nathan Fine, *Labor and Farmer Parties in the United States, 1828–1928* (New York, 1928); Greer, *American Social Reform Movements*, chaps. 1 and 2; Haynes, *Social Politics in the U.S.*, chaps. 9 and 10.

D. (Big Bill) Haywood (organizer of the Industrial Workers of the World, IWW or Wobblies), John Reed, Elizabeth Gurly Flynn, and "Red Emma" Goldman. Although Margaret admitted to some intellectual inclination toward the anarchists and avidly read their works, she joined the Socialist party. Nor was she a stranger to the consequences of poverty and excessive births. Her mother had died at the age of forty-eight after bearing eleven children. Margaret personally served as a nurse and experienced the dilemma facing those women lacking the financial means to acquire effective contraceptives, but loath to deny their husbands' sexual needs. The foundations for her future activities had thus been well laid.[12]

Like many of her compatriots of the period, Margaret Sanger was an assiduous feminist campaigner. She perceived that the forces of industrialization and urbanization were beginning to work fundamental changes in the social environment. New interests were being generated which could be aggregated to form a cohesive, articulate force for legal change.

Her earliest encounter with Comstockery occurred when one of a series of her articles entitled "What Every Girl Should Know," published in *The Call*, was suppressed by the Post Office Department (apparently because she used the words gonorrhea and syphilis) by threatening the journal with loss of mailing privileges.[13] But this only encouraged her to learn more about the impact of these laws on the availability of information concerning reproduction and its control. Wherever she turned, she was confronted by an unwillingness or an inability to discuss methods of contraception. In her *Autobiography*, Margaret Sanger recalls such conversations:

> Having no idea how powerful were the laws which laid a blanket of ignorance over the medical profession as well as the laity [or at least those who lacked the means to acquire the information], I asked various doctors of my acquaintance, "Why aren't physicians doing something?"
>
> "The people you're worrying about wouldn't use contraception if they had it; they breed like rabbits. And, besides, there's a law against it."
>
> "Information does exist, doesn't it?"
>
> "Perhaps, but I doubt whether you can find it. Even if you do,

---

[12] Margaret Sanger, *An Autobiography* (New York, 1938), chaps. 1-7. See Fryer, *The Birth Controllers*, 201-3.
[13] Lawrence Lader, *The Margaret Sanger Story* (Garden City, 1955), 36-37; Sanger, *Autobiography*, 77.

you can't pass it on. Comstock'll get you if you don't watch out."[14]

In 1914 she began to publish a journal called *The Woman Rebel*. Under the banner "No Gods: No Masters," the publication presented a clear challenge to the Comstock Act as well as the morality that had spawned it. Not only did the journal serve as a pulpit for other radical causes, but it directly discussed the taboo subject of contraception. The dangers to the pregnant mother could be shown to grow with increased incidence of birth. Margaret Sanger considered the life of the unwanted, unloved child, unable to be properly cared for, and concluded that the first right of the child was to be wanted. The rich, although inhibited by the presence of the Comstock laws, were knowledgeable and able to limit family size, but the poor lacked both knowledge and means. Her answer was a declaration of war. She asserted: "The most serious evil of our times is that of encouraging the bringing into the world of large families. The most immoral practice of the day is breeding too many children."[15] In the truest tradition of her feminist and radical leanings, she argued that it was a woman's duty "to look the whole world in the face with a go-to-hell look in the eyes, to have an ideal; to speak and act in defiance of convention."[16]

Postal authorities suppressed the first nine issues of the new journal and Margaret Sanger was indicted for violation of the Comstock laws. When the judge denied a continuance to allow her to prepare her case, she fled to Europe. There she developed a real knowledge concerning birth control (as she and her compatriots had named the subject) and fully outlined a strategy of attack. Not only did she meet individuals such as the Drysdales, Havelock Ellis, and Dr. Marie Stopes, who would have an abiding influence on her thoughts and actions, but she heard for the first time of the Bradlaugh-Besant trial.[17]

Charles Bradlaugh, founder of the English Malthusian League and publisher of the *National Reformer*, a pro-Malthusian tract, together

[14] Sanger, *Autobiography*, 93.
[15] Margaret Sanger, *Women and the New Race* (New York, 1920), 57. See Lader, *The Margaret Sanger Story*, 139; Margaret Sanger, "Birth Control—Past, Present and Future," *Birth Control Review*, V (June, 1921), 11-13.
[16] *The Woman Rebel*, Mar., 1914, quoted in Sanger, *Autobiography*, 110.
[17] *In the High Court of Justice: Queen's Bench Division, June 18th, 1877: The Queen v. Charles Bradlaugh and Annie Besant* (London, 1878) (a verbatim report of the trial and appeal). See Annie Besant, *Autobiography* (London, 1893); Arthur E. Nethercot, *The First Five Lives of Annie Besant* (Chicago, 1960); Hypatia B. Bonner, *Charles Bradlaugh* (London, 1894); Craig, *Suppressed Books*, 44-48; Fryer, *The Birth Controllers*, chap. 16.

with Annie Besant, a vigorous advocate of free thought and socialism, deliberately invited arrest for publishing Knowlton's *Fruits of Philosophy*. In fact, Bradlaugh sent a copy of the book to the police and informed them of a time and place when he would sell it. Apparently at the insistence of the English Society for the Suppression of Vice, the reformers were arrested and tried before Lord Chief Justice Cockburn. The trial had been used as a platform to publicize the legal restrictions against dissemination of contraceptive information. Every opportunity was utilized to differentiate the interests furthered by contraception from those involved in fashioning obscenity policy. Cockburn remarked: "A more ill-advised and more injudicious proceeding in the way of a prosecution was probably never brought into a court of justice.... I should very much like to know who are the authorities who are prosecuting, because that has not yet transpired. The Solicitor-General tells us it may have been the magistracy. I do not believe it." [18]

Although it appears that the reformers were found guilty (the jury returned a highly ambiguous verdict, and an appeal based on a technical error in the indictment was successful), their purpose had been achieved. For the forty years since its publication, *Fruits of Philosophy* had been selling about 700 copies a year; in the three months between the arrest and trial, it sold 125,000.[19] Further, while a causal inference is dangerous, the plunge in the English birth rate following the trial is notable.

> The Neo-Malthusian practices advocated in the pages of [*Fruits of Philosophy*] were new to the general public, and because of this it was eagerly read, and obtained a very large circulation in a comparatively short space of time. The ill effects of the abortive prosecution bear their fruits still; if it had not taken place very many would never have been initiated into this nefarious system. ... We are now becoming quite accustomed to the ever-recurring remark in the Registrar-General's returns: "This is the lowest birth-rate ever recorded".... The serious decline in the birth-

---

[18] *In the High Court of Justice*, 255. The solicitor general's argument was something less than overwhelming: "I say that this is a dirty, filthy book, and the test of it is that no human being would allow that book to lie on his table, no decently educated English husband would allow even his wife to have it.... The object of it is to enable a person to have sexual intercourse, and not to have that which in the order of Providence is the natural result of that sexual intercourse. That is the only purpose of the book, and all the instruction in the other parts of the book leads up to that proposition." *Ibid.*, 251.

[19] Fryer, *The Birth Controllers*, 162. Fryer also discusses the activities of other birth-control advocates punished in England under the general obscenity laws.

rate of the United Kingdom can clearly be traced, in the first instance, to the injudicious prosecution of Mr. Bradlaugh and Mrs. Besant.[20]

In any case, legal prosecution had brought the subject of birth control a visibility previously denied, and the Malthusian movement, a greater freedom of action.

The Bradlaugh-Besant incident provided a concrete example of a strategy for change, a dramatic illustration of using activity in the legal forum to influence social change. Ultimately, legal revision itself would have to grow out of a refashioning of the social environment.

> But the question is, can we hope that law makers will act until the public is already acting openly—as it now does secretly when it can? Do laws precede general sentiment or follow it? And does unexpressed general sentiment count? . . . So the real fight today is not in Washington, Albany, San Francisco or old Boston, but right in the heart of every community, right in the dreadful little tenement rooms, right in the mining districts, the churches, the schools and the colleges, where healthy young people go laughing into horrors, because their education fails to educate.[21]

If the Puritan restrictions were to be overcome, if the means of family limitation were to be made available to all economic classes, if free communication regarding birth control was to be achieved, the cause required public visibility. The objective to be reached defined the mode of attack to be used—agitation, education, organization, and legislation.

> Agitation through violation of the law was the key to the public which would ultimately make the other three tactics workable. We hold the law as rather a sacred thing, and the only way that you can awaken people to the question that was here before us, was to challenge that thing which all of us hold sacred. That arouses attention, and when this is done, then we come to plan the means of giving the message and educating. So the process goes, agitate, educate, organize, and legislate.[22]

---

[20] R. Ussher, *Neo-Malthusianism: An Enquiry into That System with Regard to Its Economy and Morality* (London, 1898), 3. The years following 1875-77 show a steady decline in the English birth rate. See Ethel M. Elderton, *Report on the English Birthrate: Part I. England, North of Humber* (London, 1914), viii, 233.

[21] Margaret Sanger, "Editorial Comment," *Birth Control Review*, III (Jan., 1919), 2.

[22] Margaret Sanger, *Birth Control: The Proceedings of the First American Birth Control Conference, New York, Nov. 11, 12, 1921* (New York, 1921), 91-92. She described the assumptions on which this program for change was based: "I based my program on the existence in the country of a forceful sentiment which,

Here was a credo for securing desired legal change. A favorable legal response would be possible only if a favorable social environment could be generated. Law could provide the mechanism for reaching the quiescent public.

Margaret Sanger returned to the United States now prepared for the judicial battle from which she had fled. But, as in the Bradlaugh-Besant trial, the federal indictments were bringing her a visibility she might otherwise have been denied. The Sanger martyrdom was given wide coverage by the press; advocates of the movement brought continuing pressure on federal officials. The government finally yielded by entering a *nolle prosequi*; a blow at Comstockery had been struck through the judicial subsystem without the case ever reaching court. As a leader of the nascent birth-control movement noted: "The fact remains that the prosecution for the most forthright intentional and wholesale defiance of the Federal law that had ever been undertaken to date was not carried through to a conclusion."[23]

The discretion exercised by the prosecutor in electing not to prosecute again illustrates the importance of the behavior of other decision-makers in the legal system in affecting the nature and rate of legal and social change. Indeed, perhaps the most apparent limitation of the present inquiry lies in the restriction of the framework to the behavior of

---

if coordinated, could become powerful enough to change laws. Horses wildly careening around a pasture have as much strength as when harnessed to a plow, but only in the latter case can the strength be measured and turned to some useful purpose. The public had to be educated before it could be organized and before the laws could be changed as a result of that organization. I set myself to the task. It was to be a long one, because the press did not want articles stating the facts of birth control; they wanted news, and to make them news still consisted of fights, police, arrests, controversy." *Autobiography*, 251. A primary tool for education was the *Birth Control Review*, which she edited. See generally Rilma Buckman, "Social Engineering: A Study of the Birth Control Movement," *Social Forces*, XXII (May, 1944), 420-28; Annie G. Porritt, "Publicity in the Birth Control Movement," *Birth Control Review*, VII (Apr., 1923), 88-89, 99; Margaret Sanger, "Editorial," *Birth Control Review*, V (Mar., 1921), 3-4.

It was extremely difficult to find any publishers for condemned tracts. There was a constant fear expressed of arrest and conviction. Margaret Sanger visited over twenty publishers before she found a printer for her book *Family Limitation*. See Lader, *The Margaret Sanger Story*; Sanger, *My Fight for Birth Control* (New York, 1931), 85; Caroline H. Robinson, *Seventy Birth Control Clinics* (Baltimore, 1930), xi-xii.

[23] Dennett, *Birth Control Laws*, 71. Margaret Sanger had been advised by a lawyer to agree to obey the law thereafter as a condition of her release. She refused, arguing that it was a bad law and had to be changed. She did not, however, accept the possibility of congressional action in the given social situation. Sanger, *My Fight for Birth Control*, 130. See Frederick A. Blossom, "Growth of the Birth Control Movement in the U.S.," *Birth Control Review*, I (Mar., 1917), 4.

only two of the legal actors, the judiciary and the legislature, to the exclusion of other vital components of the legal system. Given the increasing role of the executive and administrative actors, the framework must be expanded to encompass their contributions to the product. Other policy-makers within the broader legal system, e.g. attorneys, juries, also must be brought into the interaction framework. Not only is this essential for the construction of a comprehensive map of the legal process, but also for the encompassment of some of the primary work being undertaken in the field of sociology of law. While these other policy-makers might be treated as subsystems of the judicial, legislative, executive, and/or administrative systems, it would seem desirable to specify their particular role in the processes of legal change.

Following dismissal of the federal indictments in 1916, Margaret Sanger moved quickly to implement the movement's new-found momentum. Together with her sister, Ethel Byrne, and supporters, she opened America's first birth-control clinic in the poverty-ridden Brownsville section of New York. As anticipated, the clinic was closed by police and arrests were made. Unlike the earlier federal challenge, which Margaret Sanger had faced practically alone, she now had substantial public and organizational support. The press immediately brought public attention to the latest act of protest by the feminist leader; legal counsel was readily available; every opportunity to generate further visibility for the cause was utilized. Even if a favorable judicial decision could not be obtained, the trial itself would serve as a platform to increase public awareness of the injustice of Comstockery, thereby laying the basis for legal reform.[24]

Civil disobedience, which had provided access to the courts in order to recommend change, was only prefatory to the task of informing the judicial policy-maker of the need for and desirability of such policy alteration. Like the legislative process, judicial policy formation arguably is purposeful behavior even though it may involve only incremental adjustments.[25] If alternative policy approaches are to be adequately

[24] For background materials see Lader, *The Margaret Sanger Story*; Sanger, *Autobiography*; Sanger, *My Fight for Birth Control*. There evidently were a number of state cases prior to 1915. However, they appear to have followed the early federal pattern of deference to the dominant morality. See "Abstract of Mr. Ernst's Remarks," Oct. 19, 1938, p. 2 (from the files of PPLM). See Halstead v. Nelson, 36 Hun. (N.Y.) 147 (1885), in which the court held that circulating an untrue statement claiming that the plaintiff provided contraceptive information would constitute slander per se.

[25] Such an approach is suggested by Wells and Grossman, "The Concept of Judicial Policy-Making," 309, in their excellent analysis of the policy-making

evaluated and creative change fashioned, there must be devices for providing the courts with the requisite information. The judicial equivalent of the legislative proceeding, the trial, however, is governed by formalized rules and procedures, and the information-gathering and -presenting task is charged to the adversary parties themselves. Through their mutual desire for success, it is believed that necessary data will emerge. Assuming, however, that the adversaries could acquire the requisite broad data necessary for effective policy formation, archaic rules often prevent the admission of nonlegal evidence and judges tend to show a marked hostility to its use.

In the *Sanger* and *Byrne* cases, the defendants framed a challenge to the constitutionality of the New York Comstock law by arguing that the act was "arbitrary, unreasonable and oppressive" because it compelled certain women "to unnecessarily expose themselves to the hazardry of death"[26] (evidence was presented indicating the danger that conception could present to maternal health) and did not promote the health, life, morals, or welfare of the community (data was provided relating excessive fertility to low intelligence, poverty, tuberculosis, alcoholism, mental deficiency, and, most important, infant mortality. Morals were said to be transitory, a matter of time and place, and the causal relation between the morality of the citizenry and fear of conception was questioned. Even if the prohibition were held to be reasonable as to the unmarried, it was argued to be unduly harsh to apply it to married women—procreation was not the only purpose of marriage.

Considering the time, the extensive use of nonlegal data in presenting the change demands was quite impressive. The trial court, however, was apparently not favorably inclined to the social evidence, and the court of appeals in the *Sanger* case was quite explicit in rejecting its relevance: "Much of the argument presented to us by the appellant touching social conditions and sociological questions are matters for the Legislature and not for the courts."[27] While nonlegal data seems

---

process: "If it is at least feasible to conceptualize judicial policy-making as an institutional problem-solving endeavor, and not primarily as the output of individual judicial value expressions, a change of focus is required. The emphasis should be on identifying and relating the various factors which comprise the policy-making situation; that is, establishing some sort of relationship between the outcomes and the demands upon the Court." See text accompanying Introduction, notes 19–20 and 22 *supra*.

[26] Brief for Appellants in Support of Motion for Stay of Proceedings, p. 16, People v. Sanger, 222 N.Y. 193, 118 N.E. 637 (1918).

[27] People v. Sanger, 222 N.Y. 193, 118 N.E. 637, 638 (1918), appeal dismissed 251 U.S. 537 (1919).

essential to determining if the statute was a reasonable exercise of a valid state power (if that was to be the standard of judgment), the court's perspective on the role of the judiciary in processing information tends to reflect the same deferential attitude to the legislature as the sole policy-maker that characterized the earlier behavior of the federal courts.

At the prescriptive stage, the courts again acquiesced in the legislative judgment and prior judicial behavior in dealing with the constitutional issue. In the trial court, it was held that "precedent" had foreclosed the question of constitutionality, although it is difficult to determine how the minimum judicial experience had foreclosed anything. Margaret Sanger and Ethel Byrne were, therefore, both found guilty and sentenced to thirty days in the workhouse. Nor were the appellate courts impressed by the constitutional challenge. In the *Byrne* opinion, Judge Cropsey discussed the constitutional issue at length and enthusiastically legitimized the legislative policy decision. The Comstock provisions were viewed as a proper exercise of the police power designed to prevent the spread of articles "prejudicial to the public morals and inimical to the welfare and interests of the community."[28] The court determined that "the public good justified the passage of the statute and requires its enforcement."[29] Like the legislative behavior that had spawned the act, the judicial actor offered no factual basis for its finding, ignoring the reality that an adverse effect on "morals" or the "welfare and interests of the community" is an empirical fact to be proven, not a proposition to be assumed.

In *Sanger*, Judge Crane's analysis of the constitutional issue generally followed the rationale of *Byrne*. The defendant had conceded that prohibition to the unmarried would be constitutional but nevertheless argued that it was unreasonable to prevent a licensed physician from prescribing contraceptives for married persons when medically necessary. In spite of the fact that change demands were not premised on an "interpretative" re-examination of contraceptive policy, Judge Crane utilized this mechanism for circumventing the constitutional argument. Simply, the court read the statute to exclude any prohibition against proper medical provision of birth-control services. Employing an exemption included in another section of the statute covering articles "for the cure or prevention of disease," Judge Crane held that the language was "broad enough to protect the physician who in good faith gives

---

[28] 99 Misc. 1, 163 N.Y.S. 682, 686 (1917).
[29] 163 N.Y.S. at 684.

such help or advice to a married person to cure or prevent disease."[30] Although neither of the defendants was saved by such a reading (which perhaps explains why such an approach was not argued), the practical effect of the court's flexible approach to its interpretative powers was to insert a medical exemption into the Comstock provisions, in spite of the fact that the act appeared all-encompassing and there was no indication that the nineteenth-century legislature intended such a limitation. The exemption did serve the more immediate cause of the birth-control movement by not only providing a basis for opening clinics but also an impetus for the future activities of the movement in New York. Even though the exemption standard lacked the desired certainty and scope which could be furnished through legislative action, it was a marked improvement over an absolute prohibition and laid a firm foundation for subsequent development of a birth-control policy if the legislature chose to intervene favorably.

It is difficult to explain the motivations underlying Judge Crane's liberal interpretation, since he could have restricted himself to a literalist reading of the particular provisions of the Comstock Act. Instead, he chose to manipulate the legislative policy to permit a greater availability of contraceptive services. His decisional behavior may well have been only an attempt to strengthen his contention that the statute was not unreasonably prohibitive. Although he had specifically rejected the nonlegal evidence for judicial consideration, its presence also suggested the need to bolster his conclusion that the act was reasonable. His legitimization of the statute was made more acceptable by the limited effect he gave its prohibitions.

The above, however, is only speculation. Indeed, the attitude manifested by Judge Cropsey in *Byrne* seems more compatible with the dominant judicial temper of the period. The tone of his opinion appears to go beyond mere deference to legislative judgment to reflect a personal value system fully consistent with the Puritan mentality. Not only did he suggest that the birth controllers were motivated by commercialism, but he clearly expressed his personal bias against the prac-

---

[30] 118 N.E. at 637–38. The court employed the definition of "disease" in *Webster's International Dictionary*: "An alteration in the state of the body, or of some of its organs, interrupting or disturbing the performance of the vital functions, and causing or threatening pain and sickness; illness; sickness; disorder." The court of appeals' approach is contrary to the holding in People v. Hagen, 181 App. Div. 153 (1917), where a physician was convicted for a slight representation that pills delivered to decoys could prevent conception. See McWilliams, "Laws of N.Y. and Birth Control," 47–48.

tice. "One of these pamphlets is labeled 'What Every Girl Should Know.' This contained matter which not only should not be known by every girl, but which perhaps should not be known by any. The distribution of these pamphlets, especially to girls just coming into womanhood, would be a shocking disgrace to the community."[31] Judge Cropsey's comments mirror similar values expressed by Judge McInery in the 1915 trial of William Sanger, who had been tricked by Anthony Comstock himself into selling a copy of Margaret Sanger's *Family Limitation*:

> You state that you have done nothing wrong. Your crime is not only a violation of the laws of men, but of the law of God as well, in your scheme to prevent motherhood. Too many persons have the idea that it is wrong to have children. Some women are so selfish that they do not want to be bothered with them. If some persons would go around and urge Christian women to bear children, instead of wasting their time on woman suffrage, this city, and society would be better off.[32]

Alterations in the social environment appear inconclusive and, in any case, were not really directly reflected in either the *Sanger* or *Byrne* opinion. But at least in the *Sanger* case, we have an adjustment which made the legal norms more compatible with the nascent but emerging social interests. Whether this was a primary motivation in Judge Crane's behavior can remain only speculation.

LEGISLATIVE NON-ACTION IN ALBANY AND WASHINGTON

Pro-change forces had sought to maximize the gains achieved by the vast amount of publicity generated by judicial martyrdom. Convictions were transformed into triumphs as birth-control leagues sprang up around the country. In New York Margaret Sanger sought to communicate the legal policy change effectuated in the courts to those who might be affected, i.e., feedback from the judicial subsystem to the social system.[33] Change of the law in the books served as a catalyst for

---

[31] 163 N.Y.S. at 684.

[32] Editorial, "What They Said—the Sanger Trial," *America*, XIII (Sept. 18, 1915), 568. Mrs. Sanger secured Judge McInery's agreement to disqualify himself in her case.

[33] The movement did receive two setbacks in 1917 when propaganda movies were denied a license. Message Photo-Play v. Bell, 100 Misc. 267, 167 N.Y.S. 129, rev'd 179 App. Div. 13, 166 N.Y.S. 338 (1917); Universal Film Co. v. Bell, 100

further social change, which, in turn, seems to have effectuated an increased impetus for further change in the legal posture of contraception.

There was, however, a substantial segment of the nascent movement which rejected the activist approach of Margaret Sanger. The legislature, rather than the courts, was deemed the proper forum for change; lobbying, rather than agitation and judicial martyrdom, was perceived as the appropriate vehicle for reform. Mary Ware Dennett, a frequent opponent of Mrs. Sanger within the movement, decided to organize these pro-change forces for a legislative assault. Fear that agitation drove legal policy-makers into an intransigent position prompted her to pursue change through this alternative point of access to the legal system. With what appears to be a rather naive optimism, widespread legislative support for revision, which only had to be activated, was assumed to exist.[34]

While apparently lacking a developed political sense of the social support essential for generating favorable legislative response, Dennett did possess at least some recognition that organization was a vital factor for securing legislative access. In 1915 she formed the National Birth Control League and began to fashion a legislative strategy. Since the nascent movement was locally oriented, it was believed that its influence might have greater success on a state-by-state basis. But as has frequently been suggested, inarticulate, unorganized, or weakly organized social-interest groups suffer severe impediments in pressing demands in the legislative arena—even the task of initiating action takes on herculean proportions. The birth-control movement was still only a weakly organized outgrowth of the feminist protest. Its leaders were generally reform-minded women with a world of ideals but a lack of influence and expertise, challenging powerful interests with a vast amount of influence in the legislative arena.

Since the major strength of the movement was apparently concentrated in New York, it was chosen as the initial locus of activity. Although judicial action in the *Sanger* case had produced a greater leeway for social action, the standard established was deemed inadequate for the burgeoning birth-control movement. As long as the broad pro-

---

Misc. 281, 167 N.Y.S. 124, aff'd 179 App. Div. 928, 166 N.Y.S. 344 (1917). The cases manifest the great discretion given the commissioner of licenses of New York City for determining the existence of an offense against "morality, decency or the public welfare." See Fay Productions v. Graves, 253 App. Div. 475, 3 N.Y.S.2d 573, aff'd 278 N.Y. 498, 15 N.E.2d 435 (1938), again upholding a refusal of a license for a movie on sterilization.

[34] Dennett, *Birth Control Laws*, 167–75.

hibitive statutes remained in effect, the dissemination of birth-control information and services was subject to official harassment, and the scope of permissible activity remained clouded. The legislative actor, however, might provide the requisite policy reform. Little possibility of a negative legislative reaction to *Sanger* existed, but the question remained whether the legislature would assume responsibility for providing a more substantial base for the dissemination of birth-control information and services.

Initially the task was to secure access to the legislative arena. In the initial overtures in 1917, a frustrating search eventually turned up legislators willing to sponsor the bills. Even then the movement was forced to employ Socialist and Democratic sponsors in an overwhelmingly Republican legislature.[35] When the American Birth Control League, headed by Margaret Sanger, took over responsibility for the Albany operations in 1921, it experienced the same difficulty of securing effective access to the legislature. Professor Lindsay of Columbia University had drafted a more limited "doctors only" bill that would insert an exemption from the prohibitions of the act for qualified doctors, but a legislative liaison was still necessary. One legislator who had tentatively accepted the task later sent the following letter: "I very much regret, but after consulting with some of the leaders of the Assembly, I have been strongly advised not to offer your bill. . . . I was told it would do me an injury that I could not overcome for some time."[36] Another legislator refused "on the ground of levity from his associates."[37] If the legislator wasn't aware of the political realities, his colleagues and party leaders soon informed him. Fears of the reaction of vested interests formed a major impediment at every stage of the legislative process.

In 1919 the Voluntary Parenthood League, Mary Ware Dennett's successor to her earlier organization, began to press the demand for change in the national forum. But the same inability to secure effective access was again present. Four years elapsed before a legislator willing to sponsor their bill was found. Sixteen legislators who had been directly approached excused themselves with claims of time pressures, the deli-

[35] See *ibid.*, 72–93; Dennett, "Legislators, Six-Hour Weeks and Birth Control," *Birth Control Review*, III (Mar., 1919), 4–5, for an account of the early attempts at legislative repeal in New York.
[36] Margaret Sanger, "Outlines of Legislative Work at Albany," *Birth Control Review*, V (May, 1923), 107–8.
[37] *Ibid.* For a biting criticism of the Albany legislators see Margaret Sanger, "Politicians vs. Birth Control," *Birth Control Review*, V (May, 1921), 3-4; Sanger, "Intelligence Tests for Legislators," *Birth Control Review*, VII (May, 1923), 107–8.

cacy of the subject, lack of expertise or prestige, or political vulnerability. Not that they always refused; it just seemed that they felt someone else would be a preferable choice.[38] Simply, this was not the type of issue to win friends and influence people. It was a highly sensitive area which was becoming an even more intense source of social cleavage as time passed. The particular needs created by the forces of industrialization, urbanization, female emancipation, and the breakdown of the family unit, which were changing the social scene, could have justified action, but no politically oriented legislator wanted to be in the vanguard of legal change. Finally, with the introduction of the Cummins-Vaile bill in 1924, the proposal for revision of the federal obscenity laws had, at least, been placed on the legislative agenda.

The frustrations experienced by the movement in securing access to the legislature for its change demand, however, was only a prelude. The movement now had to inform the legislators of the need for and desirability of fashioning a broader legal policy toward contraception. As was indicated earlier, a primary mechanism for informing the legislative actor is the hearing. The character of this proceeding in the national forum is reflective of the pattern which appeared in all of the jurisdictions under analysis. Evidence would be presented by birth-control advocates on the medical dangers posed for the mother and child by excessive births, the problems of the unwanted child, and the dangers to the race from overproduction of defective elements in society. Movement spokesmen argued for equal opportunity for the poor to obtain assistance on fertility control and for a new morality based on adequate appreciation of the sexual act in marriage, while challenging the natural-law arguments presented by the opposition. On the other hand, the defenders of the status quo stressed primarily the moral and familial effects of the proposal and raised the specter of race suicide through declining births among native-born Americans.[39]

But the hearings were essentially emotive diatribes. Hostile legislators harassed witnesses, and the organization of arguments tended to be weak; little valuable data on the social or medical impact of the laws was presented. In these early hearings the majority of witnesses for the bill were private women relating their personal attitudes. At the Cummins-Vaile inquiry, for example, only one doctor testified. The

[38] Dennett, *Birth Control Laws*, chap. 3. See Sulloway, *Birth Control and Catholic Doctrine*, 23–27.
[39] U.S. Congress, House, Subcommittee of the Judiciary Committee, *Cummins-Vaile Bill, Hearings on H.R. 6542 and S. 2290*, 68th Cong., 1st Sess., 1924 (hereafter referred to as *1924 Hearings*).

status quo forces were also weakly organized and tended to argue solely from personal moral beliefs or those of their church, but their strength did not depend on persuasion.

Nor does there appear to have been extensive informing activity through contacts with individual legislators. Birth-control advocates were continually seeking to answer charges of race suicide, promoting immorality of the young, or attempted identification of contraception with abortion. Nor were legislators prone to accept the existence of any real need for legislative intervention; the refrain that "anybody who wants it can get it" was a probable response. The retort provided by the birth-control lobbyists provides a viable rationale for the then-muted character of public sentiment for contraception as well as an interesting commentary on the problem of effectuating legal change on behalf of the inarticulate. "We tell them that practically everyone wants it who understands it, and that brings up a most significant phase of the birth control movement, which has a unique psychology, in that the mass of people who want information and want the laws changed so they can get it, do not and will not shout their wishes from the housetops. The nature of the subject is one which largely inhibits an articulate demand."[40]

The greatest segment of the populace denied access to birth-control services by the 1920s were the poor and uneducated. Individuals at a higher socioeconomic level could obtain assistance from their physicians, who had little to fear from the police. Administrative enforcement of the Comstock provisions was increasingly directed primarily at the public dissemination of contraceptive services through clinics. While many doctors apparently continued in their refusal to defy existing legal norms, it seems that the inarticulate, invisible poor dependent on public or charitable health services bore the primary brunt of the restrictive public policy embodied in the Comstock provisions.

But even if the intelligence function had been performed ideally, it is doubtful that the results at the prescriptive stage would have been altered. Notable gains had been made by birth-control advocates in attaining social support, but they remained a minority faction confronted by powerful foes. As Protestant support for the Comstock laws had begun to wane, organized Catholic influence replaced it. Any attempt at legislative modification or repeal of the birth-control provisions had to overcome the fear of Catholic political reprisals. In the

[40] Quoted in Dennett, *Birth Control Laws*, 78.

earlier stages of the movement's efforts, medical societies, a variety of Protestant denominations, and, most likely, the greater part of public opinion supported the Catholic Church's position.[41] As this support fell away, the real or imagined influence of the Church was still sufficient to hold sway.

This was clearly true in New York; in New York City the Catholic Church was referred to as "The Powerhouse." Church authorities had demonstrated their hostility to the new movement on numerous occasions, e.g. by seeking to suppress public meetings in Albany and Syracuse. In New York City the secretary of the archdiocese had actually directed the police in closing a public meeting at the town hall in 1921, with the usual publicity triumph for the birth-control movement.[42] When legislative hearings took place, a representative of the Church was always present to reiterate its opposition to any alteration in the laws. Similarly, in the national forum, Church spokesmen clearly let the legislators know the number of voters that they purported to represent; legislative hearings effectively served to warn of the dangers of hasty action.[43] In spite of the fact that anti-change interests apparently did not employ the tactic of personal contacts to the same extent as pro-change interests, the legislator was quite aware of the possible consequences of a pro–birth control vote.

However, it would probably be error at this stage to attribute legislative unwillingness to act solely to the fear of political reprisals from the Catholic Church. Despite the lack of supportive data, the legislators were probably also reflecting the prevailing social and political realities as well as their own personal value systems.[44] Indeed, a relatively untrod area of inquiry into the bases of legislative decision-making is the effect of the legislator's personal value system on his behavior, i.e. the ideological variable. While this subject might be treated as part of interest-

[41] See, e.g., Editorial, "New York Physicians and Birth Control," *America*, VI (Jan. 6, 1917), 304–5; "The Doctors and Birth Control," *Birth Control Review*, VII (June, 1923), 144–45; *1924 Hearings*.

[42] See Editorial, "Birth Control Martyrs," *Medico-Legal Journal*, XXXIX (Jan.–Feb., 1922), 1–2; "Brief Submitted in Behalf of Paul D. Cravath and Others," *Birth Control Review*, VI (Apr., 1922), 54–55; Margaret Sanger, "Church Control," *Birth Control Review*, V (Dec., 1921), 3–5. See Fryer, *The Birth Controllers*, 213; Lader, *The Margaret Sanger Story*, 226–27; Sanger, *Autobiography*, 411, on repression in other cities.

[43] See, e.g., the testimony of Miss Sara E. Laughlin, International Federation of Catholic Alumni, *1924 Hearings*, 52.

[44] See, e.g., the comments of Representatives Major, Yates, and Hersey, *1924 Hearings*, 74–76.

group influence—the legislator's ideology is approached as a composite of his group affiliations, actual and potential—its importance would seem to justify separate consideration. It is highly unlikely that the law-maker could totally dismiss his own value system, his basic predispositions regarding the subject under consideration, and his "emotional and cognitive set toward the world around him."[45]

Roll-call studies suggest the validity of this hypothesis. For example, legislators having more formal education, longer service, and less geographic isolation tend to view the legislative process in more complex terms; those approaching party in ideological terms are less capable of identifying interest-group activity; a legislator's liberal or conservative orientation on roll-call votes tends to persist over time.[46] The influence of ideology probably varies with the salience of other motivational factors and the homogeneity in their direction—cross pressures diminish the influence of any single variable.

Ideology can also influence the character of the interactions between institutional actors in the legal system. For example, a legislator who believes that the legislature is the only instrument that can make law may be less likely to favor a delay in the legislative decision pending action by other legal actors. Hostility to the judiciary might take form in support of greater legislative action. Also relevant are the possible effects of ideology on the willingness of the legislature to act creatively in response to social change. The tendency of the legislator to resist or accept change could well be a vital determination in evaluating the role of the legislature vis-à-vis other legal institutions as a creative instrument of change. But thus far the empirical evidence is too minimal to permit any generalizations.[47]

In the present instance, ideological factors were probably still supportive of a negative response to the change demands. Birth control had

[45] John C. Wahlke and Heinz Eulau, eds., *Legislative Behavior* (New York, 1959), 241.

[46] Oliver Garceau and Corrine Silverman, "A Pressure Group and the Pressured," *American Political Science Review*, XLVIII (Sept., 1954), 687; Corrine Silverman, "The Legislator's View of the Legislative Process," *Legislative Behavior*, ed. Wahlke and Eulau, 298–304; D. R. Brimhall and A. D. Otis, "Consistency of Voting of Our Congressmen," *Journal of Applied Psychology*, XXXII (Feb., 1948), 1–14.

[47] See, e.g., Edward A. Shils, "Resentments and Hostilities of Legislators: Sources, Objects, Consequences," *Legislative Behavior*, ed. Wahlke and Eulau, 347–54; John McConaughy, "Certain Personality Factors of State Legislators in South Carolina," *Introductory Readings in Political Behavior*, ed. S. Sidney Ulmer (Chicago, 1961), 45–52.

not yet arrived; moral norms had not yet been refashioned. Religious opinion, like public opinion generally, remained hostile to the new morality. Medical and social organizations were still skeptical about the desirability of fertility control through "artificial" means. This was the environment to which the legislator responded; this was the milieu in which he had been socialized. The legislative actor still tended to reflect the dominant community morality as well as his own moral convictions that general availability of birth preventives and information would tend to promote immorality and disintegration of the family unit; that it was itself a moral perversion. This in no way denies that many legislators may well have personally sought and used contraceptives, but only suggests that they drew a fine distinction between personal and public morality.

In any case, it is difficult to avoid the conclusion that political fear was a dominant motivation in the behavior of many legislative actors.

> Every bit of direct experience with legislators augments the conclusion that the chief reason the individual legislator hangs back is because he is afraid that it will "queer him" to stand for any and the reason that "political leaders" advise the legislators to let the subject alone is precisely the same. The subject is embarrassing, that's all. As one of them advised another, "Whatever you do, don't get mixed up in any sex stuff. No man in politics can afford that."[48]

As long as the subject was taboo either with society or powerful political alliances, legislative refusal to alter the direction of policy would be the expected behavior. Birth control was still a matter to be left in the bedroom and not brought into the public arena. Need for change, as noted earlier, even if real and perceived, is only one motivational factor. When there are other, more powerful forces cross-pressuring the legislator, non-action becomes a viable alternative.

Further, the institutional factor also reinforced the feasibility of non-action. Proposals for change had to run the committee gauntlet before the legislators would be forced to declare their positions publicly in a floor fight. The structure of the legal institution and the "rules of the game" under which they operate formed the context in which legislative policy-making took place, and had a vital bearing on the

[48] Dennett, *Birth Control Laws*, 189. Another congressman explained: "We have plenty of troubles of our own—why should we add to the complications by queering ourselves with birth control." *Ibid.*, 92.

character of the decisional process—"formal structure both reflects and sustains differences in power. It is never neutral."[49]

If the bill never escaped the committee, the legislators would not be placed in the uncomfortable position of publicly declaring themselves and thus alienating a faction. This became the legislative tool for avoiding the change demands. Whenever the time for a committee vote on the congressional Cummins-Vaile bill approached, the legislators would slip away until a quorum was no longer present, and the bill would die in committee. In New York, although the *law in action* was to be constantly revised through administrative non-action and implementation of the *Sanger* exception,[50] no birth-control bill was to escape legislative committee prior to the 1960s.

[49] Truman, *The Governmental Process*, 332. Seniority, specialization, apprenticeship appear to be impediments to responsive behavior. Individual legislators are permitted to bottle up proposed legislation; young, junior legislators who may be more receptive to change are expected to serve out their apprenticeship in relative obscurity. Nevertheless, these remain only hypotheses which require testing. See Wahlke et al., *The Legislative System*, 140n3.

"Rules of the game" appear to be generally accepted by legislators in order to facilitate the manner in which business is conducted; they represent "not an absolute imposed by a superior power . . . but a convention . . . accepted by a body of equals as the first condition of their cooperation." *Ibid.*, 145. Matthews's study of Senate folkways and Fenno's analysis of the House Appropriations Committee are probably two of the best-known studies of the effects of institutional rules on congressional legislative behavior. Matthews, *U.S. Senators and Their World*; Richard R. Fenno, Jr., "The House Appropriations Committee as a Political System: The Problem of Integration," *A.P.S.R.*, LVI (June, 1962), 310–24. The same adherence to institutional norms has also been noted in state legislative behavior. Wahlke et al., *The Legislative System*, 155.

[50] See People v. Sideri (Magistrates Court, 2d District, Manhattan, May 14, 1929, unreported). When the defendant physician said she had acted in good faith, it cast the burden upon the prosecution to negate the doctor's good faith. In discharging the defendant the magistrate stated: "The Law is plain that if the doctor in good faith believes that the patient is a married woman and her health requires the prevention of conception, it is no crime to so advise and instruct them." *Laws Relating to Birth Control* (New York, 1939), 43–44.

In 1929 the police raided the Birth Control Clinical Research Bureau and arrested Dr. Hannah Stone, another physician, and three nurses. Morris Ernst based his defense on Justice Crane's decision and secured a dismissal. Nevertheless, a large quantity of medical records seized in the raid were never returned. But see Baretta v. Baretta, 182 Misc. 852, 46 N.Y.S.2d 261 (1944), in which the court denied relief to a wife seeking a separation decree. Marital difficulties had arisen over the wife's refusal to have sexual relations unless the husband employed a contraceptive. The court held: "The insistence of a wife that her husband use such knowledge and means is contrary to the principles and policy enunciated by the statutes and decisions of the State of New York, and for a court to permit plaintiff wife to recover under the circumstances and facts in the case would be contrary to our law as it now stands." 46 N.Y.S.2d at 263. In New York, 45 St. Dept. 308 (1932), it was unofficially held that the vending-machine sale of contraceptives violated section 1142.

THE MASSACHUSETTS EXPERIENCE

The strategy for recommending change initiated by Margaret Sanger in 1912 was not limited to the federal forum and New York. Driven by her example, protests against the vestiges of Comstockery spread across the country. Indeed, the impact of the New York experience on action taken in other forums demonstrates one of the major obstacles to applying the conceptual framework developed in the present study. The problem is constantly present that action taken by a legal institution in one jurisdiction can serve as a motivating force, or at least a factor conditioning the environment, to which an actor in another jurisdiction responds. Interaction takes place not only between the myriad legal institutions in a single jurisdiction, but, given our federal system, also between the various jurisdictions. It is essential, then, in analyzing legal policy formation in a particular jurisdiction, to consider possible influences from behavior taken in other jurisdictions, including both the federal and state spheres.

The Massachusetts birth-control movement, like that of New York, was born as a result of judicial action. Unlike New York, however, the martyr was not to be a leader of the nascent movement. Judicial action in the 1917 case of *Commonwealth v. Allison*[51] was initiated by the arrest of Van Kech Allison, a somewhat neurotic young man, for distributing pamphlets on contraception to factory workers. Apparently he had not consulted the leading proponents of the practice and it is doubtful that they would have selected him to represent the cause. Unlike the test case where strategy dictates the tactics of the process, the haphazard prosecution limits control by pro-change elements over the manner in which the reform demands are pressed. Nevertheless, when the opportunity for action presents itself, a response is often necessitated. A defense committee, the initial organization of the birth-control league, was formed. As a vice-president of the nascent organization commented:

> Our martyr was certainly not of our own choosing—very young, irresponsible, although well-meaning, and unfortunately, a man. There are still those who tell us how great an injury our martyr did our cause; but we are inclined to smile and say, "Yes," undoubtedly in some quarters, but the movement had to

[51] 227 Mass. 57, 116 N.E. 265 (1917). Allison was charged with violating sections 20 and 21, dealing with contraception (see Appendix D), and section 28, relating to the dissemination of lewd and obscene literature. The latter section does not specifically deal with contraception.

start somewhere, somehow, and we believe that our campaign has had a certain wide-spread educational value that it would have been hard to duplicate in so short a time without some sensational features.[52]

At the intelligence stage, an attempt was made to model the New York experience by convincing the court that the prohibitive statutes should not be applied to scientific treatises, and, if applied, would be unconstitutional. The major portion of the defendant's brief was based on the "Social and Economic Aspects of the Case."[53] Data on the negative health consequences in many cases of conception and commentary by birth-control leaders on the moral, social, economic, and medical need for preventive measures was provided. If the court chose to follow the change route, the nonlegal evidence supported the necessity for a restrictive reading of the statute to permit limited availability of birth-control services—the court could have held that the act was not intended to apply to scientific materials.

Instead, it utilized the broad, vague statutory language to encompass the defendant's acts. Although probably not necessary given the explicit proscriptions against contraception in the statute, the court employed the *Queen v. Hicklin* test, which evaluated obscenity by its possible effect on "those whose minds are open to such immoral influences,"[54] and concluded that even dignified, scientific tracts could be found by a jury to be obscene.[55] Alternatively, the act could have been declared unconstitutional, but the court held it to be a valid exercise of police

[52] Cerise C. Jack, "The Fight from Coast to Coast, Massachusetts," *Birth Control Review*, II (Apr., 1918), 7.
[53] F. C. Cowan, "Memorandum Concerning the Case of Commonwealth v. Allison," Mar. 14, 1950, p. 4 (from the files of PPLM).
[54] L.R. 3 Q.B. 360, 371, 11 Cox C.C. 19, 26 (1868).
[55] 116 N.E. at 266. Allison had distributed two pamphlets: "Don't Have Undesired Children" and "Why and How the Poor Should Not Have Many Children." Neither publication contained any pictures or diagrams. It is said they employed scientific and dignified language. Cowan, "Memorandum," 8. In the trial court, however, an extremely severe penalty of three years in the workhouse was imposed. This was later reduced to sixty days. "What the Birth Control Leagues Are Doing," *Birth Control Review*, I (Feb., 1917), 10.
The term "advertize" in the statute could have been held to exclude the distribution of scientific medical tracts that do not offer contraceptives for sale. Also the court could have required that the offending document name particular places where contraceptives could be obtained. Cowan, "Memorandum," 3-4. See Planned Parenthood Committee of Phoenix, Inc. v. Maricopa County, 92 Ariz. 231, 375 P.2d 719 (1962), where the court adopted an exceedingly narrow interpretation of the contraception statute, making it almost meaningless.

power. "Manifestly they [the statutes] are designed to promote the public morals and in a broad sense the public health and safety. Their plain purpose is to protect purity, to preserve chastity, to encourage continence and self-restraint, to defend the sanctity of the home, and thus to engender in the state and nation a virile and virtuous race of men and women."[56]

The language of the opinion suggests that, like *Byrne*, a moral orientation dominated the court's thinking; it carried the aura of Puritanism from which the act itself had evolved. The judicial actor evidenced no inclination to employ the nonlegal data available, but instead turned to the prevalent societal value system, which had not yet accepted the new morality.

But the judicial action did have practical consequences. Defeated in the judicial forum, the nascent birth-control movement next decided to press its demands to the legislature. As indicated above, interests defeated in one forum always possess the option of seeking redress in an alternative forum. However, like the New York and the national arenas, the hardships of recommendation were again operative. Twenty-five legislators were contacted, yet no sponsor could be found.[57] The movement persisted until 1920, then fell into quiescence. Without a martyr for attracting interest, without a favorable response from the legislative actor, without medical or community support, it lacked the ingredients of organizational life and temporarily dissolved. It would require another court case to revivify the dormant interests.

This impetus for renewed judicial action and reaggregation of birth-control interests came in 1928. Organizational effort in this instance was directed to the defense of Dr. Antoinette Konekow, who had conducted a lecture on family planning after advertising the meeting through handbills. She was arrested and charged with "exhibiting" articles for the prevention of conception. When the case was tried in Boston Municipal Criminal Court on March 1, 1928, the defense argued that Dr. Konekow's behavior could not be termed "exhibiting" since she neither advertised nor offered contraceptives for sale. Given the broad definition of the Massachusetts statutory provisions employed in the *Allison*

---

[56] 116 N.E. at 226. See Anthony R. Blackshield, "Constitutionalism and Comstockery," *Kansas Law Review*, XIV (Mar., 1966), 412.

[57] Jack, "The Fight from Coast to Coast," 7; Planned Parenthood League of Massachusetts, *Birth Control and the Massachusetts Law* (Boston, 1959), 3 (hereafter cited as *Massachusetts Law*). It has been contended, however, that a sponsor was found but that the bill never escaped committee.

case, the judge could have proscribed the doctor's action. Instead, the movement achieved a victory through a verdict of acquittal.

At least two possible motives might have influenced the judicial prescriptive behavior: the marked alteration of social attitudes since *Allison* and the increasingly widespread notoriety of the national birth-control movement. A more probable motivational variable, however, given subsequent judicial action, was the personal friendship existing between the defense lawyers and the trial judge.[58] In any case, the interest aggregation spawned by the judicial action in *Konekow* was not to die with the end of the case; it is the ancestor of today's Planned Parenthood League of Massachusetts.

Similar to the earlier post-*Allison* events, the movement attempted to follow up the events in the judicial arena with a favorable response from the legislative actor. In 1930 it finally succeeded in locating a legislator willing to sponsor a bill giving the state board of health the right to license physicians to handle contraceptive services. But although able to obtain access for initiating legislation, the movement lacked the strength necessary to generate a favorable response. The bill was given "leave to withdraw" by the committee.[59]

THE CONNECTICUT EXPERIENCE

In discussing maneuvers of the birth-control movement in each of the jurisdictions, our focus has been on reactions to legislation which directly sought to curtail trade in contraceptive devices and information. Connecticut, however, has had the dubious distinction of being the only state whose laws sought to proscribe the *use* of contraceptives. Prohibition of the dissemination of birth-control services was solely a product of the law dealing with accessories to the crime. (See Appendix E for the text of the Connecticut law.) Although the "use" provisions have never been enforced, and indeed appear unenforceable, this combination of statutory provisions was capable of providing its own unique *in terrorum* effects. Even aside from their actual effects on behavior, the statutes constituted a potent symbolic representation of negative public policy. But in spite of all attempts to evoke a response favorable to legal change from the legislative and judicial actors, the provisions have endured until the present decade as an excellent reminder not only

[58] Howard, "The Birth Control Law Conflict in Mass.," 13–15.
[59] *Massachusetts Law*, 3.

of the peculiar workings of the Puritan mentality, but also of the difficulty in eliminating antiquated legal norms.[60]

Although impetus for legal change appears to have been initially addressed to the legislature, closer analysis reveals that the legislative appeal was, at least partially, reactive behavior to the judicial travails of Margaret Sanger in New York. The Connecticut Legislative Committee of the American Birth Control League was one of the products of the visibility given the nascent birth-control movement by Mrs. Sanger's martyrdom. Just as Anthony Comstock came to Connecticut to initiate the state's prohibitive laws, Margaret Sanger arrived to tear down the edifice he had created. Indeed, together with Mrs. Thomas Hepburn, mother of actress Katherine Hepburn, and Mrs. George H. Day, Sr., both experienced birth-control advocates, she was instrumental in generating the initial assault on the Connecticut legislation in 1923, by assisting in the search to find a sponsor to recommend the proposed change and by appearing as a primary witness at the subsequent hearings on H.B. 504 before the Joint Judiciary Committee.[61] Her appeal and that of her cohorts at the intelligence stage was similar to that addressed to Congress and the legislatures of the other states. There was testimony relating to the medical and eugenic considerations, an appeal for equal opportunity for the poor to obtain assistance in fertility control, a challenge to the natural-law arguments of the Catholic opposition, an argument for a new morality based on an adequate appreciation of the role of the sexual act in married life. On the other hand, the weakness of the new movement was clearly evident. Only one doctor testified on their behalf; no major organizations contributed their endorsement to the appeal; the religious environment appeared to be hostile and unyielding. Although the status quo elements did not present their strongest case at the hearings, in this early period it was not really necessary. Their position, represented primarily by the Catholic Church, was based on a morality and an approach to family life which reflected the predominant mode of social thought.

The hearings did not seem to have any greater influence on legisla-

---

[60] Father John C. Murray, *We Hold These Truths: Catholic Reflection on the American Proposition* (New York, 1960), 157–58, is severely critical of the Connecticut provisions as jural norms.

[61] Sanger, *Autobiography*, 294; Lader, *The Margaret Sanger Story*, 167. Smith, ed., *Religious Thought*, 279, indicates that an unsuccessful repeal bill was introduced in 1917 (H.B. 221). At that time there was no organized birth-control movement in Connecticut. See generally "The Hearings at Hartford," *Birth Control Review*, VII (Mar., 1923), 63–64.

tive behavior than in our other jurisdictions. There would be no reason to expect the legislature or its committees to be receptive to a proposal so far removed from the dominant social mores, lacking effective political support, possibly repulsive to many law-makers, and reflecting the needs of inarticulate social interests not readily perceived by legislators. Indeed, the same analysis is applicable to the defeat of the bills offered in every session following the 1923 defeat.[62] When the bill did reach a House vote by way of a minority committee report in 1929, the legislative actor endorsed the negative reactions of the committee majority by the overwhelming vote of 226–18.

[62] 1923: H.B. 504 would have provided an exemption for physicians. It died in committee. The use of the "doctor's bill" again suggests the influence of Margaret Sanger.
  1925: H.B. 446 was again a "doctor's bill." Hearings were held but the committee reported it unfavorably, although its report did state that the bill had merit but that it was "unwise to change the law at the present time." Planned Parenthood League of Connecticut, Inc., *History of Planned Parenthood League of Connecticut, Inc.: Legislation and Legal Action* (New Haven, n.d.), 1 (hereafter cited as *PPLC History*).
  1927: H.B. 105, exempting physicians, died without any hearings. S.B. 145, a repeal bill, was referred to the Judiciary Committee, which held hearings and then reported the bill unfavorably by an 8–7 vote.
  1929: S.B. 44, a repeal meaure, was reported unfavorably. A minority, however, succeeded in securing a floor vote. The bill was defeated, 226–18.
  1931: H.B. 156 and 632 were both doctor's bills. The latter was dropped and the former was revised to exempt physicians only when contraception was indicated to safeguard life or health. Although it was favorably reported by the Judiciary Committee, it was defeated in the House by a 172–76 vote.
  1933: H.B. 519 was similar to the revised 1931 proposal. After amendments limited the bill to married women and required the concurring medical opinion of a physician nominated by the state commissioner of health, the bill was approved by the House 169–80. But it was defeated in the Senate by an 18–15 vote.
  1935: H.B. 859 sought to exempt physicians prescribing contraceptives for the health of mother or child. It died in committee.
  See generally Smith, ed., *Religious Thought*, 280n5; *PPLC History*, 1–2.

Four

Defeat and Victory in the Federal Forum

Initial legislative and judicial reaction to Comstockery had produced only a modicum of change in the formal legal norms. Institutional conservatism, born of a variety of motivational factors, had emerged as the predominant mode of behavior. But if the analysis, thus far, suggests the ability of legal norms to retard the pace at which the social environment is altered, it also raises the question of whether the norms could ever prevent change.

The social context to which the legal actor responded in the 1930s differed markedly from that which prevailed in the 1890s or even the 1920s. Social forces that had given impetus to the birth-control movement persisted and the law-in-action tended to reflect the changing reality. Comstock's laws were seldom enforced, although an occasional prosecution sufficed to sustain a fear which inhibited many, including the medical profession, thus hampering the development and distribution of preventive knowledge, especially to the poor. Forced to rely on public clinics or charitable agencies for their medical care, the poor were being denied access to contraceptive services increasingly available to other sectors of the populace. Again the legal prohibitions impeded the birth-control movement's attempt to make contraceptive services available to a wider audience through birth-control clinics. The possibility of official reprisal, and the social opprobrium frequently associated with law-breaking, can often provide as effective a restraint on social behavior categorized as "undesirable" as actual criminal prosecution.

ASSAULT ON CONGRESS

Beginning in 1930, the pro-change forces decided to launch another assault on Congress. This new phase of the repeal movement possesses neither new plot nor ending, only some of the characters and the social situation have been changed to protect the guilty. Between 1930 and 1937 eleven more attempts to alter the law would fail.[1] Recommendation for legislative action in this series of plays originated from the National Committee on Federal Legislation for Birth Control, founded by Margaret Sanger in 1928. Her reason for operating through a new interest grouping, rather than through her American Birth Control League oganized in 1921, serves as an interesting commentary on interest-group dynamics in the change process.

The birth-control movement itself reflected the changing social environment. No longer the weakly organized grouping of idealistic female radicals lacking political expertise, it had grown rapidly in membership and was becoming prosperous—"it [birth control] was being tolerated as a constructive instrument of morality."[2] The tide of public opinion was apparently turning in its favor. In some areas the movement's successes were plainly visible. Some fifty-five birth-control clinics in twenty-three cities and twelve states had opened during the 1920s and the future appeared bright.[3]

Prosperity, however, had produced changes in the movement's momentum. A conservative group which rejected the activism of Margaret Sanger was now in control. What had been a revolutionary force seeking change now chose to enjoy its success and consolidate its gains. Margaret Sanger explained this phenomenon in an intriguing thesis on the effect of time and change on interest-group activity:

> As things recede in time they become of less and less importance. One of my absolute theories is that any movement which has been based on freedom, as this had been, is like a live cell; there is a biology of ideas as there is a biology of cells, and each goes

[1] S. 4582, 71st Cong., 2nd Sess. (1930); S. 4436, 72nd Cong., 2nd Sess. (1932); S. 1842, 43rd Cong., 1st Sess. (1933); S. 600, 74th Cong., 1st Sess. (1935); H.R. 2000, 74th Cong., 1st Sess. (1935); H.R. 5600, 74th Cong., 1st Sess. (1935); S. 4000, 74th Cong., 2nd Sess. (1936); H.R. 11330, 74th Cong., 2nd Sess. (1936). A bill which would have permitted prosecution of obscene-publication cases at both the mailing and receiving points died in committee. H.R. 5370, 74th Cong., 1st Sess. (1935).
[2] Sanger, *My Fight for Birth Control*, 332.
[3] Lader, *The Margaret Sanger Story*, 219.

through a process of evolution. The parent cell splits and the new entities in their turn divide again. Instead of indicating breakdown, it is a sign of health; endless energy is spent trying to keep together forces which should be distinct. Each cell is fulfilling its mission in this separation, which in point of fact is no separation at all. Cohesion is maintained until in the end the whole is a vast mosaic cleaving together in union and strength.[4]

For Margaret Sanger, past achievement only served as a prelude to her more elusive goal—revision of the repressive Comstock legislation. Like Mary Ware Dennett, she had come to accept the federal forum as the primary focus of activity, but disagreed on the type of legislation to be pursued. Perhaps reflecting her nursing background, perhaps out of an ill-fated hope to achieve some compromise with Catholic opposition, or perhaps to appease congressional opposition, she proposed a "doctor's bill" rather than an outright repeal of the federal legislation. The medical profession was to be excluded from the prohibition in the statute.[5]

Her tactics also seemed much more organized than in earlier legislative attempts. Social change had lessened the difficulty of finding a sponsor for the bill. Legislators were contacted on a regular basis, provided with information, and their reactions noted. Organizational support was actively sought; by 1934 some 1,000 organizations had endorsed passage of a doctor's bill, including the Federal Council of Churches, containing some 23 million Protestant members.[6] The hearings were carefully planned with witnesses speaking on morals, religion, eugenics, economics, medicine, and society. Equally improved opposition forces,

[4] Sanger, *Autobiography*, 396-97. See Lader, *The Margaret Sanger Story*, 250.
[5] Compare Dennett, *Birth Control Laws*, 200-266, and James F. Morton, Jr., "Shall We Have a Limited Birth Control," *Birth Control Review*, III (Oct., 1919), 12-14, who favor the repeal approach, with Margaret Sanger, "How Shall We Change the Law," *Birth Control Review*, III (July, 1919), 8-9.
[6] Lader, *The Margaret Sanger Story*, 265-67; Sanger, *Autobiography*, 429-30. Sanger, *ibid.*, 418, provides a valuable comment on the recommending function: "We now began to be initiated into the ABC of Federal legislative procedure. After your bill had been drawn up, you had to find a Congressman to introduce it. Sometimes he believed in it a hundred percent; sometimes he sponsored it only to be accommodating and agreeable in which case it was called by request, a very weak way since you knew he wasn't going to fight for it." Some of the sponsors did manifest less than a complete commitment. See, e.g., the comments of Representative Hatfield, U.S. Congress, Senate, Subcommittee of the Judiciary Committee, *Hearings on S. 4436, Birth Control*, 72nd Cong., 1st Sess., 1932, p. 1, and Representative Hancock, U.S. Congress, House, Ways and Means Committee, *Hearings on H.R. 11082*, 72nd Cong., 1st Sess., 1932, p. 2.

however, countered with analyses of the same subjects. Regardless of the improved performance of the intelligence function, it is questionable that the data had any real impact on committee members. Emotionalism continued to be the primary characteristic of the hearings.

While other opposition groups were represented at the hearings, the Catholic Church now stood as the primary obstacle to any alteration. A papal encyclical, *Casti Connubi* (On Christian Marriage), issued in 1930, firmly expressed the severity of Catholic opposition by condemning all forms of "artificial" birth control on biblical, natural-law, and social grounds, and by asserting that this normative order binds Catholic and non-Catholic alike.[7] Catholics had a wide variety of social and fraternal groups, united under the National Catholic Welfare Council and the Catholic Bishops of the United States, which could be called upon when a show of strength was necessary in defense of the Church's policy position (each organizational representative at the congressional hearings made sure to state the numerical membership of his group).[8] Even though the numerical membership of associations declaring for change in the law exceeded the Catholic opposition, they lacked cohesion, the vital determinant of access. It would be unlikely that these loosely aligned groups would take effective reprisals against an offending legislator, but legislators could not be certain of the political repercussions of a pro–birth control vote. The obvious answer was to take no chances; as long as a bill never left committee, most legislators could avoid responsibility. Only one of the eleven bills ever reached the floor of Congress and even that was destined to be returned to committee and to die there—an example of the use of congressional "rules of the game."[9]

[7] Pope Pius XI, *Casti Connubi* (New York, 1941).

[8] See "N.C.C.M. Active in Fight against Birth Control," *Catholic Action*, XV (Mar., 1933), 27; "N.C.W.C. Executives Again Protest Passage of Contraceptive Legislation by Congress," *Catholic Action*, XVI (May, 1935), 12; "Opposition to Birth Control Bills Registered at Congressional Hearings," *Catholic Action*, XVII (June, 1932), 17; Charles A. McMahon, "The Meaning of Catholic Action," *Catholic Action*, XIV (Jan., 1932), 7–8; "Lay Organization," *Catholic Action*, XIV (Jan., 1932), 27–28. For a summary of Catholic medical and social arguments against birth control, some of which were used in the hearings, see R. DeGuchteneere, *Judgment on Birth Control* (New York, 1931); Edward R. Moore, *The Case against Birth Control* (New York, 1931).

[9] S. 1842, introduced by Senator Hastings of Delaware, was reported out of committee, placed on the unanimous-consent calendar, and passed. Shortly thereafter, Mr. McCarran, a Catholic senator from Nevada, asked unanimous consent that the vote be reconsidered since he had not been aware of the vote. Following the rules of senatorial courtesy, the bill was reconsidered (again indicating the

There were additional motivations explaining congressional non-action. As the social environment changed, birth-control laws were increasingly being ignored. While fears born of the laws still served as impediments, legal change was coming about through desuetude. Testimony before congressional committees implicitly acknowledged the impact of this motivational factor on the legislative reaction: "This committee surely should not be moved to inertia by the consideration that no real harm is being done because people will break a bad law anyway and probably with impunity. The honest thing to do is to change the bad law."[10] Most individuals wanting preventives could obtain them. Only the inarticulate poor and uneducated were effectively being denied, and equality of opportunity had not yet become a prevalent social value.

Change effectuated by the judicial actor also inadvertently strengthened conservative congressional forces. At each legislative hearing, proponents would summarize the latest judicial activity, hoping to inspire the legislature to get on the bandwagon. The testimony, however, also demonstrated that legislative non-action would neither pose severe social deprivations for most individuals nor impede change. For any legislator fearing political repercussions, non-action thus became more appealing; no serious damage would result from his failure to act. As one congressman specifically told Margaret Sanger: "You'll never get this bill passed in Congress; get yourself arrested again, that's the only way to get the law changed."[11]

Birth-control restrictions were rapidly becoming symbolic. Catholics may have recognized the general ineffectiveness of the laws, but they continued to serve as a symbolic expression of negative public policy toward contraception. As Edward Heffron of the National Council of Catholic Men expressed the objective: "We know that it [the law] is

---

importance of "rules of the game" in the legislative process). He then objected and asked that the bill be passed over. It was returned to committee, where it died. U.S., *Congressional Record*, 73rd Cong., 2nd Sess., 1934, vol. LXXVIII, pt. 10, p. 11314, pt. 7, p. 7195. See Sanger, *Autobiography*, 426–27; Sulloway, *Birth Control and Catholic Doctrine*, 23, 190–91.

[10] Testimony of Representative Walter M. Pierce, *Hearings on H.R. 11082*, 42.

[11] National Committee on Federal Legislation for Birth Control, *Birth Control News Letter*, no. 9 (Apr., 1932). In a letter from the attorney Morris Ernst to Margaret Sanger, Feb. 1, 1933, included in U.S. Congress, Senate, Subcommittee of the Judiciary Committee, *Hearings on S. 1842, Birth Control*, 73rd Cong., 2nd Sess., 1934, p. 4, this problem is recognized but the argument is made that legislative action would provide greater certainty.

not being enforced. But to remove it would be to withdraw the present stigma that the Federal law necessarily attaches to contraception."[12] More objectionable forms of action, e.g. publicly supported birth control, could be delayed through support of the prohibitions. A felt moral obligation to challenge the public immorality which might result from the use of contraceptives abetted their determination to continue the fight. Their argument appears strangely similar to that expressed by Anthony Comstock in justifying his anti-vice tactics. "National Welfare is, in the long run, identical with sound morality. To fulfill the moral law is to insure the welfare of the race."[13]

Whatever the motivations of the legislative actor (and most of those mentioned in Chapter Three were still operative) and the competing interest groups, legislative non-action was the reality. The difficulty encountered by the birth-control movement in obtaining legislative policy change suggests the hypothesis that repeal of legislation is more difficult to attain than passage of new legislation. But, even as Congress was avoiding the issue, the courts were in the process of fashioning a new legal policy more consistent with changing social conditions.

REVISION THROUGH THE FEDERAL COURTS

It has already been suggested that a primary mechanism for pressing change demands on the judicial actor arises from defending attempted prosecutions under the existing laws. This form of recommendation, however, provides only a haphazard mode of action due to lack of control over the character of the defendants and the manner in which the issues are framed. A more efficacious approach to the recommending function occurs with the test case.

Margaret Sanger's birth-control organization decided to use the latter approach to secure a judicial decision either declaring the federal laws unconstitutional or recognizing a "physician's exemption" from the federal prohibitions. Initially it was necessary to select a desirable martyr. Doctor Hannah Stone, a respected female gynecologist and leader in the birth-control movement, accepted the task of pressing the claim. It was decided to have a shipment of vaginal pessaries sent from

---

[12] *Hearings on H.R. 11082*, 81. See Joseph R. Gusfield, "Moral Passage: The Symbolic Process in Public Designations of Deviance," *Social Problems*, XV (Fall, 1967), 175.

[13] Testimony of Rev. Ryan, *Hearings on H.R. 11082*, 71.

Japan to Doctor Stone for potential use in her medical practice.[14] Efforts were made to avoid the possibility of administrative non-action by informing customs officials of the shipment. When the government filed a libel against the products, the birth-control organization had, as claimant, a distinguished physician attempting to practice her profession in the manner she believed best. The test case would thus be processed under the most advantageous circumstances.

At the intelligence stage, the case of *United States v. One Package*[15] reflected the careful planning that can be utilized in the test-case mode of pressing change demands. It was claimed that the tariff provisions should either be interpreted to permit the importation of birth-control devices for legitimate medical purposes or that the statute should be declared unconstitutional. The argument for a flexible, purposive approach to the interpretation of the act had been given substantial support by prior court decisions. The potential for such a revision, for example, had been suggested by a 1915 abortion case, *Bours v. United States*.[16] The court had employed a "rule of reasonable construction" to limit an apparently sweeping prohibition on abortion information to those instances "inimical to national life," which did not include abortion intended to preserve life. Even though the statutory words appeared all-inclusive, a judicial exception was fashioned.

Judicial behavior in developing an obscenity standard for printed materials dealing with contraception also provided an impetus for revision through interpretation. In a series of cases dealing with imported publications, the courts established that information about contraception did not per se make a work obscene. The contents would have to be judged by the general standards of obscenity—in all three cases, books dealing with birth control were admitted.[17]

[14] See Lader, *The Margaret Sanger Story*, 301-4. This approach had been suggested by governmental intervention in 1930 preventing the delivery of contraceptives to Mrs. Sanger.

[15] 13 F. Supp. 334 (E.D. N.Y. 1936), aff'd 86 F.2d 737 (2d Cir. 1936). The *One Package* case was only one of sixteen cases in which the Sanger committee was involved during this period. National Committee on Federal Legislation for Birth Control, *A New Day Dawns for Birth Control* (New York, 1937), 41.

[16] 229 Fed. 960 (7th Cir. 1915).

[17] United States v. Dennett, 39 F.2d 564 (2d Cir. 1930); United States v. One Obscene Book Entitled "Married Love," 48 F.2d 821 (S.D. N.Y. 1931); United States v. One Book Entitled "Contraception," 51 F.2d 525 (S.D. N.Y. 1931). This approach was to be implemented in later cases as well. Consumers Union of United States v. Walker, 145 F.2d 33 (D.C. Cir. 1944). The organization had sent a special report on contraceptives to 30,000 members who certified they were married and used prophylactics on advice of a physician. In United States v. Nickolas, 97 F.2d

But the primary input for change from within the judicial subsystem arose from recent cases directly dealing with the Comstock provisions on the dissemination of contraceptives. As is often the practice, these courts had called for re-examination of the legal policy through commentary extraneous to the case under consideration, i.e. dicta. The language of the court in such cases, as suggested above, may call on interested parties to press their claims for change, augur changes in doctrine, or request the legislature to intervene. In *Young's Rubber Co. v. C. I. Lee and Co.*,[18] a 1930 trademark-infringement case, Judge Thomas Swan utilized his opinion to suggest the necessity for re-examining the national policy regarding contraception. The defense had questioned the legal efficacy of a trademark on contraceptives since their dissemination was contrary to public policy, i.e., the trademark was being used in an unlawful business. Judge Swan argued that the courts had never held that the statutes barred proper medical writings, and further, that the dissemination of contraceptives would be lawful in certain localities. Most important, however, was his suggestion on the need for a re-evaluation of the legislative intent underlying the statute.

> Taken literally, this language would seem to forbid the transportation by mail or common carrier of anything "adopted" in the sense of being suitable or fitted, for preventing contraception ... even though the article might also be capable of legitimate uses and the sender in good faith supposed that it would be used only legitimately.... The intention to prevent a proper medical use of drugs or other articles merely because they are capable of illegal uses is not lightly to be ascribed to Congress.... It would seem more reasonable to give the word "adopted" a more limited meaning than that above suggested, and to construe the whole phrase "designed, adopted or intended" as requiring an intent on

---

510, 512 (2d Cir. 1938), and United States v. Himes, 97 F.2d 510, 512 (2d Cir. 1938), the court said: "Contraceptive articles may have lawful uses and statutes prohibiting them should be read as forbidding them only when unlawfully employed.... Contraceptive books and pamphlets are of the same class...and lawful in the hands of those who would not abuse the information they contained." Himes was permitted to receive the materials; Nickolas was required to come forward with evidence of his right to receive the materials. See St. John–Stevas, *Obscenity and the Law*, 18–19; Harry G. Balter, "Some Observations Concerning the Federal Obscenity Statutes," *Southern California Law Review*, VIII (June, 1935), 277–79; United States v. 31 Photographs, 165 F. Supp. 350, 357 (S.D. N.Y. 1957).

[18] 45 F.2d 103 (2d Cir. 1930). The contention that there exists a public policy against contraception per se received support in Lanteen Laboratories, Inc. v. Clark, 294 Ill. App. 81, 13 N.E.2d 678 (1938). The court claimed that the sale of contraceptives tends to corrupt morals.

the part of the sender that the article mailed . . . be used for illegal contraception or abortion or for indecent or immoral purposes.[19]

It is interesting that Judge Swan never mentioned earlier federal decisions which suggested a more sweeping prohibition of the contraceptive provisions.[20] He was delineating an approach for making the statutory prohibitions "more reasonable."

His proposal was to receive a favorable hearing three years later by the Sixth Circuit in *Davis v. United States*. The court quoted at length from *Young's Rubber*, "not as precedent, but because the soundness of its reasoning commends itself to us."[21] The lower court's exclusion of evidence designed to show "good faith" and the absence of "unlawful intent" was held to be reversible error, and a new trial was ordered— "intent that the articles . . . were to be used for condemned purposes is a prerequisite to conviction."[22] Since the court, however, failed to indicate what constituted a permissible or condemned purpose, the task remained to fashion a standard for judgment.

All of the judicial input favorable to a liberal interpretation of the Comstock Act was processed by pro-change forces to the judicial policy-maker in *One Package*.[23] Added to this array of judicial support was an impressive presentation of medical opinion indicating numerous instances in which the optimum medical treatment to prevent disease and preserve life called for the use of contraceptives. Social acceptability of the practice was stressed, and the history of the legislation was analyzed to indicate that only the "immoral" use of contraceptives was intended to be proscribed. If the judicial actor chose to fashion new legal policy, sufficient justification was provided.

The constitutional challenge was premised on the Fifth and Tenth amendments. Characterizing the purpose of the statute as an attempt to exclude immoral and obscene articles from commerce, it was argued that a blanket prohibition would not be a reasonable means to attain this legitimate objective. Contraceptives were often essential to the public welfare rather than inimical to it. The same due-process argument was

---

[19] 45 F.2d at 108.
[20] See text accompanying Chapter Two, notes 27–29 *supra*.
[21] 62 F.2d 473, 475 (6th Cir. 1933). Davis and his employee were wholesalers of druggists' rubber sundries of all kinds. They were charged with mailing circulars concerning contraceptives and the devices themselves in violation of 18 U.S.C. 334, 396.
[22] 62 F.2d at 475.
[23] Brief for Appellant, United States v. One Package, 86 F.2d 737 (2d Cir. 1936).

to arise in all of the birth-control cases and will be evaluated below. The argument based on the Tenth Amendment was premised on a claim that the amendment served as a substantive restriction on the power of the national government, a view later rejected.[24]

At the prescriptive stage, the change forces finally secured a major triumph in the national forum. In the district court, Judge Grover Moscowitz interpreted the statute as not applicable to importation of contraceptives for medical purposes. When the suit was dismissed, the government appealed. In the court of appeals, Judge Augustus Hand was confronted by the task of applying a nineteenth-century statute to twentieth-century society. He recognized that time had produced greater medical awareness of the possible dangers of conception—a point stressed by the pro-change interests through the use of nonlegal data. Then there was the precedent of *Davis*, the reasoning of Judge Swan in *Young's Rubber*, and the *Bours* inclusion of intent in the abortion provisions of the statute. Finally, there was the reality of legislative non-action; if the law on the books was to change, it appeared it would require judicial action. Generally, then, the new social situation placed birth control in a very different position from that which it had occupied in 1873. Hand elected to accept the challenge of change. Using the rule of reasonable construction, the statute was held to embrace "only such articles as Congress would have denounced as immoral if it had understood all the conditions under which they were to be used. Its design, in our opinion, was not to prevent the importation, sale, or carriage by mail of things which might intelligently be employed by conscientious and competent physicians for the purpose of saving life or promoting the well-being of their patients."[25] In spite of the fact that the statutory words appeared to be all-encompassing, seemed to admit of no exceptions, that an exception for physicians was removed by Congress in enacting the Comstock proposal, that an earlier court had re-

---

[24] See, e.g., United States v. Darby, 312 U.S. 100, 124 (1941). See generally Edward S. Corwin, *The Constitution of the United States of America: Analysis and Interpretation* (Washington, 1964), 1037-40.

[25] 86 F.2d at 739. The desire to avoid an inconsistent interpretation of the contraceptive and abortion provisions of the statute apparently was an important consideration for all members of the court. *Ibid.*, 739, 740. *Davis* had applied the mailing provisions whereas the importation provisions were involved in *One Package*. Judge Augustus Hand, however, argued: "All the statutes . . . were part of a continuous scheme to suppress immoral articles and obscene literature and should so far as possible be construed together and consistently. If this be done, the articles here in question ought not to be forfeited when not intended for an immoral purpose."

jected Hand's reading, and that Congress had consistently refused to insert this exemption into the act,[26] the law had been changed.

Judge Learned Hand, concurring, expressed his doubts concerning the court's action, and provided an excellent expression of the sociological base of legal change:

> There seems to me substantial reason for saying that contraceptives were meant to be forbidden, whether or not prescribed by physicians, and that no lawful use of them was contemplated. Many people have changed their minds about such matters in sixty years, but the act forbids the same conduct now as then; a statute stands until public feeling gets enough momentum to change it, which may be long after a majority would repeal it, if a poll were taken. Nevertheless, I am not prepared to dissent.[27]

His concern is understandable. Applying the intent and values of the Congress of 1873, all contraception would be obscene, immoral, and, hence, prohibited. But what was "obscene" and "immoral" in 1873 had changed and the court was required to apply the obscenity prohibition to this new social situation. Greater awareness of the medical necessity for conception control as well as stronger social and medical acceptance of the practice existed. As early as 1936, a national survey indicated 71 percent of those questioned to be in favor of birth control and 70 percent in support of proposed legislation revising the federal statutes.[28] Legislative response was nevertheless probably not forthcoming. Under these circumstances, judicial refusal of responsibility would have been an inappropriate response for the creative use of law.

As mentioned above, the dynamics of social change negate a simplistic, staid response to the task of statutory interpretation. As the social environment to which the laws are applied is altered, the viability of the legislative purpose may be affected. Perhaps the outstanding feature of the purposive approach is its recognition of and legal accommodation of this social change. Such an approach to statutory construction in *One Package* yielded a refashioning of legal policy to permit at least a medical exemption to the prohibitive norms. The court, informed not only of the legislative history essential to understanding the statute's purpose, but also of the changes in the social situation, responded to the input. Its decision, then, appears to be essentially a reaction to the

[26] See text accompanying Chapter Two, notes 27–29 *supra*.
[27] 86 F.2d at 740.
[28] Birth Control Federation of America, "Birth Control Education in Public Health Services Favored," *Information Service*, Apr., 1940, p. 3.

changed social milieu. As a newspaper noted at that time: "Judges, it develops, are capable of human understanding and are almost as sensitive as the rest of us to the changing winds of public opinion. To watch the weather-cock change is to watch the making of social history.... Maybe judges don't read polls. But they read the signs of the times."[29]

The *One Package* decision brought an end to the National Committee on Federal Legislation for Birth Control and its legislative efforts. Since its objective had been substantially achieved through judicial action, little impetus appeared to exist for further legislative assaults. There was no realistic possibility that Congress might react negatively and reverse the judicial action, so they disbanded. But the movement's work had not ended. The decision had to be implemented in order to give the new legal policy a social reality. Margaret Sanger announced a nationwide educational campaign to inform both the medical profession and the public.[30] The interest group now acted as a conduit for transforming legal decision into social fact, for making the decision known to those who would be affected, for using the decision as the first stage in developing publicly supported birth control—a process to be discussed in Chapter Nine.

While additional cases might be noted,[31] this discussion should indicate the change effectuated by the judiciary through revising the statutory language to bring it into closer harmony with the demands of the changed society. Unless the government could show an "unlawful purpose," an "illegal intent," importation and mailing of contraceptives

---

[29] "Public Opinion Counts," *World Telegram*, Jan. 4, 1937, quoted in *National Birth Control News*, Feb., 1937, pp. 2–4. In the same issue of the *News*, Morris Ernst commented: "The law process is a simple one, it is a matter of educating judges to the mores of the day." *Ibid.*, 6. See Notes, "Judicial Regulation of Birth Control under Obscenity Laws," *Yale Law Journal*, L (Feb., 1941), 682–89.

[30] Lader, *The Margaret Sanger Story*, 305. Margaret Sanger had approached the elimination of the prohibitions as the initial stage toward a larger objective: "Until we could clear the atmosphere and obtain a decision clarifying once and for all the meaning of the law as passed by Congress, we were unable to move forward constructively into the larger sphere where birth control is included with public health activities." National Committee on Federal Legislation for Birth Control, *A New Day Dawns*, 10. Arguably one of the immediate results of the *One Package* decision was passage of an AMA resolution approving contraception as an acceptable medical practice.

[31] United States v. Beleval (District Court of Puerto Rico, Jan. 19, 1939, unreported) "specifically limited the prohibitive statutes dealing with contraceptives in federal territories to cases of an unlawful use." See Kilborn, "Birth Control Statutes," 11–12. In United States v. H. L. Blake Co., Inc., 189 F. Supp. 930 (W.D. Ark. 1960), the court required the government to show beyond a reasonable doubt that contraceptives labeled "sold for the prevention of disease" were "designed, adopted, and intended to be used for the prevention of conception."

could not be prevented. The following commentary suggests the importance of this judicial creativity.

> United States v. One Package and the peripheral cases . . . made a significant contribution to the progress of birth control in the United States. Before these decisions, physicians, even in the states that had no laws against contraception, could not lawfully obtain contraceptive supplies and information. The mail and common carriers engaged in intrastate carriers were closed to them. Publishers had no incentive to print textbooks and articles on the subject. Research was impeded. After these decisions, the door opened to a nationwide advance in the establishment of clinics, to widespread publicity about birth control, and to the active support of the medical profession.[32]

What the legislature had been unable or unwilling to do, the courts had done. Law had been brought into a closer harmony with the changing society.

[32] Alvah Sulloway, "The Legal and Political Aspects of Population Control in the United States," *Law and Contemporary Problems*, XXV (Summer, 1960), 602. See Abraham Stone and Harriet F. Pilpel, "The Social and Legal Status of Contraception," *North Carolina Law Review*, XXII (Feb., 1944), 22.

Five

Repression and Defeat: Massachusetts and Connecticut

The judicial exemptions fashioned in *Sanger* and *One Package* severely mitigated the legal stricture on the dissemination of birth-control information and services. Similarly, court decisions, legislative action, or simply administrative desuetude were revising legal policy throughout the country. In two states, Massachusetts and Connecticut, however, both the court and legislature remained in tune, responding negatively to birth-control interests until the 1960s. Yet even in these states the legal proscriptions were neither actively enforced nor generally observed. Birth control became a thriving bootleg business complemented, in most instances, by law-enforcement officials looking the other way. But the laws stood as symbols of a negative public policy impeding acceptance of publicly supported birth control and thwarting attempts to operate private birth-control clinics. Thus, while birth-control services were generally available, the poor, dependent on free medical services, were effectively denied assistance.

THE MASSACHUSETTS STORY

Repression and Judicial Defeat

In Massachusetts, legislative abstention in the 1920s had produced a cloud of uncertainty over the legal status of physicians; judicial response had been equally unrewarding. *Allison* had not clarified the scope of the prohibitive statutory policy and *Konekow* had not really determined the status of a physician supplying contraceptive services. Birth-control interests, therefore, acted without the guidance of a definite legal policy. Nevertheless, the restrictive statutory provisions generally were not being used to interfere with physicians in the reasonable exercise of their profession. Armed with this minimal policy guide, the legal counsel of the Massachusetts Birth Control League advised that clinics could be opened to provide contraceptive care in cases of medical necessity.[1] Between 1932 and 1937, seven clinics around the state opened and serviced some 3,000 patients. Though this was only a battle, not the war, the stage for new recommendatory activity had been set.

In 1937, after Roman Catholic priests had condemned the clinics in Sunday sermons, the police launched an investigation of the Fitchburg Maternal Health Center, without, however, taking any immediate action. In June police raided the Salem center, arrested a doctor, nurse, and two social workers, and seized contraceptive and medical records. All four were convicted in the district court, although the judge, expressing his belief in their good intentions, imposed only a minimal fine.[2] Police raids and arrests following the decision closed three more clinics, and forced the league to terminate all maternal-health offices pending appeal. Even though the closure was viewed as a temporary expedient, the clinics were not to reopen in the near future. But at least the birth-control issue was again before the Massachusetts courts.

Intelligence activity centered around two alternative policies presented by the defense to the Massachusetts Supreme Court in *Commonwealth v. Gardner*:[3] (1) interpret the statute to exclude physicians and their assistants in the bona fide practice of medicine; or (2) hold the statute to be unreasonable and hence an unconstitutional exercise of police power. And again, social, medical, and religious data were processed to the judicial actor. For example, the AMA favored exclusion of responsible physicians from the statutory restrictions, and results of a poll of Massachusetts physicians also indicated wide support for a medical exemption.[4] In fact, a group of physicians filed a "Brandeis Brief" as amicus curiae—an important tool for processing nonlegal data to the courts—stressing the medical perspective.

[1] *Massachusetts Law*, 4. See "Contraceptive Advice and the Massachusetts Law," *New England Journal of Medicine*, Jan. 23, 1930 (reprint from the files of PPLM).
[2] *Transcript of Proceedings*, I, 93, Commonwealth v. Gardner, First District Court of Essex, Salem, Mass., July 20, 1937.
[3] 300 Mass. 372, 15 N.E.2d 222 (1938).
[4] Brief for Defendants, Commonwealth v. Gardner, 300 Mass. 372, 15 N.E.2d 222 (1938).

The necessity for limiting the statute was premised on the recognized danger to the infant and mother from uncontrolled births and other methods of control, e.g. rhythm, abstention, abortion, and sterilization. And the social acceptability of the practice was inferred by the existence of 350 similar clinics around the country. Even precedent from the federal and state courts inclined toward a medical exemption.[5] It was, therefore, unreasonable to apply a statute fashioned for crimes against chastity, morality, decency, and good order to the dissemination of birth-control service, especially by physicians. Application of legislative purpose to the present social environment demanded a liberal policy interpretation.

An absolute prohibition would violate the Massachusetts Constitution as unnecessarily broad and sweeping and deny the physician's patients the right to life and liberty in violation of the "due-process" guarantee of the Fourteenth Amendment of the U.S. Constitution. The state's police power, it was argued, cannot be used arbitrarily either to prevent individuals from securing accepted medical assistance or to deny physicians the opportunity to practice such techniques. While regulation might be a permissible legislative policy, complete prohibition would be unreasonable.

All sociological and medical data was castigated by the prosecution as irrelevant. The clear statutory language necessitated judicial acquiescence and the decision in *Allison* on the question of constitutionality had recognized the adequacy of the police-power justification. The legislature—not the courtroom—was the proper place to argue social questions. Here was a clear call for judicial deference, in spite of the legislative failure to act. The function of the court was not to evaluate birth-control policy, argued the prosecution, but rather to implement the legislative determination.[6]

The court, possessing this wide range of policy alternatives at the prescriptive stage, chose the route of deference and restraint. The statutory language was found to be "unequivocal and peremptory." The statutory provisions "are sweeping, absolute, and devoid of ambiguity. They are directed with undeviating explicitness against the prevention of conception by any of the means specified. It would be difficult to select appropriate legislative words to express the thoughts

---

[5] See, e.g., State v. Arnold, 217 Wis. 340, 258 N.W. 843 (1935) and the federal cases discussed in Chapter Four *supra*.

[6] Notes on the oral argument of Assistant District Attorney J. J. Ryan, Feb. 8, 1930 (from the files of PPLM).

with greater emphasis."[7] The clarity of the statutory language and lack of any demonstrable legislative intent to exclude physicians precluded reading in any medical exemption. Federal decisions were dismissed as not being determinative; the changed social and medical environment was not mentioned; the societal consequences of the decision were ignored. The court seems to have been bound by a literalist approach to interpretation to the exclusion of all other vital considerations.

On the question of constitutionality, the *Gardner* court relied on *Allison*. Arguing that the comprehensive measure taken by the legislature against what it deemed a pervasive and threatening evil was a reasonable exercise of police power, the court again legitimized the legislative behavior of 1879. Nor did the court leave any doubt as to the deferential character of its act: "The relief here urged must be sought from the law-making department and not from the judicial department of the government."[8]

Such an act of judicial deference may be approached as a form of communication, not only to the interests seeking legal change but also to the legislative actor. It may take the form of a direct call for legislative action or may consist merely of expressions on the failure of the legislature to act and/or the inability of the judiciary to provide corrective measures. The response may be born of judicial recognition of its own inability to formulate policy properly on a given subject matter, perhaps because of the lack of resources for processing complex social and economic problems, perhaps because of the need for a prompt fashioning of comprehensive legal policy in a matter that cannot wait for the slower case-by-case approach, perhaps because of a belief that the matter is properly charged to the legislature, perhaps because of agreement with the legislative judgment. In any case, "formal" judicial influences rather than the "informal" role sometimes played by judges, e.g. the role of the Supreme Court justice in the passage of the federal Comstock Act, can be exerted through the judicial decision.[9]

Indeed, a primary mechanism through which the judiciary can fulfill its role in our interactive legal system occurs when it seeks to prod the

[7] 15 N.E.2d at 223.
[8] *Ibid.*, 224.
[9] The distinction between formal and informal judicial input is derived from Murphy, *The Elements of Judicial Strategy*. The study, however, is limited in that it focuses on the behavior of U.S. Supreme Court justices and doesn't really discuss the interactions of courts and legislatures in fashioning private law. Cardozo, *The Growth of the Law*, 120–21, notes that "the channel [of communication] is essential, first, that the needs of the courts may be known to the legislature, and second, that the needs, when known, may be intelligently and promptly met."

legislature to act—when it provides impetus for legislative consideration of issues requiring action. Resembling an interest group, judicial "demands" constitute still another input to the legislative policy-maker. However, whether the judicial opinion is, in fact, an effective vehicle for communicating with the legislature and whether the legislature so perceives it require empirical investigation.

In *Gardner*, however, the judicial behavior did not appear to be a call for legislative action, but only an expression of judicial inability or unwillingness to respond. While the opinion did communicate the closure of the judicial forum for a favorable response to the change demands, thereby becoming part of the environment to which the legislature would be asked to respond, the court was in no way suggesting that the legislature *should* provide a remedy. Nor was there mention or apparent recognition in the *Gardner* opinion of the probable closure of the legislature because of motivational impediments. Under these circumstances, alleged deference to the legislative judgment and the prior decision of the Massachusetts courts was questionable.

It is difficult to explain the prescriptive behavior of the court. A remnant of Puritanism, Chief Justice Ruggs, who had written the opinion in *Allison*, also wrote *Gardner*. In both cases there appeared to be marked concern with the proper role of the courts vis-à-vis the legislature—a broad scope was provided for the state's police power and a narrow role was given to the judiciary in supervising it. There was also a manifest lack of concern with the right of Massachusetts citizens to obtain recognized medical services and with the social impact of the decision. Refusal to act, framed in abstract legal doctrine, can often be an expression of unwillingness to assume the responsibility of policy formation.[10] Whether this restraint and deference on Justice Ruggs's part reflected a personal distaste for birth control, a narrow conception of the proper role of the judiciary, or an evasion of policy responsibility cannot be determined. Probably a multiplicity of motivations influenced the court's behavior.

[10] As one commentator has noted, "To assign impugned legislation to a virtually unexaminable 'police power' may simply constitute one device for 'judicial self-restraint.'" Blackshield, "Constitutionalism and Comstockery," 412.
On the role of personal values, it should be noted that Catholics did not constitute a majority of the *Gardner* court. "It is difficult to convincingly portray the Catholics as the sole villains in the struggle." John R. Rodman, "Trying to Reform the Birth Control Law: A Study in Massachusetts Politics" (unpublished thesis, Harvard University, 1955), 17. The author attributes the decision to Massachusetts's conservative judicial tradition and the mode of argument selected by the league attorney.

In this instance an appeal was taken to the U.S. Supreme Court, but the higher court declined the opportunity to review the issues fully. Instead, it dismissed the appeal for want of a substantial federal question,[11] citing four cases in which an exercise of the state police power had been upheld against constitutional objections.[12]

Birth-control interests, faced with a sweeping prohibition, responded to the suggestion of the Massachusetts court to seek legal change in a different forum. Recommendation for revision, however, was to be processed in a new manner, the referendum. Involving initial recourse to the legislature, this reform mechanism would assure a roll-call vote on the merits. Further, failure to secure favorable legislative response would provide direct access to an alternate forum for legal change, i.e. the voting public. Since the movement was confident of widespread, inarticulate, public support, they were convinced legal change could be secured. Prior to the referendum, however, a new judicial policy was to be fashioned.

Commonwealth v. Corbett[13] involved a registered pharmacist convicted of selling a package of condoms marked "sold for the prevention of disease." The defense again sought a liberal interpretation of the statutory language in section 21, which required a determination of whether the phrase "intended to be used" was meant to modify only "for self-abuse" or was also applicable to contraceptives and abortifacients, i.e., was intention to use the article for contraception a requisite element of the offense? Once more legal and nonlegal data were presented,[14] while the prosecution relied primarily on the sweeping *Gardner* precedent for judicial deference.

Initially it seemed that the court in its prescriptive behavior would accede to the state's call for judicial restraint: "The public policy of the Commonwealth on the creation of crimes is not for the court to determine but the legislature."[15] And public policy was offended by the

[11] Gardner v. Massachusetts, 305 U.S. 559 (1938).

[12] Powell v. Pennsylvania, 127 U.S. 678, 685 (1888); Jacobson v. Massachusetts, 197 U.S. 11, 26–27 (1905); Graves v. Minnesota, 272 U.S. 425, 428 (1926); Lambert v. Yellowley, 272 U.S. 581 (1926). The *Jacobson* and *Lambert* cases, however, would seem to make an exception when the prohibition would endanger the health of the individual. But the court's *per curiam* approach failed to consider this possibility.

[13] 307 Mass. 7, 29 N.E.2d 151 (1940). See Commonwealth v. Werlinsky, 307 Mass. 608, 29 N.E.2d 150 (1940).

[14] Brief for Defendant, Commonwealth v. Corbett, 307 Mass. 7, 29 N.E.2d 151 (1940). *Gardner* was distinguished on grounds that it involved the dissemination of articles admittedly for the purpose of conception. *Ibid.*, 3.

[15] 307 Mass. 7, 29 N.E.2d at 152.

sale of articles intended to prevent conception. But the court then inserted a policy caveat. Since condoms could also be used to prevent the transmission of disease, prophylactics might be sold for this purpose. While reading the statute to embody such a limitation, the court specifically called for legislative reaction if it rejected the judicial policy formulation: "If our analysis of the statute before us shows it to be less stringent than is desired . . . the remedy must be sought in the legislature."[16] However, a vigorous dissent, reflecting the narrow conception of the judicial role in *Gardner*, was entered by Justice Donahue, who claimed that the court was usurping the legislative prerogative: "Where a public policy is thus established by the legislature in a criminal statute, which is not unconstitutional, the legislature's view as to public policy should be given effect. . . . Statutes must be interpreted as enacted. Omissions cannot be supplied by the judicial department of government."[17] The terms used by the legislature were "plain, unequivocal and peremptory."

The *Corbett* opinion was to open a wide loophole in the restrictive policy toward contraception. Prosecution would fail unless the state could prove an intent to use contraceptives for contraceptive purposes. While not impossible, as a later case was to demonstrate,[18] the decision did seriously weaken the legal impediments. Contraceptives for "the prevention of disease" or for "female hygiene" were freely sold without prescription.

However, such a resolution of the issue can scarcely approximate creative policy-making. The more effective contraceptives, e.g. diaphragms, although in practice available to anyone able to afford a private physician, were still officially prohibited. Less effective preventives could be obtained to prevent disease. Further, the legal policy encouraged subterfuge. There arose the anomalous situation that a man pursuing an illicit affair and willing to lie could purchase effective safeguards, while the husband, seeking to protect the health of his wife through fertility control, would be forced to lie or to have recourse to other, less satisfactory control methods. Most contraceptives, even though commercially available, would be excluded from proper medical usage in clinics. Nevertheless, to the extent that the *Corbett* decision increased the availability of contraceptives, it mitigated the necessity for

[16] *Ibid.*, 155.
[17] *Ibid.*
[18] See Commonwealth v. Goldberg, 316 Mass. 563, 55 N.E.2d 950 (1944), which reaffirmed the *Corbett* rule but found that adequate evidence was available to infer a purpose that the articles be used for contraception.

legislative redress by providing still another rationale for legislators unwilling to accept responsibility for fashioning creative legal policy.

Legislative Action and Public Referendum, 1941–42

There were numerous instances prior to 1940, then, in which the judicial and legislative actors were afforded an opportunity to respond creatively to changing social conditions. Whether their reaction reflected an institutional conservatism or was the product of political motivations, by 1940 Massachusetts was one of two states in which explicit legal norms seriously impeded the unhampered dissemination of birth-control services. The referendum was conceived by the Massachusetts Mothers' Health Council (MMHC) as the tool to bring the state into the mainstream.

Under 1940 Massachusetts law, a referendum, initiated through a petition, signed by ten registered citizens and endorsed by 20,000 signatures, would be submitted to the General Court (the Massachusetts legislature), where hearings would be required and a roll-call vote taken. If the bill passed, it became law; if it failed, an additional 5,000 signatures would submit the question to the voters. In September, 1940, the legal machinery was set in motion.[19] With characteristic assiduity, the MMHC obtained 43,000 certified signatures.

Before the campaign was even off the ground, however, it encountered difficulty. Frederick Mansfield, legal representative for Boston's Archbishop O'Connell, filed a protest in court that the bill was "religious" and hence not constitutionally a subject for referendum, that one of the ten original signers had recently moved, thus making her ineligible, and that some of the signatures had been fraudulently obtained. The Massachusetts courts re-entered the controversy with the Supreme Court, declaring the issue to be one of public health rather than religion: "The proposed law is purely permissive. Religion is not a factor in its application, and, if approved by the voters, it will not interfere with the freedom of any person within its scope to act in strict accordance with his religious views."[20] The following year the Massachusetts Ballot Law

[19] The proposed revision, filed September 4, 1940, would have added the following provision to section 21: "The provisions of this section and of section twenty relating to the prevention of pregnancy and the prevention of conception shall not apply to treatment or prescription of life or health by or under the direction of physicians registered in accordance with the provisions of Chapter 112; nor to teaching in chartered medical schools; nor to publication or sale of medical treatises or journals."

[20] Opinion of the Justices, 309 Mass. 555 (1941).

Commission dismissed the charges of fraud but upheld the claim that one of the signers was illegally registered. However, the Supreme Court again intervened to reverse the latter decision.[21] In these two instances, at least, it is clear that the judiciary was not merely mouthing the status quo interests. Its actions guaranteed that the bill would not die prior to legislative consideration.

The MMHC apparently had little hope of securing a favorable legislative response. The appeal, while providing a forum to reach the public as well as an opportunity to convert some legislators, was considered only a necessary formality in the attempt to effectuate the will of the people.[22] Generally, the legislative hearings were an empty ritual rather than a fact-gathering process. For legislators opposed to change, they served to fashion an argument for the requisite committee report to the General Court, and obtain support for their pre-established positions. Almost a majority of the legislators publicly announced opposition to the proposal during the hearings and delivered vitriolic attacks on birth control, labeling it subversive, filthy, un-American, un-Christian, vicious, unscrupulous, etc.—all accompanied by an appropriate audience response.[23] The proponents of birth control were equally vitriolic in their appraisal of Catholic opposition. After all, Margaret Sanger herself had condemned "the mouthpieces of the wily directors of the Church—those evil shepherds who in turn take their orders from higher up," the forces of reaction, the hopeless dogmatists, the conformists, the reactionaries who opposed "the forces of reason, of tolerance, of science."[24] There was no want of invective on either side.

On the other hand, both sides did present medical, social, and religious testimony. The case for revision, conducted by the MMHC attorney, Samuel Hoar, and Robert Dodge, the attorney who had handled the *Gardner* case, reviewed legal developments in the federal and state

---

[21] Compton et al. v. State Ballot Law Commission, 311 Mass. 643 (1942).

[22] The MMHC was quite confident that they could win a referendum contest. Interview with Mrs. Lorraine Campbell, former president of PPLM, Cambridge, May 24, 1967; interview with Mrs. Maurice Sagoff, president of PPLM, Boston, May 25, 1967.

[23] It was reminiscent of the 1931 hearings when Rev. James I. Corrigan had characterized the birth-control appeal as a "plea of animality, nauseous, disgusting, hideous." Testimony of Rev. James I. Corrigan before a committee of the Massachusetts Senate, 1931, in Sulloway, *Birth Control and Catholic Doctrine*, 84. A bill to exempt physicians became "the very essence and the odor that comes from the putrid deseased river, that had its headwaters, its fountain today in Russia." Testimony of Dr. William E. Burns before a committee of the Massachusetts General Assembly, 1931, *ibid.*, 82.

[24] Sanger, *My Fight for Birth Control*, 347-48.

forums. But the primary thrust of the argument was the need for medical freedom. Surveys of the Massachusetts Medical Society suggested substantial support for revision among physicians; medical testimony indicated the necessity of conception control under given circumstances; "natural" forms of birth prevention were evaluated and rejected. But a hiatus appeared which hostile committee members were quick to seize and emphasize. Under questioning, no statistical evidence could be provided regarding the number of women or infants who had actually died *in Massachusetts* because of uncontrolled conception. Physicians, presented by the opposition, suggested the total absence of any ill effects in the state from the lack of contraceptives.[25] However, it is doubtful that such evidence would have had any real effect—the result was preordained.

Mr. Mansfield, handling the opposition case, clarified his status immediately: "In the presentation of this case I appear for William Cardinal O'Connell, at his direction on his behalf, and on behalf of the Archdiocese of Boston, comprising in round figures, I suppose, about one million souls. I don't pretend to represent those one million souls, but I represent His Eminence who certainly does represent them."[26] Medical and religious testimony comprised the brunt of the anti-revision position. Catholic priests attacked birth control as being against God's law, destructive of the family, and, hence, destructive of community life. It was suggested that the loose construction of the proposed bill permitted widespread availability of contraceptive devices, thereby promoting immorality. As already noted, a number of physicians did challenge the medical necessity of birth control. Generally the testimony provided adequate rationalization for any legislator's decision to oppose. The Joint Committee on Public Health reported the exemption unfavorably by an 11-4 vote; the House concurred by a 133-77 vote; and the Senate joined by the narrow margin of 18-16.

If an analyst were to rely solely on the committee report to the Gen-

---

[25] See *Transcript of Hearings before the Joint Committee on Public Health of the Massachusetts Legislature on H. 2035*, Apr. 3, 1941, pp. 38-39, 45, 48-49 (from the files of PPLM) (hereafter cited as *1941 Hearings*). The majority report noted that the 1939 Massachusetts vital statistics revealed no maternal mortality from the disease indicated by the proponents as dangerous. In the prior thirteen years, the Boston City Hospital had cared for 38,312 mothers without any of them dying from the recorded disease. Massachusetts, *Journal of the House, 1941,* 1287. Contrary medical considerations were cited by the minority report. It also cited the permissive character of the bill, noted *Opinion of the Justices*, the status of birth control in other states, and the need to promote social justice. *Ibid.,* 1287-88.

[26] *1941 Hearings,* 104.

eral Court, he might conclude that the legislative behavior was motivated by a negative evaluation of the medical necessity for change and fear of the moral consequences of the proposed action: "To pass this bill we believe would open the door to untold opportunities to evade the law by unscrupulous persons, who are not physicians; and the indiscriminate dissemination of information on how to avoid conception allowed under the proposed measure would encourage promiscuous sex relations by making available to boys and girls information as to how to avoid the consequence of pre-marital relations."[27]

But considerations regarding the merits of a proposal were only part of the factors pressing for the legislator's favor. It had to be reconciled with the myriad other factors influencing legislative behavior—"Legislative policy-making appears to be the result of a confluence of factors stemming from an almost endless number of tributaries...."[28] As noted above, the ultimate behavior of the legislator arises from some resolution of these varied elements based on his perception and assessment of their relative importance.

In the case of the vote of the Massachusetts legislature, party affiliation emerges as the clearest factor influencing legislative behavior (see Table 1). Whereas Democrats were almost unanimous in opposition to the proposed change—the party formally adopted a policy position against it—the Republican party appears to have been badly split, although a majority tended to favor revision. The split within Republican ranks was heightened by the announcement by the Republican candidate for governor, Leverett Saltonstall, that he would personally vote against the proposal as a divisive issue when unity was necessary.[29]

The influence of party on legislative behavior has generally been a fruitful area for research in decision-making behavior of the legislature. But if there has been significant research undertaken, the results have been somewhat less than satisfactory, with very different conclusions reached regarding the extent to which party influences voting behavior.[30] Perhaps the best explanation is that the influence of party, like

[27] *Ibid.*, 1286.
[28] S. K. Bailey, *Congress Makes a Law* (New York, 1950), 236.
[29] *Christian Science Monitor*, Sept. 21, 1942.
[30] Compare Julius Turner, *Party and Constituency: Pressures on Congress* (Baltimore, 1941), and Malcom E. Jewell, "Party Voting in American State Legislatures," *A.P.S.R.*, XLIX (Sept., 1955), 773-79, with William J. Keefe, "Party Government and Lawmaking in the Illinois General Assembly," *Northwestern University Law Review*, XLVII (Mar., 1952), 55-71; Keefe, "Parties, Partisanship, and Public Policy in the Pennsylvania Legislature, A.P.S.R., XXXVIII (June, 1954), 450-64. See Thomas J. Anton, "The Legislature, Politics and Public Policy: 1959,"

that of other influences, varies with socioeconomic characteristics, the issue involved, the degree of party competition in the constituency, the majority-minority status of the party, the homogeneity of the party reflecting the makeup of the constituencies, the strength of the party organization, the extent to which loyalty is given to the party organization or to its ideology, the saliency of other vectors, the extent to which the party takes a stand, and a host of other factors beyond the scope of this analysis.[31]

Further, even if party is found to be salient on a selected group of roll calls, consideration must be given to the possibility that the parties may reflect deeper social cleavages. Party orientation appears to reflect a wide array of values and affiliations. The party, like the legislator, is a political instrumentality. Its strength is reflected in the interests of the individuals and groups composing it, and its orientation, to the extent it has any definite program, can be expected to be responsive to the dominant position of its constituent elements.[32]

In Massachusetts in the 1940s, the Democratic party and Democratic legislators represented Catholic, urban constituencies, whereas the Republican party generally drew its strength from nonurban, Protestant elements. Few of the motivational factors bearing on legislative judgment have been as constant a source of concern as the actual and proper relationship of the legislator to his constituency. Does he behave as a "delegate" charged with carrying out its will, or as a "trustee" obliged to pursue the wider public interest, or as a "politico" representing some combination of these role types?[33] Since the American representational pattern tends to localize the legislator's interest, a typical response has been to picture the representative as being obsessed with constituency demands and interests. On the other hand, we have the testimony of the legislators themselves, who reject the "delegate" classification.[34] Of course, it may be that this is a form of mass self-deception or a facade

---

Rutgers Law Review, XIV (Winter, 1960), 269-89; Wilder Crane, Jr., "A Caveat on Roll-Call Studies of Party Voting," *Midwest Journal of Political Science*, IV (Aug., 1960), 237-49.

[31] See Introduction, note 25 *supra*.

[32] American parties frequently tend to be loose alliances of a variety of interests: "Party discipline, where it exists, is rooted in the social and economic homogeneity of interests and political values in the constituencies of each party." Jewell and Patterson, *The Legislative Process*, 449. See Clinton Rossiter, *Parties and Politics in America* (New York, 1960). For the party to pursue actively a definite program is frequently to invite cleavages within the alliance. Usually any response must be watered down to reflect the conflicting interests.

[33] Wahlke et al., *The Legislative System*, chap. 12.

[34] *Ibid.*, 281.

TABLE 1. Relation of Party Affiliation to Voting Behavior on Birth-Control Legislation in 1941 Massachusetts General Court[a]

	COMMITTEE		HOUSE		SENATE[b]		GENERAL COURT	
	Democrat	Republican	Democrat	Republican	Democrat	Republican	Democrat	Republican
Percent Legislators Voting "Yes"	0 (0)	40 (4)	2.5 (2)	58.1 (75)	0 (0)	75 (15)	2.2 (2)	60.4 (90)
Percent Legislators Voting "No"	100 (5)	60 (6)	97.5 (79)	41.9 (54)	100 (12)	25 (5)	97.8 (91)	39.6 (59)
Number of Cases	(5)	(10)	(81)	(129)	(12)	(20)	(93)	(149)

[a] Only those who voted are included.
[b] Excludes two Democrat-Republicans (1 yes; 1 no).
SOURCE: Massachusetts, *Journal of the House, 1941*; Massachusetts, *Journal of the Senate, 1941*; Massachusetts, *Manual of the General Court, 1941*.

TABLE 2. Relation of Percentage of Catholics in Constituency to Voting Behavior on Birth-Control Legislation in 1941 Massachusetts House[a]

	20–29	30–39	40–49[b]	50–59	60–69
Percent Legislators Voting "Yes"	55.5 (12)	36.4 (8)	20 (12)	0 (0)	6.2 (1)
Percent Legislators Voting "No"	44.5 (10)	63.6 (14)	80 (48)	100 (8)	93.8 (15)
Number of Cases	(22)	(22)	(60)	(8)	(16)

[a] Only those who voted are included.
[b] If Boston is excluded, the percentages are "Yes," 36% (9); "No," 64% (16).
SOURCE: U.S. Bureau of the Census, *Sixteenth Census of the United States: 1940, Population*, I, 482–84; U.S. Bureau of the Census, *Religious Bodies: 1936*, I, 440–718; Massachusetts, *Journal of the House, 1941*.

hiding the actual behavior of the legislative actors. But additional empirical evidence suggests that the legislators may be far more publicly oriented than previously believed. This does not mean that a legislator is not concerned with his district's interests but only that he may have a greater degree of independence in his decision-making than the traditional approach suggests.[35] The "delegate" approach generally posits an interaction between the legislator and his constituency that does not seem to exist. The identity of legislators, much less their voting behavior on policy issues, has been shown to have a low saliency for the American public. Only an issue directly and seriously affecting personal interests is likely to activate the constituency. And even in the case of a salient issue, most districts contain a variety of interests and demands—it is unlikely that an issue will have saliency for the constituency at large.[36]

Nevertheless, legislative research studies have consistently maintained that constituency factors do account for some variance in roll-call behavior. With the next election around the corner no legislator can afford to lose contact with the electors; he must cope with the reality of electoral insecurity. Even if the legislator cannot directly know his constituents' attitudes, he does have a perception of the constituency composition and attitudes to guide his decision. Further, a legislator will frequently contact certain key individuals representing his "attentive publics," to act as a sounding board. Again, a number of factors apparently affect the importance of constituency in legislative decision-making: the extent of interparty competition in the district, the socio-economic characteristics of the constituency, and the nature of the issue under consideration (to what extent does it affect his constituents).[37] The saliency of constituency, then, varies with the issue, but the legislator remains a politician who must on occasion play the role of constituency partisan.

In order to obtain some estimates of the effect of the constituency's religious identification on the 1941 legislative behavior, thirty cities of over 25,000 population (1940 census) were categorized according to the percentage of Catholics (1936 census). Voting behavior of the legislators (House of Representatives) from the constituencies in the designed categories was then treated as the dependent variable (see Table 2).

[35] Lewis A. Dexter, "The Job of the Congressman," *Readings in American Political Behavior*, ed. Raymond E. Wolfinger (Englewood Cliffs, 1966), 18-19.

[36] Jewell and Patterson, *The Legislative Process*, 340-43; Wahlke and Eulau, eds., *Legislative Behavior*, 119. See Corrine Silverman, "The Legislator's View of the Legislative Process," 298.

[37] See Jewell and Patterson, *The Legislative Process*, 435-44.

For the thirty constituencies, 25.8 percent (33) of the legislators voted for the proposed change and 74.2 percent (95) voted against revision. In the constituencies not included in the analysis, 53.7 percent (44) of the legislators voted "yes," while 46.3 percent (38) voted "no." The thirty urban centers, then, evidencing the geographic concentration of Catholics and the cohesiveness of their representatives on the birth-control issue, provided the nucleus of the opposition. In our sample, Catholicity of the constituency emerges as an important consideration affecting voting behavior. Of course, many legislators from these districts may also have been Catholics reflecting Catholic values (biographical data was not available). In any case, the analysis does indicate that the opposition of the Roman Catholic Church constituted a principal impediment to legal change.

Continued emphasis by political analysts is also placed on the competition and conflict, accommodations and compromises between interest groups. Whether the lobbying activity of competing interests is damned or praised—and both positions are widely prevalent—the interaction between legislators and groups in fashioning public policy is a reality.[38] The Catholic Church, however, apparently brought little pressure to bear on legislators in this struggle. But it was not really necessary. Legislators almost certainly knew the Church's position and probably carried some perception of the probable reaction of their constituency to Church influence. If Catholic, their own value system might well be supportive. As one commentator has suggested:

> It is pointless to attend to specific instances of actual pressure on . . . legislators, when the important point is the pressure which exists in the minds of such people without having any specific stimuli. The Church is what it is; it exists; and it has shown in the past that it is capable of concerted political action. In this context, it does not need to actively pressure politicians; they come to it, so to speak, with deference, respect, and sugar plums to curry its favor; they do not need to be told that they had better oppose a measure that the Catholic bishops of Massachusetts have united in publicly condemning.[39]

In any case, the General Court had refused to fashion a new legal policy. In November, 1942, the issue was placed before the voters of

[38] See Truman, *The Governmental Process*, 45; Louis L. Jaffe, "Law Making by Private Groups," *Harvard Law Review*, LI (Dec., 1937), 201-53.
[39] Rodman, "Trying to Reform the Birth Control Law," 65.

Massachusetts, who confirmed the action of their legislature and courts in rejecting the proposed revision by a vote of 683,059 (58 percent of the votes cast; 47.7 percent of the total ballots) to 495,964 (42 percent of the votes cast; 34.7 percent of the total ballots); 17.6 percent of the voters cast blank ballots. While time and space prevent analysis of either the vote or electoral campaign, and excellent studies are already available,[40] the general tenor of the encounter can be noted.

Even though the campaign was carried on through ad hoc committees, the real combatants were obvious—the legislative foes merely transferred their confrontation to the public forum. The Catholic Church received assistance from labor interests and some other religious groups, but its primary objective was to consolidate its own membership. The birth-control movement, on the other hand, was forced to fashion a loosely knit coalition which lacked the cohesion, financial support, influence, and public relations possessed in such abundance by its opponent. Factors which had been crucial in determining legislative outcomes were also prevalent in the public sphere.

As could be expected, the referendum produced a vicious emotional battle, deeply divisive of the community. Every weapon from pulpit and confessional to pamphlet and mass media was employed. The Most Rev. James E. Cassidy, bishop of the Fall River Diocese, for example, ordered a letter containing the following comments read at all masses on November 1, 1942: "We do not believe in birth control and race suicide. We are not of your cult or party or clique for which a better name for Birth Controllers would be 'Cradle Robbers par Excellence.' Against you and your doctors we vote NO."[41] In a sermon, the Rt. Rev. Msgr. John F. McKeon, P.R., termed the bill a proposal for "legalized prostitution" and added: "Catholics can have but one thought, to do their duty as Catholics and as citizens. It is the duty of every Catholic to go to the polls and defend the law of God by voting No on the referendum. The Australian ballot is not secret from God and the teaching of the Catholic Church requires no defense. Birth Control is a deliberate attempt to thwart the purpose of marriage."[42] Sufficient antagonism between the Irish Catholic and the Boston Brahmin already existed, without adding birth control.

It is questionable that the referendum provided an advantageous

---

[40] See *ibid.*; Howard, "The Birth Control Law Conflict in Mass."
[41] "Catholics Urged to Oppose Birth Control Referendum," *Stanford-Times*, Nov. 2, 1942.
[42] *Ibid.*

method for resolving this policy question, since it did not determine the merits of the issue but only validated the recognized strength of the Catholic Church in Massachusetts politics. In fact, some 82 percent of Massachusetts residents questioned in a 1940 independent survey, including 72 percent of the Catholics, had expressed support for introducing an exemption into the law for physicians providing contraceptive services to married women.[43] But assuming the accuracy of the poll (which is questionable given the then-nascent stage of the polling art), the merits of the abstract issue were not decisive when the position of the Church magisterium was called into question. Nevertheless, the legislator and judge could take consolation in the fact that their "judgments" had been vindicated in the public forum.

Legislative Action and Public Referendum, 1948

The Massachusetts birth control laws had been legitimized by the court, legislature, and public. While evidence indicated that many people in Massachusetts were actively controlling their fertility rate, that contraceptives were readily available at any drugstore, and that most physicians would provide birth-control services to those who could afford them, the laws remained as an impediment to both family-planning clinics and an extension of birth-control services. Most Massachusetts citizens were not adversely affected by the laws, and the Catholic community, which constituted approximately 40 to 45 percent of the population, formed a sufficiently cohesive block to prevent change.

But the Planned Parenthood League of Massachusetts (PPLM)—the name change indicated the movement's new stress on family planning rather than birth control—was not convinced. Even another legislative failure in 1943, when the bill was defeated in committee by a 13-1 vote (perhaps reflecting the referendum defeat),[44] did not alter their determination to press the change demand. The legislature appeared to be a closed forum. While serious consideration was given to the possibility of a test case to generate U.S. Supreme Court review, the cost and difficulty of formulating a case of sufficient magnitude to reach the court were deemed formidable obstacles. Legal opinion suggested two

[43] Rodman, "Trying to Reform the Birth Control Law." chart 10, p. 2.
[44] The 1943 bill, H. 727, applied only to married women instead of married persons and exempted physicians "after diagnosis." *Transcript of Hearings before the Joint Committee on Public Health of the Massachusetts Legislature on H. 1748*, Apr. 6, 1948, p. 312 (from the files of PPLM) (hereafter cited as *1948 Hearings*).

possible test-case alternatives: a suit seeking to vindicate the medical rights of a woman whose health was imperiled by excess fertility or a suit based on the right to distribute treatises providing contraceptive information. The birth-control leaders, however, considered the latter situation incapable of generating the necessary interest and support, and the former case inapplicable, since the Massachusetts law did not prevent the *use* of contraceptives and *Corbett* had limited the scope of the law. Although the possibility of a test case continued to be explored until the 1960s, the impediments were viewed as sufficiently pervasive.

Officials of PPLM decided, therefore, to make another attempt at a referendum. Polls indicating widespread support for revision of the laws again bolstered their conviction that the necessary public support was present, if only it could be stimulated.[45] Other considerations also strengthened their hopes: the cumbersome and confusing text of the 1942 referendum proposition had been reworded to enhance public appeal;[46] complaints to the FCC prompted promises of equitable access to the mass media;[47] there was potential support from the large number of blank ballots cast in 1942 as well as from the return of soldiers from the war. Since the Massachusetts Constitution required a six-year interim between referendum attempts, the next opportunity for change arose in 1948. In the preceding year, the initial petition was filed with 80,450 certified signatures—four times the requisite number. The issue prompted almost a repeat performance of the earlier action.

At the intelligence stage in the legislature, the legal case for the PPLM coalition was conducted by Frank B. Wallis, who described and analyzed prior legislative and judicial behavior. He was, however, subjected to unbelievable harassment from antagonistic committee members, in spite of valiant attempts to control the proceedings by the spokesman for the Catholic Church and the committee's Catholic chairman—a pattern which continued throughout the testimony of the proponents.[48] Despite an even more convincing presentation of their case than in 1941, pro-change elements were still hampered by an inability to demonstrate serious Massachusetts mortality rates resulting from the legal prohibitions. Instead, they emphasized the general dangers to the

[45] Findings by Lee Robins, on file with PPLM, suggested that 63 percent would support the change and 5 percent were uncertain. Robins employed a stratified sample of 163 respondents. For a criticism of the sampling see Rodman, "Trying to Reform the Birth Control Law," chart 10, pp. 2-3.
[46] *Massachusetts Law*, 7.
[47] Interview with Mrs. Campbell, 1967.
[48] At one point an Episcopal bishop refused to continue his testimony under such harassment. Testimony of Rt. Rev. Norman B. Nash, *1948 Hearings*, II, 228-42.

134 : Law, Politics, and Birth Control

life and health of the mother and child, the use of abortion as a more onerous alternative preventive, the inadequacies of the alternative control methods approved by the Catholic Church, and the rights of doctors to pursue approved medical practices free of legal impediments.

The status quo forces took full advantage of the gap created by the lack of specific medical data regarding a Massachusetts-based need for action.[49] Frank Mansfield again presented their cause, introducing an impressive array of medical, social, and religious testimony, supported by an influx of legislators publicly recording their antagonism. After reading a letter from the Church hierarchy, Mansfield and his colleagues also presented a lengthy exposition on judicial precedent, including extensive citation from *Allison* and *Gardner*. The fact that some of the legislators apparently were not fully aware of this precedent at least suggests the efficacy of the hearing as a vehicle for communicating judicial output to the legislative policy-maker. In this case, however, the court's prior behavior legitimizing Comstockery merely lent added support to the status quo case and provided further justification for legislative predispositions.

As in 1941, it is doubtful that the hearings profoundly affected legislative voting—their primary value appears to have been in providing data for the majority and minority reports of the committee. However, the joint-committee vote was somewhat closer than in 1941; by an 8-6 vote it recommended defeat of the amendment. The House rejected legal change 84-130, and the Senate concurred in the negative policy action by a vote of 15-22.[50] PPLM expectations were fulfilled; the legislature again refused an opportunity to refashion legal policy.

While this prescriptive behavior might well have been given impetus by moral considerations, the 1942 referendum defeat, the general availability of contraceptives, or the oft-expressed belief that no reputable physician would be convicted for "properly" providing contraceptives

[49] The majority report cited Massachusetts vital statistics and data from public hospitals as support for the conclusion that "the incidence of death in maternity cases complicated by any of these diseases referred to by the proponents as dangerous, was either non-existent, practically negligible, or does not furnish the clear and convincing evidence prerequisite to a change in laws pertaining to the public good." Massachusetts, *Journal of the House, 1948*, 1181. It added that "the burden is upon the proponents to show by clear and convincing evidence that a public necessity exists." *Ibid.*, 1180. For a different view on the burden of proof see Christian Bay, *The Structure of Freedom* (New York, 1964); H. L. A. Hart, *Law, Liberty and Morality* (New York, 1966).

[50] The committee vote is set forth in Massachusetts, *Journal of the House, 1948*, 1180; the House vote is contained in *ibid.*, 1203-4; the Senate vote was obtained from Massachusetts, *Journal of the Senate, 1948*, 856.

(although *Gardner* should have dispelled this illusion), other motivational factors again appear salient.

The influence of party affiliation was even more pronounced than in 1941 (see Table 3). The Democratic party had achieved practical unanimity; the Republican party split on a 2:1 ratio in every forum. This pattern would seem to negate need and the public interest as primary explanations of the voting behavior. While the argument may have been framed in terms of public necessity, far deeper political forces were at work.

But as suggested in analyzing the 1941 vote, it is essential to go beyond "party affiliation" to the deeper values, interests, and pressures. It is possible to manifest this interplay of influences by once more considering the voting behavior of members of the House from constituencies of over 25,000 population, grouped by the percentage of Catholics in the district (see Table 4).

Results from communities not sampled suggest the support for revision from legislators representing nonurban areas (i.e., those areas having fewer Catholics): 76.6 percent of the legislators not included in the tabular analysis voted for legal reform; 24.4 percent voted against the change proposal. Both sets of results indicate that the religious cleavage in the legislature was becoming more severe, subject to the caveat that religious influences could include the legislator's personal values, institutional Church pressures, and the effects of a Catholic constituency; all these factors are probable motivational influences flowing into the final voting behavior.

Just as the 1948 legislative response followed the 1941 pattern, so did the electoral campaign, including the extreme hostility generated by the all-out effort of opposing factions. Although the PPLM coalition had increased access to the media, it still lacked the diverse resources of its opponents, and the results manifested the disparity. 806,829 ballots were cast for the proposition (42.6 percent of the total vote on the issue; 37.4 percent of the total ballots cast) and 1,085,350 opposed the change in the law (57.4 percent of the total vote on the issue; 50.4 percent of the total ballots cast). The percentage of blanks had declined but, contrary to PPLM's expectations, they were about equally divided by the two factions. There was still no public impetus for legal change.

PPLM almost immediately decided to make another referendum attempt in 1954, but the plan was to fail. The Republican party blamed its 1948 electoral failure on the birth-control issue, claiming that it had brought out the Catholic Democratic vote. Whatever the merits of

TABLE 3. Relation of Party Affiliation of Voting Behavior on Birth-Control Legislation in 1948 Massachusetts General Court[a]

	COMMITTEE		HOUSE		SENATE		GENERAL COURT	
	Democrat	Republican	Democrat	Republican	Democrat	Republican	Democrat	Republican
Percent Legislators Voting "Yes"	0 (0)	66.7 (6)	0 (0)	66.7 (84)	0 (0)	65.2 (15)	0 (0)	66.4 (99)
Percent Legislators Voting "No"	100 (5)	33.3 (3)	100 (88)	33.3 (42)	100 (14)	34.8 (8)	100 (102)	33.6 (50)
Number of Cases	(5)	(9)	(88)	(126)	(14)	(23)	(102)	(149)

[a] Only those who voted are included.
SOURCE: Massachusetts, *Journal of the House, 1948*; Massachusetts, *Journal of the Senate, 1948*; Massachusetts, *Manual of the General Court, 1948*.

TABLE 4. Relation of Percentage of Catholics in Constituency to Voting Behavior on Birth-Control Legislation in 1948 Massachusetts House[a]

	20–29	30–39	40–49[b]	50–59	60–69
Percent Legislators Voting "Yes"	60.9 (14)	41.4 (12)	12.7 (9)	0 (0)	0 (0)
Percent Legislators Voting "No"	39.1 (9)	58.6 (17)	88.3 (62)	100 (10)	100 (17)
Number of Cases	(23)	(29)	(71)	(10)	(17)

[a] Only those who voted are included.
[b] If Boston is excluded, the percentages are "Yes," 20% (6); "No," 80% (24).
SOURCE: U.S. Bureau of the Census, *Sixteenth Census of the United States: 1940, Population*, I, 482–84; U.S. Bureau of the Census, *Religious Bodies: 1936*, I, 440–718; Massachusetts, *Journal of the House, 1948*.

their claim, party leaders actively sought to curtail any further referendum effort.[51] In addition, the cohesion of the pro-change coalition was also beginning to deteriorate—religious groups and women's clubs expressed concern over the communal decisiveness of referendum attempts.[52] Because of these considerations, the referendum plan died. In fact, PPLM's orientation itself underwent a significant alteration with increasing concentration on education and service rather than political campaigning. Lists were compiled of doctors who would provide family-planning services and the organization became a referring agency sending patients to out-of-town clinics. The militancy had been temporarily curtailed; impetus for recommending legal change had been neutralized.

THE CONNECTICUT STORY

Repression and Judicial Defeat

Following the Massachusetts lead, the Connecticut Birth Control League (CBCL) opened nine birth-control clinics in July, 1935. If the law in the books regarding birth-control clinics could not be altered, perhaps the law in action could be revised. But while the clinics proved popular, their very success attracted the attention of hostile elements. In June, 1939, the Catholic Clergy Association adopted a resolution opposing the clinics and "publicly call[ing] the attention of the public prosecutors and demand[ing] that they investigate and, if necessary, prosecute to the full extent of the law." During Sunday masses, the resolve was read from pulpits in Waterbury, the site of the only hospital clinic. The next day Waterbury Maternal Center was raided by police, two doctors and a nurse were arrested, and the supply of contraceptives was seized. On legal advice CBCL closed all of its clinics.[53]

Again legal enforcement provided an opportunity for recommending change through the courts. As in prior judicial assaults, the birth-control movement in *State v. Nelson* suggested two alternatives at the intelligence stage: (1) the statute should be interpreted to provide an exemption for physicians prescribing for married women "where the

[51] Interview with Mrs. Campbell, 1967.
[52] See Rodman, "Trying to Reform the Birth Control Law," 47–56. Rodman's study is an excellent analysis of the group dynamics of the Massachusetts experience.
[53] On the raid on the clinics see "Ahead: Acid Test of a Law," *Connecticut Life*, July 27, 1961, p. 9. The court would later declare the seizure illegal and order the contraceptives returned. State v. Certain Contraceptive Materials, 126 Conn. 428, 11 A.2d 863 (1940).

general health and well-being of the patient necessitates it"; or (2) the statute should be declared unconstitutional as an invasion of the "retained rights" and liberties of the citizen, or as an unreasonable exercise of police power.[54] In support, the defendants cited a wide variety of evidence suggesting acceptability of contraception as a form of preventive medicine, challenging the claim that birth control tended to promote immorality, and indicating the increasing social acceptance of birth control.[55] The prosecution apparently rejected all such nonlegal data. The argument of the state was simple, if not unique: the legislature had established a policy based on its police powers against contraception in clear and absolute language, and it was the judicial function to effectuate and legitimize that policy. Just as the *Gardner* court in Massachusetts had deferred, so the Connecticut court should not assume the legislative prerogative.

Although the superior court, at the prescriptive stage, held the statute to be all-encompassing but *unconstitutional*, the Connecticut Supreme Court of Errors reversed this holding in a 3-2 decision. The opinion of Judge Hinman in *Nelson*[56] represents a classic expression of restraint in the exercise of the court's interpretative and review functions. At the outset, the court made clear that neither sociological nor physiological views could be given weight in the determination. Such evidence related to the wisdom and comprehensiveness of the legislation which properly belonged to legislative judgment. "For this reason the propaganda and arguments in support of the use of contraceptives upon advice of physicians, which are contained in and appended to the briefs on behalf of the defendants, are appropriately addressed to the general assembly rather than to the courts."[57]

But rejection of the extra-legal data was only reflective of the court's more general unwillingness to re-examine the legislative policy. Not only were the words of the statute clear but the legislature had repeatedly refused to insert the claimed exemption for physicians into

---

[54] Brief for Appellants, pp. 43-65, State v. Nelson, 126 Conn. 412, 11 A.2d 856 (1940). Two additional constitutional arguments were urged with less emphasis: (1) the statute delegates the legislative power of fixing the penalty for its violation to the courts; (2) the statute fails to fix a reasonably precise standard of guilt. *Ibid.*, 6-12.

[55] See the appendixes in *ibid.*, 67-93.

[56] 126 Conn. 412, 11 A.2d 856 (1940). See Notes and Comments, "Constitutional Law—Statutes Regulating Use of Contraceptives," *Boston University Law Review*, XX (June, 1940), 551-54; Recent Criminal Cases, "Contraceptives—Prescription by a Physician as a Health Measure (Connecticut)," *Journal of the American Institute of Criminal Law and Criminology*, XXXI (Sept.-Oct., 1940), 312-14.

[57] 11 A.2d at 862. See *ibid.*, 858.

the statute. The court failed to consider the possibility that legislative non-action might have been the product of motivational impediments—it is difficult to justify the refusal of one legal policy-maker to initiate legal change merely because another has declined to act. As an accepted standard of behavior, it would seem to frustrate any possibility of creative legal change. In rejecting federal precedent in favor of the *Gardner* approach to the judicial interpretative function, Judge Hinman had closed a vital avenue for legal adjustment to the changing social environment.

The alternative of using the court's review power to invalidate the act was also rejected; the path of legitimization based on a broad view of the state's police power was chosen. Again judicial restraint was clearly evident: "Whatever may be our own opinion regarding the general subject, it is not for us to say that the legislature might not reasonably hold that the artificial limitation of even legitimate child-bearing would be inimical to the public welfare and, as well, that the use of contraceptives, and assistance therein or lending thereto, would be injurious to public morals...."[58] The court mentioned also "the maintenance and increase of population" and the protection of public health and life as possible police-power justifications. Simply, it declined to consider whether such justifications did, in fact, presently exist and whether the statute was reasonably related to the designated purposes. Instead, the court assumed that such factors might have motivated the original legislative behavior and might explain the legislative failure to revise the statutes. Legislative refusal to change was thus transformed into a quasi-re-enactment of the provisions, regardless of the political motivations which might in reality have influenced its behavior.

Although two judges dissented without opinion from the *Nelson* decision, the courts had refused to respond to the demands for change. Even though the social environment had undergone major revisions since 1879, the conservative orientation of the court toward its role vis-à-vis the legislative policy-maker inhibited the type of inquiry that might have suggested the necessity and desirability of judicial policy reaction. Rather, Judge Hinman followed the *Gardner* court in instructing reformists to press their claims in the legislative forum. Any hope for further appeal to the U.S. Supreme Court ended when the state terminated the prosecution, claiming that the statute had been legiti-

---

[58] *Ibid.*, 861. It is interesting to note that the court reviewed the Supreme Court's refusal to hear the *Gardner* appeal as conclusive of the constitutional issue. *Ibid.*, 860.

mized and the defendants were honest individuals who had "devoted their time and energy to what they regarded as a charitable work...." Because the defendants had demurred to the charge rather than formally submitting to trial, procedural impediments foreclosed the possibility of appeal.[59]

CBCL immediately pursued the court's suggestion to seek legislative redress. But Judge Hinman had also left open a possible avenue for judicial reform by limiting his decision to a case where the "general health" of the woman was imperiled; there had been no occasion to determine if a statutory exception might be implied when "pregnancy would jeopardize life." Indeed, such an approach had been accepted by the Massachusetts courts in abortion cases. Whether or not the court intended this to be an invitation to further litigation, the CBCL accepted it as such. In 1941 a New Haven physician, Wilder Tileston, filed a civil action for a declaratory judgment recognizing the legality of prescribing contraceptives where pregnancy would endanger the life of the woman and the unconstitutionality of the statute if such an exception were not provided. The case was reserved for decision by the Supreme Court of Errors.

Extra-legal information was again provided and the Connecticut court in *Tileston v. Ullman*[60] similarly ignored it. In a 3–2 decision, the court found the statute to be all-encompassing and constitutional. The opinion, written by Judge Ellis, a new member, manifested the same conservative orientation to the judicial function that characterized *Nelson* and *Gardner*. The 1941 legislative refusal to act (discussed below) was viewed as affirming the validity of the judicial behavior in *Nelson*.

> Its refusal to make any change, in the light of the opportunity to do so, impels us to the conclusion that not even in such situation as we are presented in the instant case did the legislature wish to make exceptions.
>
> It is the legislature which must determine the requirements of public policy for the state and, if the legislature is of the opinion that the broad provisions of those statutes should remain unchanged, for us to read an exception into them is to preempt the legislative function.[61]

[59] "Ahead: Acid Test of a Law," 9.

[60] 129 Conn. 84, 26 A.2d 582, 587 (1942). On the *Tileston* case see Recent Decisions, "Constitutional Law—Connecticut Birth Control Act—Validity Contested by Physician," *St. John's Law Review*, XVII (Apr., 1943), 122–23.

[61] 26 A.2d at 585. See *ibid.*, 587.

Although the dissent noted alternative explanations for the legislative behavior, the judicial restraint was complete. Even the consequences of a prohibitive policy on the life and health of the woman provided no obstacle, since the legislature *could* have decided that an alternative was available, i.e. sexual abstention; evaluating the reasonableness of fertility-control devices was solely for the legislature.[62] While the minority emphasized evidence on the harmful medical and moral consequences that could result from sole reliance on abstention, this data was not even considered in the majority opinion.

As will be discussed below, this restrictive standard of judgment, while characteristic of judicial review in business-regulation cases, appears totally inappropriate for the vital human interests involved in birth-control litigation. But the court was adamant in its avoidance of judicial policy-making regardless of its cost to the litigants or to the capacity of the legal system to respond creatively to social change.

An attempt to obtain a favorable response from the U.S. Supreme Court also failed when it decided not to decide, an approach to be discussed in greater detail below.[63] Because the accessory provisions of the Connecticut criminal code could be unconstitutional only in conjunction with the prohibition on use, Dr. Tileston's attack would have to focus on the *use* provisions. However, the court held that he lacked standing to claim the rights of his patients to use contraceptives.[64] This was to prove the fatal flaw in his appeal. As one commentator noted: "Throughout the history of Connecticut litigation this necessity of attacking one section by attacking another has not only intensified the difficulties of showing why the Constitution is offended, but has yielded an obvious means of abstention from decision on the merits."[65] While this was the primary reason given for rejection of Dr. Tileston's appeal, the court also seemed to be concerned with the "test-case" character of the proceeding (i.e., that a test case pressed as a declaratory-judgment action would not be a true case or controversy).

In any event, the court avoided decision on the merits. It will be interesting to note below the ease with which courts can circumvent this "standing" problem when they desire to decide an issue on the merits. Whatever the motivations for avoidance in this instance, it temporarily

---

[62] *Ibid.*, 586. Compare Judge Avery's dissent, *ibid.*, 589–90.
[63] See text accompanying Chapter Six, notes 27–32 *infra*.
[64] Tileston v. Ullman, 318 U.S. 44 (1943).
[65] Blackshield, "Constitutionalism and Comstockery," 423.

foreclosed the possibility of judicial redress. Claims for legal change appeared to be restricted to the legislative arena.

Failure in the Connecticut Legislature

The behavior of the Supreme Court of Errors in both the *Nelson* and *Tileston* cases demonstrated the judiciary's ability to channel demands to the legislative system. Through its opinions, the courts indicated that the judicial forum was temporarily closed to change, while affirming the legislative preeminence in policy formation. Accepting the judicial suggestion, the birth-control league began to press its claims in the legislative forum.

The endeavor was begun with a real hope for success. In 1931 some 450 physicians had endorsed the proposal for change, reflecting the changing social conditions and the propagandizing and educative work of the growing birth-control movement. In fact, the Joint Legislative Committee had responded with its first favorable report. Although the bill was defeated in the House, it at least suggested the possibility that social changes were beginning to have an influence. In 1933 introduction of the bill by House Majority Leader Raymond Baldwin, with the endorsement of the Connecticut Medical Society, other social and religious organizations, as well as the signed support of 1,000 physicians and 4,000 citizens, had again demonstrated the growing strength of the movement. The Connecticut House of Representatives responded to the altered social conditions by passing an amended version of the bill to exempt physicians 169–80. But in this instance the Senate intervened to defeat the measure by an 18–15 vote.[66]

Given these hopeful signs and the proddings of the courts, the legislative assault was launched in 1941. In the next twelve sessions, seventeen bills were introduced; all were to die at some point in the legislative process.[67]

---

[66] *PPLC History*, 2. The 1929 measure had received the support of the Congregational Churches of Connecticut.

[67] 1941: H.B. 1813 and S.B. 2572 were public-health bills to permit hospitals, subject to state supervision, to provide birth-control services to married women. H.B. 2191 and S.B. 823 would have permitted hospitals to give contraceptive services to married persons for health reasons. H.B. 1813 was revised as a doctor's bill in health cases. This bill was passed in the House by a vote of 164–64 but was defeated in the Senate 24–10.

1943: H.B. 313, a bill for the "Establishment of Standards for Contraceptive

Analysis of the recommending and intelligence functions for each of these proposals reveals little difference and no innovation in either content or strategy from the legislative advocacy described above. Impetus for change was always from the birth-control league, i.e., the Planned Parenthood League of Connecticut, Inc. (PPLC), or some other social or religious organization acting in unison with the birth-control league.[68] The proposed change was usually an exemption for physicians, i.e. a "doctor's bill," although occasionally a repeal of the statute was advocated. When hearings were held, the league provided witnesses to speak on the legal, medical, social, economic, and religious acceptability of birth control.

Generally, adequate data was available indicating the desirability of fashioning a regulatory rather than a prohibitive legal norm. But again,

---

Devices and their Distribution," passed the House 156-83 but was defeated in the Senate 24-11.

1945: H.B. 317, a doctor's bill to save life or prevent injury, was tabled in committee after hearings.

1947: H.B. 953, similar to H.B. 317, received a favorable report from the Public Health and Safety Committee (13-16), passed the House, and was defeated in the Senate.

1949: H.B. 1110, providing a physician's exemption when necessary for the health of the woman, was reported favorably (12-5) but was recommitted and died with the end of the session.

1951: H.B. 1483, S.B. 696, H.B. 1485 were all similar to the 1949 legislation. The first was withdrawn after hearings; the second was killed in committee; the third received a favorable report (11-4). It passed the House 121-62 but was killed by a Senate committee (joint meetings were not held in this session).

1953: H.B.1452 provided an exemption for physicians prescribing for the health of married women. A House petition forced it out of committee, which then produced a straight repeal bill, S.B. 935. Both bills were killed in the Senate by a voice vote.

1955: Both H.B. 1177, a doctor's bill, and H.B. 1182, a repeal bill, were passed in the House after hearings but killed in the Senate by a voice vote.

1957: A doctor's bill, H.B. 572, passed the House 158-71 after an unruly hearing produced by a hostile committee. It was defeated in the Senate by a voice vote.

1959: H.B. 3497 manifested the increasing emphasis on freedom of conscience. It would "permit duly ordained ministers, priests and rabbis to counsel in family planning and members of such organized religious groups to use drugs, medicinal articles or instruments pursuant to the advice and prescription of licensed physicians when reasonably necessary to preserve the life and health of the patient." The bill was killed in committee after hearings.

See generally Smith, ed., *Religious Thought*, 280-81*n*49; *PPLC History*, 3-5. The bills proposed in 1961, 1963, and 1965 will be discussed below. See text accompanying Chapter Seven, notes 4-6 *infra*.

[68] H.B. 3497 in 1959, for example, was sponsored by the Connecticut Council of Churches. The American Civil Liberties Union sponsored one of the 1961 bills. See *PPLC History*, 5.

144 : Law, Politics, and Birth Control

the presence of Catholic influence was very much in evidence. The opposition would be led by Joseph Cooney, legal representative of the Archdiocese of Hartford. Counter-witnesses on each of the relevant subjects were provided with ease, though the primary thrust of the case was based on the maintenance of public morality. But whatever the character of the proceedings, their import on legislative behavior was doubtful.[69] As in Massachusetts, they served primarily to provide justification for the legislative vote (votes could be counted before the hearings), as well as to afford the spokesmen for change an opportunity to voice grievances—a safety-valve function of committees. For the league, the legislative effort at least was a mechanism for maintaining their political organization and a forum to educate the public.

Nor was there any real alteration in the salient factors in the legislature's prescriptive voting behavior. As was true in Massachusetts, party affiliation appears to have been a primary factor influencing legislative decisional behavior (see Table 5). A superficial explanation for the failure of the change proposal in 1941 is clearly revealed in Table 5. While the numerical strength of the Republican party in the House permitted passage of the legislation, the numerical strength of the Democrats in the Senate assured its defeat. It might be assumed then, that if the Republicans were ever in control of both houses, birth-control legislation would pass. However, when such a composition did occur in 1953 and 1957, legal change was still frustrated. In both instances, House passage was followed by Senate defeat of the bill by voice vote. A partial explanation would appear to be the Republican party's reluctance to assume responsibility for passage of birth-control legislation in increasingly Catholic Connecticut; they sought to avoid being tagged as the birth-control party.

In fact, as noted earlier, any analysis based solely on party affiliation would ignore the real value and interests in controversy. An adequate evaluation of legislative behavior requires consideration of the effects of religion operating through the constituency, the personal value system of the legislator, and the pressure exerted by Church interests.

Constituency influences in Connecticut, as in Massachusetts, are suggested by the relation of legislative voting behavior to the percentage of Catholics in the legislator's district. Considering cities of over 25,000 population, the relation of constituency "Catholicity" to legislative

[69] Interview with Joseph Cooney, legal representative of the Archdiocese of Hartford, Hartford, May 24, 1967.

TABLE 5. Relation of Party Affiliation to Voting Behavior on H.B. 1818 in 1941 Connecticut Legislature[a]

	HOUSE OF REPRESENTATIVES		SENATE	
	Democrats	Republicans	Democrats	Republicans
Percent Legislators Supporting Bill	24.6 (16)	90.8 (148)	95.8 (21)	20 (2)
Percent Legislators Opposing Bill	75.4 (49)	9.2 (15)	4.5 (1)	80 (8)
Number of Cases	(65)	(163)	(22)	(10)

[a] Only legislators who voted are included.
SOURCE: Connecticut, *Journal of the House, 1941*; Connecticut, *Journal of the Senate, 1941*; *Connecticut, Register and Manual, 1941*.

TABLE 6. Relation of Catholicity of County to Voting Behavior on H.B. 1813 in 1941 Connecticut Legislature[a]

	HOUSE OF REPRESENTATIVES			SENATE		
	High[b]	Medium[c]	Low[d]	High[b]	Medium[c]	Low[d]
Percent Legislators Supporting Bill	53.8 (28)	74.6 (103)	86.8 (33)	17 (2)	32 (6)	66 (2)
Percent Legislators Opposing Bill	46.2 (24)	25.4 (35)	13.2 (5)	83 (10)	68 (13)	33 (1)
Numbers of Cases	(52)	(138)	(38)	(12)	(19)	(3)

[a] Only legislators who voted are included.
[b] Includes Windham County (51% Catholic) and New Haven County (44%).
[c] Includes Litchfield County (35%), New London County (34%), Fairfield County (34%), and Hartford County (34%).
[d] Includes Tolland County (28%) and Middlesex County (28%).
SOURCE: Connecticut, *Journal of the House, 1941*; Connecticut, *Journal of the Senate, 1941*; U.S. Bureau of the Census, *Religious Bodies: 1936*, I, 729.

voting behavior again yields dramatic results.[70] The twenty-two representatives from the eleven cities over 25,000 were all Democratic; only one supported legal revision in 1941. Since Catholics tended to vote Democratic and cluster in urban areas, the same correlation of Catholicity and urbanism to resistance to legal change on the birth-control issue noted earlier was operative. If we employ the county as the basic unit of analysis and categorize the counties as having a high, medium, or low percentage of Catholics, this relationship again becomes apparent (see Table 6).

A negative correlation exists between the percentage of Catholics in the county and support for the proposed legal change. While it was only one factor bearing on decision-making behavior—as were Democratic party affiliation and urbanism—the religious makeup of the constituency apparently was extremely important.

The structure of the legislative institution was also relevant. In 1957 the Planned Parenthood League attempted to explain the institutional divergence between House and Senate and its consequent inability to secure a favorable legislative response. "The makeup of the Senate is from 36 districts and many of its members come from the central city or town in these districts, where our opposition is strongest. These centers represent the more Roman Catholic segment of the state population, which at the time of our action was about 43% of the total population. House members, on the other hand, come from the smaller towns and rural areas, generally Protestant. . . ."[71] Connecticut's apportionment pattern tended to favor the Protestant, rural, pro–birth control interests in the House while leaving the urban, Catholic elements dominant in the Senate. Since the trend was to increased urbanism, as well as to an increase in the Catholic population, political distaste for birth-control reform was understandable.[72]

Assuming that religious affiliation can represent a set of value predispositions, evidence suggests that the personal value system of the legislator also influenced his voting behavior. In 1957 the Planned Parenthood League polled each of the senators participating in the voice vote rejecting legal change. Of the fourteen senators supporting revision,

---

[70] Population data is derived from the 1940 census and voting behavior from the House and Senate journals as well as memoranda in the files of PPLC.

[71] PPLC, "Report of the Legislative Committee," 1957, p. 1 (from the files of PPLM).

[72] Miss Catherine G. Roraback, attorney for the PPLC, suggests that reapportionment would have augmented the Catholic influence. Interview with Miss Roraback, New Haven, May 2, 1967.

all were Republican and at least thirteen were Protestant, while twelve of the seventeen senators who had killed the bill were Republican and five Democrat. However, of these seventeen, fourteen were Catholic and three were Jewish.[73] This suggests not only the influence of personal religious identification, but also its predominance over party affiliation when the need arose. A very definite Roman Catholic orientation was operative.

To the extent that all of these influences were homogeneous, legislative behavior was quite predictable; to the extent they were heterogeneous, the legislator was subject to cross pressures. A common resolution of these divergent lines of force appears to have been abstention. Analysis of the 1941 vote, for example, revealed that while all Democrats representing urban areas voted, a large number of rural Democrats chose to abstain.[74] On the other hand, as noted above, the Catholic Republican legislators in 1957 voted to kill the proposed change, again reflecting the salience of the religious vector even to the extent of sequestering opposing factors.

Finally, the influence of organized interests should be noted. As time passed, the Planned Parenthood League could claim ever-increasing support from other interest groups. In 1941, for example, the league received the endorsement of 253 organizations, including the prestigious Connecticut Medical Society and the Connecticut Council of Churches.[75] But while apparently all of the accepted lobbying techniques[76] were employed, gains were, at best, marginal. Catholic opposition constituted an effective impediment to change and the proportion of Catholics in the state had constantly increased. While there was no evidence of any extensive Catholic lobbying (the more common strategy called for legislators to contact Mr. Cooney rather than for the Church representative to "buttonhole" the legislators),[77] the Church position was well known. The legislator's hesitancy to challenge the religious establishment precluded the need for organized pressure.

[73] Smith, ed., *Religious Thought*, 282. See *PPLC History*, 3. The results of a PPLC study of the 1941 legislative vote, supporting the textual analysis, is on file with the PPLC: Birth Control League of Connecticut, "An Analysis of the Vote in the House of Representatives, May 20, 1941," May 24, 1941.

[74] Birth Control League of Conn., "An Analysis of the Vote in the House," 2.

[75] See *PPLC History*.

[76] AUTHOR'S NOTE: "Lobbying" is used throughout this work in a broad general sense to encompass diverse forms of advocacy, persuasion, and education. Planned Parenthood, for example, as a tax-exempt group cannot engage in direct persuasion of legislators. Its educational efforts, of course, may influence legislators of the desirability of a particular course of action.

[77] Interview with Cooney, 1967.

Six

Modern Revisionist Efforts: Judicial Abstention and Response

Eradication of legal impediments to the availability of birth-control services through judicial and legislative action increasingly lost meaning for most citizens as time passed. But social change was generating a new host of difficulties. World War II had produced new problems in population control; inarticulate, disadvantaged elements in society were becoming aware of their common interests and ability to effectuate an alteration in their life-style; values regarding freedom of conscience, equality of opportunity, and the proper role of organized religion in society were undergoing revision. Change in the character of the family and the increasing emancipation of women, coupled with the emergence of a new and freer sexual morality, had begun to take their toll. Family planning for all social and economic classes was increasingly being viewed as a right, and cheap effective contraceptives, e.g. the pill and interuterine devices,[1] were being developed to effectuate that right, often with a demand for assistance from public authorities. In a very real sense, a changed society had already emasculated greatly

[1] See Population Council, "The United States: The Pill and the Birth Rate, 1960–1965," *Studies in Family Planning*, no. 20, June, 1967; Population Council, "United States: Methods of Fertility Control, 1955, 1960 and 1965," *Studies in Family Planning*, no. 17, Feb., 1967. In the late 1950s the Food and Drug Administration began to test contraceptives for safety, thereby further enhancing the acceptability of "artificial" birth preventives. However, recently there has been increasing concern over dangerous side effects from oral contraceptives experienced by some users. Hearings on the subject were conducted by the Senate Small Business Subcommittee on Monopoly between January and March, 1971.

the effectiveness of the legal prohibitions for the general populace; the legal system was merely being asked to catch up.

In the institutional sector, nonorthodox Protestant and Jewish values had come full circle—from a position of uncompromising hostility to birth control to fervid endorsement of its use, even making it a moral obligation to control family size. As the National Council of the Churches of Christ expressed the growing Protestant consensus:

> While responsible parenthood is the moral obligation of husband and wife, the concept has implications for society also, to assist parents in the exercise of their duty. In addition to the educational and social services called for to help equip children for their fullest development and contribution to society there are services due married couples. For most couples, family planning requires access to appropriate medical information and counsel. Legal prohibitions against impartation of such information and counsel violate the civil and religious liberties of all citizens including Protestants. Their right to means they approve in conscience does not infringe the right of others to refrain from using such means. Legislation or institutional practices that impair the exercise of moral and professional responsibilities of family-serving professions should be opposed.[2]

Only Roman Catholicism and a few orthodox churches have limited their acceptance of the new movement. And even there the concept of "responsible parenthood" achieved through the use of approved methods of family planning has been gaining increased acceptance. Disagreement tends to center on the methods of control, although the different value systems underlying the dialogue should not be minimized. Nevertheless, there had been a growing conviction within the Catholic Church that it should not impose its moral beliefs on others through public policy embodied in law. A reflection of this new tolerance is found in Richard Cardinal Cushing's commentary on the Massachusetts Comstock law: "It is important to note that Catholics do not need the support of civil law to be faithful to their religious convictions, and they do not seek to impose by law their moral views on other members

---

[2] National Council of Churches, *Responsible Parenthood* (New York, 1961). See Brief for the Planned Parenthood Federation of America, Inc., as Amicus Curiae, Appendix D, Griswold v. Connecticut, 381 U.S. 479 (1965) (hereafter cited as Amicus Brief); Planned Parenthood–World Population, *The Morality of Birth Control: What the Major Faiths Say* (New York, 1965).

of society."[3] While this live-and-let-live attitude is not universal among Catholic leaders, it does represent a modern expression and a growing development of a time-honored line of Catholic thought. There is increasing acceptance of the proposition that "Catholics in campaigning for the maintenance of such laws, gain little for public morality. They do, however, increase the fear of Catholicism in the minds of non-Catholics and increase the likelihood that when Protestants visualize the Church the image will not be of a religious body, but of a political power structure. This is a high price to pay for the maintenance of ineffectual statutes."[4] Political, civil, and social tolerance is a moral duty for Catholics. Suppression of moral evil must frequently give way to the demands of civil amity. In the matter of birth control, any moral fault is visited on the parties themselves. Neither the rights of society nor of a third party require legal protection; there has been no empirical demonstration that the common good would be seriously impaired without these provisions. Hence, negative public action would be improper.

Just as institutional religious conviction began to adjust to changing social values, so also had medical opinion and the policies of major social groups come to endorse the free availability of contraceptive services. When Margaret Sanger began her crusade she stood relatively alone. Medical opinion was either neutral or actively against her. Although some faltering discussion of the subject had been attempted in medical journals, it was generally as taboo for the physician as for the politician. Today, estimates indicate that over 82 percent of all doctors provide birth-control services.[5] The AMA has been joined by numerous other national and local medical groups as well as a wide array of social agencies in endorsing birth control as an acceptable practice.

[3] Quoted in U.S. Congress, Senate, Subcommittee on Foreign Aid Expenditures of the Committee on Government Operations, *Hearings on S. 1676, Population Crisis*, 89th Cong., 1st Sess., 1965, pt. 1, p. 17. See Norman St. John–Stevas, *Life, Death and the Law* (Bloomington, Ind., 1961); C. Thomas Dienes, "To Feed the Hungry: Judicial Retrenchment in Welfare Adjudication," *California Law Review*, LVIII (May, 1970), 555–627. See text accompanying Chapter Nine, notes 42–76 *infra*, for an analysis of the Catholic position and the changes taking place.

[4] St. John–Stevas, *Life, Death and the Law*, 96. Commenting on the tactics employed, he notes that "the hostility aroused against the Catholic community... would be hard to overestimate; they strengthen in the non-Catholic mind the ever present fear of Catholic power and do much to nullify the persuasive force of Catholic teaching." He concludes that "in proportion to their ill effect, their good effect is small, and Catholics would be well advised to abandon them." *Ibid.*, 103.

[5] See Amicus Brief, id. It should be noted that whereas 98 percent of non-Catholic doctors approve of the use of contraceptive devices, only about 25 per-

The magnitude of this institutional response would seem to be a clear reflection of the changing social attitudes accompanying altered social conditions. Gallup polls have recorded a generally constant increase in the number of individuals expressing a favorable attitude toward wider availability of birth-control services, rising to over 80 percent in 1965, including 78 percent of the Roman Catholics interviewed. In 1963 the figures were 78 percent and 53 percent respectively, suggesting the major changes taking place even in Catholic opinion. In fact, the polls indicate that 56 percent of all Catholics believe that their Church should change its position on birth control.[6] A 1960 study reveals that 81 percent of white couples in a national cross sample were using some method of conception control, an increase of 11 percent over 1955. Only 15 percent of the sample limited themselves to methods approved by the Catholic Church. In fact, only 45 percent of Catholics practicing conception control restricted themselves to Church-approved methods.[7]

Given the magnitude of the alteration of the social environment, it is not surprising that the planned-parenthood movement viewed the possibility of favorable legal response with a great deal of hope. It was true that the Connecticut legislature had continued its regular refusal to act, but the judicial forum was available as an alternate point of access to the legal system. Connecticut, the state with the most restrictive laws, thereby affording the greatest possibility of favorable action, in 1958 became the situs for still another assault on the judicial actor.[8]

---

cent of Catholic doctors hold a similar view. Guttmacher, *Babies by Choice or by Chance*, 104.

The first major breach in the medical world's negative response came in 1912, when Dr. Abraham Jacobi, a prominent pediatrician, spoke favorably of contraception in a presidential address to an AMA convention. Abraham Jacobi, *Journal of the AMA*, LVIII (June 8, 1912), 1736-37. See Fryer, *The Birth Controllers*, 199-200; AMA, Committee on Human Reproduction, "The Control of Fertility," *Journal of the AMA*, CXCIV (1965), 462-70. The first favorable AMA statement came in 1937; Amicus Brief, 28-32, Appendix B.

[6] Information Center on Population Problems, *Public Health and Birth Control* (New York, 1965), 3-4.

[7] P. K. Whelpton, A. A. Campbell, and J. E. Patterson, *Fertility and Family Planning in the United States* (Princeton, 1966), 276, 283. See R. Freedman, P. K. Whelpton, and A. A. Campbell, *Family Planning, Sterility and Population Growth* (New York, 1959), on the 1955 study. See generally Robert B. Fleming, "Contraception and a Working Public Policy," *The Pharos of Alpha Omega Alpha*, XXVIII (July, 1965), 95-98.

[8] The decision was the result of an informal conversation between Dr. Lee Buxton and the late Fowler Harper, both members of the Yale University faculty. Interview with Buxton, New Haven, May 23, 1967.

152 : Law, Politics, and Birth Control

CONSIDERATIONS OF JUSTICIABILITY:
THE POE CASE

Although complete alteration in the membership of the Connecticut Court of Errors also prompted action, the real objective of the new assault was to be the U.S. Supreme Court. In its prescriptive activity, the Warren Court had manifested an increasing commitment to an egalitarian jurisprudence; it had begun to fashion legal policy consistent with emerging social forces. In its intelligence activities, the court had not displayed the hostility toward extra-legal data that frequently characterized the behavior of state judges. Indeed, there were indications of its receptiveness to such evidence for fashioning legal policy.[9] The recommending stage had produced an increased willingness to process claims pressed by formerly inarticulate interests (e.g. racial minorities) —a responsiveness to the demands for legal revision. With the changes in both the social and medical orientation to family planning as well as the court's responsiveness to a changing society, conditions seemed ideal for a meaningful reaction from the judicial system.

Initially, however, it was necessary to overcome the jurisdictional defects that had barred access in *Tileston*; it was essential that the litigants seek redress for *personal* grievances. Dr. Lee Buxton, chairman of the Department of Obstetrics and Gynecology at the Yale School of Medicine, agreed to initiate an action based on his alleged due-process right to practice his profession according to the best available scientific principles. In a separate supporting action, three of his patients (for legal purposes Poe, Doe, and Hoe) presented a stirring portrayal of the medical indications for conception control to protect life and health. Roe, an instructor at Yale University, pressed a separate claim based on an economic desire for contraception. Economic reasons were coupled with psychological considerations in still another proceeding involving two married law students at Yale, Mr. and Mrs. David Trubek. Three additional claims were filed by ministers asserting the right to counsel in family-planning matters, i.e., an infringement of free speech and free exercise of religion.[10] The cases, then, designed to portray the

[9] See, e.g., Brown v. Board of Education, 347 U.S. 483 (1954). See generally Friedman and Macaulay, *Law and the Behavioral Sciences*, 630–98; Walter Murphy and Herman C. Pritchett, *Courts, Judges and Politics* (New York, 1961), chap. 9; Jack Greenberg, "Social Scientists Take the Stand," *Michigan Law Review*, LIX (May, 1956), 953–70.

[10] The use of fictitious names was permitted because of the nature of the issue being litigated. Jane Doe, the patient Dr. Buxton wanted to advise, was a married woman who suffered from a medical condition that would make another pregnancy

myriad of "proper" motivations impeded by an absolute prohibition on family-planning services, presented a patent demonstration that birth control was not necessarily among the obscene, indecent, immoral practices condemned in the 1879 legislation.

The intelligence function in the joined actions was directed to support the above perspective by stressing social and medical acceptance of birth-control services. It was argued that since the law prohibited recourse to the most effective methods of control, while the less reliable methods were freely available, an absolute prohibition on all recipients could not be reasonably related to the end of protecting the public morality; in their operation, the sweeping laws unreasonably encompassed married persons as well as unmarried; "contemporary community standards" suggested that birth control was no longer the immoral practice condemned by the legislature in 1879, but instead a recognized part of individual freedom and the social order; the laws unreasonably endangered the life and health of the Poes and Does; Dr. Buxton was deprived of a valuable property right in the exercise of his profession.[11]

In support of these propositions, a vast amount of nonlegal data was produced. But in this instance, the legal issues often seemed submerged in sociological and scientific evidence, especially in contrast to the ultra-legalistic arguments for the state. Medical data on the effectiveness of various contraceptives; psychological findings on the anxiety produced by unwanted conception; surveys of the medical profession regarding the reliability and acceptability of contraception and particular methods of and medical indications for control; surveys on public attitudes toward and use of family planning; data on religious attitudes toward the practice, the psychological effects of abstention, the incidence of abortion and its relation to conception, the dangers of world population growth, the socioeconomic correlates of conception control—all were processed to the judicial actor.

While the data seem clearly relevant, it might have been preferable to develop the nonlegal data primarily through the *amicus* briefs filed in

---

dangerous to her life. *Poe v. Ullman* involved a married couple who had produced three abnormal children, all of whom had died. It was questionable that a normal child could be conceived. *Hoe v. Ullman* presented the medical dangers from conception in cases of couples with incompatible blood types. The *Hoe* case became moot when the plantiff moved out of the state. The claim of the ministers was delayed pending the outcome of the other litigation and apparently was not brought to trial.

[11] Brief for Appellants, Poe v. Ullman, 367 U.S. 497 (1960).

the U.S. Supreme Court by the Planned Parenthood Federation of America, the American Civil Liberties Union, and a group of sixty-six eminent physicians. While the legal issues should not be divorced from the nonlegal data, there are questions concerning emphasis and strategy of presentation. In any case, adequate data was available to fashion a legal policy consistent with present social conditions if the courts were so inclined. The judicial actor, however, was not yet prepared to assume responsibility for creative legal change.

The behavior of the Connecticut courts was not really surprising. The lower courts succumbed to the binding effects of precedent by sustaining demurrers to the claims. The Supreme Court of Errors in *Buxton v. Ullman*,[12] citing an uninterrupted line of judicial and legislative refusals to initiate policy change in Connecticut, rejected the opportunity to fashion a physician's exemption and legitimized the existing norms. Perhaps the most interesting factor for our analysis was the court's reliance on presumed legislative acquiescence to judicial policy behavior:

> The legislature is presumed to be aware of the interpretation placed upon its legislation by the courts and the effect which its own non-action thereafter may have.... Courts cannot, by the process of construction, abrogate a clear expression of legislative intent, especially when, as here, unambiguous language is fortified by the refusal of the legislature, in the light of judicial interpretation, to change it. In short, courts cannot write legislation by judicial decree; this is particularly so when the legislature has refused to rewrite the existing legislation. The *Nelson* and *Tileston* decisions cannot be overruled by any attempt to reconstruct the statutes.[13]

This dramatically illustrates the danger which arises when precepts derived from cases are seen as immutable, dogmatic pronouncements which dictate the solution of all succeeding cases; when legislative silence is assumed to be an endorsement of past judicial action, regardless of the many motivations that might, in reality, account for inaction. This approach necessarily places a heavy burden on the legislature which, as had been true in the case of contraceptive policy, it is often unwilling to accept. Employed in this manner, the doctrine of *stare decisis* is an impediment to change, a vehicle which widens the gap between law and society. John Dewey summarized its pernicious ef-

[12] 147 Conn. 48, 156 A.2d 508 (1959).
[13] 156 A.2d at 513–14.

fects: "The effect is to breed irritation, disrespect for law, together with virtual alliance between the judiciary and entrenched interests that correspond most nearly to the conditions under which the rules of law were previously laid down."[14]

Certainly *stare decisis*, like literalist statutory interpretation, generally comports with the desire for certainty and stability through law. Men seek to impart order into their dealings, to delineate common expectations concerning human behavior as a precondition for peaceful interaction in the community, through law. Predictability is valued not only by lawyers seeking to inform their clients, but by members of society generally. Consistency with the past also serves to limit the unfettered discretion of a judge. Some uniformity of treatment is obtained. All of the above considerations are summed up in the term "the *maintenance* function of law."

But, as has been continually stressed, law must also perform a *creative* function; it must provide for change, for a more ideal legal order. The use of past legal behavior as a guide for the present, therefore, must be approached through this dual perspective. The task then is to fashion a doctrine which manifests both the limitations of precedent and the values it is designed to serve—a principle that reflects both the maintenance and creative functions. "*Stare decisis* has in the past been, now is, and must continue to be, a norm of change, and a means of change, as well as a norm of staying out, and a means of staying put."[15]

---

[14] Dewey, *Logical Method and the Law*, 26. See Roscoe Pound, "A Ministry of Justice," *Harvard Law Review*, XXXV (Dec., 1921), 115, who also warned of the problems posed by a narrow approach to *stare decisis*: "Those who know best the nature of the judicial process know how easy it is to arrive at an impasse. Some judge, a century or more ago, struck out on a path. This course seemed to be directed by logic and analogy. No milestone of public policy or justice gave warning at the moment that the course was wrong, or that danger lay ahead. Logic and analogy beckoned another judge still farther. Even yet there was no hint of opposing or deflecting forces. Perhaps the forces were not felt. The path went deeper and deeper into the forest. Gradually there were rumblings and stirrings of hesitation and distrust, anxious glances were directed to the right and to the left, but the starting point was far behind and there was no other path in sight."

The narrow conception of precedent appears to be more the resultant of the approach of the judge than a demand of the doctrine. Indeed, as Jerome Frank noted, the different facts of individual cases negate any possibility of an inflexible rule. *Courts on Trial* (New York, 1963), 14-36. Further, the variety of precedents make it quite likely that they will fall on all sides of an issue—a mechanical application is generally a practical impossibility.

[15] Karl N. Llewellyn, *Jurisprudence: Realism in Theory and Practice* (Chicago, 1962), 71. For jurists whose writings exemplify this orientation to precedent, see Cardozo, *The Nature of the Judicial Process*; Cardozo, *The Growth of the Law*; Cardozo, *The Paradoxes of Legal Science*; Hall, *Living Law*; Levi, *Legal Reason-*

Such an approach is possible if past legal behavior is perceived as only the initial facet of decision-making. The constant retesting of rules by their present social effect defines alternatives for judicial action; this sociological orientation infuses a creative element into the uses of precedent. While there are numerous ways in which precedent can be adjusted to fit modern conditions, the vital consideration is that adjustment is possible. Past behavior is viewed as a guide to decision rather than as the final determinant of decision. Understood in this manner, *stare decisis* can be an effective instrument of creative change.

Although the Connecticut Court of Errors recognized that the birth-control argument "raises an issue of public policy,"[16] it apparently negated any meaningful part for the judiciary in making such policy. Instead, by stressing the possibility that the legislature might have chosen abstinence as a viable alternative mode of conception control in cases of hardship, the court ignored the social reality that the majority of citizens either did not, could not, or would not limit themselves to such behavior. The social impact of the laws on the poor was not considered; general availability of less reliable means of control was given no effect. The court unanimously rejected the demands for legal change in *Buxton*, as it would later decide that the Trubeks' claim had been foreclosed by prior decisions.[17]

But this behavior had been generally anticipated; it was the probable reaction of the U.S. Supreme Court that was the focus of attention. Spirits soared when the court agreed to hear the *Poe* case, but they were soon to be smashed. The character of the judicial concern became apparent during the oral colloquies between the justices and the attorneys. Although there was an evident concern for the effect of denying contraceptive services on life and health, there was skepticism whether the laws in fact had this effect.[18] When the decision was rendered, the

---

ing; Llewellyn, *The Common Law Tradition*; Richard Wasserstrom, *The Judicial Decision* (Stanford, 1961).

[16] 156 A.2d at 514.

[17] Trubek v. Ullman, 147 Conn. 633, 165 A.2d 158 (1960). The subsequent appeal was dismissed by the U.S. Supreme Court even though Justices Douglas, Harlan, and Stewart would have noted probable jurisdiction. Trubek v. Ullman, 367 U.S. 907 (1961).

[18] See Poe v. Ullman, 29 U.S.L.W. 3257-60 (U.S. Mar. 7, 1961). Assistant Attorney General Raymond J. Cannon admitted under questioning by Chief Justice Warren that the statute would prevent a woman from getting contraceptive services even if death were to result from another pregnancy. *Ibid*. There is serious question concerning Justice Frankfurter's and Mr. Cannon's concurrence that the matter was merely "academic." Even Alexander Bickel, who is sympathetic to the majority position, noted: "Whether prosecution is very likely, possible, or even

court decided that there was no adequate case or controversy; the absence of any real threat of prosecution under the laws suggested a deficiency of the requisite adversity. Justice Frankfurter, speaking for the court, argued that the case lacked the "real, earnest and vital controversy between individuals"; the "rigorous insistence on exigent adversity as a condition for evoking Court adjudication" had not been fulfilled.[19] The statutes had been rendered a nullity through nonenforcement; contraceptives were freely available at drugstores throughout the state. In short, desuetude had rendered the statutes socially meaningless and made the issues inappropriate for decision. No real hardship would result from allowing the statutes to remain.

It is most fitting that this opinion was delivered by Justice Frankfurter, the paradigm of judicial restraint.[20] While a superb jurist, his orientation to judicial intervention often severely restricted the court's ability to assume responsibility in the policy-making process. In this case the decision not to decide, the use of the "passive virtues," seems quite inappropriate.

Not only did existing precedent appear contrary to the majority position, but, as Justice Harlan noted in an excellent dissent, the reasoning was also questionable.[21] It was pure conjecture to assume that open

---

improbable, the incidence of some deterrent effect cannot be gainsaid. The matter was not academic at the time of the argument; it becomes so by decision of the Supreme Court." "Forward: The Passive Virtues," *Harvard Law Review*, LXXV (Nov., 1961), 60.

[19] Poe v. Ullman, 367 U.S. 497, 506 (1961). The majority consisted of Justices Frankfurter, Warren, Clark, and Whittaker. Justice Brennan concurred, arguing, probably correctly, that the real issue involved birth-control clinics. He therefore felt that decision should be delayed until such a case was before the court. Dissents were entered by Justices Harlan, Douglas, Stewart, and Black.

[20] See, e.g., Joint Anti-Fascist Refugee Committee v. McGrath, 341 U.S. 123, 149 (1951) (concurring opinion); Rochester Tel. Co. v. United States, 307 U.S. 125 (1939); Adler v. Board of Education, 342 U.S. 485, 497 (1952) (dissenting opinion); Connecticut Mut. Life Ins. Co. v. Moore, 333 U.S. 541, 551 (1948) (dissenting opinion); Coleman v. Miller, 307 U.S. 433, 460 (1939) (dissenting opinion).

Justice Frankfurter noted (367 U.S. at 509), however, the discretion involved in the justiciability determination: "Justiciability is, of course, not a legal concept with a fixed content or susceptible of scientific verification. Its utilization is the resultant of many subtle pressures, including the appropriateness of the issues for decision by the court and the actual hardship of the litigants of denying them the relief sought."

[21] 367 U.S. at 524–39. United Pub. Workers v. Mitchell, 330 U.S. 75 (1947), lends some support to the majority position. But see Adler v. Board of Education, 342 U.S. 485 (1952); Evers v. Dwyer, 358 U.S. 202 (1958); District of Columbia v. Thompson Co., 346 U.S. 100 (1953); Notes and Comments, "Connecticut's Birth Control Law: Reviewing a State Statute under the Fourteenth Amendment," *Yale Law Journal*, LXX (Dec., 1960), 322–34; Smith, ed., *Religious Thought*, 293–95.

defiance of the law, especially through clinics, would not result in prosecutions. In *Nelson* the state had asserted its authority to punish violations subsequently. The prosecutor had specifically stated at the time: "Henceforth any person, whether a physician or layman, who violates the provisions of these statutes, must expect to be prosecuted and punished in accordance with the literal provisions of the law."[22] Further, in the years following *Nelson*, a number of police-court cases were not appealed and, according to one state official, the laws had been used to threaten prosecution.[23] The possibility of enforcement itself constitutes a restraining force. The mere fact of desuetude does not remove the statutes from the books. For those citizens who generally respect and attempt to adhere to legal norms, they may have proved a serious impediment to the desired use of contraceptives. The legislature had continually refused to abrogate the laws or even to modify their effect. Even in the instant case, not only had the state demurred to the claims, indicating its belief that the laws were still viable, but the highest court of the state had again legitimized the provisions.

Aside from all of these indications of a "real" controversy, consider the consequences of the court's decision. As Justice Douglas, dissenting, noted:

> What are these people—doctor and patients—to do? Flout the law and go to prison? Violate the law surreptitiously and hope they will not get caught? By today's decision we leave them no other alternative.... A sick wife, a concerned husband, a conscientious doctor seek a dignified, discrete, orderly answer to the critical problem confronting them. We should not turn them away and make them flout the law and get arrested to have their constitutional rights determined.[24]

The declaratory judgment was specifically designed to permit interests to challenge legal norms without violating them. But the practical effect of the court's decision was to force this behavior on social interests seeking legal change. The law would have to be broken to test its validity—this hardly seems the type of "social impact" we seek to achieve by creative social engineering through law.

It has been suggested that the judicial behavior may have been designed to motivate other legal policy-makers to produce policy change,

[22] 367 U.S. at 532. See *ibid.*, 531.
[23] Interview with Joseph Clark, who represented the state before the U.S. Supreme Court, New Haven, May 22, 1962.
[24] 367 U.S. at 513.

i.e. the Connecticut legislature.[25] However, in light of continued legislative refusal to assume responsibility, temporary judicial abstention[26] appears inappropriate. The court should not only have realized the probability of another lawsuit generated by the decision but also the improbability of favorable legislative action while the focus was on the judicial arena. To force the parties to submit to criminal processes, to undergo the time and expense of further litigation appear unnecessary. If the court had accepted its role as a coordinate policy-maker, legal change might have been effectuated. Instead, it chose to avoid the issue on the merits, thereby refusing to supplement the policy process when the other legal actor was apparently unable to effectuate the needed change. In terms of legal precedent, social necessity, and a creative policy approach to the judicial role, the decision in *Poe* seems weak. Whether born of an attitude of restraint, a desire to let the issues mature even further, or some alternative motivation, it certainly does not contribute to our perspective on law as a creative instrument of change.

While it is true that the court can circumvent the choices involved in statutory interpretation or constitutional decision-making by deciding to use diverse tools to avoid decision, the art of abstaining from the decisional process on the merits is itself a form of interaction; it involves decisional behavior. The requirements of a "case and controversy," "standing," "ripeness," "abstention," the refusal to decide a "political question," and the *Ashwander* rules generally, afford courts a wide degree of discretion in determining the extent and character of their policy role.[27] Like its discretionary jurisdiction, their effective use often suggests political decision-making.[28] While they often serve as useful

---

[25] See Bickel, "Forward: The Passive Virtues," 60.

[26] Abstention is not used in the text as a term of art referring to the federal court decision to defer in favor of a state tribunal. See, e.g., Dombrowski v. Pfister, 380 U.S. 479 (1965); Cameron v. Johnson, 390 U.S. 611 (1968). Rather, it is used in a more general sense to refer to that panoply of devices, e.g. certiorari, standing ripeness, mootness, abstention, whereby a court exercises its discretion not to decide a case on the merits.

[27] See Ashwander v. TVA, 297 U.S. 288, 346–48 (1936); William Lockhart, Yale Kamisar, and Jesse Choper, *Constitutional Law* (3rd ed., St. Paul, 1970), chap. 2.

[28] One of the prime methods through which the court can manage the extent of its intervention is control over its work load. The history of the Supreme Court has been marked by a continual struggle to keep abreast of the constantly increasing demands generated by a changing society. Through its certiorari power, the court chooses which cases are most appropriate for review. Although an "appeal" supposedly reaches the court as a matter of right, this has also become a form of discretionary jurisdiction through the court's practice of dismissing an appeal for want of a substantial federal question. Since the resources of the court are limited,

guides for a judicial decision, it seems generally true that a court can find a way of avoiding their effect if there is a real desire to act. Given the importance of this determination for understanding judicial policy behavior, it is startling to consider the paucity of systematic inquiry into their use. Studies relating to this alternative mode of decision-making appear to be primarily prescriptive rather than empirical evaluations of the behavior.[29]

As is usually the case in analyzing judicial behavior, jurists tend to fall on all sides when judging the extent to which such devices *should* be used as a judicial tool. One general approach, however, is that of Alexander M. Bickel. He fully recognizes the political character of the justiciability formulas, which he refers to as the "passive virtues," and freely accepts their use as a necessary adjunct to a principled form of constitutional decision-making. "The Supreme Court in constitutional cases sits to render an additional, principled judgment on what has already been authoritatively ordered. Its interventions are by hypothesis exceptional and limited, and they occur, not to forestall chaos, but to revise a pre-existing order that is otherwise viable and was itself arrived at by more normal processes. Fixation on an individual right to judgment by the Supreme Court is, therefore, largely question-begging."[30] The use of the "passive virtues" affords the court a leeway of expediency along the path of principle; it abstains from decision until a principled decision can be formulated. But the present analysis suggests that the rapidity of social change and situational exigencies appear to make such a perspective of limited value. The legislature simply lacks the motivational resources to respond creatively to changing

---

discretion in accepting cases is a necessity. However, additional motivation may also underlie refusal to act. These preliminary determinations, like all forms of judicial decisions, are political in character. Since the decision not to decide can be used by the court to avoid taking part in the policy process, it is all the more important to discover the standards governing the behavior. See Maryland v. Baltimore Radio Show, 338 U.S. 912, 918 (1950).

[29] But see Joseph Tanenhaus et al., "The Supreme Court's Certiorari Jurisdiction: Cue Theory," *Judicial Decision-Making*, ed. Glendon Schubert (New York, 1963), 111–32; Schubert, *Quantitative Analysis of Judicial Behavior* (New York, 1960), 25–68; Robert W. Gibbs, "Certiorari: Its Diagnoses and Cure," *Hastings Law Journal*, VI (Nov., 1955), 133–70. Game theory has also been employed by Glendon Schubert, "Policy without Law: An Extension of the Certiorari Game," *Stanford Law Review*, XIV (Mar., 1962), 284–327.

[30] Bickel, "Forward: The Passive Virtues," 173. For a criticism of the Bickel thesis see Gerald Gunther, "The Subtle Vices of the 'Passive Virtues'—a Comment on Principle and Expediency in Judicial Review," *Columbia Law Review*, LXIV (Jan., 1964), 1–25.

conditions. The Bickel approach does not restore the courts to a working partnership in the policy-making process; rather, it provides a rationale and a mechanism for staying out. But the analysis thus far indicates that the legislature is frequently unwilling to fill the gap that would be left by judicial withdrawal.

A far more acceptable approach is that suggested by Victor G. Rosenblum, who specifically calls for re-examination of the policy by which a court withdraws from controversy: "To the extent that any branch withdraws from participation as a coordinate member of this tripartite arrangement for leadership and control, it denigrates the objectives and functions of separation of powers."[31] The essential task is to open the lines of communication within our political system. There must be an understanding of the needs and aspirations of all elements of the system if a creative social order is our objective. If access to the judiciary is limited, it is usually the inarticulate and unorganized in society who suffer. "But communication and confrontation are preconditions of justice; and, to the extent the judiciary provides access to our central decision-making mechanisms for individuals or groups otherwise excluded from effective participation, it enlarges the practicability of justice as well as the commitment of the otherwise alienated populations to justice as ideal and ideology."[32]

This approach to the use of procedural techniques appears far more consistent with the perspective underlying this analysis. While both Bickel and Rosenblum accept a political role for the court, Bickel tends to implement it through abstention and delay in judicial policy action while Rosenblum advocates a wider access to the courts. The coordinate responsibility of all legal institutions for fashioning legal policy responsive to our changing social environment appears to be denigrated by the wide use of the "passive virtues." It would seem that the stress should be on the more effective processing of a wider range of social claims rather than on the narrowing of access to the system.

But perhaps the most disturbing element of the *Poe* decision was its practical effect on pro-change interests. While the Frankfurter opinion had not closed the judicial forum as a potential instrument for reform, it did force the interests to alter their tactics of recommendation, requiring them to violate the statutory norm in order to obtain access. Even though it is questionable that the interests of the legal system are

[31] Victor G. Rosenblum, "Justiciability and Justice: Elements of Restraint and Indifference," *Catholic University of America Law Review*, XV (May, 1966), 152.
[32] *Ibid.*

served by inducing violations of the law as a mechanism for changing it, the *Poe* decision did afford an excellent example of the judicial actor communicating with social interests and local authorities—the pattern for subsequent action had been defined. Despite some internal dissension within the birth-control movement[33] and the emergence of a concerted effort for legislative revision in all of the forums under consideration (discussed in Chapter Seven), it was soon decided to accept the court's suggestion for recommending legal change.

LEGAL CHANGE THROUGH THE COURTS: THE GRISWOLD CASE

On November 1, 1961, the Planned Parenthood League of Connecticut opened a public clinic providing family-planning services to married women. Every attempt was made to maximize publicity for the clinic opening. This clear defiance of the statutory norms posed a severe problem to local authorities since they would have preferred to ignore the whole issue. In fact, PPLC officials were fearful that the police might "look the other way." But pressure for enforcement of the laws developed and an investigation of the clinic's activities ensued. Finally, on November 18, Dr. Lee Buxton and Mrs. Estelle Griswold, executive director of PPLC, were charged with violation of the Comstock laws.

The manner in which the arrest was handled attested to the concern of the authorities. State officials, apparently fearing political repercussions, denied their authority to intervene; local authorities did not raid the clinic but merely requested the "criminals" to appear at police headquarters to be booked; Dr. Buxton and Mrs. Griswold were treated with extreme courtesy. As the local prosecutor noted: "All of these people had to be treated with finesse; they were all very distinguished—I was only doing my job as chief prosecutor."[34]

---

[33] There was a difference of opinion within the local organization whether the opening of a clinic was the most desirable mode of attack. Although Justice Brennan in *Poe* had recognized that the real controversy was the right to open public clinics, it was argued that the "broad right to prescribe" could not be an effective basis for review. Conflict also broke out between the national and local offices and among the legal fraternity on the proper handling of the case. Interview with Miss Roraback, 1967.
[34] Interview with Julius Martz, former chief prosecutor, New Haven, May 23, 1967; interview with Clark, 1962. See generally Record, pp. 41–46, Griswold v. Connecticut, 381 U.S. 479 (1965); Gereon Zimmermann, "Contraception and Commotion in Connecticut," *Look*, Jan. 30, 1962, pp. 78–83c.

Handling of the intelligence function more closely approximated our ideal model of informing the decision-maker than in any of the previous instances. In the lower courts, the primary objective was preserving the constitutional issues for appeal—there never was any real hope of securing a favorable response from the Connecticut courts.[35] Nor was there the extensive use of nonlegal data that would characterize the Supreme Court briefs, since the Connecticut Supreme Court of Errors apparently was not especially amenable to such evidence (which seems to reflect the attitude of many state courts). On the other hand, most of the premises from which the Supreme Court operated in the *Griswold* case could be found in the defendant's argument to the Connecticut court. The state's presentation generally followed the same lines as previous cases—the statutes had been judicially legitimized as a valid exercise of police power. Without attempting to delineate the precise interest of the state, a variety of possible interests were set forth. And, as usual, the traditional appeal to the limited character of the judicial policy role was made. "At the outset, it must be borne in mind that, in testing the constitutionality of an act of the legislature, we are not to assess it in the light of what we think of the wisdom and discernment of the law-making body in the particular instance. Rather, we are bound to approach the question from the standpoint of upholding the legislation as a valid enactment unless there is no reasonable ground upon which it can be sustained."[36]

At the U.S. Supreme Court level, the excellence of the reformist's informing activity became clearly manifest. The primary brief by Professor Thomas I. Emerson of Yale Law School and Catherine Roraback was designed essentially as a "legalistic" document, with nonlegal data clearly subordinated to the legal argument, while development of the nonlegal data characterized an excellent *amicus* brief submitted by the Planned Parenthood Federation of America.[37] Although there seems to have been no joint writing of these briefs, the authors were in contact with each other and knew what each was doing. Their complementary character reveals how legal and nonlegal data can be utilized to develop a highly effective presentation. In formulating the argument for the primary brief, careful consideration was given to the due-process ap-

[35] Interview with Miss Roraback, 1967. Mr. Clark insists that the privacy issue was not properly preserved. Interview with Clark, 1962. However, an analysis of the lower-court proceedings does suggest the issue was properly presented.
[36] Brief for State-Appellee, p. 11, State v. Griswold, 151 Conn. 544, 200 A.2d 479 (1964).
[37] Interview with Thomas I. Emerson, New Haven, May 23, 1967.

proach of each of the justices and issues were framed in an effort to maximize their appeal. Presentation of the privacy claim, for example, was framed with alternative bases reflecting some of the differing approaches suggested for this constitutional guarantee.[38] Emphasis was placed on the difference between substantive due process in economic and in civil-rights cases in an attempt to win the support of Justice Black.[39] The free-speech claim tended to be subordinated, perhaps reflecting the perspective that it had minimal relevance to the case before the court.[40] Probably the major weakness of the brief was its failure to develop an in-depth argument premised on the Ninth Amendment. Apparently this argument had been advanced by Professor Fowler Harper of Yale Law School; with his death it tended to be discounted as a viable tool.[41] The subsequent behavior of certain justices suggests that this may have been an error, though not a costly one.

In the *amicus* brief, the greater part of the argument involved analysis of "The Full Development and Present Place of Contraception in American Life Throughout the Nation."[42] In 110 pages of appendixes devoted to this subject, federal and state programs in the family-planning area, the legal status of contraception, the medical consensus on contraception, the religious consensus on family planning and responsible parenthood, and contemporary community mores were discussed. The data developed in these sections reflected a range of empirical findings too extensive to discuss in this inquiry. Suffice it to note that the evidence clearly demonstrated the archaic character of

[38] Brief for Appellants, pp. 69–89, Griswold v. Connecticut, 381 U.S. 479 (1965); see Brief for Defendants-Appellants, pp. 15–19, State v. Griswold, 200 A.2d 479 (1964).

[39] Interview with Emerson, 1967.

[40] *Ibid.* This view is also reflected in Thomas I. Emerson, "Nine Justices in Search of a Doctrine," *Michigan Law Review*, LXIV (Dec., 1965), 221–22. Alternatively, Robert G. Dixon, "The Griswold Penumbra: Constitutional Charter for an Expanded Law of Privacy," *Michigan Law Review*, LXIV (Dec., 1965), 213–17, suggests that an effectual First Amendment argument could have been presented premised on the right of access to birth-control information, i.e., making the right to privacy effective. Adoption of such a theory would provide a notable extension of the *Griswold* holding—it may suggest a potential line of development. See Commonwealth v. Baird, 247 N.E.2d 574, 576–78 (Mass., 1969), discussed in Chapter Eight *infra.*

[41] Interview with Emerson, 1967. The Brief for Appellants, pp. 82–83, treats the Ninth Amendment as the only one of the bases for deriving the right of privacy.

[42] Amicus Brief, 24–102. *Amicus* briefs were also filed by the Catholic Council on Civil Liberties stressing the right of privacy of the married couples and by Whitney North Seymour on behalf of 141 physicians arguing the medical interests involved.

the Connecticut laws when viewed against modern social values and behavior; it revealed dramatically the extensive alteration in social living since the laws were first enacted, an alteration that the court would find difficult to ignore.

Opposed to this impressive array of argument and evidence was a rather short brief from the state devoted essentially to the same recurring arguments already noted. Again the court was asked to defer to the judgment of the Connecticut courts as well as to the legislative refusal to alter the statutes. The entire argument was summarized in one terse statement: "The decision of the General Assembly of Connecticut that the use of contraceptives should be banned is a proper exercise of the police power."[43] Resort to the existence of alternative methods of fertility control, e.g. abstinence, withdrawal, rhythm, seemed to dwindle under the impact of the physiological and psychological data offered by pro-change forces on the deficiencies of these practices. While the state attempted to diminish the medical indications for conception control as well as the severity of population growth, their arguments again seemed to wane against the overwhelming evidence introduced by birth-control advocates.

If the state was to be successful, it would not be on a basis of social and medical arguments but through judicial deference to the legislative police power. Indeed, this approach did characterize the prescriptive function in the Connecticut Supreme Court of Errors. In a short unanimous opinion, the court once more legitimized the prohibitive norms with the usual expressions of deference to the legislative prerogative and to the demands of *stare decisis*.

> In rejecting this claim, we adhere to the principle that courts may not interfere with the exercise by the state of the police power to conserve the public safety and welfare, including health and morals, if the law has a real and substantial relation to the accomplishment of those objects. The legislature is primarily the judge of the regulations required to that end, and its police statutes may be declared unconstitutional only when they are arbitrary or unreasonable attempts to exercise its authority in the public interest.[44]

[43] Brief for Appellee, p. 9, Griswold v. Connecticut, 381 U.S. 479 (1965). The appellant's argument was characterized as being directed to the desirability of these statutes: "It has been held that the Supreme Court may not decide the desirability of legislation in determining its constitutionality; the forum for correction of ill-considered legislation being a responsive legislature." *Ibid.*, 28.
[44] 200 A.2d 479, 480 (1964).

The court renewed its refusal to evaluate the extent to which the statute does bear a "real and substantial relation" to the achievement of the public well-being. Rather, "police power" became a conceptual catchall permitting deference to the legislative judgment of 1879.

It might have been hoped that changing values and practices communicated to the court at the intelligence stage would have had some impact on the judicial actor's decisional behavior. But in fact it specifically refused "to consider whether or not in the light of the facts of this case, the current developments in medical, social and religious thought in this area, and the present conditions of American and Connecticut life, modification of the prior opinions of the court might not 'serve justice better.' "[45] The court thereby rejected consideration of the reasonableness of the legal norms in light of modern conditions. The practical effect of this judicial approach was to accept a past finding of legitimacy as binding on future judicial decisions despite the changing social environment. Even if we admit the constitutionality of the birth-control norms in nineteenth-century society, does this forever bar a re-evaluation in light of changed circumstances? Isn't the judicial actor under an obligation to assess the reasonableness of archaic legislative action in terms of present social reality? These are questions that the court seemingly ignored or at least declined to answer, even though their consideration would appear vital to a proper performance of the judicial function. Whether the Connecticut court was abstaining in expectation of higher court action, deferring to the legislature or following its own policy inclinations, the legislative norms had prevailed—the stage had been set for Supreme Court action.

At the prescriptive stage in the U.S. Supreme Court, the initial item on the agenda was the natural question concerning the appropriateness of review. Considering the numerous problems it had previously posed in processing the change demand to the court, the subject might have been expected to be treated in depth. Although the presence of criminal convictions rather than a declaratory-judgment action had given the claims the "exigent adversity" lacking in *Poe*, the standing problem, which had defeated the *Tileston* appeal, remained. If Dr. Tileston lacked standing to claim the rights of his patients, why should Dr. Buxton or Mrs. Griswold maintain any better position? This clearly was a source of concern for the appellants but apparently not for the justices;[46] of

[45] *Ibid.*
[46] Interview with Emerson, 1967. On the standing problem in *Griswold* see Blackshield, "Constitutionalism and Comstockery," 428–29; Dixon, "The Griswold Penumbra," 211–13.

the six opinions rendered in *Griswold*, only that of Justice Douglas dealt with the problem.

Douglas chose to distinguish *Tileston* as a declaratory-judgment action whereas a criminal conviction was involved in the instant case. A much stricter standard should be applied in the former situation "lest the standards of 'case or controversy' in Article III of the Constitution become blurred."[47] However, far more persuasive motivations than this technical distinction appear to have influenced the court's behavior. For example, it might be attributed to the general social changes since *Tileston*, or by the logic that this would be the primary method for vindicating not only the rights of the appellants but their married patients as well. Conviction of the appellants under the accessory provisions was premised on the constitutionality of the primary statute: "certainly the accessory should have standing to assert that the offense which he is charged with assisting is not, or cannot constitutionally be a crime."[48] Still another consideration was the dual character of the justiciability issue. The appellants had standing to assert their own rights by reason of the conviction; under the principles of *jus tertii* they could then assert all rights bearing on their claims.[49] Finally, we can only speculate on the importance of the absence from the court of Justice Frankfurter, who had retired. In any case, because of the court's rejection of the route of non-action on the merits, the use of the "passive virtues," the change demand would finally be passed upon by the highest judicial actor.

At no time in the policy-making process is the potential for interaction and confrontation between the judicial and legislative actors so severe as a judicial decision regarding the constitutionality of a legislative act. The legislature is charged with the primary role in formulating legal policy and then a small group of men is permitted to negate that policy. Unlike the case of statutory interpretation, a decision of unconstitutionality cannot be overcome by a clarification of intent. Unlike the case of first instance, where the courts serve as the initial decision-maker and act without prior legislative policy guidance, a decision of unconstitutionality can thrust the courts into direct defiance of the legislative will. The manner in which this power is exercised, then, is vital to any assessment of the interactive process.

[47] Griswold v. Connecticut, 381 U.S. 479, 481 (1965).
[48] *Ibid.*, 481.
[49] Dixon, "The Griswold Penumbra," 212. See Robert A. Sedler, "Standing to Assert Constitutional Jus Tertii in the Supreme Court," *Yale Law Journal*, LXXI (Mar., 1962), 599–660.

The initial problem lies in the standard against which the legislative act is to be judged. If legislative policy were in fact being judged in terms of an organic law fashioned in the eighteenth century, judicial review would be a major impediment to creative social change. In reality, however, the Constitution today is generally approached as a living institution that reflects the social needs of the period rather than a mass of static words to be read in terms of a bygone age. Words like "due process," "unreasonable search and seizure," "equal protection" attain their meaning from their usage by the courts and their effects on social behavior. "Our Constitution is not a strait jacket. It is a living organism. As such it is capable of growth of expansion and of adaptation to new conditions. Growth which is significant manifests itself rather in intellectual and moral conceptions than in material things. Because our Constitution possesses the capacity of adaptation, it has endured as the fundamental law of an ever-developing people."[50]

Recognition of the discretion that this provides the judicial decision-maker has led a number of scholars to approach courts as political agencies—they are not merely agents but a functioning part of the existing political alliance. Every time the courts favor one social interest over another, they are fulfilling their role as political institutions. The judge exercising review is not a *kadi* under a tree dispensing justice; he is a political actor whose behavior must be studied politically.

An excellent example of a theoretic study applying this perspective to constitutional decision-making is that of Karl Llewellyn. His concern with the working Constitution as an institution reflects a highly dynamic approach to constitutional decision-making: "the working Constitution is amended whenever the basic ways of government are changed."[51] If you want to understand what the Constitution means, you must watch what men are doing and how they feel; if you want to know what still remains of the original Constitution and what has changed, you study the practices and attitudes of men toward the document. Llewellyn recognized that it would be impossible to determine whether many practices are sufficiently accepted to be parts of the working Constitution; they lie within the penumbra,

---

[50] Justice Brandeis, quoted in Bickel, "Forward: The Passive Virtues," 106–7. See Robert A. McCloskey, *The American Supreme Court* (Chicago, 1960); Schubert, *Judicial Policy-Making*, 135–44, on the changing constitutional values.

[51] Karl N. Llewellyn, "The Constitution as an Institution," *Columbia Law Review*, XXXIV (Jan., 1934), 22.

and the penumbra will of necessity be in constant flux. New patterns of action develop, win acceptance (sometimes suddenly), grow increasingly standardized among an increasing number of the relevant persons, become more and more definitely and consciously "the thing to do," proceed to gain value as honored in tradition—i.e., become things to be accepted in and of themselves without question of their utility—until they take on finally, to more and more of the participants, the flavor of the "Basic."[52]

In analyzing a constitutional decision, the question is not whether it conforms to the intent of the framers, but rather, "Is this within the leeway of change which our going governmental scheme affords? And even if not, does the nature of the case require the leeway to be widened to include it?"[53] This perspective presents an explicit policy approach to constitutional decision-making which would demand of the courts a constant willingness to re-examine prior decisions—a recognition that the judiciary also determines social needs and practices. This does not mean a haphazard, case-by-case mode of constitutional decision-making. Indeed, the court throughout its history has manifested patterns of behavior in which particular values have been stressed.

Llewellyn does note a caveat. The court must control the direction of governmental activity not only by what is the going practice but also according to "the nature of what our government should be."[54] This appears to be a direct recognition of the strength of the court, by reason of its more independent position and the general higher quality of its personnel, to take a more long-range view of social needs than the exigencies of the moment. While the legislature responds to immediate pressures, the judiciary, although subject to external forces, operates in a far more calm and removed environment, permitting a more rational evaluation of competing values; the "sober second thought" can be given effect.[55]

Llewellyn's approach would seem to afford an excellent opportunity to approach constitutional decision-making not in terms of any accepted ideal model, but rather through the actual behavior involved. It permits escape from the conceptualism that develops from an excessive reliance on the words of the document; it rejects traditional models

[52] *Ibid.*, 26–27.
[53] *Ibid.*, 33.
[54] *Ibid.*, 39.
[55] Harlan F. Stone, "The Common Law in the United States," *Harvard Law Review*, L (Nov., 1936), 25.

to explore what in fact is happening. Neither the document nor constitutional precedents are disregarded, but they are not decisive. Since policy-making demands a social perspective, they must be considered in terms of the social and political situation.[56]

More recently, Miller and Howell have introduced a mode of analysis referred to as "teleological" or "purposive" jurisprudence[57] which appears quite similar to Llewellyn's behavioral perspective. Judicial review, like all decision-making, is a value-choosing process. Although the justices follow precedent and adopt orientations appropriate to the judicial role, they do not cease to have values which they should recognize and articulate. The judicial arena is a political battleground in which competing interests press their positions in an effort to influence policy. "The Court *is* a power organ which aids in the shaping of community values, whether avowedly so as in the hands of Douglas or whether abashedly so when Frankfurter seeks to convince us that he is an apostle of self-restraint."[58] "The role, then, of the Supreme Court in an age of positive government must be that of an active participant in government, assisting in furthering the democratic ideal. Acting at least in part as a 'national conscience,' the Court should help articulate in broad principle the goals of American society."[59] Judicial review demands a sense of purpose, a view of goals to be achieved, a willingness to evaluate the probable social consequences in formulating policy.

---

[56] On the uses of constitutional precedent see William O. Douglas, "Stare Decises," *The Record of the Association of the Bar of the City of New York*, IV (May, 1949), 152-79. He argues that "security can be achieved only through constant change, through the wise discarding of old ideas that have outlived their usefulness, and through adopting others to current facts." Milton R. Konovitz, ed., *Law and Social Action: Selected Essays of Alexander H. Pekeles* (Ithaca, 1950), 200-201, provides the following analysis of Pekeles's approach: "Law is too serious a business to be left to lawyers. While there are legal questions and legal problems, there are no legal solutions. The greatness of the Court is manifested in its growing awareness that the issues which confront it, no matter how legal, must of necessity find a composition social, economic, or political in nature."

[57] Arthur S. Miller and Ronald F. Howell, "The Myth of Neutrality in Constitutional Adjudication," *University of Chicago Law Review*, XXVII (Summer, 1960), 684. It also resembles the approach to legal policy-making of Harold Lasswell and Myres S. McDougall, "Legal Education and Public Policy: Professional Training in the Public Interest," *Yale Law Journal*, LII (Mar., 1943), 203-95; McDougall, "Law as a Process of Decision: A Policy-Oriented Approach to Legal Study," *Natural Law Forum*, I, no. 1 (1956), 53-72.

[58] Miller and Howell, "The Myth of Neutrality," 689. See Wells and Grossman, "The Concept of Judicial Policy-Making," 309, who provide a set of possible outcomes to which judicial policy may be directed; Murphy, *The Elements of Judicial Strategy*.

[59] Miller and Howell, "The Myth of Neutrality," 689.

Precedent and policy generally must be constantly re-examined in terms of social efficacy. As with Llewellyn's approach, this political perspective not only rejects a myopic concern with constitutional language and conceptions but also requires judicial attention to the demands of social engineering. It specifically recognizes the court as an interacting part of the legal system which bears responsibility for fashioning creative response to social change.

Although we might present other "political" evaluations of judicial behavior,[60] the above should suffice to suggest its compatibility with the present analysis. Courts are recognized as functioning elements in the policy-formation process and there is a direct concern with the manner in which judges behave in fulfilling this function. Confrontations among the legal actors are perceived as a natural product of policy-making activity. While judges are not viewed as "free decision-makers," emphasis is placed on their discretion to utilize their unique attributes in fashioning creative legal change.

Other jurists, however, have offered an alternative approach to judicial behavior far more restrictive of the exercise of judicial review. Recognizing the danger from excessive confrontations between the legal institutions, these scholars attempt to circumscribe the judicial function by advancing a narrow conception of the judicial role. Judge Learned Hand, for example, would have restricted review to those cases where court intervention is necessary to safeguard the separation of powers.[61] Thayer would have prescribed a standard whereby the court would act only when the legislation under consideration has no reasonable basis;[62] since legislatures are seldom devoid of any reason, it would appear that this approximates no review at all. Both theories seem to restrict severely the role of the judiciary in constitutional cases. While limiting the friction of the interactive process, it is questionable, given the benefits of judicial review described above, that this perspective would assist in creative social engineering.

The same criticism may well be applicable to Herbert Wechsler's thesis that the court should fashion its rules to reflect "neutral princi-

---

[60] See e.g., Dahl, "Decision-Making in a Democracy," 279–95; Victor G. Rosenblum, *Law as a Political Instrument* (New York, 1955); Martin Shapiro, *Freedom of Speech: The Supreme Court and Judicial Review* (Englewood Cliffs, 1966). For a "political" orientation to state judicial behavior, see Kenneth N. Vines and Herbert Jacob, *Studies on Judicial Politics* (New Orleans, 1962).

[61] Learned Hand, *The Bill of Rights* (Cambridge, Mass., 1958).

[62] James B. Thayer, "The Origin and Scope of the American Doctrine of Constitutional Law," *Harvard Law Review*, VII (Oct., 1893), 129–56.

ples": "I put it to you that the main constituent of the judicial process is precisely that it must be genuinely principled, resting with respect to every step that is involved in reaching judgment on analyses and reasons quite transcending the immediate result that is achieved."[63] The neutral decision transcends the immediate parties to the case to establish a principle of law. Constitutional precedents would appear to take on a new vitality since the governing principle, by definition, would be applicable to a wide variety of subsequent cases. Judicially fashioned change would be the exception and legislative adjustment the norm.

A high degree of mechanistic jurisprudence characterizes the "limited-role" approach—there is that quest for stability and certainty so common among jurists. It is not merely that it ignores the actual behavior of the courts; the concept itself is troublesome. Societal change and situational exigencies would seem to make "neutral principles" a chimera—it places constitutional interpretation in a straitjacket and leaves the task of legal adaptation to societal change excessively to the legislature. Given the motivational difficulties characterizing the legislative process, this would appear to be an extremely dangerous approach. Further, despite Wechsler's protestations, this method would demand a greater use of the "passive virtues" to avoid decisions—it is well to ponder the societal consequences of such abstention.

Criticism of Wechsler and general endorsement of a political approach to judicial review manifests a constant stress within this work on a functional role for all legal policy-makers in the policy-making process. The court brings to the process a set of attributes not possessed by the legislative decision-maker. It introduces a balance into the system to prevent any element from running roughshod over other institutions. National government versus state government, the prerogative of the various branches, the rights of the individual and of the society, of the minority and the majority—these relationships must be adjusted as society changes.[64] And the courts must play a vital role in this adjustment process if the legal system is to respond creatively to social change. With the exception of the case of first instance, no judicial act appears

---

[63] Herbert Wechsler, "Toward Neutral Principles of Constitutional Law," *Harvard Law Review*, LXXIII (Nov., 1959), 15. See Louis H. Pollack, "Racial Discrimination and Judicial Integrity: A Reply to Professor Wechsler," *University of Pennsylvania Law Review*, CVIII (Nov., 1959), 1–34.

[64] Robert H. Jackson, *The Supreme Court in American Society* (New York, 1955), 61, notes that "in a society in which rapid changes tend to upset all equilibrium, the Court, without exceeding its own limited powers, must strive to maintain the great system of balances upon which free government is based."

to offer as excellent an opportunity for creativity as the constitutional decision.

By adjusting the interpretation given to the vague terms of the Constitution, then, the limits of constitutional legitimacy can be expanded or restricted. Few cases have demonstrated the extent of this leeway as has the judicial behavior in *Griswold*. The six opinions provide a panoply of constitutional doctrine revealing the variety of judicial approaches to the character of constitutional limitations and the proper role of the judiciary in the legal system.

From the outset it was obvious that the nascent constitutional right of privacy would play a vital role in the judicial determination. Both Justice Douglas and Justice Harlan had commented at length in *Poe* on the character of this guarantee.[65] But the question remained as to where this right was to be found in the Constitution and how it would be weighed against countervailing state interests.

Justice Douglas might have been expected to follow a *flexible due-process* approach to grounding the privacy right since he had argued in *Poe* that due process had a meaning transcending the Bill of Rights and privacy was sufficiently fundamental to be included in its broad confines. On the other hand, his extra-judicial writings revealed an approach to the guarantees of the Bill of Rights which went beyond their specific content.[66] It was this latter approach that characterized his

[65] See Justice Harlan's discussion in dissent of these statutes as "an intolerable and unjustifiable invasion of privacy in the conduct of the most intimate concerns of an individual's personal life." Poe v. Ullman, 367 U.S. 497, 539 (1960). See *ibid.*, 539-55. On Justice Douglas's approach to privacy see text accompanying notes 66-68 *infra*. See generally Symposium, "The Griswold Case and the Right of Privacy," *Michigan Law Review*, LXIV (Dec., 1965), 197-288.

On the right to privacy prior to *Griswold* see generally William M. Beaney, "The Constitutional Right to Privacy in the Supreme Court," *Supreme Court Review*, ed. Philip Kurland (Chicago, 1962), 212-51; Erwin N. Griswold, "The Right to Be Let Alone," *Northwestern University Law Review*, LV (May–June, 1960), 216-26; Beard v. Alexandria, 341 U.S. 622, 628, 644 (1951); Monroe v. Pape, 365 U.S. 167 (1961); Lanza v. New York, 370 U.S. 139 (1962). See Comments, "Constitutional Law: Supreme Court Finds Marital Privacy Immunized from State Intrusion as a Bill of Rights Periphery," *Duke Law Journal*, MCMLXVI (Spring, 1966), 597n38, for more complete listing of relevant cases. See text accompanying Chapter Eight, notes 44-54 *infra*, on possible expansion of the right.

[66] Although Justice Douglas does emphasize the Fourteenth Amendment in Poe v. Ullman, 367 U.S. 497, 516-17 (1960), he did state that "it emanates from the totality of the constitutional scheme under which we live." *Ibid.*, 521. See William O. Douglas, *The Right of the People* (Garden City, 1958); Douglas, *A Living Bill of Rights* (Garden City, 1961); Paul G. Kauper, "Penumbras, Peripheries, Emanations, Things Fundamental and Things Forgotten: The Griswold Case," *Michigan Law Review*, LXIV (Dec., 1965), 241.

opinion for the court in *Griswold*. The specific guarantees of the Bill of Rights "have penumbras, formed by emanations from those guarantees that help give them life and substance."[67] The First Amendment's right of association, which itself is a derived or peripheral right, the Third Amendment's "quartering of soldiers" provisions, the Fourth Amendment's guarantee against unreasonable searches and seizures, the Fifth Amendment's self-incrimination clause, and the retained rights of the Ninth Amendment were said to create "zones of privacy." Justice Douglas, then, placed marital privacy in the realm of fundamental constitutional guarantees which were applicable to the states through the Fourteenth Amendment due-process clause. He did not foreclose the possibility, however, of a future use of due process which surpasses even this expanded version of the Bill of Rights.

Justice Douglas's use of terminology—"penumbras," "emanations," "zones of privacy"—has perhaps subjected his approach to more severe criticism than it deserves. In fact, the court has frequently recognized peripheral "rights" or "interests" not specifically guaranteed, but necessary to effectuate the primary right.[68] That these derived rights previously had a greater degree of propinquity to a particular guarantee than does the right of privacy vis-à-vis any particular guarantee does not belie recognition that the right to be let alone is pervasive to the constitutional scheme and vital to the exercise of the enumerated guarantees. It is this flexibility of the constitutional guarantees that permits the instrument to be adjusted to social realities, to become a living Constitution. While the language of the Douglas opinion might be considered ambiguous, the decision itself is grounded on the prior behavior of the court and provides the flexibility requisite for constitutional adjustment to social change.

The penumbrial approach was accepted by Justice Goldberg, who nevertheless felt it was necessary to develop further the relation of the nascent right to the Ninth Amendment.[69] Joined by Chief Justice War-

---

[67] 381 U.S. at 484.

[68] See, e.g., NAACP v. Alabama, 357 U.S. 449 (1958) (freedom of association); Gibson v. Florida Legislative Investigation Committee, 372 U.S. 539, 544 (1963) (privacy of association); Pierce v. Society of Sisters, 268 U.S. 510 (1925) (right to educate children as one chooses); Meyer v. Nebraska, 262 U.S. 390 (1923) (right to study a foreign language); Martin v. Struthers, 319 U.S. 141, 143 (1943) (right to distribute, receive, and read); Wieman v. Updegraff, 344 U.S. 183, 195 (1952) (freedom of inquiry and thought and freedom to teach). See Comment, "Constitutional Law—Connecticut Contraceptive Ban v. Right of Privacy," *University of Missouri at Kansas City Law Review*, XXXIV (Winter, 1966), 106–7.

[69] For prior discussions of the Ninth Amendment see Bennett B. Patterson,

ren and Justice Brennan, Goldberg rejected the "total incorporation" of the Bill of Rights in favor of *selective incorporation* of only those rights which are fundamental to the concept of ordered liberty, not to be limited to the specifics of the Bill of Rights—due process encompasses guarantees beyond those provided in the Bill of Rights. It was argued that the Ninth Amendment lent support to the claim of rights other than those specifically mentioned in the Bill of Rights—"fundamental principles of liberty and justice which lie at the base of all our civil and political institutions."[70] In order to determine which rights are sufficiently fundamental, the court looks to the "traditions and (collective) consciences of our people."[71] Accepting this reasoning necessarily entails reference to social behavior, to social experience. Goldberg, in applying this perspective, leaves little doubt that he considers privacy, at least marital privacy, as central to the constitutional scheme, fundamental to ordered liberty.

It is difficult, however, to understand why Goldberg felt it necessary to utilize the Ninth Amendment to bolster his argument for an interpretation of due process exceeding the specific guarantees of the Bill of Rights. Perceived as an independent source of constitutional guarantees, e.g. privacy, such reliance would become more comprehensible, but Goldberg specifically negates this rationale.[72] As a rejection of the necessity of analogizing the penumbrial rights with the specifics of the first eight amendments—as Douglas's approach suggests—it lends credence to Justice Black's critique that a "natural justice" is being imported into the Constitution.[73] While Douglas's perspective arguably permits a malleable building process on stated constitutional guarantees to encompass new social developments, it has been suggested that Goldberg's

---

The Forgotten Ninth Amendment (Indianapolis, 1955); Knowlton H. Kelsey, "The Ninth Amendment of the Federal Constitution," *Indiana Law Journal*, XI (Apr., 1936), 309-23; Norman Redlich, "Are There Certain Rights...Retained by the People?," *New York University Law Review*, XXXVII (Nov., 1962), 787-812.

[70] 381 U.S. at 493, quoting from Powell v. Alabama, 287 U.S. 45, 67 (1932).

[71] 381 U.S. at 493, quoting from Snyder v. Massachusetts, 291 U.S. 97, 105 (1933). On the fundamental character of the right to marital privacy, the justice commented: "The entire fabric of the constitution and the purpose that clearly underlies its specific guarantees demonstrate that the right to marital privacy and to marry and raise a family are of a similar order and magnitude as the fundamental rights specifically protected." 381 U.S. at 495.

[72] *Ibid.*, 492.

[73] 381 U.S. at 524-25 (Black, J., dissenting). For an analysis of the Douglas and Goldberg opinion based on this distinction and a severe criticism of the Goldberg approach see Mitchell Franklin, "The Ninth Amendment as Civil Law Method and Its Implications for Republican Form of Government: Griswold v. Connecticut; South Carolina v. Katzenbach," *Tulane Law Review*, XL (Apr., 1966), 487-522.

use of the Ninth Amendment would introduce a type of "free-decision" theory into constitutional decision-making. The approach is said to lack the foundations and ordered pattern for growth present in Douglas's perspective and suggests a rather haphazard process of legal change instead. On the other hand, the Goldberg rationale, minus its unnecessary references to the Ninth Amendment, represents a traditional technique for due-process adjudication. Reliance on a version of the Fourteenth Amendment not limited by the provisions of the Bill of Rights has received considerable prior support. Justice Goldberg appears only to have generated misunderstanding with his Ninth Amendment discussion.

Justices Harlan and White, in separate concurring opinions, adopt perhaps a somewhat more orthodox approach to due-process decision-making. True to the tradition of Justice Frankfurter, both reject incorporation in any form in favor of a case-by-case determination of the fundamental character of the right being pressed; due process does not receive its meaning from the Bill of Rights but from the independent determination that the claim is fundamental to the concept of ordered liberty. For Harlan, reliance on the Bill of Rights only limits the full richness of due process: "The Due Process Clause of the Fourteenth Amendment stands, in my opinion, on its own bottom."[74] And on due process, standing alone, rests the right of marital privacy. Justice White concurs with Justice Harlan's grounding of the privacy guarantee but stresses another aspect of due-process inquiry utilized by some members of the court, i.e., the balancing of the constitutional guarantee with the alleged interest of the state. Given the "clear effect of these statutes, as enforced... to deny disadvantaged citizens of Connecticut, those without either adequate knowledge or resources to obtain private coun-

[74] Franklin, "The Ninth Amendment," 500. The following commentary is illustrative of the Harlan approach to due-process questions: "However it is not the particular enumeration of rights in the first eight amendments which spell out the reach of Fourteenth Amendment due process, but rather, as was suggested in another context long before the adoption of that Amendment, those concepts which are considered to embrace those rights 'which are ... fundamental; which belong ... to the citizens of all free governments' ... for 'the purposes [of securing] which men enter into society.'" Poe v. Ullman, 367 U.S. 497, 541 (1961). "Due process has not been reduced to any formula; its content cannot be determined by reference to any code. The best that can be said is that through the course of the court's decisions it has represented the balance which our Nation, built upon postulates of respect for liberty of the individual, has struck between that liberty and the demands of organized activity." Ibid., 542. See Pointer v. Texas, 380 U.S. 400, 408-9 (1965), and Gideon v. Wainwright, 372 U.S. 335, 352 (1963), for other statements of the Harlan perspective. Harlan's discussion of privacy in Griswold is very brief since he discussed the character of the right at length in Poe. See 367 U.S. at 548-55.

seling, access to medical assistance and up-to-date information in respect to proper methods of birth control," the effect of the statute on the intimacies of the marriage relationship and the restrictive effect on doctors in preventive medicine, the statute bore "a substantial burden of justification."[75] In oral argument White had probed the counsel for the state as to the justifications for the laws, and this testimony was utilized to formulate his argument.[76] Although the Connecticut courts had offered a number of possible justifications for the statute and the appellants had attempted to destroy each of those claims,[77] Justice White reduced all claims to the single police-power policy against all forms of illicit sexual relationships. While the justice might have attacked the validity of the purpose, he chose the more common approach of challenging the means used to effectuate the goal. Actual social behavior demonstrated that the policy was not really being pursued through the statute. Simply, the need for the statute did not offset its detrimental effects.

Although the above opinions reach the same policy decision by very different routes, suggesting the richness of constitutional terminology, they do possess one primary common attribute: all provide for flexible legal adjustment to changing social demands. Whether arguing due process standing alone, the penumbras of the Bill of Rights, or a Ninth Amendment retained-rights perspective, the Constitution provides a viable instrument for adjusting the legal system to the changing social environment. *Griswold* may cause some consternation to those who seek a craftsmanlike development of principled constitutional decision-making, but it does recognize the necessity of fashioning legal tools consistent with a changing society. The development of the tools then awaits subsequent claims being pressed on the courts.

Unfortunately, the same evaluation cannot be applied to the separate dissenting opinions of Justices Black and Stewart. Both reveal a restric-

---

[75] 381 U.S. at 503, citing three equal-protection cases. The possibility of serious equal-protection attack on the statute had been rejected by the appellants. Nevertheless, the first issue raised by Justice Brennan in oral argument probed this basis. Interview with Emerson, 1967; see text accompanying Chapter Eight, notes 65-66 and 76 *infra*.

[76] Interview with Emerson, 1967; interview with Clark, 1962, who presented the state's case to the court.

[77] Five possible "legislative purposes" were cited by appellants for attack: (1) dangers to health or life; (2) population control; (3) to restrict sexual intercourse to the propagation of (legitimate) children; (4) to promote public morals by preventing the use of extrinsic contraceptive aids; (5) to discourage extramarital relations. Brief for Appellants, p. 25, Griswold v. Connecticut, 381 U.S. 479 (1965). See State v. Nelson, 126 Conn. 412, 425, 11 A.2d 856, 862 (1940).

tive approach to the role of the court and the process of constitutional decision-making. While this may appear to be a harsh criticism of Justice Black, an early leader in formulating the new egalitarian jurisprudence, his perspective on the process of legal change seems to warrant this evaluation. The concern of the justice is understandable; like the courts in Massachusetts and Connecticut, he fears a relapse to the pre-New Deal days when the court stood as a super-legislature passing on the wisdom of the legislatively fashioned policy.

> My point is that there is no provision of the Constitution which either expressly or impliedly vests power in this court to sit as a supervisory agency over acts of a duly constituted legislative body and set aside their laws because of the court's belief that the legislative policies are unreasonable, unwise, arbitrary, capricious or irrational. The adoption of such a loose, flexible, uncontrolled standard for holding laws unconstitutional, if ever it is achieved, will amount to a great unconstitutional shift of power to the courts which I believe and am constrained to say will be bad for the country.[78]

It is questionable, however, that Justice Black's analogy to the pre-New Deal era is really appropriate in this instance. While the courts have recognized a broad range of legislative discretion in fashioning economic regulations, when vital personal rights are infringed the legislative enactment has been subjected to a much closer scrutiny.[79] Thus,

[78] 381 U.S. at 520–21. Justice Black also comments: "While I completely subscribe to the holding of Marbury v. Madison, I Cranch 137, and subsequent cases, that our court has constitutional power to strike down statutes, state or federal, that violate commands of the Federal Constitution, I do not believe that we are granted power by the Due Process Clause or any other constitutional provisions to measure constitutionality by our belief that legislation is arbitrary, capricious or unreasonable, or accomplishes no justifiable purpose, or is offensive to our own notions of 'civilized standards of conduct.' Such an appraisal of the wisdom of legislation is an attribute of the power to make laws, not of the power to interpret them." *Ibid.,* 513. See Charles A. Reich, "Mr. Justice Black and the Living Constitution," *Harvard Law Review,* LXXVI (Feb., 1963), 673, 754.

[79] On judicial reviews of economic regulations see, e.g., Dandridge v. Williams, 397 U.S. 471 (1970); Two Guys from Harrison—Allentown, Inc. v. McGinley, 366 U.S. 582 (1961); McGowan v. Maryland, 366 U.S. 420 (1961); Morey v. Dowd, 354 U.S. 457 (1957); Williamson v. Lee Optical Co., 348 U.S. 483 (1955); Giboney v. Empire Storage Co., 366 U.S. 490 (1949); Lincoln Union v. Northwestern Co., 335 U.S. 525 (1949); Goesaert v. Cleary, 335 U.S. 464 (1948); Kotch v. Board of River Port Pilot Commission, 330 U.S. 552 (1947); Olsen v. Nebraska, 313 U.S. 236 (1941). An excellent summary of the standard used in business-regulation cases is contained in Lindsley v. Natural Carbonic Gas Co., 220 U.S. 61, 78 (1911). See Dienes, "To Feed the Hungry," 591–625; Comment, "Developments in the Law—Equal Protection," *Harvard Law Review,* LXXXII (Mar., 1969), 1076–87.

Justice Douglas utilized this differential standard in *Griswold* when he declared: "We do not sit as a super-legislature to determine the wisdom, need and propriety of laws that touch economic problems, business affairs, or social conditions. This law, however, operates directly on the intimate relation of husband and wife...."[80] When fundamental human interests are involved, the state cannot succeed merely by demonstrating a rational relationship between the statute and a state interest. Rather, the state must demonstrate a compelling interest; the regulation must be subjected to "closer scrutiny" to determine if it is necessary to achieve a permissible state objective; or, as Justice White put it in *Griswold*, the state "bears a substantial burden of justification when burdened under the Fourteenth Amendment."[81]

The different approach utilized by the courts in cases involving personal, individual liberties reflects in part the judicial sensitivity to the importance of the interests involved. It is highly questionable for a political system which purports to exalt human values to treat alleged violations of these interests in the same manner as challenges to the validity of ordinary economic controls. If we do purport to follow a hierarchy of values, our legal policy must be fashioned in such a way as to reflect these differences. The elevation of human values over economic values in constitutional adjudication is a logical manifestation of this principle. To blandly throw basic human needs and aspirations into the same mix as business and industrial concerns goes far to vindicate the accusations of those critics of our system who claim we have distorted value priorities. For the courts to abdicate their responsibility to protect scrupulously these basic human needs, while other institutions of government are increasingly perceived as being closed to reform, is to invite chaos.

Closely related to this justification for special treatment of "human-rights" cases is the special need of the inarticulate, disadvantaged minori-

---

[80] 381 U.S. at 482. Levy v. Louisiana, 391 U.S. 68, 71 (1968), similarly, involved the "intimate, familial relationship between a child and his own mother," which demanded the special protection of the court. See Loving v. Virginia, 388 U.S. 1, 12 (1966); Griswold v. Connecticut, 381 U.S. 479 (1965); McLaughlin v. Florida, 379 U.S. 184 (1964); Prince v. Massachusetts, 321 U.S. 158 (1964); Skinner v. Oklahoma, 315 U.S. 535 (1942); Pierce v. Society of Sisters, 268 U.S. 510, 534-35 (1925).

[81] 381 U.S. at 503. Justice Goldberg also relied on this doctrine in his concurring opinion in *Griswold*, 381 U.S. at 497: "Where fundamental personal liberties are involved, they may not be abridged by the states simply on a showing that a regulatory statute has some rational relationship to the effectuation of a proper state purpose." It must be "necessary, and not merely rationally related, to the accomplishment of a permissible state policy." McLaughlin v. Florida, 379 U.S. 184, 196 (1964). See Poe v. Ullman, 367 U.S. 497, 554 (1961) (Harlan, J., dissenting).

ties often involved for political representation. Harrington noted: "It is one of the cruelest ironies of social life in advanced countries that the dispossessed at the bottom of society are unable to speak for themselves.... as a group, they are atomized. They have no face; they have no voice."[82] Whereas regular access to the system can be secured by aggregated, articulate groupings, the poor and minorities generally are especially dependent on a meaningful judicial response. It is precisely this dependency that has moved the courts to extend special protection to "insular minorities."

> For these groups are not always assured of a full and fair hearing through the ordinary political processes, not so much because of the chance of outright bias, but because of the abiding danger that the power structure—a term which need carry no disparaging or abusive overtones—may incline to pay little heed to even the deserving interests of a politically voiceless and invisible minority. These considerations impel a closer judicial surveillance and review of administrative judgments adversely affecting racial minorities, and the poor, than would otherwise be necessary.[83]

Finally, the special scrutiny employed for laws affecting personal human liberties has reflected an assessment by the court of its competence vis-à-vis the legislature to decide complex social, economic, technical issues as opposed to those involving basic human freedoms guaranteed by the Constitution. Whereas legislatures usually have the capability for marshaling the intelligence necessary for effective policy formulation in the former area, the courts generally possess a greater insulation and the capacity for commitment to long-range principles vital to the preservation of personal guarantees. As has been noted: "Knowledge about civil and individual right, unlike some economic data, is neither so technical nor so esoteric as to lie beyond the legitimate cognizance of the court."[84]

It is clear, nevertheless, that the heart of Black's dissent and judicial

---

[82] Michael Harrington, *The Other America* (Baltimore, 1962), 13.

[83] Hobson v. Hansen, 269 F. Supp. at 507-8 (D.D.C. 1967). The need for special judicial protection of "insular minorities" was suggested by Justice Stone in United States v. Carolene Products Co., 304 U.S. 144, 152n4 (1938). This rationale is most applicable when strict scrutiny is invoked in equal-protection adjudication when the classifying trait is "suspect," e.g. race, alienage, nationality. See Dienes, "To Feed the Hungry," 600-604.

[84] Joseph Tussman and Jacobus Tenbroek, "The Equal Protection of the Laws," *California Law Review*, XXXVII (Sept., 1949), 341, 373.

restraint generally lies in concern for the proper institutional role of the courts in the legal system. In order to assure against transgression on the prerogatives of the other legal actor, the judicial decision-maker must limit himself to the specifics of the Constitution. For Justice Black, due process is not a catchall but receives its meaning solely from the Bill of Rights, i.e. *total incorporation,* and only by those guarantees specifically provided. The court, he argues, lacks the machinery to determine "fundamental rights"; it has no Gallup poll.[85] Privacy is a "broad, abstract and ambiguous" word not specifically guaranteed: "I like my privacy as well as the next one, but I am nevertheless compelled to admit that government has the right to invade it unless prohibited by some specific constitutional guarantee."[86] Justice Black has been in the forefront of civil-rights jurisprudence because of his view of the guaranteed rights, not because he has a flexible approach to the judicial function or the process of constitutional decision-making.

But if the Black perspective, also reflective of Justice Stewart's dissent, lends a definitiveness to the court's exercise of its review power, it lacks creative adjustment to social change. Justice Black specifically addresses himself to this problem:

> I realize that many good and able men have eloquently spoken and written, sometimes in rhapsodical strains, about the duty of this Court to keep the Constitution in tune with the times. The idea is that the Constitution must be changed from time to time and that this Court is charged with a duty to make those changes. For myself, I must with all deference reject that philosophy. The Constitution makers knew the need for change and provided for it. Amendments suggested by the peoples' elected representatives can be submitted to the people or their selected agents for ratification. That method of change was good for our fathers, and being somewhat old-fashioned I must add it is good enough for me.[87]

It is difficult to believe that Justice Black really believes constitutional adjustment to our rapidly changing environment could effectively be handled through the cumbersome and time-consuming amendment process. In any case, creative legal adjustment would appear to be severely

---

[85] 381 U.S. at 519. Justice Black adds: "And the scientific miracles of this age have not yet produced a gadget which the court can use to determine what traditions are rooted in the (collective) conscience of our people."
[86] *Ibid.,* 510.
[87] *Ibid.,* 522.

hampered by such a perspective on the constitutional decision-making process. Creative legal change would appear to require a recognition of the flexibility of legal concepts and their capacity for growth.

The judicial behavior in *Griswold*, then, reflects the importance of the judge's role orientation in influencing his decision-making. All of the justices were agreed that "this is an uncommonly silly law,"[88] and the personal reactions of the majority may have played a part in their determinations. Indeed, some of the commentary by the justices on marriage and the family clearly manifests deep value predispositions.[89] But at best this would appear to constitute only a partial explanation of the decisional behavior. Equally as important were the justices' perspectives on the role of the courts in the legal system and the character of constitutional decision-making. While Justice Douglas, like Justice Black, expressed concern lest the court regress to its pre–New Deal days, he nevertheless believed that the court must approach civil-liberties claims in a different manner than economic questions.[90] Justice Harlan, a student of Justice Frankfurter and a noted advocate of restraint, specifically rejected a personal interpretation approach to the constitutional task but recognized that such an approach was possible even with Justice Black's specifics approach. On self-restraint in dealing with due-process issues he noted: "It will be achieved in this area, as in other constitutional areas, only by a continual insistence upon respect for the teachings of history, solid recognition of the basic values that underlie our society, and wise appreciation of the great roles that the doctrines of federalism and separation of powers have played in establishing and preserving American freedoms."[91] Members of the majority did not merely concur in the result but framed their decision according to the considerations which they felt were vital. While the dissent may not have accepted the social policy behind the Connecticut laws, they felt constrained by their understanding of the judicial function and the character of constitutional decision-making.

Nor should we ignore the effects of the changing social environment on the court. Although no member of the majority specifically cited the

[88] *Ibid.*, 525 (Stewart, J., dissenting).

[89] Justice Douglas, for example, expresses his conception of the marital relationship: "Marriage is a coming together for better or for worse, hopefully enduring, and intimate to the degree of being sacred. It is an association that promotes a way of life, not causes; a harmony in living, not political faiths; a bilateral loyalty, not commercial or social projects. Yet it is an association for as noble a purpose as any involved in our prior decisions." *Ibid.*, 486.

[90] *Ibid.*, 481–82. See text accompanying note 80 *supra*.

[91] *Ibid.*, 501.

nonlegal data provided in the intelligence state (the nonlegal data in *Brown v. Board of Education* had received only a footnote), this information would lend support to their approach. It would be impossible for them to be unaware of the tremendous changes in social values and practices regarding birth control or the activist position increasingly being assumed by government in this area.[92] While we can only speculate, continual references in the opinions to social behavior and values tend to lend credence to a belief that social variables played a vital role in the judicial decision process.

Insofar as *Griswold* affected the status of birth-control legislation nationally, the decision could be read very narrowly. Since marital privacy served as the focus for review rather than some broader constitutional guarantee urged by disseminators of family-planning services, the decision might apply only to the *use* statute of Connecticut and only to married persons. On the other hand, the spirit and language of the decision appear far more pervasive. Although the court did not say there was a right to contraceptive information or to distribute such information, proponents of such a view, as will be discussed in Chapter Eight, could use the opinion for support.[93] Like so many judicial actions, the court merely dealt with the immediate issue, but at the same time forged new tools for constitutional review and suggested possible lines for further constitutional development. To the extent that the court acts in this manner, the judicial actor is not merely responding to the social situation, but is also influencing it.

[92] Interview with Mrs. Nancy Wechsler, attorney with the firm of Greenbaum, Wolff & Ernst, New York, May 17, 1967. Mrs. Wechsler, who participated in the writing of the Planned Parenthood *amicus* brief, believes its function in *Griswold* was primarily supportive.
[93] See the discussion of the cases generated by the revised Massachusetts statute in Chapter Eight *infra*. See generally Harriet F. Pilpel, "Birth Control and a New Birth of Freedom," *Ohio State Law Journal*, XXVII (Fall, 1966), 688, who presents a thought-provoking analysis of the potential impact of *Griswold*: "As pointed out above, Griswold established the right of voluntarism in family planning. The establishment of this right was a significant achievement, but what does the right mean to those who have no access to the information or supplies which make birth control possible? Unless the government recognizes an obligation to provide birth control information and supplies where needed, the right of voluntarism will be meaningless to many citizens." See Comments, "Privacy after Griswold: Constitutional or Natural Law Rights," *Northwestern University Law Review*, LX (Jan.-Feb., 1966), 828-33.

Seven

Modern Revisionist Efforts: Legislative Abstention and Response

Perhaps the greatest strength of the legislature as a creative instrument for legal change is its ability to bargain and compromise conflicting interests and to fashion an appropriate remedy. While there is wide discretion in judicial fashioning of policy, its primary effect will be to recognize certain interests and to deny others. The legislature, on the other hand, can seek to formulate a policy acceptable to all contending parties—negotiation and accommodation are hallmarks of the legislative process. We have already noted the potential scope of the legislative fact-finding inquiry that makes such a creative fashioning of policy possible. If the interests can be brought to the legislative arena—and the difficulties in this process have been noted—the legislative mode of adjusting interests appears to support the potential of law as a creative instrument for managed social change.

Another phase of the creative ability of the legislature is the scope of the social problem that can be encompassed in its policy. While a court is generally limited to a case-by-case fashioning of policy, the legislature can seek to reach all facets of the problem.[1] When the legal system

[1] Gelhorn, "The Legislative and Administrative Response," 100, notes: "Moreover, the legislature has the advantage of being able to attack a many-sided problem on all its sides at once. Often it fails to do so, either because of lack of forethought or because what Lon Fuller calls the polycentric nature of the problem causes the sides to shift about so quickly that even the most nimble legislature cannot keep up with the shiftings. At any rate, the legislature, unlike a court, need not be dependent upon the fortitudes of litigation to bring issues within its reach." Llewellyn, *The Bramble Bush*, 76–77, also recognizes this scope of statutory coverage: "But statutes are made relatively in the large, to cover wider sweeps and looking forward. They

Legislative Abstention and Response : 185

deals with complex social or economic change presenting a wide range of legal issues, this legislative resource is vitally important. Such a policy decision, although not a final legal settlement, can provide the general contours for handling the social problem as well as an impetus to the further fashioning of policy by nonlegal and other legal policy-makers. The competing social interests need not be left in a complete limbo of uncertainty as to their legal status.

Equally as important as the form of legislative settlement and the scope of the problem that can be dealt with by statute is the range of tools through which the legislature can implement its policy determinations. Unlike the judiciary, whose range of choice seems more restricted, the only real limitation on legislative policy formation appears to be constitutional restrictions and political and social realities. Legislation may be permissive, prohibitory, or regulatory. It can carry affirmative or negative sanctions or can merely be an expression of policy. Through the use of licensing, taxing, report requirements, the legislature may not only make an immediate determination on a policy issue, but can seek to provide for its subsequent implementation. Special agencies can be created to maintain a continuing surveillance.[2] A statute may provide for the government itself to perform a desired behavior or it may seek to induce others to perform it by persuasion or the offer of reward or assistance. While these are only a sampling of the tools the legislature has for creative law-making, it is suggestive of the ability of the legislature to fashion the remedy to the situation.

It should be noted, however, that "the situation" refers not only to the need generated by social change, but also to the political, personal, and institutional factors discussed above. Regulation may be preferable to permissive legislation not because continued regulation is necessary, but because certain elements salient to the legislator may have to be appeased. The stringency of a sanction may reflect not only a desire to prohibit a practice but to express the appropriate degree of contempt. Again, there seems to be a paucity of empirical evidence bearing on such behavior but there is no reason to believe that these influences

---

apply only to events and transactions occurring after they have come into force; that element of caution disappears. They represent not single disputes, but whole classes of disputes. They are political not judicial in their nature, represent readjustment along the lines of balance of power, decide not single cases by a tiny shift of rule, but the rearrangement of a great mass of clashing interests."

[2] See the dissent of Justice Brandeis in International News Services v. Associated Press, 248 U.S. 214, 264–67 (1918), who comments on this wider range of tools available to the legislature.

cease to be operative at this phase in the performance of the prescriptive function.

The *Griswold* case might not have been necessary if the legislative policy-makers had utilized their capabilities for creatively responding to the change demands and the altered social environment. Whereas the Supreme Court could respond only by declaring the Connecticut statute unconstitutional, thereby leaving Connecticut "wide open" without any legal controls directly relating to dissemination of contraceptives, the legislature could consider "desirable" and "undesirable" practices— considered regulation would be a viable alternative to either free license or prohibition. Further, the competing interests seeking protection of the public morality and those stressing individual freedom of and opportunity for choice in family planning could be compromised to reflect the vital concerns of each. Instead, the legislature had followed the path of non-action. Even as the Supreme Court was assuming responsibility in *Griswold*, legislators in the various forums hesitated and stumbled. Nevertheless, legislative revision would at last be realized.

CONSISTENT IF NOT CREATIVE:
THE CONNECTICUT LEGISLATURE ABSTAINS

Each session of the Connecticut legislature since the 1920s had witnessed an attempt for revision of the laws by the Planned Parenthood League and its allies with unvarying frustration and defeat. The Senate bulwark, with its entrenched Catholic power, had remained steadfast against the birth-control demands. In fact, pro-change forces apparently had little hope of altering this pattern, but, as has been consistently noted, an appeal to the legal system served as an educative device for the public, a forum for articulating the increasing acceptability of birth-control practices, a vehicle for articulating disgust at the intransigence of the status quo interests. Further, judicial behavior could have repercussions on behavior in the legislative arena.

Indeed, it might have been hoped that the failure to secure reform from the courts in *Poe* or the sweeping affirmative action of the U.S. Supreme Court in *Griswold* would produce some deviation in the legislative pattern. But for those who harbored such optimism, the Connecticut legislature would provide little comfort.[3]

[3] 1961: H.B. 3741, a bill to exempt "persons married to each other," sponsored by the ACLU, was withdrawn in favor of H.B. 3753, an outright repeal bill. Hearings

Prior to the 1960s the anti-change presentation to the legislative actors had been skillfully organized by Joseph Cooney, who had continually marshaled medical, religious, and economic evidence providing some objective basis for rejection of the change demand. But in 1961 the opposition was represented solely through a letter from the Catholic hierarchy expressing its continued opposition to the proposed reform and noting the pending judicial determination: "Pending the judicial decision of the Supreme Court of Errors, it would not be necessary, and it may not be advisable, in effect, to argue the case before the legislative branch of government."[4] Here was a direct appeal for legislative deference to the judicial policy-maker. Given the primary responsibility of the legislature for effectuating change in the policy it has formulated, continued judicial acquiescence, and the need for carefully managed change, such a deferential approach would seem of dubious propriety. But it did offer a viable approach for the legislator wishing to avoid potential political risks of decision-making. While pro-change interests continued to press their moral, religious, medical, social, and economic arguments, although with much less assiduity than in earlier campaigns,[5] abstention remained a viable alternative to action.

In 1961 legislative determination to avoid decision was plainly evident. In spite of a favorable House committee report on the bill, it was never debated on the floor and died with legislative adjournment. In 1963, with the judicial response in *Poe* forming part of the legislative input, the House did pass the bill in spite of numerous abstentions. But the Senate again rejected the invitation to act by killing the bill in committee; structural impediments to effectuating change in birth-control policy had again been utilized to defeat the reform appeal.

The 1963 legislative behavior appears to reflect the same motivational considerations discussed above. In the 1961 abstention, however, the legislature could have been avoiding decision in expectation of a ju-

---

were held but the committee failed to vote on the bill prior to adjournment.

1963: H.B. 3790, a repeal bill, was introduced. Hearings were held in the House, a favorable report was given, and the House passed the measure 149–66 with 79 abstentions. The chairman of the Senate committee announced that the bill would be considered in committee; the bill died without coming to a vote.

1965: H.B. 2462, a repeal bill, and H.B. 3028, regarding sterilization, were introduced. H.B. 2462 received a favorable report of the House Committee on Public Health and Safety on May 12, 1965. The Senate, considering the bill after *Griswold*, killed it.

[4] See "Birth Control Law Opponents Dominate Hearing," *Hartford Times*, Apr., 21, 1963; "Birth Control under Fire in 24th Assembly Repeal Try," *New Haven Register*, Apr. 12, 1963.

[5] Interview with Miss Roraback, 1967; interview with Cooney, 1967.

188 : Law, Politics, and Birth Control

dicial determination.[6] With the failure of the courts to assume responsibility for dealing with change demands in *Poe*, the legislature was denied this convenient basis for avoiding decision. Its refusal to act reflects the motivational impediments to effectuating change through the legislative forum. In fact, even after *Griswold*, the Connecticut legislature refused to enact a repeal bill; nor was any more limited policy fashioned.

CONGRESS: A BREACH IN OUR COMSTOCK HERITAGE

One Package had fashioned an exemption to the federal birth-control prohibitions for scientific and medical purposes, and generally opened the channels of interstate commerce to dissemination of birth-control information and materials. Judicial action had not, however, abrogated the laws, nor, prior to 1970, had any action of Congress. In spite of the social acceptance of birth control, the federal Comstock statutes drafted in 1873 remained on the books. Although not regularly enforced, they continued as a symbol of a negative public policy which had ceased to exist. The cause of a creative legal order was hardly being served by the maintenance of antiquated, seldom-enforced statutes, nor was it wise to provide administrative officials with a constant opportunity to harass individuals and businesses dealing in contraceptives. While there has been a recent furor over the safety of oral contraceptives, regulations do exist to control the quality of birth-control devices.[7] In any case, such concern would not justify the prohibitive policy embodied in the Comstock laws. In the light of the active role presently being played by the federal government in assuring wider availability of contraceptive services (discussed in Chapter Nine), the negative legal policy represented by the law increasingly emerged as an anomaly. The decision of the Supreme Court in *Griswold v. Connecticut* also suggested the disparity of the statutory policy with the present value system. Interests given recognition in that decision are ill

---

[6] Interview with Miss Roraback, 1967; see Emerson, "Nine Justices in Search of a Doctrine," 219*n*2.

[7] See U.S. Congress, Senate, Small Business Subcommittee on Monopoly of the Committee on Banking and Currency, *Hearings* [on Oral Contraceptives], 91st Cong., 2nd Sess., 1970; "The Pros and Cons of the Pill," *Time*, May 2, 1969, pp. 58–59; "The Pill on Trial," *Time*, Jan. 26, 1970, pp. 60–62. Gallup polls reflect a deepening concern about the safety of oral contraceptives with 46 percent in January, 1970, expressing the belief that "the pill" is not safe, and 32 percent unsure.

served by the maintenance of the antiquated legal norms, and *Griswold* could be perceived as still another input suggesting the necessity for a legislative re-examination of our restrictive statutory policy. Nevertheless, there was little concentrated social pressure exerted to have the laws revised or removed.

In 1966 Representative James H. Scheuer of New York introduced H.R. 8440, "to remove the prohibitions against importing, transporting and mailing in the U.S. mails, articles for the prevention of conception, and advertisements with respect to such articles," and H.R. 8451, "to eliminate the prohibition against the importation of drugs, medicine and other articles for the prevention of conception"; both bills would merely have eliminated the offensive language from the respective statutes.[8] The immediate impetus for the legislative action appears to have been the behavior of a customs officer in requiring a woman to dispose of her diaphragm before entering the country. This was, in fact, only one in a series of incidents where postal authorities suppressed, or threatened to suppress, the mailing of nonprescription contraceptive materials.[9] The potential for administrative abuse from the maintenance of broad, sweeping prohibitions, even after judicial amendment, is a major impediment to the viability of a rational legal system.

H.R. 8440 was sent to the House Judiciary Committee and H.R. 8451 went to the House Committee on Ways and Means. Since it was considered "minor" legislation, formal hearings were not held. However, testimony dealing with the "Population Crisis" given before the Subcommittee on Foreign Aid Expenditures of the Senate Committee on Government Operations, chaired by Senator Gruening, had provided ample background information for policy formation.[10] Further, various governmental departments sent letters to the committee chairman,

---

[8] The information on the history of the revision of the federal laws, unless otherwise indicated, was provided in a letter from Representative James H. Scheuer to the author; a personal interview with then Representative George Bush, Houston, Tex., May 22, 1970; and telephone interviews with Mr. Jerome Koenig (May 19, 1970) and Mr. Gordon Kerr (Feb. 15, 1971), members of Representative Scheuer's staff.

[9] Mr. Koenig noted that a number of pharmaceutical companies dealing in contraceptives, especially those dealing in nonprescription devices (e.g. vending-machine sales), have had mail shipments seized by the Post Office Department. Interview, 1970. See generally Amicus Brief, 16a–18a.

[10] U.S. Congress, Senate, Subcommittee on Foreign Aid Expenditures of the Committee on Government Operations, *Hearings on S. 1676, Population Crisis*, 89th Cong., 1st Sess., 1965 (hereafter cited as *1965 Hearings*); ibid., 89th Cong., 2nd Sess., 1966 (hereafter cited as *1966 Hearings*); ibid., 90th Cong., 1st Sess., 1967 (hereafter cited as *1967 Hearings*).

either endorsing the proposals or assuming a neutral position,[11] and organizations supporting repeal provided still another source of data. No formal opposition to the repeal measures emerged. Nevertheless, the 1966 proposal was to fail.

As Representative Scheuer's staff had anticipated, the Judiciary Committee proved an insurmountable obstacle. The committee chairman, Representative Emanuel Celler, who has no deep affection for Representative Scheuer, sent the bill to a hostile subcommittee, headed by Representative Feighan of Ohio (a state having a number of Catholics), where it died. It was hoped, however, that the House Ways and Means Committee might be willing to accommodate the proposed revision. But the bill was minor legislation requiring unanimous consent for a favorable report. When Representative Burke of Boston objected, the battle was lost.

In the next term only one repeal bill was submitted, covering both the mailing and tariff provisions. It went to the House Ways and Means Committee, which was still deemed the more favorable forum. At the request of the Post Office Department it was amended to continue the prohibition against the mailing of unsolicited contraceptives (except to doctors, nurses, hospitals, clinics, etc.), which was to be handled as a regulatory matter rather than through the obscenity statutes.[12] Again, however, the bill died in committee when, for some undetermined reason, Representative Martha W. Griffiths of Michigan objected.

On January 27, 1969, Representative Scheuer, joined by Representative George Bush of Texas (subsequently our UN ambassador), introduced H.R. 4605, which would remove the mailing and tariff prohibitions; Senator Tydings of Maryland introduced S. 1537, a companion bill, in the Senate. The Scheuer-Bush proposal was sent to Ways and Means and S. 1537 went to the Senate Finance Committee. The willingness of Representative Bush, a strong advocate of family-planning legislation, to co-sponsor (a strategy made possible by recent revisions in

---

[11] Copies of these replies sent to the chairmen of the House committee were obtained from Representative Scheuer. Undersecretary Wilbur J. Cohen of the Department of Health, Education and Welfare said that "there is no reason, in this enlightened era, why . . . (contraceptive) importation, transportation, and mailing should be prohibited and denounced in the Code as associated with the immoral and obscene." The U.S. Tariff Commission suggested that the statute might not be consonant with constitutional policy as stated in Griswold v. Connecticut. General Counsel Robert E. Giles suggested the statutory situation was being reviewed by the executive branch.

[12] This would amend 39 U.S.C. 4001, dealing with the seizure and disposal of nonmailable matter.

Legislative Abstention and Response : 191

the House rules) was of vital importance since he was a member of the House Ways and Means Committee. Having a member of the designated committee with a personal stake in the legislation fervidly urging action on the measure—especially since committee members' bills are given special consideration on "members' day"—is extremely valuable in overcoming legislative inertia.

One obstacle, however, arose as a result of the changeover in administration. The postal department urged that unsolicited advertisements for contraceptives, as well as the aforementioned contraceptive materials themselves, be retained (with the exception of doctors, clinics, etc.) in the postal laws. This apparently would not include solicitation for business in magazines to which the individual subscribes. The primary effect of the provision would be to continue the power of the postal department to seize unsolicited material dealing with contraception, thereby inhibiting competition in nonprescription contraceptives. While there may be some question regarding the constitutionality of such seizure, in light of the First Amendment guarantees and the *Griswold* decision, the Supreme Court has recently given approval to limited postal controls on unsolicited obscenity.[13]

In any case, the bill, amended to meet Post Office objectives, was favorably reported. It then had to face the obstacle of the House unanimous-consent calendar for minor legislation. However, the fact that it came to the floor favorably reported by the House Ways and Means Committee, chaired by the extremely influential Wilbur Mills, gave the bill added impetus. On June 22, 1970, it passed the House by unanimous consent; on December 18, after making technical adjustments required by the postal reorganization act, the Senate concurred; on December 22, 1970, the House accepted the Senate amendments; and President Nixon signed Public Law 91–662 on January 8, 1971.[14] Finally, nearly a hundred years after its passage, the essential federal Comstock provisions regarding contraception were removed from the statute books.

As the above discussion indicates, institutional factors have played a vital part in preventing earlier repeal of the federal Comstock laws regarding contraception. Classed as minor legislation, it has been forced

[13] Rowan v. United States Post Office Department, 90 S. Ct. 1484 (1970), recognizes the ability of the Post Office, upon complaint of the recipient, to prevent further mailings of material which the recipient finds to be "erotically arousing or sexually provocative."

[14] Public Law 91–662, 84 Stat. 1973 (1971), is set forth in *U.S. Code Congressional and Administrative News* (Jan. 15, 1971), 8012–14.

to overcome obstacles, including unfavorable committees, the requirement of unanimous consent, the power of committee and subcommittee chairmen. Support from a committee member with a personal stake in the outcome and the status of the reporting committee, on the other hand, provided impetus for action. Structural impediments took on added importance in this instance, possibly because of religious influences (although there is no apparent institutional opposition), certainly because of time pressures imposed by legislation deemed more critical and by the timidity and inertia which continually plague "sex-liberalization" proposals. The lack of felt need for effective congressional action, given increased impetus by prior court rulings mitigating the effect of the prohibitions, coupled with increased interest in publicly supported family planning, had their effect. Former Senator Tydings, in a letter to the author dated April 22, 1970, commented on these impediments to effective action.

> The principal reason Congress has failed to act on legislation introduced to amend the Tariff Act of 1930 to remove the prohibitions on the importation of contraceptives is best understood in the context of legislative priorities. The principal focus of those of us interested in population in Congress has been the enactment of a comprehensive family planning bill. For such a measure, if enacted, would provide family planning services for the roughly 5 million women in this country who currently cannot afford them, and would also allocate substantially more money for much needed contraceptive research.
>
> Since the provisions of the Tariff Act of 1930 prohibiting the importation of contraceptives has been rendered fully ineffective by "court rulings," the feeling among my colleagues has been that this is simply not a matter on which legislative efforts ought to be concentrated at this time when more important matters are at issue. My guess is that Congress will get around to removing this measure from the law books after some of the fundamental legislation in the family planning field has been enacted.

Given the changes that have taken place in the family-planning activity of government, in Roman Catholicism and religion generally, in medical practice, and in social values and attitudes, there seems to be no justification for such legislative inertia. To permit the postal department officials and customs inspectors to exercise broad discretion in seizing and suppressing materials under antiquated penal provisions is of dubious propriety. Indeed, the delay in removing these remnants of

Comstockery, which contradict actual government policy toward contraception (discussed in Chapter Nine), seriously challenges any perspective of law as a creative influence in social change.

NEW YORK: THE LEGISLATURE RESPONDS

As a result of the liberal application of the Comstock statute by the New York courts and the absence of any real attempt to resurrect the legal prohibitions, no major effort had been launched in New York to secure legal revision prior to the 1960s. The policy fashioned by the judiciary and actual social behavior had become the governing policy. But in the mid-1960s conditions suggested the need for a renewed effort to secure legislative revision or repeal of the statutory norms. The principal motivating factor for such a re-examination was the developing concern over publicly supported birth control. Although this subject will be discussed in detail in Chapter Nine, we might note the nature of the problem. While the general populace had no difficulty obtaining birth-control services, the poor, who relied on public facilities for medical care, were often denied the means to control effectively the incidence of birth, in spite of the *Sanger* exception.

> Whatever the justification for these laws may have been in the 1880's they are totally obsolete and irrelevant today—in the context of medical practice, socio-economic realities, and public opinion of the 1960's. In effect, the New York statutes are discriminatory. They penalize our poorer families.
>
> The limitation that physicians prescribe contraceptives only for "the cure and prevention of disease" has created two standards of medical practice. It is well known that the physician prescribing contraceptives in his private practice applies the widest possible interpretation to "health and disease." On the other hand, the physician treating the poorer patient in public hospitals or public health services, under the closer security of the law, will often use a much narrower interpretation. Furthermore, the prohibition of section 1142 to disseminate contraceptive information has been interpreted by some as prohibiting referrals to family planning services.[15]

[15] "Memorandum in Support of Senate Intro. 3980 by Senator Thompson and Senator Metcalf" (from the files of Planned Parenthood–World Population, PP-WP). See testimony of Harriet F. Pilpel before the Commission on Penal Law Revision, Nov. 24, 1964 (from the files of PP-WP).

The state welfare board had already approved family-planning services for married public-aid recipients and consideration was being given to assisting the unmarried. However, a number of local public officials were challenging the spread of publicly supported birth control and were using the Comstock laws to question the legality of the new welfare policies.[16] In addition, a number of the public-health agencies were concerned over the permissible scope of activities—there was an archaic cloud over the entire issue. Coupled with the opposition of the Catholic Church to the new welfare family-planning programs, an effective obstacle was clearly present.

In 1964 a unique opportunity for recommending change in the laws arose when the Bartlett Commission began formulating proposals for revision of the New York Penal Code. A number of organizations came forward recommending repeal of sections 1461 and 1465 (the contraceptive provisions) and it appeared that the commission might well accede to the demand. Political expediency, however, resulted in a study bill which would have transferred the two provisions from the Penal Code to the public-health law.[17]

In March, 1965, with the support of a number of social organizations pressing for change, three bills were introduced in the Assembly and two bills entered the Senate hopper;[18] on April 5, 1965, S. 3980, the Thompson-Metcalf bill, joined the other proposals in the Senate Codes Committee. Although there were no public hearings, a major campaign was launched as part of the intelligence function to influence and inform the legislature of the need for change. Evidence indicating the alterations in social, medical, and religious attitudes and values was made available; a special representative of the pro-change groups, with prior lobbying experience, acted as liaison with the legislative actors. Personal contacts were made, letter-writing campaigns promoted, organizational endorsements secured. The Planned Parenthood Association,

---

[16] See "Old Law Imperils Birth Control Aid," *New York Times*, Feb. 21, 1965, p. 1, col. 5; "Birth Control Aid Assailed Up State," *New York Times*, Feb. 27, 1965, p. 26, col. 5.

[17] "Memorandum from Beekman H. Pool to Messrs. Brown, Ibery, McMahon," Jan. 12, 1965 (from the files of PP-WP); letter from Harriet F. Pilpel to Frederick Jaffe, Nov. 9, 1964 (from the files of PP-WP).

[18] A. 5292, introduced Mar. 23, 1965, by Assemblyman Browne, and S. 2331, introduced Mar. 31, 1965, by Senator Warner, deleted "for the prevention of conception" from the statute. All other bills sought to repeal sections 1142 and 1145: A. 3959, introduced Mar. 3, 1965, by Assemblyman Sutton; A. 5558, introduced Mar. 23, 1965, by Assemblyman Manley; S. 2863, introduced Mar. 10, 1965, by Senator Thompson.

although barred from direct lobbying because of its tax status, nevertheless lent its full support to the campaigners. Generally the undertaking was well organized and effective, providing adequate information for any interested legislator. The movement had become far more experienced in the intelligence function and strategy of influence than its earlier days in Albany, but for a time it appeared to have all been for naught. One by one the bills were killed in committee, and Assemblyman Bartlett indicated that it would be fruitless to press for any new proposals.[19]

While one can only speculate about the motivations for the committee action, the primary reason would seem to be Catholic opposition. Charles Tobin, representative of the New York State Catholic Welfare Committee, the voice of the Catholic bishops of New York, had indicated that the hierarchy opposed the suggested change. It was feared that elimination of the restrictions would promote immorality, especially among the young.[20] Catholic opposition also reflected its concern over the expanding family-planning activities of welfare agencies; removal of the prohibitions, it was argued, contributed to the development of a contraceptive mentality. An additional motivation could be found in the expectations of the Catholic community. While Catholic opinion had undergone substantial alteration, significant elements still believed the Church was under an obligation to oppose this "public immorality." Finally, the chairmen of both codes committees and approximately one-third of the membership of each of the committees were Catholic, and personal value systems may well have come into play. But whatever the explanation for the religious opposition, it seems probable that it played a major part in the defeat of the repeal measures. Although the Church was no longer perceived as a monolithic entity, it was still a powerful force to be considered.[21]

Failure of the initial repeal legislation, however, did not preclude the possibility of obtaining a liberalization of the law. And the intervention of Mayor Wagner of New York City may have played a vital role in

[19] "Albany Kills Bill to Repeal Law against Birth Control," *New York Times*, May 6, 1965, p. 1, col. 2. A *New York Times* editorial, "Our 1881 Legislature in 1965," May 11, 1965, p. 38, col. 1, was extremely critical of this "political" decision.
[20] Interview with Charles Tobin, representative of the New York State Catholic Welfare Committee, Albany, May 19, 1967.
[21] Frederick Jaffe, vice-president of Planned Parenthood–World Population, suggested that the 1959 public birth-control controversy in New York City (see p. 266 *infra*) had revealed the possibility of overcoming Catholic resistance. It could be viewed as the opening battle of the repeal effort. Interview with Jaffe, New York, May 15, 1967.

achieving this objective. A delegation of citizens visited him shortly after defeat of most of the repeal bills and secured his agreement to discuss the matter with legislative leaders.[22] Shortly thereafter a series of amendments transformed S. 3980 from absolute repeal legislation into a more limited form of statutory amendment. References to the "prevention of conception" were to be deleted from section 1142 of the Penal Code and the following provision was added to the public-health law: "The sale or distribution of any instrument or article or any recipe, drug or medicine for the prevention of conception, is authorized only by a duly licensed pharmacy and such sale or distribution to a minor under the age of sixteen years is prohibited. An advertisement or display of said articles, within or without the premises of such pharmacy is hereby prohibited."[23] The bill passed the Senate by a vote of 40–14 and the Assembly by a vote of 85–50.

We come then to the problem of motivations and the obvious question arises: What effect did the Catholic Church's opposition have on the final vote? A simple tabulation based on the probable religious affiliation of the legislators[24] suggests the effect may have been considerable (see Tables 7 and 8). Using a chi-square test, probable religious affiliation proved statistically significant at the .01 level of confidence for both roll-call votes. But, as previously noted, such a result may well reflect the combined influence of the Church's position, the legislator's personal value system, and the religious values of his constituency.

The competing interests generally agree that the Catholic Welfare Committee did not really bring its full power to bear on the birth-control issue.[25] While Charles Tobin, the committee's legislative rep-

[22] Interview with Mrs. Carita Bersohn, consultant for Public Programs, Planned Parenthood–World Population, New York, May 15, 1967; letter to the author from Beekman H. Pool, director of the Legislative Information Service, State Communities Aid Association, July 18, 1967; Gordon E. Brown, executive director of the State Charities Aid Association, "Report on Meeting with Mayor Wagner, Concerning Repeal of Sections 1142 and 1145 of the Penal Law," May 3, 1965 (from the files of the State Communities Aid Association, formerly State Charities Aid Association).
[23] Senate Intro. 3980, print 4421, 5404, 5690, 5787.
[24] Religious affiliation was determined by organizational membership and educational background.
[25] Interview with Jaffe, 1967; interview with Tobin, 1967. On the other hand, Catholic opposition defeated a 1963 repeal attempt on Minnesota. "A Study Is Urged of Birth Control," *New York Times*, Jan. 24, 1965, p. 55, col. 1. Planned Parenthood–World Population, *Just Delete Six Words and a Comma* . . . (New York, 1965), 1, a report on the revision effort, notes that "although it is easy to say that most of these laws can be left on the books and interpreted administratively, our experience was a closed door policy from public health and welfare officials."

TABLE 7. Relation of Probable Religious Affiliation[a] to Voting Behavior on S. 3980 in 1965 New York Senate[b]

	Catholic	Non-Catholic
Percent Legislators Voting "Yes"	37.5 (6)	89.5 (34)
Percent Legislators Voting "No"	62.5 (10)	10.5 (4)
Number of Cases	(16)	(38)

[a] Based on background data from *The New York Red Book*, 1965–66 (Albany, 1965), 570–97.
[b] Only those who voted are included.

TABLE 8. Relation of Probable Religious Affiliation[a] to Voting Behavior on S. 3980 in 1965 New York Assembly[b]

	Catholic	Non-Catholic
Percent Legislators Voting "Yes"	24.1 (13)	88.9 (72)
Percent Legislators Voting "No"	75.9 (41)	11.1 (9)
Number of Cases	(54)	(81)

[a] Based on background data from *The New York Red Book*, 1965–66 (Albany, 1965), 570–97.
[b] Only those who voted are included.

resentative, did circulate a memorandum explaining the basis for opposition, no real campaign was organized in contrast to the Church's response to an abortion-liberalization bill that had been introduced in the New York legislature. This lack of any real reaction suggests the changing values within Catholicism (i.e., the differing attitudes concerning sex practices and the proper role of the Church in civil society). Indeed, there was even a Catholic group among the organizations endorsing change. But whatever the explanation, the Catholic opposition of the 1960s differed markedly from that of the formative years of the birth-control movement.

The personal value system of the legislators also appears to have been a vital element in the voting behavior. The character of the approved amendment reflects legislative fears concerning public morality, especially among the young. As one legislator explained: "It's necessary to maintain certain moral standards for effective community thinking. Any society without moral standards is going to fall." Since anyone who wanted contraceptives could get them, why make it public?—"all you do is impress it on youth before he reaches an age where he is ready to evaluate it."[26] Some legislators conjured up visions of street-corner

[26] Interview with Municipal Judge Joseph Corso, former chairman of the New

selling and vending machines permitting the young to purchase prophylactics freely.[27] While the legislators interviewed frequently argued that their religious norms were not determinative of their behavior, that the legislator had no right to impose his moral views on others, it seems impossible that they could ever divorce themselves completely from deeply imbedded moral predispositions. A legislator socialized in Catholicism with its defined moral values will most likely be influenced in his response to issues such as birth control.

Unfortunately, data on the possible influence of the religious affiliation of the constituency on voting behavior is not available. Based on the findings in Massachusetts and Connecticut, however, there is every reason to believe that this element may have played an important role, especially when it supported other negative religious and moral influences.

Although the motivations favorable to change were discussed above, a summary provided by the sponsors of S. 3980 suggests the myriad influences at work.

1. To remove the aura of illegality from the concept of family planning which has been culturally accepted for decades and which is endorsed as a beneficial medical measure.
2. To recognize today's socio-economic realities by lifting the ban on contraceptive devices, which now are labeled "indecent articles."
3. To remove a legal anachronism—one of the Comstock Laws of 1881—that makes technical "criminals" of millions of New Yorkers.
4. To help wipe out the discrimination against the poor who must depend on public or private aid. The well-to-do can decide whether or not to use contraceptives, but the poor do not have this choice as long as professional persons are confused or inhibited by the presence of this legal relic.
5. Also, while family planning has a basic medical aspect, it is unrealistic in 1965 to limit contraceptive devices to "preven-

York State Assembly Codes Committee, Brooklyn, May 17, 1967. This same approach was evident in an interview with Thomas Duffy, former chairman of the New York State Senate Codes Committee, Queens, May 17, 1967.

[27] This fear was augmented by the arrest of William Baird, who drove a van around the New York area distributing contraceptives. The New York charge was dismissed on passage of the 1965 legislation even though the statutory change would not seem to negate the charges against him. Baird has been arrested in both New Jersey and Massachusetts for violation of the birth-control norms. See text accompanying Chapter Nine, notes 2–5 *infra*.

tion or cure of disease" only—no matter how broadly this provision is construed.
6. The Temporary State Commission on Revision of the Penal Law and Criminal Code (the Bartlett Commission) recommended deleting these provisions from the Penal Law.[28]

Even though total repeal was not achieved, the motivations for liberalization do seem to reflect these considerations. Minimal church opposition, widespread acceptance of the desirability of greater availability of birth-control services, and community support for the bill evidenced by the numerous endorsements in policy statements and letters provided strong motivation for legislative policy change.

Another influential factor, of special importance to the present study, lies in the aforementioned Supreme Court decision in *Griswold v. Connecticut*. While interviews revealed wide differences of opinion regarding its impact, newspaper commentary and statements by some of the legislators on the proposed revision reflected much of the "privacy" orientation provided by the decision.[29] Its psychological effects probably aided pro-change interests by lending greater support for their efforts. Further, there almost certainly would have been an impediment to a favorable legislative outcome if the court had decided to legitimize the Connecticut norms. An interactive effect may take many forms—legitimizing policy by the court could have lent support to the status quo interests. Instead, its strong language regarding the value of privacy and marital rights strengthened the argument for legal change.

In any case, legal revision had been employed to remove barriers to further social and legal change. Moreover, the safeguards inserted into the act compromised opposing interests, accommodating those concerned with the uncontrolled, haphazard spread of conception control while providing only minimal impediments of a nonpenal character to legitimate commerce in birth-control information and services. Generally, the resolution of New York birth-control policy suggests the potential for a creative use of the legal process.

[28] "Memorandum in Support of Senate Intro. 3980."
[29] Assemblyman Metcalf, for example, stated that the bill was designed to "set up a private right, one that should not be interfered with by law." He specifically noted the Supreme Court decision. "State Bill Gains in Birth Control," *New York Times*, June 15, 1965, p. 32, col. 3. Assemblywoman Constance E. Cook stated: "We seem to have recognized that here is an area of private morality where the Legislative frankly has no business. We are telling the people: 'The responsibility is yours. Take it and see that it is properly handled.'" "Legislature Voids Birth Control Ban in Effect 84 Years," *New York Times*, June 17, 1965, p. 1, col. 4.

MASSACHUSETTS: DELAY BUT REVISION

Revision of the Massachusetts laws is in process as these words are being written. As will be discussed in the next chapter, the U.S. Supreme Court even now awaits argument on a case challenging the validity of the state laws. But the legal provisions which the court will review will not be exactly those fashioned by the nineteenth-century Puritan legislature. Not only have the courts altered the formal law and actual social behavior, the law in action, but the Massachusetts legislature in the mid-1960s also drafted an amendment to the legal norms.

Recommendation for legal change was again to come from external sources. At a 1964 World Affairs Council symposium in Boston, a number of key individuals, including Catholic leaders, reached an informal consensus concerning the need for some revision of the birth-control laws. Pursuant to this willingness to explore the possibility for change, an article appeared in the *New England Journal of Medicine*[30] written by a young Catholic doctor, calling for united action free from the interference of old antagonisms. Of course, in Massachusetts, changes in moral-legal norms could not be effectuated without consideration of the position of the Catholic Church. But as the article suggested, the Church might adopt a neutral position. Cardinal Cushing of Boston had written the author a letter in which he noted: "In no way will I feel it my duty to oppose amendment to the law." In addition, the article carried a foreword by Rt. Rev. Msgr. Francis J. Lally, editor of the archdiocesan newspaper *The Pilot*, endorsing study aimed at revision.[31] The strategy for recommending legal alteration had been laid. Although some members of the birth-control movement still wanted to fight an anti-Catholic campaign, the more moderate faction prevailed. In December, 1964, Drs. Reid and Rutstein, acting through Representative Dukakis, introduced H. 1401, designed to legalize dissemination of contraceptives by doctors and pharmacists as well as the furnishing of information about where such preventatives could be obtained.[32]

---

[30] Joseph L. Dorsey, "Changing Attitudes toward the Massachusetts Birth Control Law," *New England Journal of Medicine*, CCLXXI (Oct. 15, 1964), 823–27. See PPLM, "Bill H-1401: Before and After the Hearing," *Planned Parenthood News*, Spring, 1965, p. 4.

[31] Dorsey, "Changing Attitudes," 823. Msgr. Lally suggested that "most people in the community . . . feel . . . that the time is ripe for reconsidering the question in the light of the claims of a plural society."

[32] H. 1401 would have added the following section: "The provisions of sections twenty and twenty-one shall not apply to the furnishing by a registered pharmacist

The changes wrought by time were clearly evident in the character of the intelligence function. At the hearings before the Joint Committee on Public Health, legislators no longer trooped in to announce their opposition to and disgust for the proposal; the proceedings were conducted in a relatively calm atmosphere compared to the carnival aspect of past hearings; harassing tactics, although present, were minimal. New social interests were also apparent—the presence of NAACP and Urban League representatives, as well as spokesmen from other social agencies, manifested the changes that had taken place in the pro-change coalition. Testimony now emphasized freedom of conscience and the need for tolerance in a pluralistic community, although the physicians, lawyers and religious leaders continued to discuss the medical, legal, and moral aspects of the issue.

But all of this evidence was offset by the testimony of Henry Leen, representative of Cardinal Cushing. The cardinal had been a leader in the campaign for a strong declaration on religious liberty at Vatican II and frequently had indicated his appreciation of the demands of pluralism. His statement concerning revision of the laws reflected this liberal orientation. While affirming the traditional Catholic position on the immorality of birth control, he asserted that the demands of public morality are not coextensive with private morality. "In the present case, especially in the light of the position taken by other religious groups in our plural society, it does not seem reasonable to me to forbid by civil law a practice that can be considered a matter of private morality."[33] Although his reaction exemplifies the ecumenical spirit, the cardinal nevertheless advocated rejection of H. 1401. The bill, he argued, did not provide adequate safeguards for the public morality, especially for the young. Instead, he advocated the creation of a broadly based study commission to fashion a proposal "to satisfy the conscientious opinions of the whole community."[34] Once this statement was

---

of drugs or articles intended for the prevention of pregnancy or conception; nor to the furnishing of information as to where such drugs or articles may be legally obtained." See PPLM, "The Time Has Come—a bill Is Filed in Mass.," *Planned Parenthood News*, Winter, 1965, p. 1; Irene Saint, "How and Why Mass. Birth Control Law Is Likely to Be Amended," *Boston Sunday Herald*, Jan. 31, 1965, p. 5.

[33] *Transcript of the Hearing on House Bill No. 1401 before the Public Health Committee*, Boston, Mar. 2, 1965, p. 19 (from the files of PPLM). For the views of Cardinal Cushing see his introduction to Dorothy Bromley's *Catholics and Birth Control: Contemporary Views on Doctrine* (New York, 1965).

[34] *Hearing on 1401*, 20. There is evidence that the reformists, organized as the Committee to Support H. 1401, had advance notice that the cardinal might oppose the bill as premature. Nevertheless, they felt that the campaign would be extremely

made, the hearings became meaningless with respect to the final result. The next day the committee voted unanimously to recommend the creation of a study commission, and shortly thereafter Governor Volpe proceeded to name a twenty-one-member panel.

H. 4089, the bill produced by the commission, was given public airing before the Joint Committee on Public Health, although the actual purposes of these deliberations seemed to be the clarification of the Church's position rather than an evaluation of the merits of the proposal. Mr. Leen, testifying in behalf of the bill as a private citizen, declared that the cardinal had no additional comments. This statement left the position of the Church authorities in grave doubt. The confusion was intensified by the fact that the three abstentions from the study commission's report were all Catholics, including Bishop Riley and Rt. Rev. Msgr. Lally. Apparently many individuals, including legislators, believed this reflected Church opposition.[35] Nevertheless, the bill passed the legislative committee by a vote of 13–3. When it reached the House, however, the debate brought back unpleasant memories of earlier campaigns. Charges were made of murder, violation of God's law—all of the old invective that had seemingly been eliminated. The bill was defeated by vote of 119–97.[36]

In analyzing the legislative behavior, we can again refer initially to party affiliation. While the tabular results reveal the breakdown of earlier sharp party cleavages, the Democratic party still reflected the opposition orientation (see Table 9). And, once more, the party variable appears to have been surface manifestation of deeper values and commitments. The Catholic value orientation found expression in the negative Democratic position on the measure. While there was, in this

---

educational and there was reason to hope that some satisfactory revision might be developed. PPLM, "An Evaluation of H. 1401 and the Hearing," Mar. 10, 1965 (from the files of PPLM).

[35] See Rt. Rev. George W. Casey, "Implications of the Death of the Massachusetts Birth Control Bill," *Boston Sunday Herald*, Aug. 8, 1965, sec. 4, p. 3. In a letter from Representative Joseph E. Brett to Mr. and Mrs. Harry A. Sweetes, Aug. 10, 1965 (from the files of PPLM), the legislator notes that "two monsignors of the Church, directly responsible to the Cardinal declined to vote on the matter, thus indicating their disapproval." It should be noted, however, that *The Pilot*, July 3, 1965 (from the files of PPLM), editorially stated that "Catholic legislators certainly have no obligation to oppose a change in the law and should work for a law that protects freedom of conscience for all the people."

[36] On the 1965 campaign see generally Joseph L. Dorsey, "Massachusetts Liberalizes Birth Control Law," *Dartmouth Medical School Quarterly*, III (Summer, 1966), 9–10.

TABLE 9. Relation of Party Affiliation to Voting Behavior on H. 4089 in 1965 Massachusetts House[a]

	Democrats	Republicans
Percent Legislators Voting "Yes"	25 (37)	89 (65)
Percent Legislators Voting "No"	75 (111)	11 (8)
Number of Cases	(148)	(73)

[a] Only those who voted are included.
SOURCE: Massachusetts, *Journal of the House, 1965*; Massachusetts, *Manual of the General Court, 1965*.

instance, no organized Church opposition, it has been suggested that parish priests with hostile attitudes toward the revision effort exerted some influence on legislative behavior (often the views of the local priest can be a more vital religious influence than the official position of the Church hierarchy). In many cases, it would have been politically impossible for a legislator to vote for legal change.[37]

It might be noted, however, that a great part of Catholic legislative opposition was not born of hostility toward *any* legal revision, as in the past. Rather, the Catholic value system demanded a far more limited bill than was offered in 1965. Safeguards that many Catholic legislators felt were essential to the protection of *public* morality, e.g., against indiscriminate pharmaceutical sales, vending-machine sales, and street-corner sales of contraceptives, providing services to the unmarried, widespread public advertising of the merits of contraceptives and the denigration of the statutory abortion provisions, had not been provided. While many of the above fears might have been groundless, the absence of a carefully coordinated campaign by the pro-change elements, perhaps reflecting overconfidence, failed to reveal and confront these lingering doubts. A lobbyist was employed, but little pressure was brought to bear; no strategy of influence was formulated and pursued. Although the mass media, major organized interests, and probably the greater part of the public supported some revision, the reformists failed to maximize their advantage.[38]

[37] See Casey, "Implications." A roll-call analysis relating the percentage of Catholics in the constituency to voting behavior similar to that provided for the 1942 and 1948 legislative campaigns was not possible since the religious census was terminated in 1936. Later studies only provide data on religious makeup of counties. Since the basic political units in Massachusetts are towns and cities, this appeared to be too gross a measure.

[38] Interview with Edward J. Collins, former legislative coordinator of the Massachusetts Public Health Association, Chicago, Apr. 7, 1967.

Among reformists the immediate reaction to the 1965 legislative defeat was shock. There was support for trying the alternative route of access to the legal system by developing a test case, especially since *Griswold* had suggested that the court might entertain such an action. But the court's decision had rested so heavily on the rights of the married couple violated by a "use" statute that *Griswold*, while indicative of a line of argument for challenging the narrower restrictive Massachusetts legislation, was not really determinative. In addition, a number of PPLM leaders were convinced that legislative redress was still the most effective source of change.[39] If favorable response was to be generated, however, a number of defects in the 1965 recommendation activity would require correction.

An initial step toward this objective was taken by having the recommending function performed primarily by legislative actors. It was believed that a proposal fashioned in part by their colleagues would invoke a more favorable response from legislators. Nine representatives joined in a coalition sponsoring H. 2965. Although the timing was questionable (it was an election year when controversial issues tend to be avoided whenever possible), the coalition was convinced of the possibility of success.[40] The proposed revision was designed to satisfy the objections which had apparently generated much of the 1965 negative reaction: pharmacists would be permitted to provide contraceptives only with a doctor's prescription; restrictions on advertising were specifically retained and vending-machine sales were prohibited; only a private, nonprofit, or public-health or welfare agency could furnish information regarding the source of contraceptive services.

But the most significant alteration in the 1966 effort appeared to involve the manner in which the strategy of influence was performed for both the intelligence and prescriptive functions. Edward J. Collins, a Catholic, was selected legislative coordinator of the Massachusetts Public Health Association (MPHA) which would head the reform drive. He concentrated primarily on sixty legislators whom he viewed as "switchables"—they had voted against change in 1965, but might be

---

[39] Interview with Dr. Joseph L. Dorsey, New Haven, May 22, 1967. In fact, the attorneys for National Planned Parenthood–World Population were requested to prepare a legal memorandum outlining the argument for a test case if it should become necessary. "Preliminary Memorandum of Law re Unconstitutionality of Massachusetts Birth Control Statutes," Oct. 18, 1965 (from the files of PPLM).

[40] Interviews with Representatives Kathrine Kane and Theodore Mann, Boston, May 25, 1967. See James McGlincy, "A New Challenge Is Sounded against Birth Control Law," *Boston Sunday Herald*, Mar. 6, 1966, sec. 4, p. 3; PPLM, "Massachusetts Tries Again!!," *Planned Parenthood News*, Winter, 1966, p. 1.

susceptible to influence. Although information was provided to all members of the General Court, these "targets" were given additional treatment. Among the MPHA handouts was massive quotation of local and national Catholic clerics suggestive of the change in Catholic perspectives since the 1940s. Another example of the impact of Collins's activity was a petition circulated among Massachusetts colleges favoring revision, signed by 500 faculty members, including 200 from Catholic colleges.[41]

The hearings before the Joint Public Health Committee on April 12, 1966, mirrored the 1965 proceedings with one exception: in this instance the cardinal merely reiterated his views on the proper relation of public and private morality and expressed his confidence that the legislature would fashion an acceptable policy. In order to obtain maximum visibility for the hearings, reform elements arranged to have them televised. Unlike the 1965 campaign, they were maximizing their advantages. The committee reported the bill favorably with only one dissenting vote.

In the General Court every effort was made to control the course of the legislative deliberations; the external efforts of Collins were designed to complement the internal activity of the coalition, especially Representatives Kathrine Kane and Theodore Mann. Attention to structural variables in studying legislative behavior has tended to focus primarily on the impact of rules of procedure and organization. Another institutional variable that may have an important bearing on legislative decision, however, is the character of the informal groupings which develop. The legislature is not a group of discrete bodies moving in space; it is composed of cliques and personal friendship ties which can influence behavior. A legislator "is part of the informal structure of the legislative group and is affected by the norms of these informal groups in his own decision-making behavior."[42]

The actual effect of these formal alignments is nevertheless difficult to assess. In many cases they may merely reinforce existing party, state, or regional groupings. It has been suggested, for example, that the greatest number of contacts occur within the majority party and members tend to give a high degree of support to legislation proposed by their friends.[43] However, when party and length of service are held constant, friendship decisions apparently account only for a small percentage of

---

[41] Interview with Collins, 1967.
[42] Wahlke et al., *The Legislative System*, 218.
[43] Garland C. Routt, "Interpersonal Relationship and the Legislative Process," *Annals*, CXCV (Jan., 1939), 129–36.

voting behavior.[44] Nevertheless, where other variables are not especially salient, friendship alliances may explain some otherwise inexplicable voting behavior.

In any case, the insiders in the Massachusetts legislature employed personal contacts while Collins made sure that external constituency pressure would be present. The leaders of the two houses, for example, both of whom had expressed some opposition to the proposed change, were contacted by faculty members of their alma mater. During floor debate the opposition appeared to be reduced to the extremist elements (e.g., Representative Ianello's remark that the legislature should wait for "a green light or a red light from Rome") primarily because the more responsible opposition members had agreed to remain silent. Nevertheless, the House did insist on imposing additional safeguards in the proposal, limiting it to married women and allowing only a limited range of activity to practicing physicians, public-health agencies, registered nurses, and hospital health clinics. The House approved the amended bill 136–80 and shortly thereafter the Senate concurred 29–11. When Governor Volpe signed the act on May 19, 1966, Massachusetts had finally experienced at least a formal modification of its Comstock laws.[45] A new section, 21A, had been fashioned to embody exceptions to sections 20 and 21, which, however, remained as vague and sweeping as they were originally intended. (See Appendix D for the revised text.) The basis for further legal challenge was being laid even as the law was revised.

Motivations for change or adherence to the status quo in the legislative action again appear to have been varied. A questionnaire sent by the author to the "switchers," while not producing responses adequate for definite conclusions, nevertheless suggests that a primary motivation for revision was the altered character of the proposal through the inclusion of safeguards, thus making it more acceptable to legislators concerned with health and the public morality.[46] Coupled with non-opposition from the Catholic hierarchy, the primary obstacles to change had been overcome. It is generally agreed that legal revision would

[44] Wahlke et al., *The Legislative System*, 234–35.
[45] See Appendix D for the text of the revised law. See generally Dorsey, "Massachusetts Liberalizes Birth Control Laws," 10–11.
[46] For example, an interview with Representative Donald Manning, Boston, May 25, 1967, indicated his deep moral reservations concerning a wide-open bill. The limitation to married women was an essential amendment for his vote. Indeed, based on questionnaire and interview responses, it seems that this was an essential item for many of the Catholic legislators.

have been impossible if Cardinal Cushing had actively opposed legal change. The strength of the Catholic Church had not disappeared in the years since the referendums of the 1940s, but its approach to moral-legal questions had been considerably altered.

Naturally, for some legislators any change was unacceptable. Either personal values or the political dangers of "voting for" birth control predetermined their behavior. In fact, reform lobbyists generally avoided any attempt to influence these legislators; time and energy were directed instead at the "switchables." The character of these untouchables is suggested by the continuing effect of the party-affiliation vector (see Table 10).

While opposition to repeal was still embodied in the values and interests represented by the Catholic, urban Democrat, the Democratic party itself was split. Whereas the Republican party in the 1940s had divided on the birth-control issue, in the modern legislature the Democratic party experienced the cleavages. Conversations with some of the legislators revealed their extreme difficulty in relating to the effects of the changes in Catholicism. The Catholic, socialized according to a particular value system, is undergoing severe strains as his Church adjusts to modern conditions and the Catholic legislator suffers these same stresses.[47] Even if his personal value system accepts the revision, the legislator from the Catholic constituency must still consider the extent to which the changes have permeated his district. And even hierarchical support of revision may be insufficient if the legislator's personal values or those of his district or local parish priest have not made the transition. The divisiveness within the Protestant community which characterized the early years of the birth-control movement is now being experienced by Catholicism. While the Church possesses an organization and hierarchical authority without parallel in the Protestant community, it is by no means the monolithic structure some have contended.

One other possible motivation must be mentioned, i.e., the effect of the *Griswold* decision. While there was wide difference of opinion in Massachusetts over the impact of the court's decision, it was generally agreed—even assuming that it did not directly affect the vote—that it

[47] This stress was clearly evident in an interview with Representative Paul J. Cavenaugh, Boston, May 25, 1967. He voted against the bill because he couldn't give up the moral tenets he had always known. Sex was becoming only a physical act; thirteen-year-old kids were getting the pill in Baltimore. Even if the law had no real inhibiting effect, "the change is another affirmative step toward condoning promiscuity." He admitted that his vote was a personal moral decision which he often had difficulty in justifying.

TABLE 10. Relation of Party Affiliation to Voting Behavior on H. 2965 in 1966 Massachusetts General Court[a]

	HOUSE OF REPRESENTATIVES[b]		SENATE	
	Democrats	Republicans	Democrats	Republicans
Percent Legislators Supporting Bill	50.9 (78)	92.1 (58)	59.3 (16)	100 (13)
Percent Legislators Opposing Bill	49.1 (75)	7.9 (5)	40.7 (11)	0 (0)
Number of Cases	(153)	(63)	(27)	(13)

[a] Only legislators who voted are included.
[b] House vote no. 134 on a motion for reconsideration was received as the decisive vote.
SOURCE: Massachusetts, *Journal of the House, 1966*; Massachusetts, *Journal of the Senate, 1966*; Massachusetts, *Manual of the General Court, 1941.*

was relevant that Massachusetts remained the only state with effective prohibitive laws. This isolation may have had a profound psychological impact, especially coupled with the growing tax-supported family-planning activity. Further, as was noted above, an opinion by the Supreme Court legitimizing the Connecticut statute might well have produced a profound negative impact. The court's decision, then, probably contributed some support and added justification for legislators, and, as suggested in the next chapter, helped define the content of the proposed revision. But it clearly was not the dominant motivational force. In any case, the legislature had acted and the stage was set for still further action in the implementation and review of the legislative work product.

Eight

Modern Revisionist Effort: A Judicial Epilogue

The legislative revision of the Massachusetts laws had been far from a total rejection of the Comstock legacy. Sections 20 and 21, embodying the sweeping prohibitions against contraception, remained intact. The added section (21A) did provide for increased legitimate availability of contraceptives *under medical supervision* but limited this exception to assistance of married persons. Indeed, the legislative work product could be perceived as a minimal response to a very narrow reading of *Griswold*. In fact, this is precisely the approach taken by the courts that have reviewed the 1966 amendment. Each court approached the amendment as a direct revision of the law to conform to the Supreme Court mandate.[1] While the previous analysis of this legislative action indicates that a number of other forces were at work and that the judicial reading is probably an oversimplification of the legislative behavior, it does indicate the judicial perception of the process involved. The legislature had revised its legal norms in response to judicial action and the courts were now being called upon to review the legislative work product. Action and reaction, challenge and response, the interplay of legal institutions in fashioning policy once more emerges as vital reality.

NOTE: A more comprehensive analysis of the legal issues discussed in this chapter is provided by C. Thomas Dienes, "The Progeny of Comstockery—Birth Control Laws Return to Court," *American University Law Review*, XXI (Sept., 1971), 44-123.

[1] Baird v. Eisenstadt, 429 F.2d 1398, 1401 (1st Cir. 1970); Baird v. Eisenstadt, 310 F. Supp. 951, 956 (D. Mass. 1970); Commonwealth v. Baird, 355 Mass. 746, 247 N.E.2d 574, 576 (1969).

Recommendation for change in the law came from William R. Baird, a thirty-four-year-old zealot of the birth-control movement.[2] On April 6, 1967, pursuant to an invitation, Baird addressed approximately 2,000 students in Hayden Auditorium at Boston University on the relative merits and limitations of various birth-control devices. During the speech he employed diagrams, exhibited some of the contraceptives being discussed, and criticized the legal prohibitions. Following the address, Baird told the students to "come on up to the stage and get some devices," and he personally handed a package of Emko vaginal foam to a coed. At this point, officers from the vice squad intervened, told him to "wind it up," and took him (accompanied by an ACLU attorney) to police headquarters, where he was charged with violating section 21 by exhibiting and giving away articles for the prevention of conception.

This was not, in fact, Baird's first encounter with the Comstock legacy. In New York he had driven around in a van, stopping occasionally to discuss and demonstrate various birth-control devices.[3] When he was arrested, it appeared that there would finally be further challenge to the prohibitions remaining in the New York statutes following the *Sanger* decision. But legislative revision of the statute thwarted Baird's martyrdom, and he was forced to settle for an appointment as a consultant on birth-control problems to the New York state legislature and an invitation to participate in Harvard University's distinguished-lecturer series. In New Jersey he was again arrested when he took his van to Freehold, displayed his wares, and explained their use. This time he was more successful in securing a judicial hearing. The New Jersey Supreme Court, while not invalidating the state birth-control law, did find Baird's conduct was not "without just cause" as required by the statute.[4] The character of the court's opinion leaves little substance to the prohibitions, but the norms do remain on the books, potentially inhibiting behavior and serving as a symbolic expression of a value system out of harmony with present-day realities.

It is clear, then, that Baird was not merely the unwitting victim of oppressive laws. On every occasion he was engaging in the recom-

---

[2] Although accounts of the facts of the case tend to vary, the material was derived from the opinions and briefs in the cases cited in note 1 *supra*; A. Goldberg, "Perils of the Pill," *Ramparts Magazine*, VII (May, 1969), 45–46; and articles appearing in the *New York Times*, Apr. 7, 1967, p. 14, col. 7, and the *Boston Globe*, Apr. 8, 1967, p. 6.

[3] See Goldberg, "Perils of the Pill"; also text accompanying Chapter Seven, note 27 *supra*.

[4] State v. Baird, 50 N.J. 376, 235 A.2d 673 (1967).

mendation function; he was seeking to fashion a test case. In New Jersey he telephoned local police to inform them of his intent to break the "archaic laws" and invited arrest. In his Boston speech Baird frequently noted that he was breaking the law and wished to be arrested. At the conclusion he yelled: "If the good police don't step forward and arrest me, they're not acting responsibly."[5]

The judges passing on Baird's convictions were extremely critical of these tactics, noting the availability of an alternative legal remedy, i.e. declaratory judgment. But as the Supreme Court of Massachusetts suggested, Baird was most likely addressing his challenge not only to the courts but to the public generally. Like Margaret Sanger, Baird almost certainly saw criminal prosecution not only as an opportunity to test the laws but as a vehicle for achieving public notoriety. Whether his purpose was to dramatize his cause and educate the public or to seek personal publicity for himself is unknown and immaterial; the criminal process was again being used as a platform for reaching the public.

In all fairness to Baird, it should be noted that challenges to the birth-control laws via the declaratory-judgment route have not proven very successful (e.g. *Poe*). In fact, even as Baird's case was being processed through the courts, a declaratory-judgment action brought by physicians failed to overturn the laws. In *Sturgis v. Attorney General*, Justice Reardon of the Massachusetts Supreme Court rejected the plaintiff's arguments that the prohibitions against serving the unmarried violated the physician's due-process right to practice his profession, and that the limitations regarding access to contraceptives denied equal protection of the laws to the poor.[6] Instead, the laws were found to serve as a rational means for the state to protect the public health and morals. Indeed, Justice Reardon directly told the plaintiffs that the proper forum for their appeal was the General Court (i.e. the state legislature) and not the courts.[7] Whether this lack of success experienced in using the declaratory-judgment route to challenge the birth-control laws is

---

[5] *Boston Globe*, Apr. 8, 1967, p. 6. On the New Jersey arrest see 235 A.2d at 674.

[6] Sturgis v. Attorney General, ———Mass.———, 260 N.E.2d 687 (1970). The litigation was a direct result of the decision of the Massachusetts Supreme Court in *Commonwealth v. Baird*. Since the *Baird* Court had validated the laws on medical grounds (see text accompanying note 23 *infra*), this declaratory-judgment action argued that the laws permitting the physician to use his medical skills only for his married patients limited the ability of a physician to practice his profession in violation of the Fourteenth Amendment due-process guarantee and the Massachusetts Bill of Rights, articles 1, 10, and 12. The equal-protection argument will be discussed below. See text accompanying note 76 *infra*.

[7] 247 N.E.2d at 691.

only a matter of circumstance or whether it represents the inability of this mode of adjudication to dramatize sufficiently the need for judicial action to the same degree as a criminal conviction, resort to more successful avenues of attack is not very surprising.

In any case, Baird was to have his day in court and then some. The processing of his case affords still further evidence of the myriad avenues for recommending change through the judicial system. As might be expected, Baird was found guilty by the trial judge and the usual motions to dismiss were denied. Following an available Massachusetts procedure, however, the trial judge did not immediately impose sentence. Finding the questions of law doubtful and important, he reported the case directly to the Massachusetts Supreme Court. As will be noted below, although Baird was to obtain a partial victory in the higher court, his conviction was upheld by a 4–3 vote. His petition for certiorari was denied[8] and he was subsequently sentenced to three months' imprisonment. Nevertheless, this only began his trek through the courts. Baird now addressed his constitutional claims to the federal forum through a petition for a writ of habeas corpus. While the district court sustained the judgment of the Massachusetts Supreme Court by denying the petition, the Court of Appeals accepted Baird's challenge. The court held the Massachusetts statute violative of the U.S. Constitution and ordered the district court to grant the writ discharging Baird.

It is in this context that the Supreme Court has agreed to hear the case.[9] When Baird initially petitioned the court to intervene, he was asking for review of a conviction under a seldom-used statutory prohibition. He could not point to other convictions or widespread negative impact from the maintenance of the law. Indeed, *Griswold*, legislative reaction, and administrative desuetude gave promise of substantially mitigating any real negative effects remaining. While Baird's constitutional challenge was certainly substantial and important, given the court's work load and the very pressing national issues demanding its attention, its initial refusal to hear the case is hardly surprising and certainly not shocking. But when the Court of Appeals decision was handed down, the context was changed considerably. Not only had a state statute been declared unconstitutional and the requested review was by appeal rather than certiorari (i.e. allegedly mandatory), but the decision stood directly contrary to the previous decisions of the highest state court and a federal district court. In this context it would have been

[8] Baird v. Massachusetts, cert. denied 396 U.S. 1029 (1970).
[9] Eisenstadt v. Baird, prob. juris. noted 91 S.Ct. 921 (1971).

questionable to dismiss for want of a substantial federal question. In any case, Baird's recommendations for legal change will now be heard and acted upon by the U.S. Supreme Court.

At the intelligence stage, in addition to the briefs presented by the principle parties to the Supreme Court of Massachusetts, *amicus* briefs were filed by the Massachusetts Civil Liberties Union and Planned Parenthood League. Again there is evidence of the capacity of the judicial forum to accommodate argument from a variety of interests. Further, the increasing use of *amici* suggests the potential increased flow of information to the courts in the policy-formation process. Certainly there were a variety of alternatives available. The court could sustain the conviction and legitimize the statute; it could void the conviction for failure to satisfy the statutory requirements, thereby avoiding the more difficult underlying constitutional questions;[10] it might find the statute, or a particular provision thereof, unconstitutional *as applied* to the defendant and thereby avoid the broader challenges to the statute in its entirety (i.e., void on its face); or it might declare a particular provision or provisions of the statute or the entire statute unconstitutional. And the constitutional tools were readily available. In addition to challenges based on the Massachusetts Constitution, the various briefs in *Baird* (and *Sturgis*) offered challenge to the validity of the statutes based on free speech, the rights of privacy, substantive due process generally, vagueness, equal protection, and even cruel and unusual punishment.[11] In analyzing the primary issues, it is vital to reiterate again the dynamic character of constitutional decision-making. The Constitution is not a mass of simple rules to be mechanically applied to problems. It is organic

[10] The contention was made that the state had failed to introduce any evidence that Baird *intended* the contraceptives given away to be used to prevent conception, a necessary element of the offense. Compare Commonwealth v. Corbett, 307 Mass. 7, 29 N.E.2d 151 (1940), with Commonwealth v. Goldberg, 316 Mass. 563, 55 N.E.2d 951 (1944). See text accompanying Chapter Five, notes 13-18 *supra*. Given the fact that Baird was seeking to force a decision on the constitutionality of the Massachusetts statutes, it is difficult to understand why counsel offered the court this opportunity to evade constitutional decision. In any case, the court declined the invitation, holding that the nature of the item (Emko foam) and the plea in Baird's speech for use of contraceptives provided sufficient evidence of his unlawful purpose. 247 N.E.2d at 579.

[11] Baird had contended that the maximum penalty set by section 21, five years, violated the Eighth Amendment guarantee against cruel and unusual punishment. He noted that the penalty was grossly disproportionate to that provided for more serious offenses and to that provided for similar violations in twenty-three states. While the Massachusetts court evidenced clear discomfort over the sentencing scheme, it avoided the issue by noting that Baird had not yet been sentenced. 247 N.E.2d at 579. He was later sentenced to three months.

law, embodying broad principles capable of growth and change as the social context which it governs changes.

THE LIMITS OF FREE SPEECH

This perspective is clearly seen in the contention which served as the primary focus of the *amicus* briefs: that the statutory prohibitions against both exhibiting and giving away birth-control devices violated the guarantee of freedom of speech. From the initiation of the Comstock laws, serious question had been raised concerning the free-speech implications of the vague, sweeping prohibitions, and the vice hunter himself had vigorously undertaken to defend the laws against such criticism.[12] Although free-speech norms had not sufficiently developed during these early years to support effective legal challenge, modern doctrinal development asserting broad constitutional protection for speech interests offered real hope for a successful challenge.

But it may bewilder the reader how the guarantee of free speech has anything to do with exhibiting and/or distributing birth-control materials. On its face, the First Amendment would appear to be directed to verbal utterances, whereas the proscribed criminal activity involves *conduct*. Consider, however, the nature of saluting a flag, a silent prayer on your knees before a crucifix, applause after a theatrical presentation. Each instance is an expression of an idea, a belief, an opinion. Is it so difficult, then, to perceive the desecration of a flag, the burning of a draft card, the carrying of a picket sign, the wearing of a black armband to protest the Vietnam war, or the exhibition and distribution of contraceptives as symbolic expressions of ideas, opinions, beliefs? Increasingly, the courts have recognized that the mere labeling of certain actions as conduct instead of pure speech only begins, rather than ends, the First Amendment inquiry. "There is no doubt that, in connection with the pledge, the flag salute is a form of utterance. Symbolism is a primitive but effective way of communicating ideas. The use of an emblem or flag to symbolize some system, idea, institution, or personality is a short cut from mind to mind.... Symbols of State often convey political ideas just as religious symbols come to convey theological ones."[13]

The First Amendment *perceived functionally* does not extend only

---

[12] See Comstock, *Traps for the Young*, 226–30.
[13] West Virginia Bd. of Educ. v. Barnette, 319 U.S. 624, 632 (1943).

to words but affords some protection to such conduct as may be used to express and/or communicate ideas, beliefs, opinions. For individuals unskilled at verbal communication or seeking to communicate concerning complex subjects, symbolic acts may provide the only real form of speech available. For the politically disadvantaged, symbolic speech which draws the attention of the mass media may be the only effective means of communicating an idea to the public. Often words are totally inadequate to express the depth or importance of a belief; if the First Amendment is designed, at least in part, to achieve psychological satisfaction through expression, symbolic action may provide a viable alternative. As Marshall McLuhan cogently put it: "The medium is the message";[14] or, as some courts have recognized: "It may be that particular considerations surrounding a specific symbolic act justify clothing it in the concept of speech. Thus, picketing, like sit-ins, may be the poor man's printing press; similarly, the techniques of a 'silent and reproachful presence' may be the only means of true communication in certain areas of the civil rights struggle."[15]

But what of the anarchist who throws a bomb into a legislative chamber or assassinates a public official? Or what of the person who appears nude in public to express disdain for society's sex values; blacks who burn and loot in an outpouring of frustration; students who use rocks or more violent means to express antagonisms; or, on a different level, what of the student's use of long hair, beards, or disheveled clothing to manifest rejection of society's cultural values? All this conduct may well be expressing personal beliefs and opinions or even communicating ideas of importance to the public, but is it entitled to First Amendment status as speech? Unfortunately, the courts have not yet provided viable criteria for handling conduct partaking of speech interests. As Justice

---

[14] Marshall McLuhan, *Understanding Media: The Extensions of Man* (New York, 1964), 7.
[15] United States v. Miller, 367 F.2d 72, 79 (2d Cir. 1966). Compare Browne v. Louisiana, 383 U.S. 131, 141–42 (1966), and Thornhill v. Alabama, 310 U.S. 88 (1940), with Cox v. Louisiana, 379 U.S. 536, 555 (1965), where the court rejected the contention that the Constitution "afford[s] the same kind of freedom to those who would communicate ideas by conduct such as patrolling, marching, and picketing in streets and highways, as these amendments [First and Fourteenth] afford to those who communicate ideas by pure speech."
On the functions served by the free-speech guarantee and consideration of problems in light thereof see Thomas I. Emerson, *Towards a General Theory of the First Amendment* (New York, 1967); Dean Alfange, Jr., "Free Speech and Symbolic Conduct: The Draft-Card Burning Case," *Supreme Court Review: 1968,* ed. Philip Kurland (Chicago, 1968), 22–38; Note, "Symbolic Conduct," *Columbia Law Review,* LXVIII (June, 1968), 1105–26.

Harlan has noted: "The Court has, as yet, not established a test for determining at what point conduct becomes so intertwined with expression that it becomes necessary to weight the State's interest in proscribing conduct against the constitutionally protected interest in freedom of expression."[16]

Recognition of the fact that not all conduct is expressive or communicative has led to a variety of attempts to draw a line between conduct and speech. It has been suggested, for example, that the conduct must be intended as communication and capable of being recognized as communication.[17] Such an approach, however, would seem to exclude conduct intended only to express the personal feelings, ideas, beliefs of the individual—conduct may be solely a means of self-expression furthering the psychological well-being of the individual and not intended to convey a message to others. Further, the individual's expression of an idea, while it may have only minimal or even no social value when uttered, may over time, when joined with other ideas, produce social worth. On the other hand, by requiring a relational interest between a "speaker" and a "hearer," the suggested standard for identifying First Amendment speech does stress the primary emphasis of the guarantee—the free flow of ideas, beliefs, opinions in the marketplace of ideas. It recognizes "a profound national commitment to the principle that debate on public issues should be uninhibited, robust, and wide-open" even if the communication is "vehement, caustic and sometimes unpleasantly sharp."[18]

The difference is not really between speech and conduct but between speech or conduct that expresses and/or communicates ideas, beliefs, opinions and that which does not. Given a communicative interest, the activity is entitled to speech status in a regular First Amendment adjudication, and this, in turn, requires the showing by the state of a compelling interest in controlling the particular speech activity. Whether this judgment is framed in terms of a formula (e.g., the state must demonstrate a clear and present danger of lawless action if it seeks to proscribe advocacy of action) or a general balancing test of the state and speech interests, there must be a preference for speech interests. The central place of the First Amendment in our constitutional hierarchy, its essential role in democratic theory, its importance to the exer-

[16] Cowgill v. California, 396 U.S. 371 (1970).
[17] "Symbolic Conduct," 1109–17. The author of this note discusses some of the objectives raised in the text at p. 1110. See Louis Henkin, "Forward: On Drawing Lines," *Harvard Law Review*, LXXXII (Nov., 1968), 78–80.
[18] New York Times v. Sullivan, 376 U.S. 254, 270 (1964).

cise of all other constitutional guarantees, demands that purported state interests be carefully scrutinized and that only the most vital state interests, which cannot be satisfied in any other way less destructive of First Amendment values, be accepted as justifying restrictions on speech.[19]

At first glance this appears to be what the court had in mind in *United States v. O'Brien* when Justice Warren enunciated a fourfold test for use in judging the power of the federal government to punish draft-card burning.

> This Court has held that when "speech" and "nonspeech" elements are combined in the same course of conduct, a sufficiently important governmental interest in regulating the nonspeech element can justify incidental limitations on First Amendment freedoms. To characterize the quality of the governmental interest which must appear, the Court has employed a variety of descriptive terms: compelling; substantial; subordinating; paramount; cogent; strong. Whatever imprecision inheres in these terms, we think it clear that a government regulation is sufficiently justified if it is within the constitutional power of the government; if it furthers an important or substantial governmental interest; if the governmental interest is unrelated to the suppression of free expression; and if the incidental restriction on alleged First Amendment freedom is no greater than is essential to the furtherance of that interest.[20]

In reality, the court's *use* of this test in *O'Brien* indicates that it provides inadequate protection to the communicative interests involved. It is not judging "speech," it is judging conduct associated with speech, i.e. "speech plus," which is entitled to a lesser degree of constitutional protection from the courts than "pure speech." The *O'Brien* court's focus is almost entirely on the importance of the governmental interests in maintaining the requirement (and its evaluation of those interests is itself highly questionable). There is almost no attention to the vital interests of O'Brien in employing his mode of protest. Even treating O'Brien's conduct as "speech plus," the court should consider the severi-

[19] See *ibid.*, 269–70; NAACP v. Button, 371 U.S. 415, 429, 438, 444 (1963); Thomas v. Collins, 323 U.S. 516, 530 (1945); Bridges v. California, 314 U.S. 252, 262, 263 (1941); and cases cited in United States v. O'Brien, 391 U.S. 367, 376–77nn 22–27 (1968). See generally Alexander Meiklejohn, *Political Freedom* (New York, 1965); Shapiro, *Freedom of Speech*, 58–72, 102–73; Black, *The People and the Court*, 220–21; Robert B. McKay, "The Preference for Freedom," *New York University Law Review*, XXXIV (Nov., 1959), 1182–1227; Annotation, "The Supreme Court and the Right of Free Speech and Press," 21 L.Ed.2d 976 (1969), especially sec. 6.
[20] United States v. O'Brien, 391 U.S. 367, 376–77 (1968).

ty of the "incidental" limitations on First Amendment freedoms. If balancing is to be used, the competing values must be fully explored and evaluated—one-sided balancing is no balancing at all.

An alternative approach can be seen in *Tinker v. Des Moines Independent Community School District,* involving an attempt by school authorities to discipline high school students who wore black armbands in a silent protest against the Vietnam war in direct contravention of school policy. The court initially recognized that the conduct constituted a symbolic act "closely akin to 'pure speech' which, we have repeatedly held, is entitled to comprehensive protection under the First Amendment...."[21] There is to be a balancing of interests but the First Amendment requires that added weights be placed on the free-speech side of the scale. The court in *Tinker* weighed the nature of the state interests, the special position of the educational institution as a place for disputation of ideas, and the importance and character of the student's speech.

> Under our Constitution, free speech is not a right that is given only to be so circumscribed that it exists in principle but not in fact. Freedom of expression would not truly exist if the right could be exercised only in an area that a benevolent government has provided as a safe haven for crackpots. The Constitution says that Congress (and the States) may not abridge the right of free speech. This provision means what it says. We properly read it to permit reasonable regulation of speech-connected activities in carefully restricted circumstances. But we do not confine the permissible exercise of First Amendment rights to a telephone booth or the four corners of a pamphlet, or to supervised and ordained discussion in a school classroom.[22]

The court concluded that in absence of any evidence of reasonable probability of disturbance or disturbance in fact, the passive "witness of the armbands" was constitutionally protected.

The *Tinker* case, then, suggests the need for an amendment to the fourfold *O'Brien* standard. We must also ask: How important is the conduct to the effective communication of the opinion or idea and how important to the individual and society is it that the idea be expressed

---

[21] Tinker v. Des Moines Community School Dist., 393 U.S. 503, 505 (1969).

[22] *Ibid.,* 513. Justice Fortas, dissenting in Street v. New York, 394 U.S. 576, 616 (1969), again accepted that "action, even clearly for serious protest purposes, is not entitled to the pervasive protection that is given to speech alone.... The test that is applicable in every case where conduct is restricted or prohibited is whether the regulation or prohibition is reasonable, *due account being taken of the paramountcy of First Amendment values*" (emphasis added).

and/or communicated? This would restore some of the balance in the balancing test. If conduct is accepted as partaking of First Amendment speech, the guarantee cannot be diluted with a lesser standard of protection. The need for free, full, effective communication, especially in modern society, which so often induces personal anonymity and alienation and where power frequently dictates access to policy-makers, demands full consideration of the speech interests involved.

It was against such a background that the Supreme Court of Massachusetts was called upon at the prescriptive stage to judge the constitutionality of the state's statutory prohibitions against exhibiting and giving away birth-control devices. Both provisions of the statute were attacked as violative of free speech, and therefore the speech interests and state interests relating to each required consideration. Turning first to the proscription against exhibiting contraceptives, the court cited the broad language of Justice Douglas in *Griswold*: "The State may not, consistently with the spirit of the First Amendment, contract the spectrum of available knowledge. The right of freedom of speech and press includes not only the right to utter or print, but the right to distribute, the right to receive, the right to read ... and freedom of inquiry, freedom of thought, and freedom to teach...."[23] It noted further that concern for free-speech interests had induced the Supreme Court of New Jersey, while not declaring its birth-control statute unconstitutional, to find that conduct by Baird similar to that in Massachusetts was not "without just cause," as required by the statute for conviction. The court concluded that Baird's exhibition of contraceptives "was incidental to, and part of the lecture, and thereby within the protection of the First Amendment. The display of those articles was essential to a graphic representation of his subject." That portion of section 21 prohibiting exhibition was, therefore, deemed unconstitutional *"as applied to the defendant in this case."*[24] This does not mean, however, that the statute itself was declared unconstitutional and void but only that it was not constitutionally applied in his case.

Nor was recognition of the speech interest (limited as the holding may be) to be defeated by invocation of court decisions denying obscenity free-speech status (i.e., obscenity is not the "speech" or "press" protected by the constitutional guarantee). In a different era, the view

---

[23] Griswold v. Connecticut, 381 U.S. 479, 482 (1965).
[24] Commonwealth v. Baird, 355 Mass. 746, 247 N.E.2d 574, 578 (1969) (emphasis added).

that contraception was itself obscene might well have lent credibility to such an assertion. Courts have, however, rejected the contention that discussion of contraceptives is necessarily obscene.[25] Further, the extensive use of contraceptives in modern society and, most important, judicial acceptance of the permissible use of contraceptives in *Griswold* denigrate any such claim. While many of Baird's remarks during his address may have been of questionable value and taste,[26] this did not make his verbal speech or the exhibition of contraceptives obscene. At the very least, as the Massachusetts Supreme Court noted, the speech unquestionably had "redeeming social importance" and hence could not satisfy the requirements fashioned by the U.S. Supreme Court for identifying obscenity.[27]

But the Massachusetts court had not finished with Baird or his free-speech claim: his conviction for giving away contraceptives remained. The court, in a 4-3 decision, held this to be a permissible exercise of police power. It is, however, somewhat difficult to determine if Chief Justice Wilkins, writing for the majority, held that the conduct was not speech because "the bestowal of this item upon an individual in the audience added nothing to the understanding of the lecture,"[28] or whether he was asserting that the distribution was speech but that the state interest was sufficient to overcome the interference with the constitutional guarantee. In either case, Baird's conviction was permissible and the statutory restraint was legitimized.

Whatever the merits of the result, the Massachusetts court's opinion leaves much to be desired. The court seems correct that the exhibiting of contraceptives was an integral part of the full, effective communication of Baird's message. That he also desired to be arrested in order to test the law may detract from the purity of his intent but it does not deny an intent to communicate an enhanced understanding of his subject matter. While the court never discusses how the use of the visual

[25] See Chapter Four, especially note 17 *supra*.
[26] The Commonwealth noted, for example, Baird's references to Emko as an "amusement tax," that a diaphragm, "if improperly fitted, is like the Grand Canyon being left wide open," that a cervical plastic device was "like hitting a brick wall; cools the whole idea," that "people who take chances are called parents," and that the rhythm system was "Catholic roulette." Brief for Commonwealth, p. 2, Commonwealth v. Baird, 247 N.E.2d 574 (1969).
[27] 247 N.E.2d at 577. See A Book Named John Clelend's Memoirs of a Woman of Pleasure v. Attorney General, 383 U.S. 413 (1966), setting forth a threefold test defining obscenity.
[28] *Ibid.*, 578.

aids made the speech more meaningful, it is not too difficult to accept that understanding of a complex subject such as birth control could be aided by an exhibition of the material itself.

However, after having decided speech was involved, the Massachusetts court failed to consider the possibility of countervailing state interests. If the court were affirming an "absolutist" position regarding free speech, denying any permissible state interests, this might be understandable. But its disposition of the "exhibiting" phase of the free-speech argument and its references to the need for a "clear and present danger" in order to justify state interference with free-speech interests suggests that such was not the case.[29]

While a full evaluation of the state interest in regulating the availability of birth-control materials will be presented below, even cursory consideration of the possible state interests in prohibiting exhibition would seem to support the court's holding. Whatever the state interest in preventing uncontrolled distribution of contraceptives, there seems to be no basis for a total prohibition on *all* "exhibiting" of *all* contraceptives. This is not a limited regulation of public displays or commercial advertising or a minimal prohibition for the protection of children. It is a total prohibition on exhibition generally. Nothing that Baird did in exhibiting his wares to a college audience would seem to invoke the need for state intervention. Indeed, to borrow the language of the court in *Tinker*, the conduct is "closely akin to pure speech" and there is little question that the state would be barred from suppressing Baird's verbal message.[30]

The court's treatment of the distribution count is even more problematical. While noting the argument of *amicus* that the distribution of contraceptives was designed to implement the ideas and message provided by the speech, the chief justice concluded that it added nothing to the understanding of the subject matter of the lecture and therefore was not a protected exercise of free speech.[31] However, the distribution does seem to add potency and support to Baird's overall message regarding the desirability and need for wider availability and use of contraceptives. This is especially true when the speech is perceived also, as his references to the Massachusetts laws indicated, as a protest against

---

[29] *Ibid.*, 577.

[30] Justice Stewart's dissent in *Griswold* (381 U.S. at 529n3) reflected this principle: "If all the appellants had done was to advise people that they thought the use of contraceptives was desirable, or even to counsel their use, the appellants would, of course, have a substantial First Amendment claim."

[31] 247 N.E.2d at 578–79.

the maintenance of such legal norms. While it may not stand high in importance on the hierarchy of free-speech values and may well pale when weighed against state interests, it does appear that Baird's conduct in giving away the contraceptives should, as Judge Spiegel argued in his dissent, "be considered part of constitutionally [protected] free speech and protest."[32]

Having concluded that Baird's conduct was not an exercise of the speech guarantee, the court's First Amendment inquiry should have ended. But instead, consideration was given the state interest involved, thereby at least suggesting that the constitutional guarantee afforded some protection to Baird's activity. In any case, the court argued that the state had a definite interest in preventing the distribution of contraceptives by indiscriminate persons: "The Commonwealth has a legitimate interest in preventing the distribution of articles designed to prevent conception which may have undesirable, if not dangerous, physical consequences. In these circumstances, absent any definite intimation, we shall not guess as to the probable attitude of the Supreme Court of the United States.... The legitimacy of the purpose depends upon a distinction as to the distributor and not as to the marital status of the recipient."[33]

Whatever the merits of other constitutional challenges to the Massachusetts statutes, this phase of the decision appears formidable. Although Baird's conduct should be perceived as partaking of speech for First Amendment purposes, the speech interests seem minimal. On the other hand, the state has a real interest in controlling indiscriminate distribution of contraceptive devices, many of which could be harmful to particular persons or harmful if improperly used. While a total prohibition of *all* distribution by *all* persons not within the statutory exception for *all* contraceptives is somewhat broader than necessary, and it is a command of the free-speech guarantee that statutes be drawn with precision,[34] the state interest does appear substantial. Use of the balancing test seldom provides answers in constitutional adjudication. Rather, it helps to articulate relevant considerations—decision is still born of judgment reflecting the values of the policy-maker.

There is, however, another aspect of the free-speech issue which the Massachusetts court failed to consider. The reader may recall that its

[32] *Ibid.*, 582. Justice Spiegel cited Nat'l Labor Relations Bd. v. Int'l Longshoremen's Assn., 332 F.2d 992, 999 (4th Cir. 1964), arguing that each of these acts was "implementary conduct... in the nature of advocacy."
[33] 247 N.E.2d at 578.
[34] See text accompanying notes 81–87 *infra*.

holding was limited to a declaration that the statute was unconstitutional *as applied* to *Baird* under the given facts. But the challenge posed by the various briefs was much more far-reaching: the claim asserted was that the statute itself constituted an overly broad infringement on free speech (i.e., it is void on its face). While its narrow holding on the exhibiting conviction might permit an avoidance of this issue, its affirmance of the conviction based on giving away contraceptives against the free-speech claims would seem to necessitate consideration of the broader issue.

In fact, there appears to be substantial merit in the argument, especially in light of the court's holding. As the Supreme Court has made clear, especially in First Amendment cases, a "governmental purpose to control or prevent activities constitutionally subject to state regulation may not be achieved by means which sweep unnecessarily broadly and thereby invade the area of protected freedoms."[35] or "Broad prophylactic (rules in the area of free expression) are suspect.... Precision of regulation must be the touchstone in ... area[s] closely touching our most precious freedoms."[36] Even assuming there is activity which the state might constitutionally regulate or even prohibit, the *Baird* case itself demonstrates that there is a wide range of activity that is beyond state reach. "In applying the rule against vagueness or overbroadness something, however, should depend on the moral quality of the conduct. In order not to chill conduct within the protection of the Constitution and having a genuine social utility, it may be necessary to throw the mantle of protection beyond the constitutional periphery, where the statute does not make the boundary clear."[37]

Certainly the *Baird* decision provides no criteria regarding the conduct that can be constitutionally proscribed. Nor is this infirmity of the

---

[35] NAACP v. Alabama, 357 U.S. 449, 460–61 (1958). In Keyeshian v. Bd. of Regents, 385 U.S. 589, 602 (1967), the court stated that "even though the governmental purpose be legitimate and substantial, that purpose cannot be pursued by means that broadly stifle fundamental personal liberties when the end can be more narrowly achieved." See Interstate Circuit, Inc. v. Dallas, 390 U.S. 676 (1968); Shuttlesworth v. City of Birmingham, 394 U.S. 147 (1968). Government must, therefore, pursue its legitimate concerns "by means which have a less drastic impact on the continued vitality of First Amendment freedoms." United States v. Robel, 389 U.S. 258, 268 (1967).

[36] NAACP v. Button, 371 U.S. 415, 438 (1963). "Because First Amendment freedoms need breathing space to survive, government may regulate in the area only with narrow specificity." *Ibid.*, 432–33.

[37] Bouie v. City of Columbia, 378 U.S. 347, 362 (1964), citing Paul A. Freund, "The Supreme Court and Civil Liberties," *Vanderbilt Law Review*, IV (Apr., 1951), 540.

Massachusetts law limited to the "exhibiting" provision. Section 21 makes criminal all advertising, regardless of the character of the advertisement or the status of the writer, relating to drugs, medicines, instruments, or articles "for the prevention of conception or for causing unlawful abortion." Advertisements are not limited to commercial ads, even if that might represent a permissible state control. All writings communicating where contraceptives can be obtained are criminalized by sections 20 and 21. No distinction is drawn between communications directed to the married and unmarried; no exception is made for communications by doctors—the exceptions developed in section 21A apply only when doctors "administer to or prescribe for any married persons." Indeed, it might well be argued that even if the Massachusetts statutes do not prohibit the *use* of contraceptives to married persons protected in *Griswold*, statutory restriction of the effectuation of that right through severe limitations on access to contraceptive information is itself impermissible.

This is, in fact, an essential fault of the 1966 legislative revision. The General Court did not attempt to revise sections 20 and 21 but merely added a caveat in section 21A. The primary provisions remain, as they were originally intended, vague, sweeping, all-encompassing, visiting their inhibiting effects on all communications regarding contraception. Indeed, this was recognized in the Commonwealth's brief when it defined the issue involved as the state's ability "to regulate and control the dissemination and distribution of contraceptive *knowledge* among the unmarried...."[38]

Even if we were to assume that the state may *prohibit* the communication of knowledge to the unmarried consistently with First Amendment guarantees—a highly questionable assumption—the Massachusetts statute is not so limited. Even if the statute is constitutionally applied to *Baird*, this is not conclusive of a challenge to the statute as void on its face because of overbreadth.[39] Even if it were possible through some legerdemain to revise the statute judicially to take account of the potential free-speech interests impaired, it is probable that the resulting statute would be so vague as to violate due process. Justice Douglas recently noted: "The requirement of a narrowly drawn statute when the regulation touches a protected constitutional right ... is only another

[38] Brief for Commonwealth, p. 5, Commonwealth v. Baird, 247 N.E.2d 574 (1969) (emphasis added).
[39] Dombrowski v. Pfister, 380 U.S. 479 (1965); NAACP v. Button, 371 U.S. 415 (1963); Thornhill v. Alabama, 310 U.S. 88 (1940); Near v. Minnesota, 283 U.S. 697 (1931).

facet of the void-for-vagueness problem."[40] As will be discussed below, this problem of vagueness permeates the state prohibitions. Nevertheless, in this instance, while the argument based on vagueness and overbreadth in relation to the fundamental guarantee of free speech and press was accepted by the dissent, it was not even considered by the majority of the Massachusetts Supreme Court.

Nor was majority taken with the argument that the various provisions of the statute are inseverable—if one fails they all fail. In fact, since the court did not invalidate any of the provisions totally, the argument does not really seem even applicable. But whatever the merits of the court's approach to the free-speech issues, it does seem correct that even the excision of the "exhibiting" provision would not necessarily void the whole statutory scheme. The various proscribed acts are described in the disjunctive and there is no indication whatsoever that either the nineteenth-century legislature that framed the laws or the 1966 legislature that revised them wanted all or nothing at all. The cursory dismissal of this argument by all the courts passing on the Baird conviction (it was, however, accepted by the dissenting judges in the Massachusetts Supreme Court)[41] seems fully justified. On the other hand, if vagueness and overbreadth could be shown to permeate the statutory scheme then it is arguable that the entire statute (including Baird's conviction under the distributing provision) should fall.

The federal district court, in judging the free-speech issues, adopted a somewhat different approach than the Massachusetts court to reach the same result. Like the Massachusetts court, however, the opinion is framed totally in terms of the statute *as applied* in the *Baird* case. Returning to cases involving mass picketing, the court urged a lesser degree of constitutional protection for speech-plus-action than is afforded pure speech. Conduct is distinguished from pure speech, and the state interest in regulating the *"non-speech"* interest, even though involving incidental limitations on free speech, is then determined. Again, this approach to the line-drawing problem severely impairs the essential inquiry. All conduct involves activity, just as all speech involves activity. The dichotomy is not between conduct and speech but rather between

---

[40] United States v. Vuitch, 91 S. Ct. 1294, 1302 (1971) (Douglas, J., dissenting). See text accompanying notes 35-37 *supra*.

[41] Compare the dissents of Justices Whittemore and Cutter (247 N.E.2d at 581) and Justice Spiegel (*ibid.*, 583) with the opinions of Chief Justice Wilkins (*ibid.*, 579-80), Chief Judge Aldrich for the Court of Appeals (429 F.2d at 1399), and District Judge Julian (310 F. Supp. at 956).

action that furthers First Amendment interests in expression and communication and that which does not. Excluding expressive and/or communicative conduct from full First Amendment protection introduces an unnecessary bias into the decision-making process. Nevertheless, the district court applied the *O'Brien* test and concluded:

> Sections 21 and 21A meet all these requirements. First, from the discussion above it should be clear that a legitimate purpose of the statute was to safeguard the health of citizens, unmistakably a traditional police power objective. Second, prohibiting the "giving away" of contraceptives is manifestly "unrelated to the suppression of free expression." Finally, the restriction on alleged First Amendment freedoms is, at best, incidental. The petitioner was not convicted for any beliefs or views that he espoused or urged upon others, nor for exercising his right of free speech or of assembly, nor for any intellectual, moral or other opposition he may have expressed against the Massachusetts statutes in question. He stands convicted solely for "giving away" a certain contraceptive medicine or article in violation of §21.[42]

Unlike *O'Brien*, however, the above quotation indicates some consideration for the free-speech interests asserted by Baird. The restraints imposed by the statutory prohibition on giving away contraceptives are visited only remotely on his beliefs and his protest against the laws; there are numerous, fully effective, alternative means to express and communicate his opposition. At least under this provision of the statute, he remains free to exhibit, protest, and challenge—to air his views fully and have their merits considered in the marketplace of ideas.

The Court of Appeals was cursory in its dismissal of Baird's free-speech claims. Following the lead of the previous decisions, the opinion is limited to the question of the statute's constitutionality *as applied*. Comparing the interests of Baird in giving away contraceptives as a means of communication with the "speech" interests of O'Brien in his conduct, the court, correctly I believe, found the former far less persuasive. Indicating that it was also considering the state interests involved, the court noted that it was "unimpressed by the argument that the right of free speech justifies the performance of an act which has been reasonably prohibited on independent state grounds."[43] While it

[42] Baird v. Eisenstadt, 310 F. Supp. 951, 955 (D. Mass. 1970).
[43] Baird v. Eisenstadt, 429 F.2d 1398, 1399 (1st Cir. 1970).

was to invalidate the Massachusetts laws on other grounds, the Court of Appeals could find no free-speech difficulty with upholding the conviction.

RIGHTS OF THE UNMARRIED

But regardless of the free-speech issue, what of the effect of *Griswold*; hadn't the Supreme Court held such birth-control prohibitions unconstitutional? That the answer must be "no" points to a very real problem with effectuating legal change through judicial action. In the first place, a judicial decree is enforceable only in relation to the parties then before the court. Its application to other parties, and fact contexts, requires further time and expense in litigation. Further, as previously noted, the judicial opinion is a weak vehicle for dealing with complex problems involving multifaceted issues. While it is true that an opinion can anticipate questions and provide indicators of probable disposition, decision must await a concrete fact situation embodied in litigation raising unsettled issues.

Griswold had declared a statute prohibiting the *use* of contraceptives violative of the right of *marital and familial privacy* embodied in the due-process guarantee of the Fourteenth Amendment. But what implications does this have for a statute like that of Massachusetts, which permits the use of contraceptives but prohibits a variety of other activities associated with their use, subject to an exception for medical services, but limits the exception solely to married individuals? Read narrowly, *Griswold* is totally inapplicable to the problem raised by the Massachusetts prohibitions. A broader approach to the decision, focusing on the underlying principles involved, however, suggests that *Griswold* is very much involved.

Consider the following statement made by former Supreme Court Justice Tom C. Clark referring to *Griswold* and related cases:

> The result of these decisions is the evolution of the concept that there is a certain zone of individual privacy which is protected by the Constitution. Unless the State has a compelling subordinating interest that outweighs the individual rights of human beings, it may not interfere with a person's marriage, home, children and day-to-day living habits. This is one of the most fundamental concepts that the Founding Fathers had in mind when they drafted the Constitution.[44]

[44] Tom C. Clark, "Religion, Morality and Abortion: A Constitutional Appraisal,"

This would suggest that constitutional privacy extends beyond the marital-familial rights invoked as part of due process in *Griswold*. It suggests further that when these fundamental interests are invoked, as was indicated in discussing *Griswold*, that the courts will impose a higher burden of justification on the state than is typical in due-process adjudication. No mere showing of some rational state interest will suffice; "the state may prevail only upon showing a subordinating interest which is compelling."[45] Courts afford "strict scrutiny" to the purpose and operation of such enactments and demand that the state demonstrate an overriding interest to infringe the vital interests at stake.

Here was the basis for a more viable due-process attack by pro-change interests on the Massachusetts prohibitions. If the interests at stake in the litigation could be analogized to those vindicated in *Griswold* and the "compelling state interest" approach to due-process adjudication invoked, it might be possible to denigrate any purported state police power claims. The statute might be declared an unconstitutional invasion of due process. Although there was again the problem of the standing of Baird to raise some of these privacy rights, since he was married and fully able to obtain contraceptives legally, the approach taken in *Griswold* to the right of a third party to challenge the validity of the statutes under which he was convicted suggested that this was not a serious obstacle.[46] Far more difficult was the task of fashioning some constitutionally cognizable interest being violated by the state law; how could you successfully assert a right in an unmarried person to obtain contraceptives?

One way would be to approach privacy as a generic right protecting a variety of interests. This might include, for example, the person's stake in mental and emotional tranquillity. The language employed by Justice

---

Loyola University Law Review, II (Apr., 1969), 8. See Levy v. Louisiana, 391 U.S. 68 (1968); Loving v. Virginia, 388 U.S. 1, 12 (1966); McLaughlin v. Florida, 379 U.S. 184 (1964); Skinner v. Oklahoma, 315 U.S. 535, 536, 541 (1942); Pierce v. Society of Sisters, 268 U.S. 510, 534-35 (1925); Meyer v. Nebraska, 262 U.S. 390 (1923). See generally Dienes, "To Feed the Hungry," 618-23.

[45] Bates v. City of Little Rock, 361 U.S. 516, 524 (1960). The "compelling state interest" or "strict scrutiny" standard is discussed in the text accompanying Chapter Six, notes 79-84 *supra*.

[46] See text accompanying Chapter Six, notes 46-49 *supra*, on the problem of standing. The *amicus* brief of the Massachusetts Civil Liberties Union, p. 6, Commonwealth v. Baird, 242 N.E.2d 574 (1969), argued: "As a general proposition a party lacks standing to rely on the constitutional rights of others. However, a well recognized exception exists when the nature of the constitutional rights and the governmental action alleged to violate them are such as to render it impracticable for the adversely affected persons to present the issues themselves."

Brandeis in his classic statement on privacy certainly transcends marital-familial privacy: "They [the makers of our Constitution] recognized the significance of man's spiritual nature, of his feelings and of his intellect. They knew that only a part of the pain, pleasures and satisfactions of life are to be found in material things. They sought to protect Americans in their beliefs, their thoughts, their emotions and their sensations."[47] In fact, prior to his ascension to the bench, Brandeis referred to the underlying principle as being "that of an inviolate personality," and later writers have taken up this theme.[48] Search-and-seizure cases can be narrowly described in Fourth Amendment terms or emphasis can be placed on the broader *privacy* rights of the individual under surveillance, on his right to be free from unwarranted intrusion.[49] Even the state interest in control of obscenity has been held not to justify police intrusion into the privacy of an individual's home.[50]

Given the psychic suffering occasioned by the fear of pregnancy, and the subsequent mental and emotional anguish occasioned by the forthcoming birth of an unwanted child, the negative implications for privacy come into clearer focus. It is not surprising that advocates of revision in the abortion laws cite the psychic injury to the woman as a vital consideration. And this same psychic damage can be occasioned by inability to obtain safe and effective contraceptives. Yet the Massachusetts laws, while making medical services available to the married, deny similar medical assistance to the unmarried. This is not to say that such treatment is not warranted, but it does argue that the state must demonstrate a compelling interest, that the stricter standard of due process should be applied.

Closely related to this argument, and more intensely urged by the pro-change interests, is the claim of the individual to control over his or her own bodily processes. Finding support in a number of recent court

[47] Olmstead v. United States, 277 U.S. 438, 478 (1928). See generally the sources cited in Chapter Six, note 65 *supra*, and Dienes, "To Feed the Hungry," 618–19nn 321–24, on the broader implications of the privacy right.
[48] Louis Brandeis and Simon Warren, "The Right to Privacy," *Harvard Law Review*, IV (Dec., 1890), 205. See Edward J. Bloustein, "Privacy as an Aspect of Human Dignity: An Answer to Dean Prosser," *New York University Law Review*, XXXIX (Dec., 1964), 1000–1007; Pavesich v. New England Life Ins. Co., 122 Ga. 190, 195–96, 50 S.E. 68, 70 (1905), which are, however, stressing tort-law privacy.
[49] See, e.g., Katz v. United States, 389 U.S. 347, 361 (1967). See generally Kent Greenwalt, "The Right of Privacy," *The Rights of Americans*, ed. Norman Dorsen (New York, 1970), 299–325.
[50] Stanley v. Georgia, 394 U.S. 557 (1969).

decisions overturning abortion laws, the argument is made that "as a secular matter a woman's liberty and right of privacy extends to family, marriage *and sex matters*"[51] or that "the woman's right to life is involved because child birth invokes risks of death,"[52] or again, that "these protected areas are the women's rights to life, to control over their own bodies, and to freedom and privacy in matters relating to sex and procreation...."[53] It was such considerations that led the Citizens Advisory Council on the Status of Women, appointed by the president, to recognize that "the right of a woman to determine her own reproductive life is a basic human right...."[54] Privacy, then, is not necessarily limited to rights arising from marriage, but extends to the intimacies of sexual relations.

Alternatively, decisions regarding pregnancy may be perceived as questions of health and physical well-being.[55] When the state undertakes to burden the individual's ability to receive health care, it should be required to demonstrate a compelling interest. Sexual relationships outside of marriage as a reality that cannot be ignored, and the negative consequences flowing from unwanted pregnancies, as will be noted below, is similarly a reality that must be faced. Again, this is not to deny state power to control sexual relationships, but the nature of the interests at stake does suggest the need for more careful scrutiny and a more intense burden of justification than is typical in due-process adjudication.

[51] United States v. Vuitch, 305 F. Supp. 1032, 1035 (D.D.C. 1969). See Skinner v. Oklahoma, 315 U.S. 535 (1942); In re Cavitt, 182 Neb. 712, 157 N.W.2d 171, 175 (1968).

[52] People v. Belous, 80 Cal. Rptr. 354, 359 (1969).

[53] Doe v. Scott, 321 F. Supp. 1385, 1389 (N.D. Ill. 1971). See Roe v. Wade, 314 F. Supp. 1217, 1221–22 (N.D. Tex. 1970); Babbitz v. McCann, 310 F. Supp. 293, 298–300 (E.D. Wis. 1970). See generally Charles Lister, "The Right to Control the Use of One's Body," *The Rights of Americans*, ed. Dorsen, 348–64.

[54] Quoted in Peter M. Horstman, "Problem Areas in the Federal Provision of Family Planning Services," *Clearinghouse Review*, IV (Feb., 1971), 463. The Family Law section of the American Bar Association has recognized that "the changes in our decisions and statutory law expresses a general recognition that the right to limit family size is a basic human right—that the individual has a right to free choice and self-determination in regard to procreation." See the International Covenant on Civil and Political Rights, article 17.

[55] Editorial, "Medical Indications for Contraception: Changing Viewpoints," *Obstetrics and Gynecology*, XXV (Feb., 1965), 285, suggests: "Good health embraces more than mere absence of disease. The World Health Organization has defined health as a 'state of complete physical, mental and social well-being.'" See Eva H. and John L. Hanks, "The Right to a Habitable Environment," *The Rights of Americans*, ed. Dorsen, 146–71.

The above analysis has proceeded primarily in terms of a broadened right of privacy, or at least an assertion of broad rights associated with an "inviolable personality" that might inhere in the due-process guarantee. In fact, it should not be necessary to assert the existence of a constitutionally based right in order to elicit the more stringent standard of judicial review. Regardless of whether or not a "right" exists, the interests being asserted by the pro-change forces differ significantly from the interests which induce the courts to defer to the legislative judgment.[56] This is not a case involving business and economic affairs, where legislative competency and the law-making prerogative are maximized. The state in this instance undertakes to control vital human relationships, the most intimate, personal interests of the individual. When the personal liberty of the individual over these interests is curtailed, judicial deference is highly inappropriate. This is not to defend sexual or other practices violative of state laws but only to argue that such assertions of state power be carefully scrutinized. It should be noted, however, that while the Court of Appeals and the dissenting justices in the Massachusetts Supreme Court accepted the "fundamental" character of the interests asserted by Baird, they never really came to grips with what made the interests "fundamental" and failed to articulate clearly their standard of review.

But regardless of the standard of review, what are the state interests in maintaining these laws? The state at the intelligence stage wisely avoided any moral judgment regarding the use of contraceptives which might challenge *Griswold* or any restraint on the availability of contraceptive devices for the prevention of disease since that had been legitimized in *Commonwealth v. Corbett*. Instead, the state defined the issue before the courts in the following terms: "What is presently involved is the right of the Commonwealth to regulate and control the dissemination and distribution of contraceptive knowledge among the unmarried, and place the traffic in contraceptives in responsible hands."[57] *Griswold* was not applicable since it was specifically addressed only to contraception within the marital relationship. In fact, a concurring justice in *Griswold* had even expressed the belief that "the State ... does have statutes, the constitutionality of which is *beyond doubt*, which prohibit adultery and fornication." For the state, then, this was "an emphatic recognition of the principle that the State may consti-

[56] See Dandridge v. Williams, 397 U.S. 471, 520 (1970) (Marshall, J., dissenting); Rothstein v. Wyman, 303 F. Supp. 339, 347 (S.D. N.Y. 1969).

[57] Brief for Commonwealth, p. 5, Commonwealth v. Baird, 247 N.E.2d 574 (1969).

tutionally prescribe and punish private sexual conduct."[58] Evidence introduced by the defendant regarding the socioeconomic costs of illegitimacy, argued the district attorney, is properly for the legislative policy-maker and not the courts. It is not the function of a court to substitute its judgment for that of the legislature. Then, in one sentence, discussing the free-speech issue rather than due process, the state offered its only real delineation of the state interests that might be involved: "... the state might find that the public interest involved in preventing greater sexual activity among unmarried persons and the prevention of venereal disease as a result of such activity, justified a deprivation of free speech."[59]

There was no attempt to analyze the importance of such interests or the relation of the birth-control regulation to the effectuation of such interests, or to denigrate the importance of the private interests asserted. In ordinary due-process adjudication, courts are expected to defer to the legislative judgment and not to substitute their determinations of wisdom for those of the state. If the state *might* have had any rational police power interest in the laws, that is sufficient. However, the state's argument seems weak even under these traditional due-process standards. The mere assertion of a possible state interest hardly proves the existence of a rational justification.

At the prescriptive stage, Chief Justice Wilkins followed even the Commonwealth's mode of assessing the state interest. There was no separate treatment of the due-process issue. Instead, as was indicated above, the court limited its analysis to the assertion that the state had a viable health interest, overriding any possible *free-speech interest* of Baird in giving away the contraceptives.[60] Even if this were accepted, however, it should not be conclusive of the due-process inquiry.

Nevertheless, the federal district court utilized Chief Justice Wilkins's findings regarding the health interests of the state:

> It is a matter of common knowledge that contraceptive substances may have harmful effects on the health of those who use them and for that reason are still the subject of extensive medical research. The statutes in question have a clear relationship to the legislative purpose of safeguarding the health of members of the community by placing the distribution of such substances exclusively in the hands of registered physicians and pharmacists. The

---

[58] *Ibid.*, 7, citing Griswold v. Connecticut, 381 U.S. 479, 498 (1965) (Goldberg, J., concurring) (emphasis added).
[59] *Ibid.*, 9.
[60] See text accompanying note 33 *supra*.

statutes, therefore, can reasonably be regarded as furthering an important and substantial government interest.[61]

This does seem a fair explanation of why William Baird and other non-licensed persons might be controlled in distributing *some* contraceptives. But this, of course, is not the essence of the defendant's claim. Whatever the merits of a narrowly drawn law regulating the distribution of certain contraceptives, the Massachusetts laws are not so limited. Baird was asserting the interests of the unmarried and of doctors to provide health services to the unmarried. But the district court avoided this issue by asserting that such were not the facts in the case before the court, and that Baird lacked standing to press the rights of those "with whom he had no legally significant relationship."[62]

But the broader health impact of the statutes had been raised in *Sturgis v. Attorney General* and, in that instance, by licensed practitioners. Utilizing a traditional due-process standard of review rather than the compelling-interest standard urged by the petitioners, the Massachusetts court concluded: "In short, the legislature is free to conclude that some harm may conceivably attend the employment of contraceptive devices. If such be so, the prohibition against their distribution bears a real and substantial relation to the legislative purpose."[63] While admitting that the statute might create "factual situations which at best can be described as unhappy," the court found nothing which *compels* a legislature to investigate available scientific and medical opinion when legislating. Even the fact that there were a number of contraceptive devices, including the foam distributed by Baird, which clearly posed no health hazard was not an insuperable obstacle, since, as will be noted below, the *Sturgis* court was to find other grounds for supporting the state's enactments.

The Court of Appeals and the dissenting justices in the Massachusetts Supreme Court in the *Baird* case also directly confronted the broader issues concerning the impact of the law. Unlike Chief Justice Wilkins, these judges found no difficulty with the standing of Baird to raise these

---

[61] 310 F. Supp. at 954.

[62] *Ibid.*, 957. See text accompanying note 46 and Chapter Six, notes 46–49 *supra*, and note 64 *infra* on the issue of standing.

[63] 260 N.E.2d at 690. The court, quoting from previous decisions, claimed: " 'Unless the act of the Legislative cannot be supported upon any rational basis of fact that reasonably can be conceived to sustain it, the court has no power to strike it down as violative of the Constitution.' We further test the legislation on the basis that all rational presumptions are made in favor of the validity of every legislative enactment. Enforcement is to be refused only when it is in manifest excess of legislative power." *Ibid.*

issues, since the challenge was to the validity of the law on its face. Since Baird was being jailed under the statute, argued Chief Judge Aldrich for the Court of Appeals, "he must have as much standing to protest as anyone else."[64] Indeed, the Massachusetts court itself had criticized Baird for seeking arrest rather than utilizing a declaratory judgment. Yet, according to its rationale, the only possible way of establishing the requisite personal harm would be arrest. In light of Justice Douglas's treatment of standing in *Griswold*, there would appear to be substantial merit in Judge Aldrich's position.

Nor were these judges willing to accept the assertion of health as a sufficient interest to sustain the law. Chief Judge Aldrich contended that the asserted health interest was a late-blooming justification born in the 1966 amendments, and appeared more as a legislative attempt to avoid *Griswold* than a real interest in promoting health. But at least in dealing with the health measure, the Court of Appeals did not rest on an inquiry into purpose. Instead, it found the statute, treated as a health measure, unreasonable in its "total exclusion of the unmarried, and because of its palpable overbreadth with respect to the married."[65]

If the statute is treated as a health measure, the health of the unmarried is in as great if not greater danger than the married. Instead of permitting approved medical assistance, these laws force individuals to use any preventives they can get regardless of their safety or effectiveness. If they are unable to secure a device or the device fails, they are subjected to the health hazards of pregnancy, or perhaps, as will be noted below, the often extreme dangers of an illegal abortion. Nor should the probable differential impact of such provisions be ignored. It is most likely the poor and the uneducated who are successfully inhibited by this legislation from access to safe and reliable contraceptives used under medical supervision. Indeed, this differential impact of the birth-control laws led the doctors in *Sturgis* to challenge the laws on equal-protection grounds as discriminating against the poor. To label as health measures provisions which exclude persons from obtaining medical assistance and which prohibit competent doctors, under threat of criminal sanction, from providing medical services which they reasonably believe to be necessary health measures does seem to reach the level of an absurdity.

Married persons are forced by the statute to utilize medical assistance for *all* contraceptive assistance, even though there is no question that many contraceptives are not dangerous. Availability of contraceptives,

[64] 429 F.2d at 1402. See text accompanying notes 46, 62, and Chapter Six, notes 46–49 *supra*.
[65] 429 F.2d at 1400.

especially to the poor, is thus curtailed. "The legislature made no attempt to distinguish, in the statutory restriction, between dangerous or possibly dangerous articles, and those which are medically harmless."[66] Although there might be some merit in trying to assure the effective use of contraceptives through medical supervision, this certainly was not the health purpose of the state. Further, it is questionable that even this objective would justify a total prohibitory law, the natural effect of which is to deny meaningful contraceptive services to those without ready access to medical assistance (especially the poor).

Whatever the purpose of the 1966 exceptions fashioned in section 21A of the laws, however, health care was definitely not the original state interest in enacting sections 20 and 21. While contraceptives as such or the use of contraceptives can no longer be branded obscene and prohibited, could the provisions be justified as laws to promote the public morality, especially as embodied in the criminal prohibitions on fornication? Such a state interest had been recognized in 1916 in *People v. Byrne*: "The information [about contraception] would make people generally believe that by using the means suggested the act of intercourse could be had without the fear of resulting pregnancy. While there are other reasons that keep unmarried people from indulging their passions, the fear that pregnancy will result is one of the potent ones. To remove that fear would unquestionably result in an increase of immorality."[67]

Justice Reardon, speaking for the five-judge majority in *Sturgis*, had clearly rested his decision on this basis. While accepting an interpretation of *Griswold* that would invalidate prohibitions on distribution as well as the use of contraceptives by married persons, he argued that the Supreme Court had "affirmed 'beyond doubt' the right of the State ... to enact statutes regulating the private sexual lives of single persons, stating that the discouraging of extra-marital relations is 'admittedly a legitimate subject of state concern' and that the statutes within the basic purpose of protecting marital fidelity are available to Connecticut without the need to 'invade the area of protected freedoms.' "[68] While the *Sturgis* majority is certainly correct that *Griswold* had not established the rights of the unmarried relating to contraceptives, it is highly questionable to utilize dicta from a concurring opinion (Justice Gold-

[66] *Ibid.*, 1401.
[67] People v. Byrne, 163 N.Y.S. 680, 686 (1917). See Sir Patrick Devlin, *The Enforcement of Morals* (Oxford, 1959); James Fitzjames Stephen, *Liberty, Equality, Fraternity* (London, 1873).
[68] 260 N.E.2d at 690.

berg) as conclusive of an issue. Further, whatever the merits of Justice Goldberg's opinion concerning the viability of the state interest in fornication laws, the Massachusetts provisions at issue do not criminalize fornication. They relate to birth control, and the question is more properly whether the use of these laws properly furthers the same permissible state interests, whatever they may be, as the fornication statutes. Indeed, the very existence of the fornication laws, if these birth-control provisions are only repetitive of the same interests, raises added question as to the need for sections 20 and 21—the state interests are already being furthered by the more specific laws. Finally, even the determination that a permissible state interest is involved does not conclude the inquiry. It must still be determined whether the particular means chosen by the state to effectuate the interest satisfy due-process demands. The *Sturgis* court, however, dealt with none of these questions.

Neither the majority of the Massachusetts Supreme Court nor the federal district court in *Baird* dealt with the state morality interests, perhaps reflecting their acceptance of the health interests as sufficient (at least to meet the free-speech challenge). On the other hand, the dissenters in the Massachusetts Supreme Court and the opinion of the Court of Appeals directly confronted this possible state interest and rejected it.

Chief Judge Aldrich had difficulty with the true character of the morality concerns of the state. Noting that prior to 1966 the restrictive statutes ran against married and unmarried alike, he concluded that "it is contraceptives per se that are considered immoral. . . ."[69] Whether or not it is deemed desirable for a court to probe the legislative purpose in constitutional adjudication, in this instance the inquiry would appear misleading. Whatever the purpose of the nineteenth-century legislature that enacted sections 20 and 21, the 1966 legislature had reconsidered the laws and "affirmed" the two provisions, adding the section 21 proviso. Concern for premarital sex activity is not only consistent with the statutory language, but the earlier analysis of the legislative motivation in 1966 indicated that this strongly influenced the final work product.

But whatever the true purpose, the opinions did probe the viability of the possible state interest in controlling the sex activities of the unmarried. Treated as a support for the fornication laws, Chief Judge

[69] 429 F.2d at 1401-2. See John H. Ely, "Legislative and Administrative Motivation in Constitutional Law," *Yale Law Journal*, LXXIX (June, 1970), 1205-1341; Comment, "Legislative Purpose and Federal Constitutional Adjudication," *Harvard Law Review*, LXXXIII (June, 1970), 1887-1903.

Aldrich found serious problem with the sentencing structure.[70] In Massachusetts fornication is a misdemeanor punishable by a $30 fine or three months in jail. The birth-control provisions, however, involving a felony charge, carry a maximum punishment of five years' imprisonment. To support a ninety-day misdemeanor with a five-year felony not only raises due-process concerns but suggests again the cruel and unusual punishment prohibitions of the Eighth Amendment. Also questionable is an attempt to justify a generally unenforced law by still another widely unenforced law.

Whether treated as a support for the fornication laws or, more generally, as supportive of the public morality, there are, however, more serious challenges to the use of these prohibitions against the unmarried. Again, it should be noted that the state interest would not rest on any demonstrated tangible harm to society or its inhabitants but solely on the desire to enforce community moral judgments through the criminal law. To restrain the liberty of the individual and to visit punishments on her and her offspring without any demonstrable harm but solely to effectuate the dominant morality is of questionable propriety. Further, even if it were assumed that a "public morality" exists and that it is ascertainable, both of which are highly questionable in our changing, heterogeneous society, it is clear that not every means of implementing moral values is justifiable even under the narrowest standard of judicial review.[71]

The opinion of Chief Judge Aldrich also summarized the views of the dissenters in *Commonwealth v. Baird*:

> [To say that contraceptives] . . . are to be forbidden to unmarried persons who will nevertheless persist in having intercourse, means that such persons must risk for themselves an unwanted pregnancy, for the child, illegitimacy, and for society a possible obligation of support. Such a view of morality is not only the

[70] 429 F.2d at 1401.
[71] For a criticism of using criminal law to enforce public morality see Hart, *Law, Liberty and Morality*; Murray, *We Hold These Truths*, 165–66; C. Thomas Dienes, "Moral Beliefs and Legal Norms: Perspectives on Birth Control," *St. Louis Law Journal*, XI (Summer, 1967), 536–69; Comments, "Private Consensual Adult Behavior: The Requirement of Harm to Others in the Enforcement of Morality," *University of California at Los Angeles Law Review*, XIV (Aug., 1967), 581–603. The classic statement of the position is that of John Stuart Mill, "On Liberty," *Essential Works of John Stuart Mill*, ed. Max Lerner (New York, 1971), 263: "The sole end for which mankind are warranted, individually or collectively, in interfering with the liberty of action of any member, is self-protection. That the only purpose for which power can be rightfully exercised over any member of a civilized community, against his will, is to prevent harm to others."

very mirror image of sensible legislation; we consider that it conflicts with fundamental human rights. In the absence of demonstrated harm, we hold it is beyond the competency of the State.[72]

To use pregnancy for women, many of whom lack capacity to control their behavior, and illegitimacy of an innocent child as sanctions (males may well escape the impact of the sanction) for enforcing the values of a particular group, even if it constitutes a majority, not only fails under a compelling-interest standard, it also fails to satisfy even the rationality demanded for traditional due process. "The serious risk of an undesired pregnancy and the unwanted child, disastrous alike to the married as to the unmarried parents and to society as a whole, is utterly disproportionate in harm to any slight public benefit to be gained from a probably ineffective attempt to discourage fornication."[73] An alternative way of stating the same conclusion is to argue that it cannot be assumed that the legislature would have intended such a result.

The nonlegal data processed during the intelligence stage and judicial recognition of the increasing body of data on the negative effects associated with unwanted pregnancy had come to fruition, as they had in a number of abortion cases. For the woman, the fear and then the reality of unwanted pregnancy threatens serious psychic injury.

> One can't help but imagine the panic that exists in the minds of some of these girls when the meaning of the "missed period" becomes evident. For in a futile attempt to bring on their menses, they ran the gamut from praying that they were not pregnant to strenuous exercise, swimming, highdiving, horseback riding, to taking quinine pills, bodily trauma, back bends, hot douches, starvation, having the boy forcibly strike them in the lower abdomen, and in a few cases even attempt to get an abortion. As one girl put it, "Everything possible without killing myself."[74]

The increasing number of illegal abortions, often with serious health hazards for the woman, provides further testimony to the health hazards of unwanted pregnancy. Estimates range from ¼ million to 2 million

---

[72] 429 F.2d at 1402. See Commonwealth v. Baird, 247 N.E.2d at 581, 582.
[73] 247 N.E.2d at 582 (Spiegel, J., dissenting). He reached this conclusion after citing a number of nonlegal sources.
[74] Clyde Von der Ahe, "The Unwed Teen-age Mother," *American Journal of Obstetrics and Gynecology*, CIV (May 15, 1969), 283. See generally Group for the Advancement of Psychiatry, *The Right to Abortion: A Psychiatric View* (New York, 1969).

criminal abortions annually, resulting in about 40 percent of all maternal deaths.[75]

These negative health effects become even more compelling when consideration is given to the economic discrimination thus effectuated (which also raises serious equal-protection issues). Wealthier women can probably secure contraceptive advice and services, married or unmarried, and, if pregnancy does develop, can afford safer, effective abortions. Even if abortive services are not available in her immediate area, she can bear the costs of travel. The unwanted child can be quietly disposed of, leaving the woman free of any social stigma that might attach to out-of-wedlock pregnancy. In all of this, the fornication laws and the birth-control provisions stand as testimonials to the ineffectiveness of some laws. Similarly, the laws appear to be equally ineffective in deterring the poor unmarried woman or teenage girl from having sexual relations outside of marriage. But even if there were some inhibiting effect on those who appreciate their inability to pay to avoid the possible consequences of illicit sex, as the judges recognized, it is totally disproportionate to the harm visited on those not deterred. It is the poor who lack the means to avoid pregnancy effectively, who must forgo abortion or utilize the butcher, who suffer the most severe trauma at the thought of still another child to care for, who are unable to escape any social stigma if they choose to bear the child.[76]

Similarly, the racial implications of these laws cannot be ignored. As will be discussed in the next chapter, poverty tends to correlate affirmatively with race. Since the laws have their greatest impact on the poor, it is not surprising that inability to avoid the birth of the unwanted child safely and effectively is greatest among racial minorities. During the 1960s, 93 percent of all hospital abortions in New York City were performed on white women. During the same time maternal deaths as a result of illegal abortions were, in a typical year, 56 percent black, 23 percent Puerto Rican, and only 21 percent white.[77]

---

[75] "Abortion Laws, under Challenge, Are Being Liberalized," *Congressional Quarterly*, July 24, 1970, p. 1915.

[76] Group for the Advancement of Psychiatry, *The Right to Abortion*, 207-8. See S. Kleegman, "Planned Parenthood: Its Influence on Public Health and Family Welfare," *Abortion in America*, ed. H. Rosen (Boston, 1967), 254-65. See text accompanying Chapter Nine, notes 2-14 *infra*, on the relationship of poverty and unwanted pregnancy. In Sturgis v. Attorney General, 260 N.E.2d at 691, the court disposed of the equal-protection question by finding that the record was devoid of facts to overcome the presumption of fair treatment.

[77] "Abortion Laws under Challenge," 1915. See text accompanying Chapter Nine, notes 7-18 *infra*, on the relationship of race and unwanted pregnancy.

And the negative effects of utilizing pregnancy or the threat thereof as a sanction is also visited on the child. From the outset of her campaign, Margaret Sanger had stressed the need for contraception to avoid harm to the unwanted child. Branded as an illegitimate, society and the law alike visit burdens on the child. He is unlikely to receive the love and affection available to his legitimate counterpart—maternal rejection is a major factor in human psychopathology.[78] While the U.S. Supreme Court has recognized that it is impermissible to punish a child for the sins of the parents, this is the practical effect of the morals justification.

Finally, there are the negative consequences for society in overpopulation and the soaring public-assistance costs, which will be treated extensively in the next chapter.[79] It might be noted, however, that when governmental resources are increasingly being directed toward fertility control and curbing population pressures, the Massachusetts prohibitions contrarily limit the ability to control fertility. Similarly, as society seeks to curb the incidence of illegitimacy and the soaring welfare rolls, especially in the Aid to Families with Dependent Children program, the Massachusetts law produces opposite tendencies. As already has been suggested, it is the poor who suffer the primary negative effects if the "deterrence" fails, and it is precisely these women and children who swell the welfare rolls. It is well known that illegitimacy rates are disproportionately high among women on welfare. It is not surprising, therefore, that contraceptive services under federally supported welfare services are now available to married and unmarried alike.[80]

Most of these arguments should sound familiar. They were among the basic contentions processed by the Planned Parenthood Federation in its *amicus* brief in *Griswold* and which have been argued in all the court cases discussed in this book. In addition, they portend the analysis of publicly supported family planning in the next chapter. In each instance, the negative effects associated with unwanted pregnancy and the differential wealth impact of laws seeking to control the availability of such services raise serious legal issues. In *Baird*, at least in the Court of Appeals and among the dissenters in the Massachusetts Supreme

---

[78] J. Bowlby, *Maternal Deprivation* (New York, 1966); Group for the Advancement of Psychiatry, *The Right to Abortion*, 109–10, on the sources cited therein. V. Anderson et al., "The Medical, Social, and Educational Implications of the Increase of Out-of-Wedlock Births," *American Journal of Public Health*, LVI (Nov., 1966), 1866–73. See Brief for Defendant, pp. 9–20, Commonwealth v. Baird, 247 N.E.2d 574 (1969).

[79] See text accompanying Chapter Nine *infra*, notes 19, 20–34, on the costs of unwanted pregnancy.

[80] 45 C.F.R. 220.21. See Horstman, "Problem Areas," 483–84.

Court, as in *Griswold*, the arguments and supporting data were successfully processed to the judicial policy-maker and accepted. While it might have been preferable if the legislature had examined the data and fashioned a more precisely drawn regulatory measure taking cognizance of the diverse interests involved, the failure of the legislative policy-maker to assume this responsibility fully laid the groundwork for further judicial intervention. *Griswold* had provided the impetus for a careful re-examination of the issues but the legislature had chosen a narrow response meeting only the minimal implications of the court's opinion. The U.S. Supreme Court will now be called upon to determine if this was sufficient to meet constitutional requirements. For the purpose of this study, the desirability of such seriatum policy formation raises serious question concerning the capacity of the legal system to meet the demand of social change.

DEFINING CRIMINALITY

Still another argument urged by pro-change interests at the intelligence stage, i.e., that the statute was excessively vague and overbroad, has already been discussed in some depth in analyzing the free-speech issues. But this infirmity was not limited to the inhibiting effects on the exercise of free speech alone. Instead, it was argued that the statute failed generally to inform citizens of the boundaries of permissible and proscribed conduct and failed to provide guidance to law-enforcement officials and judges on the limits of proper application: "A statute which either forbids or requires the doing of an act in terms so vague that men of common intelligence must necessarily guess as to its meaning and differ as to its application, violates the first essential of due process. . . ."[81] Simply, if citizens are expected to conform their behavior to the commands of the law or suffer punishment, and if law-enforcement personnel and courts are expected to apply the legislative policy judgment, it is only basic fairness and reasonableness that the legislature provide sufficient guidance regarding the parameters of criminality.

The dissent in *Commonwealth v. Baird* and the Court of Appeals decision both accept the contention that the statute is void for vagueness and overbreadth although the approaches do differ. Justice Spiegel

[81] Connally v. General Constr. Co., 269 U.S. 385, 391 (1926). See generally Note, "The Void-for-Vagueness Doctrine in the Supreme Court," *University of Pennsylvania Law Review*, CIX (Nov., 1970), 67–116.

summarized his conclusion as well as that of the other dissenting opinion: "Its scope of application is indefinite and vague . . . and is a 'hodgepodge' of uncertainties."[82] The exceptions that had been fashioned or suggested through the years (principally by the courts) had rendered the sweeping language of sections 20 and 21 confused and inexact. In *Commonwealth v. Corbett*, for example, the Massachusetts Supreme Court had held that the prohibition did not reach the use of the designated articles when they were intended to be used for the prevention of disease. We are forced to guess at the meaning of this judicially fashioned exception or the extent to which it survived the 1966 legislative addition of section 21A. Perhaps even unmarried persons can obtain contraceptives unless the state is able to prove an intent to use the devices for the prevention of conception. Further, given the physical and psychiatric evils frequently associated with unwanted pregnancy, the condition itself might suffice as a "disease" (it is, for example, susceptible to treatment).[83] Whether a doctor could furnish contraceptives to an unmarried person to preserve her health also remains in doubt. As Justice Black recently observed: "Generally, doctors are encouraged by society's expectation, by the structure of malpractice law and by their own professional standards to give their patients such treatment as is necessary to preserve their health," and health "includes psychological, as well as physical well-being."[84] Nevertheless, the broad words of the statute raise serious doubt whether adequate protection is afforded to the doctor's due-process right to practice his profession.[85]

Further, there are the myriad of free-speech problems cited above, generated by the broad and sweeping language, even given the narrow exception carved into section 21's reference to "exhibiting" by the Massachusetts Supreme Court on behalf of Baird. Finally, there is the

[82] 247 N.E.2d at 583. See *ibid.*, 580-81, for a detailed specification by Justices Whittemore and Cutter of the vagueness created by changes in the law.

[83] N. Wagner, "Sexual Behavior of Adolescents," *Postgraduate Medicine*, XLVI (Oct., 1969), 71, supports the need to treat unwanted pregnancy as a disease. See text accompanying Chapter Three, note 30 *supra*, on the broad definition of disease used in *Sanger*. See text accompanying Chapter Five, notes 13-18 *supra*, on *Corbett* and related cases.

[84] United States v. Vuitch, 91 S. Ct. 1294, 1302 (1971).

[85] But see Sturgis v. Attorney General, 260 N.E.2d at 690-91, where the court disposed of the physician's claims: "We can only say that such well recognized right as does exist is constantly subject to those laws and regulations which have the design of protecting the public health by any rational means. . . . The physician's obligations to his conscience and to his profession is entirely consonant with his obligation also to abide by appropriate regulation imposed by the body politic in the public interest."

uncertain status of those provisions of the statutes requiring medical supervision for *all* contraceptives used by married persons and the excessive intrusion, discussed above, into the private lives of the unmarried under the constitutional mandates of *Griswold*. Even if we were to assume a valid state interest for limited, precisely drawn regulations, this is certainly not the character of the Massachusetts laws.

The Court of Appeals rested its finding of unconstitutional vagueness on the results of its inquiry into the sufficiency of the state interest: "To preserve the statute as one directed towards health [the only permissible state interest involved] would necessitate judicial excision of the expressed distinction between married and unmarried users. Even then, there would be difficulties. Deletion of unsupportable overbreadth, encompassing articles not reasonably believed dangerous to health, would leave the statute with an element of vagueness, a burden we would be reluctant to impose upon the fundamental rights at stake here."[86] Simply stated, the statute could not be judicially revised through interpretation to preserve its constitutionality and still be sufficiently precise to satisfy the demands of due process.

The problem Chief Judge Aldrich faced is common when attempts are made to save statutes from constitutional attack by ignoring the true (but impermissible) objectives of a statute in favor of secondary or unintended (but permissible) state interests. Sections 20 and 21 were enacted to provide a complete state prohibition on dissemination of contraceptive knowledge which was deemed obscene, and the broad, sweeping language served this objective admirably. Obscenity was not entitled to First Amendment protection and the moral evil to be apprehended justified the breadth and vagueness of the prohibitions. But if the purpose and language of the prohibition have remained constant, the status of birth-control materials and information has not. Today, the use of contraceptives (at least by married persons) is protected by constitutional command, and the dissemination of knowledge concerning contraception serves vital social functions deserving constitutional protection. In such a context there is no place for such overly broad, vague prohibitions.

Nevertheless, the majority of the Massachusetts Supreme Court chose to ignore the vagueness issue just as it had avoided the statute's overly broad intrusion into protected free speech. The district court, while noting the problem, blithely dismissed it by noting that the 1966 amendment had fashioned the exemption in section 21A with full knowledge

[86] 429 F.2d at 1402.

of prior judicial action.[87] How the narrow exceptions drawn in section 21A cured the vagueness in sections 20 and 21, which remained intact, was not, however, explained. Under the exception, registered physicians are permitted only to *prescribe and distribute* contraceptives to married persons; registered pharmacists can *furnish* contraceptives to married persons with a prescription; and public-health agencies, registered nurses, and maternity-health clinics may furnish information to married persons as to sources of professional advice regarding contraception. The broad prohibitions of sections 20 and 21 regarding advertising contraception are explicitly retained. (See Appendix D.) And the numerous other sources of vagueness and overbreadth discussed above are in no way affected by the exceptions. Indeed, the limited character of the 1966 legislative action and its failure to review and revise the broad language employed by nineteenth-century legislators, who operated in a different social context to enact laws designed to achieve objectives rejected by modern constitutional interpretation, could hardly be expected to produce any other result. Given the pervasiveness of this infirmity, the entire statutory scheme should fail.

It is now for the Supreme Court to pass judgment on the work product of the state legislature and the state and federal courts. The author's personal evaluation of the desirable outcome must certainly have become apparent. In terms of free speech, due process, and equal protection, the state's legal norms have been found wanting. Again, it is the problem posed when laws are artificially preserved after their reason for enactment has ceased. It is the problem posed when a legislative body fails to assume responsibility to review and revise laws consistently with legal and social change. And it is the problem posed when the criminal law is made the handmaiden of a particular morality without regard for the absence of any demonstrated harm to persons or society.

ADDENDUM

Following completion of this book, the Supreme Court decided *Eisenstadt v. Baird*, holding the Massachusetts law to be unconstitutional.[88] The majority opinion, written by Justice Brennan, initially disposed of the standing issue, primarily along the lines suggested in the text.[89] Just

[87] 310 F. Supp. at 955-56.
[88] 92 S. Ct. 1029 (1972). Justices Powell and Rehnquist did not participate.
[89] *Ibid.*, 1033-35. See text accompanying Chapter Six, notes 46-49 *supra*, and Dienes, "The Progeny of Comstockery," 72-75.

as in *Griswold*, the relationship of the parties (i.e., "between an advocate of the rights of persons to obtain contraceptives and those desirous of doing so")[90] required relaxation of the judicially imposed third-party rule and provided Baird with standing to argue the rights of other persons to acquire contraceptives. Even more important was "the impact of the litigation on third-party interests" since "enforcement of the Massachusetts statute will materially impair the ability of single persons to obtain contraceptives."[91] In this instance, the inability of users of contraceptives to protect their own rights (i.e., they are not subject to prosecution for *use*, as was the case under the Connecticut statute struck down in *Griswold*) necessitated recognition of Baird's standing to raise the constitutional claim.

Turning to the merits, Justice Brennan held the Massachusetts law violative of the equal-protection guarantee of the Fourteenth Amendment. Although recognizing the possibility that a more stringent standard of equal protection might be applicable given the "fundamental freedoms" claimed,[92] he concluded that the statute failed to satisfy even the more lenient standard of review. Simply, there was no rational basis for the different treatment accorded unmarried persons under the act.[93]

First, the court rejected deterrence of illicit sex as the purpose of the statute. It would be unreasonable to assume that the state would punish the misdemeanor of fornication by unwanted pregnancy.[94] The numerous exceptions to the statute suggested that the law could not realistically be directed toward such an objective.[95] Finally, the disparity in sentencing between the birth-control and fornication statutes denigrated the contention that the former was designed in aid of the latter.[96]

Nor was section 21A a health measure. Certainly it was not prior to the 1966 legislative revision, and that was, argued Justice Brennan, only an adjustment to *Griswold*.[97] As a health measure, the provision would

---

[90] 92 S. Ct. at 1034. Since the court was to hold that the Massachusetts law was not a health measure, the fact that Baird was neither a doctor nor druggist was not deemed relevant. *Ibid.*, 1033–34.

[91] *Ibid.*, 1034.

[92] *Ibid.*, 1035n7. See text accompanying Chapter Eight, notes 76–80 *supra*, and Dienes, "The Progeny of Comstockery," 97–118, for an analysis of the equal-protection issue.

[93] 92 S. Ct. at 1035. See Dienes, "The Progeny of Comstockery," 117–18, for an equal-protection analysis using the rational basis test.

[94] 92 S. Ct. at 1036. See text accompanying notes 67–87 *supra*, and Dienes, "The Progeny of Comstockery," 93–96, on the morals interest of the state.

[95] 92 S. Ct. at 1036.

[96] *Ibid.*

[97] *Ibid.*, 1037.

be discriminatory and overbroad. The health needs of the unmarried are as great as those of the married—the statute therefore would discriminate. Not all contraceptives are dangerous—the statute would be overbroad with respect to married persons.[98] Further, the existence of federal and state laws regulating harmful products would make such a health measure unnecessary.[99]

Finally, the court asked whether the laws could be sustained as a prohibition on contraception. But it was deemed unnecessary to determine if a person has a right of access to contraceptives since, whatever the right, there still was no basis for differentiating between the married and unmarried and *Griswold* had established that "the distribution of contraceptives to married persons cannot be prohibited. . . ."[100] Then, in a passage that bespeaks the due process–privacy issue more than the equal-protection issue, Brennan stated:

> It is true that in *Griswold* the right of privacy in question inhered in the marital relationship. Yet the marital couple is not an independent entity with a mind and heart of its own, but an association of two individuals each with a separate intellectual and emotional make-up. If the right of privacy means anything, it is the right of the individual, married or single, to be free from unwarranted governmental intrusion into matters so fundamentally affecting a person as the decision whether to bear or beget a child. See *Stanley v. Georgia*, 394 U.S. 557 (1969). See also *Skinner v. Oklahoma*, 316 U.S. 535 (1942); *Jacobson v. Massachusetts*, 197 U.S. 11, 29 (1905).[101]

By providing different treatment for married and unmarried persons, without any rational basis, Massachusetts had violated the equal-protection guarantee.

Although I certainly concur with the decision reached, there is an aura of unreality to the Brennan opinion. While he argues that health and the deterrence of illicit sex could not be the objectives of the Massachusetts legislation, the above investigation of the 1965–66 legislative travail indicates these were, in fact, the objectives of the statutory revision.[102] A preferable approach would have been to argue that the classi-

[98] *Ibid.* See text accompanying notes 60–66 *supra*, and Dienes, "The Progeny of Comstockery," 88–91, on the health interest of the state.
[99] 92 S. Ct. at 1037.
[100] *Ibid.*, 1038. See Dienes, "The Progeny of Comstockery," 82–86, on the right to distribute.
[101] 92 S. Ct. at 1038. See text accompanying notes 47–56 *supra*, and Dienes, "The Progeny of Comstockery," 65–71, 75–84, on the right of privacy.
[102] See text accompanying Chapter Seven, notes 30–47 *supra*.

fication between married and unmarried persons was not rationally related to these purposes. Although judicial inquiry into the "rationality" of classifications usually has manifested a broad deference to the legislative judgment, there have been occasions when members of the court have been more exacting.[103] Alternatively, the court might have adopted the more stringent standard of review accorded fundamental rights such as privacy, and held that the classification was not *necessary* to effectuate a *compelling* state interest.[104] Or Brennan might have used the privacy right–due process rationale employed in *Griswold*. Certainly his opinion supports acceptance of such a holding. Indeed, the cases cited by Justice Brennan in the foregoing quotation suggest the potential breadth of such a privacy right: *Stanley v. Georgia*, an obscenity case, reflecting mental privacy; *Jacobson v. Massachusetts*, involving compulsory vaccination, suggesting physical integrity as an aspect of privacy; *Skinner v. Oklahoma*, dealing with compulsory sterilization, reflecting privacy in procreative matters.[105]

Any of these alternate approaches would seem to provide more acceptable foundations for the decision. In trying to take the narrower, more traditional route to equal-protection questions, the opinion introduces unnecessary confusion and affords opportunity for criticism. But in any case, recognition that *Griswold* potentially protects the right to *distribute* and *receive* as well as to *use* contraceptives and the broad language used in characterizing the privacy right does provide ammunition for further adjudicatory development. And the limited character of the holding invites a more precisely defined state legislative response designed to regulate distribution of certain contraceptives in light of possible health hazards.

Indeed, the excessive breadth of the Massachusetts prohibitions is the focus of the concurring opinion of Justice White, joined by Justice Blackmun. They accept the statute as a health measure and recognize the power of the state to regulate in spite of the intrusion on privacy interests.

[103] See, e.g., Morey v. Doud, 354 U.S. 457 (1957); Shapiro v. Thompson, 394 U.S. 618, 638 (1969); Dandridge v. Williams, 397 U.S. 471, 528-30 (1970) (Marshall, J., dissenting); Labine v. Vincent, 91 S. Ct. 1017, 1027 (1971) (Brennan, J., dissenting); Reed v. Reed, 92 S. Ct. 251 (1971).

[104] See text accompanying notes 44-45 *supra*, and Dienes, "The Progeny of Comstockery," 70-72, 97-98, on the more stringent standard of review.

[105] See text accompanying Chapter Six, notes 65-93 *supra*, and Dienes, *The Progeny of Comstockery*, 65-70, on *Griswold*. See material cited in note 101 *supra* on the application of *Griswold* to the Baird litigation. All three dimensions of the privacy right noted in this addendum are discussed in Dienes, "The Progeny of Comstockery," 75-79.

Had Baird distributed a supply of the so-called "pill" I would sustain his conviction under this statute. Requiring a prescription to obtain potentially dangerous contraceptive material may place a substantial burden upon the right recognized in *Griswold*, but that burden is justified by a strong State interest and does not, as did the statute at issue in Griswold, sweep unnecessarily broadly or seek "to achieve its goals by means having the maximum destructive impact upon" a protected relationship. *Griswold v. Connecticut*, 381 U.S. at 485.[106]

But in this instance the state control encompassed contraceptives not proven hazardous to health, Baird had been convicted for distributing such a nonhazardous device, and this burdened the constitutional right to privacy of married persons. "Due regard for protecting constitutional rights requires that the record contain evidence that a restriction on distribution of vaginal foam is essential to achieve the statutory purpose, or the relevant facts concerning the product must be such as to fall within the range of judicial notice."[107]

Even if Baird could constitutionally be convicted for distributing contraceptives to unmarried persons, there was nothing in the record indicating the marital status of the recipient of the foam. Therefore, since Baird *could* have been convicted for distributing nonhazardous contraceptives to married persons, his conviction could not stand. It was unnecessary to reach "the novel constitutional question whether a State may restrict or forbid the distribution of contraceptives to the unmarried."[108] Justice White's opinion, then, is limited solely to the law treated as a health measure and its impact on the privacy of married persons. But it implicitly recognizes that the privacy right of married persons does afford a degree of constitutional protection to a distributor of contraceptives.

Justice Douglas, concurring, joined the opinion of the court, but also found the Massachusetts law violative of the First Amendment free-speech guarantee. However, instead of following the argument suggested in the text that the statute was *on its face* an overly broad intrusion on free-speech interests,[109] he held that the distribution provisions were unconstitutional *as applied* to Baird. Recognizing that this right

[106] 92 S. Ct. at 1043.
[107] *Ibid.*
[108] *Ibid.*, 1044.
[109] See text accompanying notes 35–40 *supra*, and Dienes, "The Progeny of Comstockery," 60–63, on the constitutionality of the distribution provision on its face. See text accompanying notes 31–34 *supra*, and Dienes, "The Progeny of Comstockery," 59–60, on its constitutionality as applied.

was "not confined to verbal expression" but "embrace[s] appropriate types of action," the distribution of articles was deemed "a protection of the visual aid," which "should be a permissible adjunct of free speech."[110] There was no substantial governmental interest justifying this regulation of conduct associated with speech since no evidence had been presented that Baird intended the recipient to keep the foam.[111] But there is again an aura of unreality to this argument—Baird had told his audience to come up and get some of the contraceptives. What might have been argued is that the government's interest in controlling distribution of this contraceptive was not sufficiently compelling. But the importance of the conduct to effectuating the speech interest seems relatively minor and challenges such a conclusion. In pursuing the narrower holding, Douglas, like Brennan, provided an unnecessary basis of attack for those critical of a broad reading of the free-speech guarantee. On the other hand, renewed recognition that the First Amendment guarantee does protect associated conduct affords an additional tool for further constitutional adjudication.

Chief Justice Burger dissented, hardly a unique situation. For Burger, the other opinions "seriously invade the constitutional prerogative of the States and regrettably hark back to the heyday of substantive due process."[112] The rights of the distributor and those of the recipients are distinguishable and Baird lacked standing to raise the latter[113]—privacy rights and the constitutionality of the married-unmarried classification are thereby excluded from consideration. (He did, however, acknowledge the choice of a means of birth control to be "a highly personal matter.")[114] But the focus was to be solely on the ability of the state to regulate health matters without assessing the impact of the regulation on the rights of users of the contraceptives. Contrary to the majority, the state court had determined that the law served a health purpose and it was not a proper function of the Supreme Court "to dismiss as dubious a state court's explication of a state statute absent overwhelming and irrefutable reasons for doing so."[115] Here is a clear rejection of the more stringent standard of review in favor of an approach emphasizing Supreme Court deference to local judgment. Since the fundamental right of

[110] 92 S. Ct. at 1041–42.
[111] *Ibid.*, 1041.
[112] *Ibid.*, 1045.
[113] *Ibid.*, 1044.
[114] *Ibid.*, 1047.
[115] *Ibid.*, 1046.

privacy had been dismissed from consideration, such a determination logically followed.

While acknowledging the majority's reference to the overbroad character of the law when treated as a health measure, Chief Justice Burger noted that they had not rested on or even developed the argument.[116] The approach of Justice Brennan avoiding a probing inquiry into the relation of the classification and the claimed purposes of the state lent itself to such an offhand dismissal. Still, the remainder of Burger's opinion, rejecting Justice White's approach, leaves little doubt that he would have similarly rejected any of the alternative equal-protection or due-process formulations suggested above.

Chief Justice Burger argued that it was not for the court to probe the evidence, as Justice White had done, to determine if the permissible state purpose would in fact be furthered by application of the statute to the fact situation in question.

> The actual hazards of introducing a particular foreign substance into the human body are frequently controverted, and I cannot believe that unanimity of expert opinion is a prerequisite to a State's exercise of its police power, no matter what the subject matter of the regulation. Even assuming no present dispute among medical authorities, we cannot ignore that it has become common-place for a drug or food additive to be universally regarded as harmless on one day and to be condemned as perilous on the next. It is inappropriate for this Court to overrule a legislative classification by relying on the present consensus among leading authorities. The commands of the Constitution cannot fluctuate with the shifting tides of scientific opinion.[117]

For Burger, the state was merely regulating distribution of medical substances, a traditional local prerogative. There was no interference with the legitimate need for information concerning birth control or with its use. *Griswold*, which was viewed as resting on "tenuous moorings," was not rejected; it simply wasn't deemed applicable. "By relying on *Griswold* in the present context, the Court has passed beyond the penumbras of the specific guarantees into the uncircumscribed area of personal predilections."[118]

By avoiding issues relating to the impact of the law on the rights of

[116] *Ibid.*, 1046*n*2.
[117] *Ibid.*, 1046.
[118] *Ibid.*, 1047.

married and unmarried persons, and focusing instead solely on the state regulation of the distributor, Burger's opinion conveys a greater sense of credibility than it deserves—the effect of the law on personal rights is the essence of the issue. Still, contrary to Burger's contention, there is nothing in the majority or concurring opinions which opens the door to the "curbstone quack." What is demanded is that state legislation be narrowly drawn and applied to further its actual interests in health or morals. It is the sweeping governmental intrusion into private matters of individual choice that is condemned. Indeed, the opinions invite the state legislature to clarify its vital objectives and more carefully delineate what interferences with individual liberty are necessary to effectuate them—only then is it possible to determine if the benefits are worth the costs. Indeed, Chief Justice Burger is correct that this is essentially substantive due process, whether cast in the language of due process or equal protection. But when fundamental interests of citizens are at stake, the exercise of the legislative prerogative demands close judicial scrutiny.

While I have some difficulty, then, with the rationale of the majority and concurring opinions in *Baird*, they do provide ample opportunity for constitutional development through adjudication and invite state legislation furthering vital interests but having a less intrusive impact on fundamental rights. Only four justices rejected the power of the state to distinguish between married and unmarried persons in their right to receive contraceptives. Indeed, the opinions do not clearly establish a general due-process right to receive contraceptives. And there are now two additional justices. Still, the language of the Brennan opinion regarding privacy and the limitations on the state's ability to differentially treat married and unmarried persons provides potent ammunition for civil-rights lawyers challenging laws involving abortion, homosexuality, sodomy, etc. There is, in short, ample impetus for further constitutional development, for additional legal change.

Nine

The Dynamics of Change: Publicly Supported Birth Control

The developments discussed in the previous three chapters were not isolated events, but part of a general legal response to a changing social environment. Legislatures and courts across the country were actively refashioning or eliminating their restrictive birth-control provisions; frequently, sweeping prohibitions were replaced by more flexible regulatory tools or by no control at all.[1] Indeed, it appears that there has been increasing acceptance, at least in this area, of the tenet that private moral beliefs are not properly translated automatically into legal norms, that legal action must be justified only by demonstration of social necessity or desirability. This rationale can be extended even further to suggest that a presumption against the necessity of such restrictions exists and a strong burden of proof must be placed on those who would restrict individual liberty to demonstrate clearly an overriding requirement of the public well-being. Relating these jural considerations to the birth-control issue, it could then be argued that there is no empirical demonstration of serious danger to the public well-being without these provisions. In this instance, then, prohibitive use of civil power would not be justified.

But neither a general consensus on the inefficacy of the Comstock provisions nor the achievement of a temporary social adjustment marks

[1] On legislative and judicial revisions prior to and after *Griswold* see Planned Parenthood–World Population, *Ending Comstockery in America*, I–V, Sept., 1966; Amicus Brief; Planned Parenthood–World Population, *Laws Relating to Birth Control and Family Planning in the U.S.* (New York, 1968), and subsequent addenda to the 1968 report.

the end of this interaction process. As indicated in the Introduction, the "settlement" of a legal dispute is merely a temporary refuge as new interests are aggregated and new demands articulated. Even as the consensus on prohibitive legal norms was being fashioned, new demands were pressed based on changing social needs. Government was being asked to change roles, from a prohibitor of the dissemination of birth-control services to an active participant in its distribution. In the present chapter this dynamic character of the legal-change process will be analyzed through examination of the social needs that prompted the new change demands, as well as the controversy and legal response they engendered. Although our general focus will be on the national forum, reference will also be made to the changing patterns of legal action in states which reflect the national developments.

THE SOCIAL IMPETUS FOR CHANGE

Impetus for the government's domestic intervention has centered on two primary issues: (1) the need to assure equality of access to birth-control services; and (2) the effect of the continuing population explosion on the quality of American life.

As of 1967, some 26 million Americans, approximately 13 percent of our population, lived on incomes below the Social Security Administration's "poverty level" of $3,335 for an urban family of four.[2] An additional 19 million citizens would be encompassed in the "near-poor" classification—if a person forced to live on 90 cents per day for food can realistically be classified as only near-poor.[3] Consideration of the consequences of uncontrolled fertility for this sector of the populace pro-

[2] U.S. Congress, House, Ad Hoc Subcommittee on Urban Growth of the Committee on Banking and Currency, *Hearings on Population Trends*, 91st Cong., 1st Sess., 1969, pt. 1, p. 56, table 19 (hereafter cited as *Population Trend Hearings*). A study of the cost of living in thirty-nine metropolitan areas and several nonmetropolitan regions by the Bureau of Labor Statistics of the U.S. Department of Labor estimated that it would cost $9,076 for a "moderate" living for a family of four in our urban areas as of spring, 1967, $5,915 for a "lower" level, and $13,050 for a "higher" level. U.S. Bureau of Labor Statistics, "3 Standards of Living for an Urban Family of Four Persons," bull. 1570-5, Mar., 1969. See Bureau of Social Science Research, Inc., *Living Costs and Welfare Payments* (Washington, 1969); L. A. Ferman, J. L. Kornbluh, and A. Haber, eds., *Poverty in America* (rev. ed., Ann Arbor, 1968), chap. 1, for a variety of other cost-of-living standards.

[3] Planned Parenthood–World Population, *When More Is Less* (New York, 1968).

vides an initial impetus for extension of publicly supported family planning.

Differential fertility among our differing socioeconomic classes is a reality that can no longer be ignored. Mothers in the upper SES have approximately two to three children; in the lowest SES group they have between five and six children.[4] There are approximately 15 million indigent children in the United States. Of these, 6.5 million, or 43 percent, are from families with at least five members under age eighteen. There are 148 children among the poor for every 100 productive adults; among the non-poor, the ratio is 79 per 100 adults. Chicago's poor, for example, are said to have a birth rate equal to that of India.[5] The poverty ratio among families with one child is 9 percent; when there are six or more children, the rate soars to 42 percent.[6] Over one-fourth of all families with three or more children were living in poverty in 1966 and 40 percent were poor or near-poor.[7]

And it is precisely these families, living on below-subsistence incomes, who can least afford the addition of another member. The proper care of children is directly related to the financial ability of the family to provide for their physical and emotional needs. The effects of deprivation on physical and mental well-being are too well documented to contest. With hunger and malnutrition come higher infant and maternal mortality rates, organic brain damage to the child, retarded growth and

[4] Planned Parenthood–World Population, *The Poverty of Abundance* (New York, 1966).
[5] Mollie Orshansky, "Who's Who among the Poor: A Demographic View of Poverty," *Social Security Bulletin*, July, 1965, pp. 2, 14–15. See Harold L. Sheppard, *Effects of Family Planning on Poverty in the United States* (Kalamazoo, 1967), 2.
[6] Joseph D. Tydings, "Family Planning: A Basic Human Right," reprint of a speech delivered before the U.S. Senate, May 8, 1969, p. 2.
[7] Mollie Orshansky, "The Shape of Poverty in 1966," *Social Security Bulletin*, Mar., 1968, table 4. See Frederick S. Jaffe and Allan F. Guttmacher, "Family Planning Programs in the United States," *Demography*, V, no. 2 (1968), 910–23, reprinted in Center for Family Planning Program Development, *Family Planning Programs in the United States*, pub. 7 (New York, 1969), 2–3; testimony of Philip M. Hauser, *1966 Hearings*, 110. The National Academy of Sciences, in its report on the growth of the U.S. population, states that excess fertility "is one of the factors that puts prosperity out of reach of millions of our citizens. The burden of unwanted children among impoverished mothers in the United States is much like that experienced by mothers in underdeveloped countries." It adds that "most Americans of higher income and better education exercise this right (to control family size) as a matter of course, but many of the poor and uneducated are, in fact, deprived of the right. No family should be fated through poverty or ignorance to have children they do not want and cannot properly care for." "The Growth of the U.S. Population," *1966 Hearings*, 148.

learning rates, greater susceptibility to disease, and numerous psychic damages—"social unrest, distrust, alienation, withdrawal, and frustration."[8] The 1955 and 1965 nationwide household-consumption studies conducted by the Department of Agriculture documented the direct relationship between the adequacy of a child's dietary intake and the amount of income available.[9] The following commentary, from the report of the Council of Economic Advisors, summarizes the consequences of the "cycle of dependency" produced by an inadequate income.

> *The vicious circle.* Poverty breeds poverty. A poor individual of a poor family has a high probability of staying poor. Low incomes carry with them high risks of illness; limitations on mobility; limited access to education information, and training. Poor parents cannot give their children the opportunities for better health and education needed to improve their lot. Lack of motivation, hope and incentive is a more subtle but no less powerful barrier than lack of financial means. Thus the cruel legacy of poverty is passed from parents to children.
>
> Escape from poverty is not easy for American children raised in families accustomed to living on relief. Recent sample studies of AFDC recipients found that more than 40% of the parents were themselves raised in homes where public assistance has been received. It is difficult for children to find and follow avenues of living out of poverty in environments where education is deprecated and hope is smothered. This is particularly true when discrimination appears as an insurmountable barrier. Education may be seen as a waste of time if even the well-trained are forced to accept menial labor because of their color or nationality.[10]

---

[8] Citizen's Board of Inquiry into Hunger and Malnutrition in the United States, *Hunger, U.S.A.* (Washington, 1968), 31. For further documentation of the effects of deprivation suffered by children in families having below-subsistence incomes see U.S. Congress, Senate, Subcommittee on Employment, Manpower, and Poverty of the Committee on Labor and Public Welfare, *Hearings on Hunger and Malnutrition in America*, 90th Cong., 1st Sess., 1967; C. S. Chilman, *Growing Up Poor* (Washington, 1966); Harrington, *The Other America*; Ferman, Kornbluh, and Haber, *Poverty in America*.

[9] U.S. Department of Agriculture, *Household Food Consumption Survey, 1955 and 1965, Food Consumption of Households in the United States*, rpt. 1.

[10] U.S., *Economic Report of the President* (1964), 69–70. A graphic description of the "culture of poverty" is also presented in former President Johnson's "Message on Poverty," Mar. 16, 1964: "The young man or woman who grows up without a decent education, in a broken home, in a hostile and squalid environment, in ill health or in the face of racial injustice—that young man or woman is often trapped in a life of poverty. He does not have the skills demanded by a complex society, he does not know how to acquire those skills. He faces a mounting sense of

Parents lacking an adequate income are severely impaired in their ability to provide an adequate diet, decent housing, educational opportunity, psychic well-being, recreational advantages, physical and mental care, and the countless other elements essential to a decent living standard. Consider, for example, the life-style and the treatment of the children in one such family.[11] The house in which the family lives does not comply with minimum standards of decency and health. Children are forced to sleep two and three to a bed or cot. None of them have more than one change of clothing and all need shoes. There are inadequate funds to pay school expenses including the cost of lunches, often forcing the children to skip this meal. One of the children missed approximately twenty-two days of school last semester because of illness and hunger, producing trouble with the truant authorities. Another child three years old weighs only twenty pounds because of worms and a deficient diet. All of the children require dental care, but there is no money available for such "extras." Refrigeration equipment is in poor condition, permitting air to enter and spoil the food.

Nor can we shrug off the problem by a simplistic "It's their choice. If they want kids, they have to pay the piper." In the first place, certainly the child has no choice. Lacking any option as to his birthright, he is thrust into a life-style of minimal opportunity and destructive of hope. Nor does the parent really make a free choice. Women in the poverty sector have a fertility rate 55 percent higher than those non-poor in spite of the fact that they aspire to the same size family as their more fortunate counterparts;[12] it has been estimated that women in the poverty sector experienced some 450,000 unwanted births during 1966.[13] Indeed, a 1960 study concluded that the problem of unwanted pregnancies is most severe in the lower-income and -education groups, and cited as the reason the lack of knowledge of effective contraceptive techniques. The study also indicated that, while the poor and uneducated tended

---

despair, which drains his initiative and ambition and energy." U.S. Congress, House, *Misc. Doc. 243*, 88th Cong., 2nd Sess., 1967, p. 2.

[11] The facts are derived from Memorandum for Plaintiff, pp. 5-6, Robinson v. Hackney, Civ. No. 68-4-294 (S.D. Tex., filed Apr. 2, 1968).

[12] Arthur A. Campbell, "The Role of Family Planning in the Reduction of Poverty," *Journal of Marriage and the Family*, XXX (May, 1968), 237. See Campbell, "Family Planning and the Reduction of Poverty in the United States," in Oscar Harkavy, Frederick S. Jaffe, and Samuel Wishik, *Implementing DHEW Policy on Family Planning and Population* (New York, 1967) (hereafter cited as Harkavy Report), reprinted in *1967 Hearings*, 186-90; Jaffe and Guttmacher, "Family Planning Programs," 1.

[13] Campbell, "The Role of Family Planning," 237; Campbell, "Family Planning and the Reduction of Poverty," 190.

to want fewer children than the higher SES groups, they expected to have more.[14] Research done thus far, then, seems to indicate that while motivation is present among lower SES groups, the knowledge and access to means of effective conception control is lacking, and there are no statistics available on the number of these women who, fearing another birth, turned to an illegal abortion as a last resort.

While higher SES groups have access to their family physicians for family-planning assistance and generally have the education to regulate fertility effectively, the poor have almost invariably been forced to depend upon public-health services, which, until recently, assiduously avoided family planning. It has been estimated that there are some 5.4 million American women aged eighteen to forty-four who are in need of a subsidized family-planning service. In 1968 only 773,000 of these women were served by all public and private sources—less than 15 percent of those needing assistance.[15]

This is not to say that providing family-planning services to this unserved segment is claimed to be a panacea for poverty and the problem it entails, but many view it as a vital weapon in the struggle. This fact, the importance of family planning in the struggle against poverty, has led some persons to refer to it as a "fundamental human right": "For the right to be able to plan one's family is as essential a part of full freedom of opportunity as the right to a decent home, the right to an education commensurate with ability and the right to a good job. Indeed, the denial of the right to plan the number and spacing of children denies equal opportunity in housing, education and employment."[16]

---

[14] Whelpton, Campbell, and Patterson, *Fertility and Family Planning*, 239-43. The highest proportion of those who lack the knowledge and means to control effectively the incidence of births are non-whites who live in the rural South or who have such a background. See N. B. Ryder and C. F. Westoff, "Relationships among Intended, Expected, Desired and Ideal Family Size: United States, 1965," *Population Resources*, Mar., 1969, 1-7; "Child Bearing Aspirations of Public Health Maternity Patients," address by R. Browning and L. L. Parks, American Public Health Association, 1963; testimony of Dr. Joseph D. Beasley, *1966 Hearings*, 474-91.

Judith Blake, "Population Policy for Americans: Is the Government Misled?," *Science*, CLXIV (May 2, 1969), 522-29, is extremely critical of findings such as those set forth in the text. For an effective refutation of her critique see Oscar Harkavy, Frederick S. Jaffe, and Samuel M. Wishik, "Family Planning and Public Policy: Who Is Misleading Whom?," *Science*, CLXV (July 25, 1969), 367-73.

[15] U.S. Office of Economic Opportunity, *Need for Subsidized Family Planning Services: United States, Each State and County, 1968* (prepared by PP-WP, Center for Family Planning Program Development), 4-5; Planned Parenthood-World Population, *Five Million Women* (New York, 1969).

[16] Tydings, "Family Planning," 3. The 1966 U.N. "Declaration on Population"

Nor can we divorce this problem from considerations of racial justice. It has been estimated that of the 5.4 million American women presently requiring subsidized family-planning services, approximately 70 percent are white. However, because non-whites are disproportionately poor, more than half of fertile non-white women seeking to avoid pregnancy need subsidized family-planning services. Further, non-white fertility is still 40 percent higher than white fertility. Births of the fifth order or higher totaled nearly one-third of all non-white births—almost twice the proportion for white women, in spite of the fact that non-white poor manifest a desire for even smaller families than the poor and non-poor white.[17] Although poverty among whites and non-whites alike has steadily decreased (although at a much slower pace for the latter), the deprivation ratio among the non-white poor with five or more children has actually increased.[18] Given the relation of fertility rates to poverty and of poverty to the Negro population, the problem seems clear.

Aside from the human consequences of poverty and racial injustice, there is the more mundane but relevant consideration of economic cost. The burden of maintaining a constantly increasing Aid to Families With Dependent Children (AFDC) program, the costs of public housing and health-care facilities and the manifold other economic repercussions of the welfare state have brought increased attention to the causes of the poverty problem. Given the desire, but inability, of the poor to control their family size, and the correlation between poverty and the fertility rate, there is a real potential for savings in tax dollars. In fact, it has been estimated that every dollar invested in assuring the availability of effective family-planning services produces a savings of $25 to $70.[19] On a

---

provides that "the opportunity to decide the number and spacing of children is a basic human right." "Statement by Secretary-General U Thant on Population," U.N. Press Release S6/SM/620, Dec. 9, 1966.

[17] Adelaide C. Hill and Frederick S. Jaffe, "Negro Fertility and Family Size Preference: Implications for Programming of Health and Social Services," *The Negro American*, ed. Talcott Parsons and Kenneth B. Clark (Boston, 1966); PP-WP, *Five Million Women*, 9. On the fertility desires of the poor see U.S. Congress, Senate, Subcommittee on Health of the Committee on Labor and Public Welfare, *Hearings on Family Planning and Population Research*, 1970, 91st Cong., 1st Sess., 1970, pp. 64–65, 121 (hereafter cited as *S. 2108 Hearings*).

[18] Sheppard, *Effects of Family Planning on Poverty*, 5–6.

[19] Tydings, "Family Planning," 5; Sheppard, *Effects of Family Planning on Poverty*, 19–20. The latter author notes that the cost-benefit ratio involves private individual benefits of $450 million and $250 million in reduced public expenditures. Planned Parenthood–World Population estimates the potential benefits at $13 billion annually—even the most conservative estimate indicates a saving of $3.5 billion annually. *When More Is Less*, 14.

simple cost-benefit basis, then, the impetus for providing family-planning service to those unable to afford assistance is clearly present.

We turn now to the second impetus for modern governmental intervention. If you have ever visited Walden Pond, Thoreau's spot of seclusion and isolation, or spent time at a popular national park during the peak tourist season, or gone to the beach on a hot summer day, or even driven the expressways of a major city during rush hour, you perhaps have a better appreciation of the meaning of the population explosion. Americans have been prone to associate population problems with Asia and Latin America with their teeming millions approaching the point of starvation. It is quite true that this country has and probably will have the food and capital to provide sustenance for our increasing population. But where do we put the people and what kind of life will they lead? Americans have long valued growth, large families, and have poured into the cities in search of new opportunities, but the consequences of the continuation of such patterns for the future might well be disastrous.

Population growth has already intensified problems of urban congestion, educational quality, transportation, air, water, and noise pollution, sanitation, provision of recreational facilities, unemployment, crime, taxation, freedom from excessive governmental interference, and race relations. Our present population is 205 million, and in spite of a steady decline in the birth rate between 1958 and 1968 it will increase by approximately 100 million in the next thirty years.[20] What do we do with our projected 300 million-plus Americans in the year 2000 driving their 240 million automobiles?[21] Where do we find the 1.5 million jobs every year for the next decade and a half to absorb new workers?[22] And where do you go if you just "want to get away from it all?" Babies born in the first boom years following World War II are now reaching their high fertility ages. Between 1960 and 1980 the number of women aged twenty to twenty-nine will double, with a doubled potential for fer-

[20] U.S. Bureau of the Census, *Statistical Abstract of the United States: 1970*, 5, 6, tables 2, 3; President Richard M. Nixon, "Message on Population Growth," *House Doc. 91-139*, July 21, 1969, p. 4 (hereafter cited as Nixon, "Population Message"). See Philip M. Hauser, "The Population of the United States, Retrospect and Prospect," *The Population Dilemma*, ed. Hauser (2nd ed., Englewood Cliffs, 1969); "Population Activities in the United States," *Population Bulletin*, XXVI (Dec., 1970), 7–8.

[21] "Anti-Pollution Funds Are Short, Time Lags Are Long," *Congressional Quarterly*, May 23, 1969, p. 817 (hereafter cited as *CQ* Pollution Fact Sheet). See Population Reference Bureau, "Outdoor Recreation Threatened by Excess Population," *1965 Hearings*, 491.

[22] Planned Parenthood–World Population, *The Poverty of Abundance*, 30.

tility. An average reduction of one birth per woman would still leave us with a population in the year 2000 of 290 million.[23] Coupled with a continuing decline in the death rate, an increase in the marriage rate, and a continued expectation of many Americans for families of three to four children, the population dilemma poses one of the most severe issues our nation faces.

Nor is the American population dispersing uniformly throughout the nation. We have increasingly become a nation of urban dwellers and there is no reason to expect this trend to change. A nation 95 percent rural in 1790 is almost three-fourths urban in 1970, and is projected to reach over 80 percent urban by the turn of the century. Equally as dramatic is the projected increase in the segment of the population living in metropolitan areas—from 64 percent today to approximately 75 percent in the year 2000.[24] The concept of the "megalopolis" is rapidly being transformed into reality as rural farmlands are absorbed into the urban complex. Flying over the northeast coast of the United States will illustrate the fact of urbanization more than any words. The packing of people into an ever-diminishing amount of personal space suggests a life-style more akin to a bee or an ant than a human being.

But population is not only a problem of numbers or even population concentration. The words "environment" and "ecology" are taking on a new meaning for many citizens as we experience the consequences of the havoc we are inflicting on ourselves.

Stagnant streams, dying lakes, and water rationing attest to our unwillingness to preserve decent water supplies so essential to life processes. Not only do we seem willing to poison the water we drink with pollutants, but we inflict our destructive tendencies on the other inhabitants of the planet who look to the waters, and of course we again reap the harvest to the extent that we depend on them for our life-styles. It has been estimated that the demand for water, presently totaling 24 billion gallons daily, will reach 34 billion gallons daily by 1980. By the year

[23] "U.S. Population Prospects," address by Robert C. Cook, National Conference on Family Planning, Planned Parenthood–World Population, May 5–6, 1966. See Hauser, "The Population of the U.S.," 91, 95–96.

[24] U.S. Census, *1970 Statistical Abstract*, 16, table 15. See testimony of Philip M. Hauser, U.S. Congress, Senate, Committee on Government Operations, *Hearings on S. 2701 to Establish a Commission on Population Growth and the American Future*, 91st Cong., 1st Sess., 1969, pp. 207–8 (hereafter cited as *American Future Hearings*); Hauser, "The Population of the U.S.," 102. It has been estimated that some 75 percent of the nation's population in 1975 will live on 11 percent of the land. Testimony of Dr. William E. Moran, Jr., president of the Population Reference Bureau, Inc., *Population Trend Hearings*, 70.

2000, two-thirds of the annual stream flows in our country will consist of polluted waters[25]—polluted by the willingness of man to dump his wastes freely and by his unwillingness to take steps to preserve and reclaim this vital resource.

The fact that Los Angeles residents continue to breathe has provided a dramatic example of the capacity of the human animal to adapt to his changing environment. But there is increasing concern that even adaptation has its limits. It is established that air pollution is associated with higher mortality rates due to cancer of the respiratory tract, cancer of the stomach, esophagus, and arteriosclerotic heart disease. Yet we continue to spew 142 million tons of toxic matter every year into our air from motor vehicles, industrial emissions, and just plain waste incineration.[26] Decreasing amounts of oxygen and increases in carbon dioxide in the atmosphere pose an obvious, even though often ignored, threat to our survival, not only from the air we breathe, but also from its potential impact on other life forms on which our own place in the ecological system depends. When one reads of the sale of oxygen to the residents of Tokyo during the peak periods of atmospheric pollution or the threat of mass death from an atmospheric depression in Los Angeles, the importance of air quality becomes apparent.[27]

And then there is the garbage! Consider the following commentary on our willingness to care for our environment:

> We spread 48 billion (rustproof) cans and 26 billion (nondegradable) bottles over our landscape every year.... We produce 800 million pounds of trash a day, a great deal of which ends up in our fields, our parks, and our forests. Only one-third of the billion pounds of paper we use every year is reclaimed. Nine million cars, trucks, and buses are abandoned every year, and, while many of them are used as scrap, a large though undetermined number are left to disintegrate slowly in backyards, in fields and woods, and on the side of highways.[28]

[25] *CQ* Pollution Fact Sheet, 817. See the chapter on "Water: Filthier and Farther," in Mitchell Gordon, *Sick Cities* (Baltimore, 1965), 110–35; "President Nixon's Message on the Environment," *Congressional Quarterly*, Feb. 13, 1970, pp. 435–36 (hereafter cited as "Nixon's Environment Message").

[26] "Pollution: Will Man Succeed in Destroying Himself," *Congressional Quarterly*, Jan. 30, 1970, p. 279 (hereafter cited as *CQ* Environment Fact Sheet); Gordon, *Sick Cities*, 86–109.

[27] Gordon, *Sick Cities*, 86–109. See Rufus E. Miles, Jr., "Whose Baby Is the Population Problem," *Population Bulletin*, XVI (Feb., 1970), 12.

[28] Jean Mayer, quoted in Luther J. Carter, "The Population Crisis: Rising Concern at Home," *Science*, CLXVI (Nov. 7, 1969), 725.

I remember seeing a TV special on the environment in which the reporter pictured the cans and debris along the roads and my somewhat incredulous response that he was overdramatizing the problem. Then I walked down some roads and drove my car down the highway and experienced firsthand how accurate the portrayal really was. There is an aggregate of some one billion pounds of solid wastes each day in our urban areas, six to eight pounds per person per day. It is expected that the latter figure will double in the next twenty years[29]—more people, more wastes, and more pollution, more impact on the ecological system.

And even this dreary picture does not begin to explore the dimensions of the problem. Pesticides poisoning our foods and destroying vital components of the eco-system; the noise of our cities threatening our aural capabilities, the loss of privacy so essential to psychological well-being and even our physical health; the oil spills destroying beaches and valuable wildlife; the consumption of natural resources; the intentional or negligent destruction of irreplaceable species of wildlife—all go into man's environmental crises. As the Department of Health, Education and Welfare suggested: "An individually acceptable amount of water pollution, added to a tolerable amount of air pollution, added to a bearable amount of noise and congestion can produce a totally unacceptable health environment."[30]

In the righteous indignation of citizens directed at government, industry, and technology, we seem somehow to have ignored the real culprit. Industry produces because we consume; the more we consume, the more industry produces. And Americans with only 6 percent of the world's population consume 34 percent of the world's energy production, 29 percent of the steel production, and 17 percent of the cut timber.[31] Aside from our natural reluctance to cut back on our own pollution, how many of us would be willing to curtail the consumption— our high standard of living—which is responsible for the demand to which industry responds?

As we begin to perceive this relationship of demand for consumption purposes with pollution and environmental destruction in meeting that

[29] *CQ* Pollution Fact Sheet, 817. The estimate of a doubling in the amount of solid waste by 1990 was made by the Public Health Service.

[30] HEW, quoted in *CQ* Pollution Fact Sheet, 817.

[31] Carter, "The Population Crisis," 725. Paul Ehrlich, *The Population Bomb* (New York, 1968), 133, estimates that with less than one-fifteenth of the population the United States consumes over half of the raw materials produced each year and suggests this figure might reach 80 percent in twenty years. For an account of the debate over the relationship of pollution and population see *Population Bulletin*, XXVI (Dec., 1970).

demand, we also begin to perceive the relationship of pollution to population pressures. Population is not merely a problem of the consequences of overcrowding, as vital as this may be. It is also a problem of increasing demand. People consume; more people tend to consume more. Increased demand for goods, increased wastes requiring disposal, further utilization of our resources to supply the increased demand—this is the by-product of excessive population, and it is a problem as crucial as any we face today.

There is, however, a tendency to confuse the population-environmental issue with the problem posed by the need of indigents for family-planning assistance and the value of family planning generally. While women in the lower SES sectors are overproducing, it is our white, middle-class suburban family that is largely responsible for the population crisis. If the poor had the capacity to control fertility pursuant to their desire for limited family size, the annual birth rate would drop, but, as the National Academy of Sciences report in 1965 noted, "the importance of high fertility among the under-privileged lies not so much in its contribution to the national birth rate, as in the difficulties that excessive fertility imposes on the impoverished themselves."[32] Whereas the ideal family among the population generally was once considered to be two to three children, it has more recently been three to four. Whereas the problem in the indigency sector is knowledge and access, in this area it is motivation. With our affluence we feel that we can afford a third or fourth child. To stress population problems in relation to the indigent without considering the problem posed by fertility rates among the white middle class can only serve to lend credence to the claims that the birth-control drive among Negroes and the poor generally is really a device for racial and quality control.[33]

Although the subject will be discussed in more detail below, it should be noted at this point that family planning is only partially a meaningful response to the population problem. As noted above, insofar as the poor control their fertility there would be a diminution in the national birth rate. It would not, however, be a particularly meaningful response to the population problem. Family planning assumes freedom of the

[32] National Academy of Sciences, *The Growth of U.S. Population* (Washington, 1965). See Miles, "Whose Baby," 19; *S. 2108 Hearings*, 121.

[33] Hannah Lees, "The Negro Response to Birth Control," *The Reporter*, May 19, 1966, p. 46, Mary Smith, "Birth Control and the Negro Woman," *Ebony*, Mar., 1968, and Moran testimony, *Population Trend Hearings*, 80, discuss the black militant opposition to publicly supported birth control as a form of genocide.

parties to choose their family size. If couples, however, decide to have three or four or more children, the population continues to mount. Family planning is essentially a device for spacing and timing of births rather than the limitation of births. The need for *population* or at least *fertility* control,[34] then, is not the same problem as the need for expanded family-planning services, although the latter is a vital tool in implementing a meaningful population policy.

THE LEGAL RESPONSE

It is these two problems, then—indigency and population—that have provided the case for the government's entrance into the family-planning field. But as has continually been the case in this volatile area of policy formation, legal response has been conditioned by severe motivational impediments. As will be discussed below, opposition from the Catholic Church, at both the national and local levels, has provided a formidable barrier to any creative public response. And perhaps an even greater impediment to effective governmental intervention in family planning has been the silence which has surrounded the subject. In spite of a "generally" favorable public attitude toward the subject of birth control, public officials generally viewed it as fit only for the bedroom and not for the arena of public debate. But the rise in welfare costs, modern emphasis on assuring equality of treatment and opportunity, desire of the poor to control their family size and participate in the good life, increasing recognition given to the detrimental effects of the postwar baby boom, development of simple, efficient methods of fertility control—all have combined with changing values and the widespread activity of private interests, such as Planned Parenthood–World Population, to spell the end to this wall of silence. As was the case in the elimination of government prohibitions on the availability of birth-control services, social, religious, scientific, and medical associations have been instrumental in manifesting the developing consensus in favor of governmental intervention. Again the Gallup polls have indicated the changed social attitudes. Sixty-three percent of Americans in 1965 favored the

[34] Kingsley Davis, "Population Policy: Will Current Programs Succeed?," *Science*, CLVIII (Nov. 10, 1967), 731, makes the useful distinction between "population control," attempts to influence all attributes of a population or, at least, growth and size, which involve considerations of birth, migration, and death; "fertility control," influencing the reproductive processes; and "family planning," which is premised on voluntary choice and does not really attempt to influence most determinants of reproduction.

proposition that "the United States government should give aid to states and cities for birth control programs if they request it," including 59 percent of Catholics interviewed.[35] The social atmosphere for the dissemination of birth-control services is gradually being transformed, and the character of the legal response reflects this gradual evolution. The social revolution is making a political revolution practically inevitable.

The Slow Awakening

The initial crack in the wall appeared in 1958, when the Draper Committee, appointed by President Eisenhower, issued its report on foreign aid containing a recommendation favoring increased governmental attention to birth control. Catholic reaction was clear and negative. The Catholic Bishops of the United States completely rejected the suggestion and declared that Catholics would not support any public assistance, at home or abroad, to promote artificial birth prevention or sterilization. Major elements of the non-Catholic community joined the battle primarily in opposition to the Catholic position. But in the late 1950s government was not prepared to enter the field of combat. President Eisenhower clearly repudiated the intervention policy, stating: "I cannot imagine anything more emphatically a subject that is not a proper political or governmental activity or function or responsibility.... This government will not... as long as I am here... have a positive political doctrine in its program that has to do with this problem of birth control. That is not our business."[36] He would later repudiate this stand, but at this time it accurately reflected government's noninterventionist policy.

However, the widely publicized controversy had brought the issue out in the open. The topic had been moved from the realm of private morals and theology and into that of public discussion and political action.[37] Additional publicity developed when a controversy broke out in New York over the rights of doctors and municipal hospitals to prescribe contraceptive devices. Catholic organizations stood almost alone while a vociferous, united non-Catholic community forced the Board of Hospitals to lift the ban. As news of the New York confrontation spread, similar drives were launched in a number of cities.

Change was being experienced in the national sector as well. Although

[35] "American Attitudes on Population Policy," *1966 Hearings*, 28, 29.
[36] Dwight D. Eisenhower, quoted in *1966 Hearings*, 219.
[37] Arthur Kroch, quoted in William D. McElroy, "A Special Report on Birth Control," *John Hopkins Magazine*, May, 1963, pp. 6, 11.

the Kennedy administration had generally been favorable to increased governmental activity in family planning, it was during the Johnson years that the fashioning of interventionist policy norms had really begun. In his health and welfare message on March 1, 1966, President Johnson had clearly expressed the administration's support for a more active program of publicly supported family planning: "We have a growing concern to foster the integrity of the family and the opportunity of each child. It is essential that all families have access to the information and services that will allow freedom to choose the number and spacing of their children within the dictates of individual conscience."[38]

This policy orientation was also reflected in a directive issued by the Department of Health, Education and Welfare on January 24, 1966. Reaffirmed in more detail in 1969, it has not only provided guidelines for the myriad HEW activities, but has also been expressive of the general approach of the Office of Economic Opportunity (OEO) and other agencies engaged in providing subsidized services. Family-planning programs would be provided with federal support in order "to improve the health of the people, to strengthen the integrity of the family and to provide families the freedom of choice to determine the spacing of their children and the size of their families. Programs conducted or supported by the department shall guarantee the freedom from coercion or pressure of mind or conscience. There shall be freedom of choice or method so that individuals can choose in accordance with the dictates of their conscience."[39] Equally as important, the policy norms were slowly being implemented at the local level. In 1963 only thirteen states offered some tax-supported programs; by the middle of 1966 over forty states had acted (although the actual number served was minimal). The number of publicly financed birth-control clinics increased from 400 to 700.[40]

The Congress, however, had been extremely reluctant to respond. While Senate hearings on bills introduced by Senators Gruening and Tydings, which would provide federal financial support for greater availability of birth-control services, had provided a forum for articulating social demands, for urging administrative responsiveness, for explor-

[38] Lyndon B. Johnson, quoted in *1966 Hearings*, 381.
[39] U.S. Department of Health, Education and Welfare, *Report on Family Planning* (Sept., 1966). See HEW, *The Role of Public Welfare in Family Planning* (n.d.).
[40] Information Center on Population Problems, *Public Health and Birth Control*, 1.

ing problems engendered by public intervention, and for defining alternative lines of policy formation,[41] legislative reaction had been disappointing to those seeking a creative legal response to extremely serious social problems. As noted above, the primary explanation for reluctance to act would appear to arise from the motivational area—from the fear of adverse political reaction given the opposition of the Roman Catholic Church and a general reluctance to become involved in the highly sensitive area of sexual relations.

The Rubrics of Controversy

In spite of the transition being effectuated in Catholic thought, fear of reprisal or personal value orientation inhibited many legislators. Many Catholics, in spite of their own personal behavior, have been unwilling to challenge the moral condemnations of the institutional church. Whatever their views toward the substantive merits of the abstract issue of publicly supported birth control, they would generally remain silent or even support the actions of the Church hierarchy in opposing government subsidization of family planning. Socialized into a particular value system, it has been difficult for Catholics to accept the challenges to Church authority and doctrine. Further, the latent, uncertain character of the response of Catholics has been supported by official hostility from the Catholic hierarchy and Catholic social organizations in their appearances before legislative and administrative decision-makers. While much of the vituperation and hate had been purged from the debate and the strength of the hierarchy had somewhat diminished, the lawmaker still had to consider the potential for retribution on this sensitive issue.

A prime example of the Church's intransigence to the change demand being forwarded by the various social, medical, and religious groups, and increasingly receiving a favorable hearing from law-makers, came in November, 1966, in a statement by the Catholic Bishops of the United States on the increasing public involvement in family-planning matters. The objective of the declaration was to "call upon all—and especially Catholics—to oppose, vigorously and by every democratic means, those campaigns already under way in some states and at the national level towards the active promotion, by tax supported agencies, of birth prevention as a public policy, above all in connection with welfare benefit

[41] See *1965 Hearings*; *1966 Hearings*; *1967 Hearings*.

programs."[42] (See Appendix G for the full text.) Because this constituted a policy statement from the highest institutional authority challenging the new demands, arguments underlying the protest require consideration. It should be noted at the outset, however, that while I am a Catholic, I, like many other Catholics including a number or prominent theologians, disagree with the conclusions reached by the bishops and, more recently, by Pope Paul VI.

The bishops clearly indicated their concern: "The good of the individual person and that of human society are intimately bound up with the stability of the family. Basic to the well-being of the family is freedom from external coercion in order that it may determine its own destiny.... Let our political leaders be on guard that the common good suffer no evil from public policies which tamper with the instincts of love and the sources of life." Their call for opposition to tax-supported birth control seems to rest on three basic premises: (1) the coercive character, both inherent and actual, of government action; (2) the infringement of the individual's right to privacy; and (3) the "camel's-nose" argument—if you let in government birth control, more objectionable programs will follow. Underlying the entire statement has been the theme that inherent in the concept of consensus developed for American pluralism is the limitation that public funds cannot be used for purposes contrary to the moral dictates of an element of that consensus.

Regarding the "inherently coercive" character of the government's action, the bishops cited the effect of placing, even by implication, the power and prestige of government behind birth-control services.[43] There is an element of validity to this claim. Consider a possible situation: on one side of the table is the public-aid recipient, from the rural South, poor, black, with little education; across from her is the white social worker, with an M.A. degree and a wide range of power over the recipient's life-style and income. What is the likely effect of a suggestion by the social worker that the recipient can receive assistance to

[42] National Catholic Welfare Conference, Administrative Board, "On the Government and Birth Control," Nov. 14, 1966. A similar statement was presented in 1969. See Appendixes G and H for the text of both statements. Many of the issues raised by the bishops are discussed in Harriet Pilpel and Nancy Wechsler, "Memorandum of Law on Constitutional Liberties and Publicly Supported Family Planning Programs Presented to the Subcommittee on Foreign Aid Expenditures of the Senate Committee on Government Operations on Behalf of Planned Parenthood–World Population," Mar. 1, 1966.

[43] See William B. Ball, "Government Birth Control: Reply to George M. Sirilla, S.J.," *Catholic Lawyer*, XII (Summer, 1966), 221.

control the number of children she has? The situation is quite clearly a delicate one and it does little good to ignore the dangers. But it is also a situation which exists whenever government welfare is involved. If the bishops' argument were accepted, there would be few welfare programs today. The problem requires careful attention to the selection and training of welfare workers, close supervision of their subsequent relationship with the welfare recipient, and a firm commitment on the part of government agencies to freedom of choice, but it does not justify rejecting the entire program. Further, another form of coercion arises from the inability to make a free choice regarding family planning because of the lack of information. Private sources do not have the resources to carry the burden alone; only government possesses the means to make a truly free choice possible. But extreme caution is necessary to prevent any actual coercion—to assure that the individual poverty recipient's decision remains free as to acceptance or rejection and choice of method as is possible. Assistance to the poor must not become a vehicle for imposing fertility control on the poverty sector while other citizens reserve their prerogatives in choosing family size.

The claim of the bishops that "government activities increasingly seek aggressively to persuade and even coerce the underprivileged to practice birth control" suffers from a lack of proof. Presidential and congressional directives as well as HEW and OEO policy, at least verbally, clearly guarantee "freedom from coercion."[44] Funds are provided to local agencies only after assurances are given that this policy will be effectuated, and similar guarantees are generally contained in state programs. In spite of the fact that the states have generally adopted policies of referring public-aid recipients for requested family-planning services and some 1,200 counties now have at least some experience with tax-supported birth control,[45] there does not appear to be any widespread coercion. Although a welfare recipient might be hesitant to report an offending social worker given their power relationship and the coercion

[44] See "Public Policy, Birth Control and Freedom of Choice," statement by George N. Lindsey in response to the bishops' declaration, Planned Parenthood–World Population, Nov. 16, 1966; Editorial, "The Prelate's Accusation," *New York Times*, Nov. 17, 1966, p. 46, col. 1. Both HEW and OEO issued statements reiterating their policy of free choice and noncoercion. HEW Secretary Gardner indicated that he had specifically requested evidence from the National Catholic Welfare Conference and that eight to nine months had elapsed and there still was no reply. Statement of the Department of Health, Education and Welfare, Nov. 15, 1966 (from the files of PP–WP). See further George M. Sirilla, "Government Policy and Family Planning," *Catholic Lawyer*, XII (Summer, 1966), 209, who notes the increasing awareness by the poor of their legal rights.

[45] OEO, *Need for Subsidized Family Planning Services*, 5.

is likely to be indirect, the absence of complaints and substantiated accusations suggests that abuse is not prevalent. While the bishops' argument indicates the vital necessity of carefully assessing the implementation of government policy, it relates precisely to that subject and not to the policy itself.

The bishops' defense of the right of privacy appears to involve the personal information that would have to be furnished by any applicant. And, indeed, there does seem to be a diminishing amount of information that remains in the personal domain of the individual. But again, the argument is directed at government intervention of any kind—it is a price that the individual pays if he wishes to take advantage of this program and is an essential aspect of an effective program. While we can guard against an excessive amount of information-taking and carefully protect this information, some "privacy" will be lost if the government intervenes. However, this danger must be balanced against the danger that the indigent will be denied the opportunity to choose family planning freely if the government does not intervene.

The "camel's-nose" argument is perhaps the most disturbing to many citizens.[46] In accepting a policy of tax-supported birth control, are we fostering a "contraceptive mentality" which will open the door to practices such as coerced abortion, compulsory sterilization, or even governmental control of fertility? What is the effect of the widening use of contraceptives on the family and the value placed on human life? Is this the first step toward building our own "Brave New World"? Yet what is the alternative to permitting an interventionist policy? Continued mounting of our population; continued denial of the right of the poor to make their own ethical decisions; continued rise in the rate of criminal abortion; continued birth of unwanted, illegitimate children who cannot be properly cared for; continued upward spiral of welfare costs, equally inviting more repressive forms of governmental intervention. None of the measures indicated above are beyond the realm of possibility; all have been suggested; some have already been approved by governments here and abroad.[47] These possibilities are sufficiently

[46] Father Dexter Hanley has noted the danger that "any concession which permits the establishment of these programs becomes in the hands of others either a wedge to try to change the Catholic's private morality or a weapon to achieve total political victory for another point of view." "Religious and Political Values in Population Policies," address by Dexter L. Hanley, S.J., National Conference on Family Planning, Planned Parenthood–World Population, May 6, 1966.

[47] In Mississippi a plan was considered which would have required a woman bearing an illegitimate child to go to a Planned Parenthood clinic. The proposal was soundly criticized by the Planned Parenthood Federation as "betraying an

uninviting to emphasize the importance for the poor of promoting the voluntary curbing of family size, which, in turn, necessitates governmental intervention based on a policy consistent with the freedom and dignity of the individual.

We turn, finally, to the character of the consensus embodied in the creed of American pluralism. Contained in all of the dialogue on this subject is acceptance of the fact that the strength of the consensus lies in the willingness of all major elements of our pluralist society to respect the moral beliefs of the other elements. But does this mean that any policy which is not in conformity with the moral dictates of all major elements should be rejected? While this seems to be the import of the bishops' declaration, it appears to be mistaken interpretation of the character of the obligations imposed by pluralism. What is guaranteed by this concept is the freedom to pursue one's own ethical convictions consistent with the same right existing in others. Catholics can properly demand that governmental programs for the poor guarantee freedom of acceptance or rejection and free choice of method and that government research include projects designed to improve the effectiveness of the rhythm method, considered morally licit by the Church (this apparently is being done in present government-supported projects). But it would seem violative of the pluralistic creed to offend the ethical norms existing in the non-Catholic community, to prevent them from freely pursuing a practice they believe to be morally licit. No Catholic need participate in these programs, but they should not deny to others the right to participate.

It is important to note that the bishops explicitly endorse government support for research into "morally acceptable" methods of family limitation. Catholic resistance, therefore, seems to be based on the belief that the government is endorsing public immorality. At the outset, it is important to recall that private morality and legal policy should not be confused—the fact that "artificial" contraception is viewed as immoral does not alone justify opposition to the government activity; some harm to the public well-being must be shown.

---

appalling insensitivity to the human dignity of even the least of us." Planned Parenthood Federation of America–World Population Emergency Campaign, *Birth Control and Public Policy* (New York, 1962), 25. There is also a movement for the compulsory sterilization of such women. Thomas J. Reese, "Catholic Charities and Family Welfare," *The Problem of Population: Practical Catholic Applications*, Conference on Population Problems (South Bend, 1964), 18. See generally John Thomas, "Problems of the Future; Sterilization, Abortion and Other Issues," *ibid.*, 28–61; *1966 Hearings*, 462.

Lacking or rejecting the guidance of the Catholic Church, men, even those of utmost good will, can differ about questions of private morality. Thus the decisions reached by non-Catholics and by Catholics are religious decisions. Thus, as a matter of practical and political fact, neither position may be said to be right in the political order. And, just as we recognize religious freedom for theological convictions, we must grant civic freedom to moral convictions. Here too is the common good, the regulating norm.[48]

Condemnation of "promoting public immorality" is sometimes stated as a demand for government neutrality, which thus comes to mean nonaction.[49] In either form, the argument would appear to have merit only if the government were endorsing or promoting a particular method of family limitation or if it refused to provide support for research and services in morally acceptable methods. Neither of these situations seems to exist.

Finally, it is claimed that by accepting and supporting government intervention, Catholics are cooperating in the material sin of another. Since artificial contraception is sinful for all, Catholic support of programs which provide the vehicle for moral transgression would itself be sinful. Again the basic answer must be that government programs do not require acceptance of services nor do they promote a particular form of control. What is provided is the right of the married couple to reach their own ethical decision, to accept responsibility for their own

[48] Testimony of Dexter L. Hanley, S.J., in U.S. Congress, Senate, Subcommittee on Employment, Manpower, and Poverty of the Committee on Labor and Public Welfare, *Hearings on S. 2993, Family Planning Program*, 89th Cong., 2nd Sess., 1966, pp. 28–29 (hereafter cited as *Tydings Hearings*). See Thomas McDonough, "Distribution of Contraceptives by the Welfare Department: A Catholic Response," *The Problem of Population*, Conference on Population Problems, 109, who observes that Catholic resistance can properly rest only on "effects, results, and consequences socially harmful and reasonably predictable." Robert P. Drinan, "Catholics, Birth Control and Public Policy," *U.S. Catholic*, XXXI (May, 1965), 6, also recognizes the moral basis of the Catholic opposition but endorses state action to help fulfill their duty of responsible parenthood. Ball, who opposes present government policy, accepts the moral foundations of the Catholic protest when he notes that Catholic resistance to repeal of the Connecticut statute and its resistance to tax-supported programs both swing on the "pivotal point of Catholic moral teaching on contraception." "Government Birth Control," 217.

[49] Father Hanley suggests that "neutrality is not found in any one-sided surrender of interests." True government neutrality requires that "government will not express a preference for one medical procedure over another nor lend its authority to one moral position rather than another." It is "to be found in encouraging the free exercise of choice in these matters of public concern just as much as in running away from the problem." *Tydings Hearings*, 19, 21, 28.

moral life. Pope Paul's 1967 encyclical, *Populorum Progressio*, clearly recognized this principle: "It is for the parents to decide, with full knowledge of the matter, on the number of their children, taking into account their responsibilities toward God, themselves, the children they have already brought into the world, and the community to which they belong. In all this they must follow the demands of their own conscience enlightened by God's law authentically interpreted, and sustained by confidence in Him."[50]

The bishops' declaration against publicly supported family planning, reaffirmed in 1969,[51] was not an isolated instance of Catholic opposition. At the local level the potential or reality of adverse reaction among Catholics has often proved a severe motivational impediment to the lawmaker. Consider the reaction of a Catholic legislator from an old Polish Catholic district regarding a program for publicly supported birth control after his parish priest indicated strong disapproval. Although no statistical evidence on the actual incidence of such pressure can be presented, two examples of controversy engendered by publicly supported birth control suggest the basis for the concern.

The issue of providing birth-control services to unmarried mothers receiving welfare benefits broke out in Illinois in 1962.[52] The Illinois Public Aid Commission had voted 6-4 on straight religious lines (all four Catholics voted against the change) to provide services "to any recipient with a spouse or child who requests such assistance." The Chancery of the Archdiocese of Chicago, the largest archdiocese in the United States, then representing 2.5 million Catholics (the archbishop as well as the governor had a No. 1 license plate), issued a statement that "this means that the citizens of Illinois are asked to abet, facilitate and subsidize illicit extramarital relations. This is bad public policy and those commissioners who voted in favor of it must assume responsibility for any resultant breakdown in public morality." Pro-

[50] Pope Paul VI, "Populorum Progressio" (On the Development of Peoples), *New York Times*, Mar. 27, 1967, p. 34, col. 1 (city ed.).
[51] "Statement of the Bishops of the United States in Protest of U.S. Government Programs against the Right to Life." (See Appendix H for the text.)
[52] The factual data on the Illinois controversy was derived primarily through interviews and the following materials: Thomas B. Littlewood, "The Politics of Birth Control" (unpublished mimeo, Eagleton Institute Case Studies Program, 1965); H. L. Bruno, "Birth Control Welfare Funds and the Politics of Illinois," *The Reporter*, June 20, 1963, pp. 32–35; Planned Parenthood Association, Chicago Area, *Chronological History of the Birth Control Controversy in Chicago* (Chicago, 1964).

change forces stressed that existing proof did not indicate a substantial causal relationship between the availability of contraceptives and increased incidence of illicit sex relations.[53] Questions regarding moral priorities were also emphasized: wasn't bringing an unwanted child into the world perhaps a greater immorality than fostering illicit sex relations? The competing interests had been delineated and the battle was on.

Shortly after the commission's vote, bills were introduced in the state legislature (by Catholic legislators) which, after amendment, would have limited the welfare plan to married recipients, thereby eliminating 87 percent of Illinois AFDC mothers. The bill passed the Senate by a vote of 42-5. As the size of this vote margin suggests, not only Catholics resisted the proposal for change by the Public Aid Commission; the "fostering of sin" and "promoting promiscuity" arguments coupled with the amendment limiting the plan to married recipients had fostered a coalition of urban Catholics and downstate Protestants.[54] In the House, however, the speaker made the unprecedented decision to prevent the bill from ever reaching the floor even though it had been favorably recommended by committee. The interactive process continued as the courts were asked to intervene through a suit filed by the Republican mayoral candidate on the day before election to enjoin the Public Aid Commission from acting on its resolution. On the day after the election, the Catholic attorney general, who would normally act as legal representative for the commission, entered an appearance *against* the commission, claiming that the policy would make the state accessory "to sexual promiscuity and prostitution" and violate the public policy of the state. The judge, noting that the matter was pending before the legislature, continued the case indefinitely.

Back at the ranch, a legislative compromise was reached through the creation of a legislative commission charged to study the matter for two

[53] See, e.g., testimony of Francis A. Allen before the Illinois Birth Control Commission, Mar. 4, 1964 (from the files of the Planned Parenthood Association, Chicago Area).

[54] Littlewood, "The Politics of Birth Control," 29, noted: "The issue had now been nicely removed from the framework of religious doctrine—Catholic versus non-Catholic. Sponsors of the legislation could no longer be accused of trying to impose Catholic morality concepts, namely their opposition to artificial contraception, on all the people of the State. They had joined together the Catholic rejection of birth control and the Protestant vision of mass Negro fornication encouraged and subsidized by the State without regard for the sacred institution of marriage."

years during which family-planning services would be limited to married mothers.[55] The makeup of the body turned out to be eight Catholics and seven non-Catholics—its three officers were Catholic, including, as chairman, the sponsor of the original Senate bill and, as secretary, its House sponsor. Things looked dark indeed for the pro–birth control forces.[56] But Catholic Church authorities had decided not to fight a major campaign, perhaps in response to changing values or in appreciation of the community hostility engendered by such campaigns.[57] In the subsequent legislative commission hearings, i.e. the intelligence stage, the Planned Parenthood Association secured the services of speakers who presented overwhelmingly favorable testimony. An independent citizens' committee, fostered by Planned Parenthood, also obtained the support of social, religious, and medical associations, sponsored letter-writing, and handled the lobbying.[58] Opposition came only from a few Catholic organizations. The rising costs of welfare, the growth of the Negro population in Chicago—91 percent of AFDC mothers were Negro—and the plight of the unwanted child all appealed to different segments of opinion. Surveys could be cited indicating the public support for the proposed policy[59] as well as the desire of the poor to have access to family-planning services.[60] The politics of birth control can certainly

[55] Senate Bill No. 66, approved Aug. 28, 1963, by the Seventy-third General Assembly. Section 2 of the bill authorized the commission "to study the legal, social, moral, health and financial implications" of the proposed program.

[56] Littlewood, "*The Politics of Birth Control*," 23, cites the experience of Claire Driscoll, lobbyist for the Catholic Church. Representatives generally came to him for advice negating any need for pressure tactics. He quotes a legislator to the effect that "if you're Catholic and reasonably intelligent, you ought to be able to recognize that the Church wants you to proceed in a certain way without signals being given." Littlewood concludes: "The Church is automatically a political force, therefore, without the need for 'hot lines' between the chancery and the offices of public officials. Though he tends to underplay the Church's influence in secular affairs, Driscoll conceded there is bound to be considerable 'respect for anything that big.' "

[57] Some Catholic legislators have some hostile memories arising from this decision. Many feel they were let down by Church authorities. Interview with Representative Paul Elward, Chicago, Mar., 1963.

[58] Interview with Dr. Lonnie Meyers, former chairman of Citizens for the Extension of Birth Control Services, Chicago, Feb., 1967; interview with Mrs. Mary Jane Snyder, coordinator of Public Relations, Planned Parenthood Association, Chicago Area, Chicago, Feb. 20, 1967.

[59] Of those interviewed 63 percent thought it was a good idea to distribute birth-control information and materials to persons on relief; 26 percent thought it was a poor idea; 11 percent had no opinion. "Birth Control and Public Responsibility," address by Arnold H. Maremont, Planned Parenthood–World Population, Oct. 16, 1963.

[60] See testimony of Donald J. Bogue, "Birth Control 'Works' for the Poor as

make strange bedfellows: the dollar-conscious, the anti-Negro, and the humanitarians had found a common cause. The final vote of the commission was 14-1 to provide birth-control services to all mothers over the age of fifteen. A resolution to that effect was passed by large majorities in both houses of the legislature. (See Appendix I for the text of the resolution.)

As early as 1949, Pennsylvania had formulated a policy of referring public-aid recipients, upon request, to maternal-health centers for birth-control information. Change again came from the administrative decision-maker. On December 17, 1965, the Office of Public Assistance issued a policy directive introducing a fundamental alteration of the public role in the family-planning field in that staff would be permitted to initiate discussion on the subject of family planning when "serious problems of family functioning exist because of the inability of parents to limit the number of children born to them in accordance with their own interest and the health and welfare of family members." A caveat was inserted for recipients with religious convictions against the practice, although the means of determining this conviction were not indicated. Adoption of the policy was premised on "the deepening social problems created by increased population," equality of access to medical services, "assuring freedom of choice," and the increasing problems posed by illegitimacy.[61]

As in Illinois, the Catholic hierarchy's reaction was prompt and antagonistic. Archbishop John J. Krol of Philadelphia laid the foundations for opposition by declaring that birth-control activities "are not the business of the state and they are serious threats to civil liberty."[62] Un-

---

Well as the Rich," State of Illinois, Birth Control Commission, June 24, 1964; testimony of Philip M. Hauser, State of Illinois, House Committee on Public Aid, May 14, 1963; address by Illinois Representative William H. Robinson, Planned Parenthood Conference, Minneapolis, May 16, 1961 (from the files of the Planned Parenthood Association, Chicago Area).

[61] Pennsylvania, Office of Public Assistance, *Policy of the Department of Public Welfare Concerning Family Planning, Memorandum No. 870*, Dec. 17, 1965, sec. 3. See "Birth Control Plan Set Up for State's Relief Recipients," *Evening Bulletin*, Dec. 17, 1965, p. 1; "Rosen Defends Aid to Unwed Mothers, Cites Child's Needs," *Philadelphia Inquirer*, June 19, 1966. For a historical study of the Pennsylvania policy see Ad Hoc Committee on Family Planning and Public Assistance in Pennsylvania, *What about Pennsylvania's Family Planning Program?* (Harrisburg, 1966), pp. 1–5.

[62] "Krol Says Birth Control Is Not State's Business," *Evening Bulletin*, Dec. 17, 1965, p. 1. William B. Ball summarized the position of the Catholic hierarchy in Ad Hoc Committee, *What about Pennsylvania*, 1: "The main thrust of our objection to the Department's birth control program is with respect to moral principles upon which the whole community is agreed: that rights of human privacy should not be

like previous battles fought on the basis of the moral beliefs of Catholicism, the hierarchy, in this instance, formulated the issue in terms of the right of privacy and danger of coercion of the poor—a utilization of the *Griswold* thesis to attack change demands. In addition, the archbishop gave clear expression to the continuing Catholic fear that such public involvement was only the first step toward state-supported abortion and sterilization.

Also, as in Illinois, legislative action was initiated to reverse the administrative decision. The Catholic chairman of the House Appropriations Committee, Representative Martin Muller of Philadelphia, introduced a rider on the appropriation bill that "no moneys herein appropriated may be used for birth control information." [63] The practical effect of the rider would have been to eliminate not only the liberal 1965 changes but also the general involvement of public authorities in the family-planning field. Hearings on the appropriation bill, which were mirrored by severe clashes in public debate, became a forum for the direct confrontation of opposing interests.

Whereas Catholic interests in Illinois had chosen to avoid a major confrontation, in Pennsylvania they were mustered, using the device of an ad hoc committee. William Ball, general counsel of the Pennsylvania Catholic Conference, became a leading spokesman for anti–birth control forces. In addition to presenting testimony before the Appropriations Committee, a full-scale campaign was launched against the administrative action. Pulpits were used to denounce the policy; an emotional pamphlet, *Betty and Jack Talk about Government Birth Control*, was distributed;[64] a full-page ad, signed by all of the Catholic bishops of Pennsylvania, was run in sixty papers across the state. Although the Planned Parenthood League attempted to combat the impressive chal-

---

violated, that the dignity of the poor should be protected, that the public power ought not to be used to support adultery or fornication. The dispute in Pennsylvania is not over *these principles*—which, I take it, all accept—but rather with the application of *these principles* to Pennsylvania's program."

[63] "State Discloses Birth Control Aid to Unwed Mothers," *Philadelphia Inquirer*, June 9, 1966. The House Appropriations Committee in executive session endorsed inclusion of the provision. "House Unit Backs Ban on Birth Control," *Philadelphia Inquirer*, May 24, 1966.

[64] The pamphlet is a disturbing piece of emotional propaganda. The following comment from the publication, which is accompanied by a picture of a woman hugging a baby, is illustrative: "Gosh, I wonder how many people realize that government birth control is intended eventually to tell us how many children we're allowed to have? Sort of frightening, isn't it?" Pennsylvania Catholic Conference, *Betty and Jack Talk about Government Birth Control* (Harrisburg, n.d.).

lenge, it lacked the equipment needed to neutralize the pressure in a state where the Catholic Church is so strong.[65]

Given community cleavages on this policy, legislative review of administrative behavior would seem appropriate in order to permit clarification of competing interests and to maximize the possibility of a policy fashioned with greater safeguards for the problems which justly concerned Church authorities.[66] But the prescriptive behavior in the Pennsylvania case did not produce such a resolution of interests. A compromise was reached, not embodying a carefully drawn plan for public involvement, but rather a capitulation of family-planning interests. The new policy not only prohibited family-planning services to unwed recipients but also prohibited caseworkers from initiating discussion of the subject with their clients. Nor was the policy fashioned by evaluating competing considerations. Rather, it appears that Representative Mullen employed his position to threaten state appropriations unless there was a cutback in the state's family-planning involvement.[67] While the concern of the Church with protecting the rights of welfare recipients from abuse deserves respect and consideration, the manner in which change was impeded in this instance seems indefensible. Whether Representative Mullen reacted on the basis of his own value system or in response to external pressures, the resolution of the dispute represents a negative commentary on the creative capabilities of the legislative actor. The ability of an individual to coerce submission to a policy seems in-

---

[65] In 1960 there were 3,905,314 Catholics in a state population of 11,582,000. Thomas B. Kenedy, *Official Catholic Directory* (New York, 1967), 225, 243, 328, 339, 466, 526, 531, 673, 685, 786; U.S. Bureau of the Census, *Statistical Abstract of the United States: 1967*, 12.

[66] The administrative introduction of the original policy was cited by Ball as raising serious legal issues: "But the thing that excites our attention is the fact that government birth control rarely comes in by the front door—with open-faced honesty submitting its proposals to the representatives of the people for them to weigh and judge, coming candidly before the legislature as most other social programs do, offering their evidence, offering their proponents as witnesses to be questioned in the give-and-take of the democratic process. Instead government birth control appears to prefer to bypass the common assemblyman and to establish itself through the more cloistered processes of executive order." Ad Hoc Committee, *What about Pennsylvania*, 5-6. If Ball's position were followed to its conclusion, administrators would be excluded from creative law-making. The legislature possesses review powers if the scope of delegated power is exceeded, but initial delegation is usually necessarily framed in broad and vague terms permitting wide discretion.

[67] See "Bitter Pill," *Greater Philadelphia Magazine*, Sept., 1966; memorandum from Frederick S. Jaffe to PP-WP Affiliates et al., Sept., 1966.

compatible with our model of the effective utilization of law for meeting social problems.

While time and space necessitate limiting analysis of the modern controversy over public involvement at the state and local levels, the above should suffice to indicate the effect of motivational impediments to legislative change. In Illinois, Catholic resistance delayed implementation of the administrative decision-maker's policy alteration for three years. In Pennsylvania, opposition produced a temporary delay in the change process. While further legal alteration will almost certainly occur, again there will be a burdensome delay.[68] Given the pressing character of the social problems outlined at the beginning of this chapter, it is questionable that such impediments are really in the public interest.

But as has been previously noted, the Catholic position on the morality of contraception has been undergoing a searching re-examination in recent years. Many Catholic religious and laity have found in the concept of "responsible parenthood" a viable compromise between the importance of procreation to the marital state and the very compelling reasons for contraceptive control of fertility. The position of Vatican II toward marriage and family life, while not endorsing the change in Catholic birth-control doctrine, had raised the hopes of many that a revision was imminent.[69] Pope Paul's sympathetic treatment of the problems engendered by population and his recognition of fertility control as part of responsible parenthood in *Populorum Progressio* had added to the anticipation. And when a papal commission reported in favor of a relaxation of the moral standards relating to artificial birth control, there appeared no question that a change was at hand.[70] If the moral condemnation of artificial "birth control" were removed, the basis for op-

[68] In June, 1969, Illinois enacted S.H.A., Chap. 91, sec. 18.7, which permits doctors to provide birth-control services without parental consent to defined classes of minors.

[69] "Pastoral Constitution on the Church in the Modern World," *The Documents of Vatican II*, ed. Walter M. Abbott and Joseph Gallagher (New York, 1966), 249–58. See John T. Noonan, Jr., "Contraception and the Council," *The Catholic Case for Contraception*, ed. Daniel Callahan (New York, 1969). On the changes in Catholicism on this issue, in addition to the above, see Leon J. Suenans, *Love and Control* (Westminster, Md., 1961); Bromley, *Catholics and Birth Control*; Louis Dupre, *Contraception and Catholics: A New Appraisal* (Baltimore, 1964); G. Egner, *Contraception vs. Tradition: A Catholic Critique* (New York, 1967); John A. O'Brien, "Family Planning in an Exploding Population," *Ave Maria*, Aug. 24, 1963, p. 5; O'Brien, "Let's End the War on Birth Control," *Ave Maria*, Nov. 2, 1963, p. 5.

[70] See *National Catholic Reporter*, Apr. 19, 1967, p. 1, col. 2.

position to a governmental interventionist policy would also be seriously undermined.

But on July 25, 1968, these hopes were smashed with the issuance of *Humanae Vitae* (On the Regulation of Birth), reiterating the traditional condemnation of artificial birth control as violative of natural law.

> Likewise, if they consider the matter, they [the married couple] must admit that an act of mutual love, which is detrimental to the faculty of propagating life, which God the Creator of all, has implanted in it, according to special laws, is in contradiction to both the divine plan, according to whose norm matrimony has been instituted, and the will of the Author of human life. To use this divine gift destroying, even if only partially, its meaning and purpose is to contradict the nature both of man and of woman and of their most intimate relationship, and therefore it is to contradict also the plan of God and His will. On the other hand, to make use of conjugal love while respecting the laws of the generative process means to acknowledge oneself not to be the arbiter of the sources of human life but rather the minister of the design established by the Creator. In fact, just as Man does not have unlimited domain over his body in general, so also, with particular reason, he has no such domain over his generative faculties, as such, because of their intrinsic ordination towards raising up life of which God is the principal. "Human life is sacred," Pope John XXIII recalled; "from its very inception it reveals the creating hand of God."[71]

To be excluded as illicit means of regulating birth (in addition to abortion and direct sterilization) "is every action which, either in anticipation of the conjugal act, or in its accomplishment, or in the development of its natural consequences, proposes whether as an end or as a means, to render procreation impossible."[72] The encyclical went on to solidify the foundations for condemnation of government intervention in support of wider access to family-planning information and services.

> Let it be considered also that a dangerous weapon would be placed in the hands of those public authorities who take no heed of moral exigencies. Who could blame a government for applying to the solution of the problem of the community those means acknowledged to be illicit for married couples in the solution

[71] Pope Paul VI, *Humanae Vitae* (Washington, 1968), 8. See Callahan, ed., *The Catholic Case for Contraception*, pt. II, for critiques of the papal position.
[72] Pope Paul VI, *Humanae Vitae*, 9.

of a family problem? Who will stop rulers from favoring, from even imposing upon their people, if they were to consider it necessary, the method of contraception which they judged to be most efficacious? In such a way men, wishing to avoid individual, family, or social difficulties encountered in the observance of divine law, would reach the point of placing at the mercy of the intervention of public authorities the most personal and most reserved sector of conjugal intimacy.[73]

Regardless of the merits of the papal decision, and this is not the place to discuss it, the basis for continued church opposition to public support for family planning had been laid. While *Humanae Vitae* was not presented as an infallible pronouncement demanding obedience, but rather was rested on the authority of the Church as *mater et magistra* of communicants of the Catholic religion, it nevertheless carries a high degree of authority, requiring Catholics to weigh its teachings carefully. There is little indication, however, that the document will substantially alter the life-style of American Catholics regarding fertility control, or impede the forward movement of publicly supported family planning. In fact, it appears more probable that the papal position will produce still further disruptions in the authority relationships within the Church. Polls indicate that a majority of American Catholics do not accept the argument of the encyclical and will continue to control their birth rate using "artificial" means.[74] A large segment of the religious, priests and nuns alike, have publicly announced their rejection of *Humanae Vitae*, often bringing them into direct conflict with their hierarchical superiors. Rather than submit to doctrinal discipline, they have asserted the overriding mandate of conscience. The nature of the authority relationship between the pope and the Church in Rome, the bishops, the religious, and the laity are increasingly being called into question. Large numbers of religious have felt compelled to renounce their vows and even to sever formally their membership in the Catholic Church. It is questionable, however, that these disruptions are attributable solely to the papal encyclical. Rather, it demonstrates the reality that the Catholic Church is not a monolith; that its communicants possess a variety of beliefs and values while adhering to a core of religious beliefs; that it is subject to a

[73] *Ibid.*, 11.
[74] "Pope's Birth-Control Stand: How U.S. Reacts," *U.S. News and World Report*, Sept. 9, 1968, p. 11. On the institutional crisis within the Catholic Church generated by the encyclical see "The Catholic Church and Birth Control," *U.S. News and World Report*, Aug. 12, 1968, pp. 38 *et seq.*; "Catholic Church Moves toward Biggest Crisis in 400 Years," *U.S. News and World Report*, Sept. 30, 1968, pp. 66–67.

breakdown in temporal authority patterns as are other social institutions.

In any case, there is a substantial segment of Catholic opinion that not only tolerates but in fact endorses tax-supported family-planning programs and does so "with full respect and adherence to traditional Catholic teachings."[75] Father Dexter Hanley, director of Georgetown Institute of Law, Human Rights and Social Values, has offered five policy principles which stand in marked contrast to the position enunciated by the American hierarchy and supported by the tenor of *Humanae Vitae*.

> 1. In a legitimate concern over public health, education, and poverty, the government may properly establish programs which permit citizens to exercise a free choice in matters of responsible parenthood in accordance with their moral standards.
> 2. In such programs, the government may properly give information and assistance concerning medically accepted forms of family planning, so long as human life and personal rights are safeguarded and no coercion or pressure is exerted against individual moral choice.
> 3. In such programs, the government should not imply a preference for any particular method of family planning.
> 4. While norms of private morality may have special dimensions so affecting the common good as to justify opposition to public programs, private moral judgments regarding methods of family planning do not provide a basis for opposition to government programs.
> 5. Although the use of public funds for purposes of family planning is not objectionable in principle, the manner in which such a program is implemented may pose issue requiring separate consideration. These opinions are submitted as being morally justified and in accordance with the traditional Catholic position on birth control. These opinions are expressed out of a concern for civil liberty and freedom, and are based upon respect for the sincere consciences of our fellow citizens in this pluralist society.[76]

It is this perspective which appears to be obtaining increasing support among American Catholics, since it reflects not only the change in social

---

[75] Address by Dexter L. Hanley, S.J., Family Law Section, American Bar Association, Aug. 9, 1965. If the government were to *promote* a particular form of birth control or utilize coercion, Father Hanley indicates the Catholic should condemn the program on moral grounds. Testimony of Father Hanley, *1965 Hearings*, 1262. See Dienes, "Moral Beliefs and Legal Norms," 536–69.
[76] Testimony of Father Hanley, *1966 Hearings*, 1373.

values and practices but also an ecumenical re-evaluation by many Catholics under the stimulus of John XXIII and the Vatican Council. In any case, the changing character of the "Catholic interest" suggests the potential for legal compromise, for the formation of a family-planning policy consistent with the jural norms of the contending interests. It is in this context that the present legal response must be analyzed.

The Emergence of Family-Planning Policy

In spite of the controversy, however, it is clear that government intervention in the family-planning area is an accomplished fact. While the sensitivity of the subject has retarded the rate of change, it has not been an insurmountable barrier. At least a verbal commitment to a policy of closing the gap by providing access to family-planning services to the poor has been articulated by the administration, administrative agencies, and Congress. But the question remains as to the pace at which performance will match the promise.

In the closing years of his administration, President Johnson appointed an Advisory Committee on Population and Family Planning to review federal policy and programs and recommend steps for future development. In its 1968 report, *Population and Family Planning: The Transition from Concern to Action*, the committee expressed its recognition of the need for research and training, education, and especially provision of family-planning services for the poor.

> This section outlines the role for the federal government in achieving a society in which all parents can have the number of children they want when they want them. For the majority of American people, this goal will be attained by research programs yielding superior contraceptive methods and increased knowledge about human reproduction, by training programs for physicians and other family-planning professionals and by programs of public education.
>
> For the one-fifth of Americans who are poor or nearly poor, however, these programs will not be enough. The current availability of family planning is of little help to those who cannot afford the services, who do not know that they are available, or who live where medical services are scarce.[77]

[77] President's Committee on Population and Family Planning, *Population and*

Pursuant to this definition of the domestic problem, the committee recommended a commitment to assure the availability of family-planning information and services to the 5 million women in need of subsidized assistance within five years. HEW and OEO would develop five-year plans and implement appropriate programs to achieve this objective; the Department of Education would undertake an expanded program of educating the public on the problems associated with population growth and family life; an expanded program of bio-medical and social-science research and training would be launched by the recently created Center for Population Research and the National Institute of Child Health and Human Development, which would be transformed into a National Institute for Population Research by 1970; and the president would create a permanent commission to deal with the problems of population growth. These governmental activities would be made possible by a substantial increase in expenditures for family-planning and population programs and would be supplemented by additional support for similar programs in the private sector.

On July 18, 1969, President Nixon committed his administration to development of such a program in a message on population growth. Here was clear presidential recognition of the relation of poverty to uncontrolled fertility, and the potential use of family planning in the war against poverty.

> In my first message to Congress on domestic affairs, I called for a national commitment to provide a healthful and stimulating environment for all children during their first five years of life. One of the ways in which we can promote that goal, is to provide assistance for more parents in effectively planning their families. We know that involuntary childbearing often results in poor physical and emotional health for all members of the family. It is one of the factors which contribute to our distressingly high infant mortality rate, the unacceptable level of malnutrition, and the disappointing performance of some children in our schools. Unwanted or untimely childbearing is one of several forces which are driving many families into poverty or keeping them in that condition. Its threat helps to produce the dangerous incidence of illegal abortion. And, finally, of course, it needlessly adds to the burdens placed on all our resources by increasing population.[78]

Family Planning: The Transition from Concern to Action (Washington, 1968), 15.
[78] Nixon, "Population Message," 5.

Further, the recognition of this problem was accompanied by at least a verbal acceptance of a five-year target deadline for closing the gap in access to effective family-planning services.

> Both the Department of Health, Education and Welfare and the Office of Economic Opportunity are now involved in this important work, if their combined efforts are not adequate to provide information and services to all who want them. In particular, most of an estimated 5-million low income women of childbearing age in this country do not now have adequate access to family planning equipment, even though their wishes concerning family size are usually the same as those of parents of higher income groups. It is my view that no American woman should be denied family planning assistance because of her economic condition. I believe, therefore, that we should establish as a national goal, provision of adequate family services within the next 5 years to all those who want them, but cannot afford them. This we have the capacity to do.[79]

In the Congress, also, this new public mood has become increasingly evident. Not only has the subject of family planning become a more acceptable topic for discussion, but Congress has seen fit to initiate vital steps toward assuring the availability of family-planning services. The year 1967 produced some of the most important legislation yet enacted to assure broader dissemination of family-planning information and services consistent with the conscience of the individual. The Child Health Act required that 6 percent of grants for maternal and child health and maternal- and infant-care projects be used for family planning and provided that 10 percent of authorized funds for child-health programs be allocated for family-planning research and training of personnel; amendments to Title IV of the Social Security Act *required* (HEW policy directives previously had made the program optional) participant states to offer family-planning services to public-assistance recipients (the Medicaid program in Title XIX of the act also provides for family-planning assistance to recipients); the Partnership for Health amendments of the Public Health Service Act provided that project and formula grants could now be used for family-planning programs.[80] At

[79] *Ibid.*, 8.
[80] Changes in the AFDC program are set forth at 42 U.S.C. 602(a) (14) and (15) (Supp. V, 1970). Revision in the Maternal Child Health provisions are cited at 42 U.S.C. 705(a) and 706(e). HEW has indicated that under 42 U.S.C. 1905(a) (15), states are *urged* to include family planning as a health service. S. *2108 Hearings*, 175. See Sar A. Levitan, *Programs in Aid of the Poor for the 1970's* (Baltimore, 1969), 87–91; Levitan, *The Great Society's Poor Law* (Baltimore, 1969), 207–13.

the informational level as well Congress was active. Congressional hearings have continued to provide valuable data on the need for assistance and have served as a platform for public disclosure of the inadequacies of existing programs and the often lethargic attitude of national and local agencies in the implementation of governmental policy.[81]

But to portray the fashioning of a policy is only part of the story. What is even more important is an appreciation of the tasks that remain to be done and the actual extent to which the articulated policy has been implemented. As Senator Tydings pointed out in 1967 hearings on the population crisis: "Policy statements are not worth anything if you do not do anything about them."[82] And it is here that the reality is frequently far removed from the promise.

Unfortunately, the difference between promise and fulfillment in the area of family planning, in the prosaic words of Senator Ralph Yarborough of Texas, "makes the Grand Canyon look like a Texas creek."[83] While Texas creeks do run big, in this instance it appears that the gap is wide indeed. In 1967 a group of HEW departmental consultants published the Harkavy Report on the state of HEW family-planning programs.[84] It was extremely critical of the lack of coherence in service, research, and training and education programs of the department, of the absence of any distinguishable priorities, and of the failure of HEW to request adequate funding or to utilize the funding already available (a consideration which caused many legislators to urge increased earmarking of family-planning funds). The report carefully documented the fragmentation of programs and responsibilities within the department—a myriad of agencies, each with some role in family planning with little coordination between them. At the local level, administrators were found to be lagging in developing meaningful programs for providing family-planning services to the target population; they failed to perceive any clear mandate from the top that this was, *in fact*, to be a priority program. HEW's own reluctance to request adequate funds to organize the department, to stress the importance of family planning, to

[81] See, e.g., U.S. Congress, House, Subcommittee on Public Health and Welfare of the Committee on Interstate and Foreign Commerce, *Hearings on Family Planning Services*, 91st Cong., 2nd Sess., 1970 (hereafter cited as *1970 FPS Hearings*); U.S. Congress, House, Subcommittee of the Committee on Government Operations, *Hearings on the Effects of Population Growth on Natural Resources and the Environment*, 91st Cong., 1st Sess., 1969 (hereafter cited as *Environment Hearings*); S. 2108 Hearings.
[82] *1967 Hearings*, 40.
[83] *S. 2108 Hearings*, 35.
[84] See note 12 *supra*.

use general funds available for family-planning purposes, to provide meaningful constant supervision over local activity only fortified local administrators' evaluation of the reality of the departmental policy. In 1967 congressional hearings on domestic family planning, HEW officials were literally raked over the coals for their foot-dragging response.

> Unfortunately the top leadership in HEW either lacks the foresight or the courage to meet the problem headon. Despite the numerous speeches of the Presidents of the United States, the department's attitude has been, in my judgment, extremely cavalier in this whole problem.
>
> In terms of the national debate that is going on today there are some real lessons we can learn from this report [the Harkavy Report]. I think we can draw some conclusions from the record of the pusillanimous and faint-hearted administration that HEW has given these programs, the almost total lack of effective leadership, drive, direction, and forward thrust in getting the services to where the action is in the neighborhood of America.
>
> I sometimes think that the top officials in the federal bureaucracy who want to innovate are simply unable to leave the bureaucracy that they are straddling. They are, in effect, trying to fight their way out of a bag of wet Kleenex. And it is very rough.[85]

The situation had apparently not altered substantially by 1970, when legislation was introduced to reorganize and intensify the federal effort in family planning and population (S. 2108). In congressional hearings, HEW was again roundly criticized for failing to take action consistent with its verbal promises. And the congressional wrath was further intensified when HEW had its own more limited bill introduced the night before the hearings (S. 3219).[86]

One of the primary distinguishing characteristics of the proposals was their differing approach to the problem of departmental organization. While HEW was praised by proponents of S. 2108 for the department's recent efforts to end some of the extreme fragmentation of power and responsibility in family-planning matters, it was severely

[85] Harkavy Report, 15. 17, 29.
[86] Both bills are set forth in *S. 2108 Hearings*, 2-19. Companion bills to S. 2108 were introduced in the House. See *1970 FPS Hearings*. The most severe criticism of HEW performance was offered by former Senator Joseph Tydings, the principal sponsor of S. 2108, but a number of the senators and speakers utilized the opportunity to castigate the agency. See, e.g., *ibid.*, 24-36, 40, 59-62, 137-38, 153-59, 282-89. See generally Richard Lincoln, "S. 2108: Capitol Hill Debates the Future of Population and Family Planning," *Family Planning Perspectives*, II (Jan., 1970), 6-12. HEW's rejoinder is set forth in *S. 2108 Hearings*, 119-29, 153, 169-81.

castigated for its continued opposition to total coordination of family-planning and population activities in a single center. At the time of the hearings, *most* of HEW's service grants were handled by a newly created National Center for Family Planning Services; research was the *primary* (but not exclusive) responsibility of the Center for Population Research in the National Institute of Child Health and Human Development; policy coordination was the prerogative of the Office of the Deputy Assistant Secretary for Family Planning and Population (although there was serious question whether this was accompanied with the power to achieve coordination). While coordination of research and service activities had been extremely weak in the past, HEW argued that the Office of the Deputy Assistant Secretary would serve to "orchestrate" the programs.[87] Given the past failure of the department to perform this task, however, legislators had difficulty in understanding why the suggested scheme offered any greater probability of assuring a coherent strategy.

Nor were they satisfied with HEW assurances concerning the level of expenditures for family-planning activities and population research. The agency-sponsored bill (S. 3219) provided only for "such sums as may be necessary" each fiscal year under a five-year authorization. Although HEW could point to congressional cutbacks of its 1970 authorization requests, its past performance (even using its own statistics, which have been challenged) indicated that it would fail to meet the five-year deadline indicated by President Nixon in providing family-planning services to those who wanted them.[88] While there were some 5 million women in need of subsidized services in fiscal 1968, only about 773,000 patients were serviced by all public and private agencies; while approximately 1,200 counties had some public or private subsidized family-planning services in 1968 (frequently only of a minimal character), more than 60 percent of all U.S. counties (1,872) had no identifiable program.[89] Given a cost of $50 per patient for family-planning services, the

---

[87] See *S. 2108 Hearings*, 157, 168. The restructuring and activities of the new centers are discussed by Secretary Finch in *ibid.*, 126–29. For a critique of the reorganized structure see the remarks of Senator Tydings in *ibid.*, 27–28, 158, 282–89.

[88] It was argued in the hearings that HEW data had previously proved inaccurate. *Ibid.*, 137–38, 150–52. In fact, Senator Tydings's statistics relating to federal family-planning activity are markedly different from those offered by HEW. Compare *ibid.*, 27–28, with *ibid.*, 134–35, 136–37, 142.

[89] See OEO, *Need for Subsidized Family Planning Services*; "Family Planning Services in the U.S.: A National Overview," *Family Planning Perspectives*, I (Oct., 1969), 4–12; Center for Family Planning Program Development, *Family Planning Programs in the U.S.*

HEW expenditure of $35.8 million for fiscal 1970 was clearly inadequate.[90] The President's Committee on Population and Family Planning, for example, had recommended a minimum of $30 million for support of research and training in 1970; HEW requested only $15.5 million for the Center for Population Research in fiscal 1970.[91] Similarly, HEW funding requests and expenditures and its leadership in stimulating general education in family planning and population and in training manpower for service and research programs were felt by many to be seriously deficient. In total, the congressional bill would have provided some $991 million over the next five years for family-planning and population services, research, education, and manpower training.[92]

In contrast to HEW, the Office of Economic Opportunity had generally provided imaginative leadership in getting family-planning services to recipients. Since 1967, when family planning was designated a "special-emphasis program" for OEO by Congress, the agency has actively pursued a policy of providing an alternative for "poor women burdened by unplanned and unwanted pregnancies that endanger their health and keep their families locked in the poverty cycle."[93] It has accepted the proposition that "family planning, the way that individuals can determine the number and spacing of their children, is an essential element in improving the health and economic well-being of the poor." Provision has been made for assuring the voluntary character of the program consistent with the individual's social and religious beliefs, and emphasis has been placed on the need for a "dignified and professional atmosphere as well as maintaining the confidence and trust of the participants." Further, since the programs are administered under the community-action provisions of Title II of the Economic Opportunity

[90] *S. 2108 Hearings*, 137, table K-11, 139. As the table indicates, HEW proposed to spend $67.7 million for fiscal 1971, which, when coupled with OEO spending, would service 2.2 million women.

[91] *Ibid.*, 134-35. The President's Committee proposal is set forth in *Population and Family Planning*, 36. See the testimony of Dr. John Rock on the inadequate funding of reproductive research in this country in *S. 2108 Hearings*, 36-43. Senator Gaylord Nelson argued that $175 million was needed in 1971 and $1 billion over the next five years. *Ibid.*, 263. Again, HEW envisioned an increase in research funds to $36.4 million in 1971.

[92] A detailed breakdown of present funding and the funding under S. 2108 and S. 3219 is provided by Lincoln, "S. 2108," 7, table 1. See "Government Seeks Way to Limit Population Growth," *Congressional Quarterly*, June 12, 1970, pp. 1554-58.

[93] Unless otherwise indicated, the material is derived from U.S. Office of Economic Opportunity, *The Office of Economic Opportunity Family Planning Program* (Oct. 6, 1969), 2. See OEO, *Conference Report on Family Planning* (1969); testimony of Dr. Gary London, *S. 2108 Hearings*, 79-85; OEO, *Community Action for Health: Family Planning* (Oct., 1967).

Act, attention has been given to involvement of the poor themselves in developing and carrying out the program. Through direct operation of a family-planning program conducted by a community-action agency, or through a delegate agency under a contractual arrangement, the growth of the OEO-supported projects has been extremely rapid. Since 1964, when OEO initiated the first federal family-planning project, the program has grown from 14 projects designed to serve 12,500 individuals in 1965 to 230 projects designed to serve 350,000 individuals in 1969. Whereas OEO spent only $436,184 in fiscal 1965 on family-planning activities, its budget request for 1970 was $22 million.[94] Equally as important, however, as the growth in numbers served and expenditures, has been the willingness of OEO to innovate, to carry the program directly to the target community and to provide leadership for local community-action agencies. The treatment afforded OEO programs at the congressional hearings when contrasted to that provided HEW serves as a testimonial to the greater willingness and success of the poverty agency to involve itself directly with the potential recipients of subsidized family planning.[95]

In any case, the Ninety-first Congress was prepared for a major legislative initiative in the area of population research and family planning. On December 24, 1970, President Nixon signed Public Law 91-572, the Family Planning Services and Population Research Act of 1970. The act set forth as its purposes:

> (1) to assist in making comprehensive voluntary family planning services readily available to all persons desiring such services; (2) to coordinate domestic population and family planning research with the present and future needs of family planning programs; (3) to improve administrative and operational supervision of domestic family planning services and of population research programs related to such services; (4) to enable public and non-profit entities to plan and develop comprehensive programs of family planning services; (5) to develop and make readily available information (including educational material) on family planning and population growth to all persons desiring such information; (6) to evaluate and improve the effectiveness of family planning service programs and of population research; (7) to assist in providing trained manpower needed to effec-

[94] OEO, *Family Planning Program Fact Sheet* (n.d.). See "Past, Present, Future: An Interview with Gary D. London," *Family Planning Perspective*, I (Oct., 1969), 18-22.
[95] See *S. 2108 Hearings*, 83.

tively carry out programs of population research and family planning services; and (8) to establish an Office of Population Affairs in the Department of Health, Education, and Welfare as a primary focus within the Federal Government on matters pertaining to population research and family planning, through which the Secretary of Health, Education, and Welfare . . . shall carry out the purposes of this Act.[96]

Reflecting its origins in S. 2108, all HEW activities relating to population research and family planning are centered in an Office of Population Affairs under a deputy assistant secretary (Dr. Louis Hellman became the first appointee). As approved by the Senate without opposition and by the House of Representatives by a vote of 298-32, the act authorizes $382 million over three years—a compromise from the original Senate proposal of approximately $991 million over five years.[97]

While the new legislation represents a dramatic congressional initiative to prod federal support for population research and family planning (the act, however, specifically prohibited the use of appropriated funds "where abortion is a method of family planning"), the extent to which it achieves its potential remains for future determination. The articulation of public policy is only the initial step; transformation of the policy through the legal system into action lies ahead. Nevertheless, there appears to be little question that government has accepted a commitment to publicly subsidized family-planning services. While the Catholic hierarchy continues to caution against the dangers of coercion and local officials often grow timid from the fear of controversy or personal bias, the direction seems clear. Although there may well be further stuttering by the bureaucracy, while courts may on occasion be asked to intervene to correct alleged abuses, while congressional appropriations may be inadequate for a full-scale effort, and while the executive may reshuffle priorities, it seems safe to assume that governmental policy has been defined in this area and that it will be implemented.

[96] Family Planning Services and Population Research Act of 1970, sec. 2, Public Law 91-572 (1970).
[97] The authorized funding (in millions) is as follows:

	FY 1971[a]	FY 1972	FY 1973
Family Planning Services—project grants	$30	$60	$90
—formula grants	10	15	20
Training Grants, Contracts	2	3	4
Population Research Grants, Contracts	30	50	65
Information and Education Grants, Contracts	.75	1	1.25
	$72.75	$129	$180.25

[a] funding is in addition to current programs for FY 1971.

POPULATION CONTROL: HARBINGERS OF TURMOIL AND CRISIS

Emergence of a family-planning policy, however, is not a panacea for the problems discussed at the beginning of the chapter. The "culture of poverty," the "cycle of dependency," the realities of discriminatory treatment denying opportunity for economic advancement—these are too pervasive in our system to be rooted out by any single measure, however vital. Even less is the emerging family-planning policy a definitive response to the problems of population and pollution. As indicated above, the primary source of the population-pollution crisis lies not in the procreation decisions of the poor, but in the voluntary decisions of Americans generally to have three, four, or more children. And family planning postulates freedom of choice regarding procreation. By definition, the decision as to the number and spacing of children is left to the parents free from external pressures. It is a complete misnomer, then, to speak of family planning as population control; it is highly questionable to consider present governmental family-planning policy to be a population policy.

> Logically, it does not make sense to use *family* planning to provide *national* population control or planning. The "planning" in family planning is that of each separate couple. The only control they exercise is control over the size of *their* family. Obviously, couples do not plan the size of the nation's population, any more than they plan the growth of the national income or the form of the highway network. There is no reason to expect that the millions of decisions about family size made by couples in their own interest will automatically control population for the benefit of society.[98]

Whereas comprehensive population policy would involve delineation of objectives and programs relating to mortality and migration as well as fertility, governmental decision-making thus far cannot even be deemed a viable policy of fertility control. Consideration of authoritative policy statements and "fertility-related" legislation prior to 1970 reveals a preoccupation with assuring availability of contraceptive services primarily to the poverty sector, in order to implement the voluntary private decisions of the married couple. While there has been increasing recognition of the potential negative consequences of exces-

[98] Davis, "Population Policy," 732.

sive population and legislation to promote population research, there has been no definitive authoritative statement declaring a policy of limiting population growth. As Oscar Harkavy, Frederick Jaffe, and Samuel Wishik indicated: "To our knowledge, there has never been an official policy regarding the virtue or necessity of reducing U.S. population growth, much less achieving population stability. Nor has there emerged among Americans generally a 'virtually unchallenged' consensus on what should constitute an official U.S. population policy."[99]

There have been a number of statements by governmental officials, however, at least looking toward a policy of fertility limitation and population stability. For example, on February 18, 1970, the former secretary of HEW, Robert Finch, suggested that Americans might limit their family size to two children and referred to the possibility of employing "disincentives" to discourage excess fertility. As might be expected, this invoked a scathing denunciation by Rev. James McHugh, director of the Family Life Division of the Catholic Conference, and the administration was quick to deny any policy implication in the Finch statement.[100] On the other hand, on October 30, 1969, Roger Egebert, HEW secretary for Health and Scientific Affairs, declared:

> What does freedom of choice and family planning imply for the present state of our society? It implies enormous population growth for the simple reason that the typical American family, if it can, will elect to have three children, not two.... I think we are going to have to work towards changing national mores, a change based on the public acceptance of the demographic facts of life. I think we are going to have to help the people of this country understand that their vital interest and that of their children demand that we control the growth of population.[101]

And Lee DuBridge, White House science and technology advisor, set an even more precise objective for limiting population growth: "Can we not invent a way to reduce our population growth to zero? Every human institution... should set this as its prime task."[102]

Similar statements from executive and legislative officials might be cited, but the fact remains that such statements, while vital indicators of

[99] Harkavy, Jaffe, and Wishik, "Family Planning and Public Policy," 368.
[100] See James T. McHugh, "The Government's Baby Limit," NC Feature, Mar. 9, 1970; "Population Activities in the United States," 13.
[101] Address to Planned Parenthood–World Population, Oct. 30, 1969, quoted in *Population Bulletin*, XXV (Dec., 1969), 127–28.
[102] Address to the Thirteenth National Conference of the U.S. Commission for UNESCO, Nov. 25, 1969, *ibid.*, 128.

the thinking of key policy-making officials, are not definitive policy pronouncements. Indeed, careful consideration of authoritative declarations indicates that the government's approach, thus far, is not population limitation, but population accommodation. Thus, President Nixon speaks of anti-pollution programs, environmental protection, new cities to house the increasing populace, expansion of the transportation facilities to assure adequate mobility. Policy-making is thus directed to ameliorating the impact of excess population, rather than seeking to strike at the source of the impact directly.

It is, however, questionable that such a policy orientation can effectively impede the negative consequences of excess population discussed earlier. It is doubtful that we have either the resources or the willingness and capability to allocate our resources effectively to protect even our surface life-style. Assuming *arguendo*, that such resources were effectively committed, it still would not effectively confront the pure psychological pressures of an anthill existence. Like all animals, man seeks *Lebensraum*, territoriality, areas of privacy—it is difficult to conceive a meaningful life-style in a world of people bunched together.[103]

What then would be a viable policy objective? The real need seems to be for an *optimum* policy whereby population is brought into balance with available resources—and the term "resources" is used in a broad sense to encompass those ingredients deemed essential to a decent life-style. Given the projection of the consequences of present population growth discussed above, the most reasonable approach would be to define a zero population growth as our objective, which would require that Americans limit themselves to two children per family. This policy objective can be seen in Joint Resolution 214, introduced June 18, 1970, by eighteen senators. (The proposal died in committee.) The resolving clause declared "that it is the policy of the United States to develop, encourage, and implement, at the earliest possible time, the necessary policies, attitudes, social standards and actions which will, by voluntary means, be consistent with human rights and individual conscience, stabilize the population of the United States and thereby promote the future well-being of the citizens of this nation and the entire world."

Given political realities, however, it is perhaps more probable that

[103] See Fairfield Osborn, *Our Crowded Planet: Essays on the Pressures of Population* (Garden City, 1962); Louise B. Young, ed., *Population in Perspective* (New York, 1968), 355–97; Ehrlich, *The Population Bomb*; Alan F. Westin, *Privacy and Freedom* (New York, 1967).

initially the goal will be left more inexact and the orientation will be toward a policy of seeking to limit the fertility to approximate the optimum more closely. Kingsley Davis stated:

> Most discussions of the population crisis lead logically to zero population growth as the ultimate goal, because *any* growth rate, if continued, will eventually use up the earth. Yet hardly ever do arguments for population policy consider such a goal, and current policies do not dream of it. Why not? The answer is evidently that zero population growth is unacceptable to most nations and to most religious and ethnic communities. To argue for this goal would be to alienate possible support for action programs.[104]

In any case, it is increasingly necessary to delineate some policy guidelines for fashioning action programs directed at limiting fertility. Two of the most important have been suggested by recent decisions of the judicial actor. As in *Griswold*, emphasis in policy implementation should be placed on maximizing voluntariness, privacy, human dignity. Not only is this a political necessity, but the values therein defined are themselves deserving of protection. Intrusion of the state into the marital union is necessarily suspect given the importance we place on a viable marital relationship. Individual freedom of choice regarding this most intimate decision must not be ignored, but rather deserves the most careful attention and maximum protection. While fertility limitation may be necessary to protect personal liberties for the future, we must be careful that we do not destroy personal liberty in the present. Recognition of the importance of voluntariness in the procreative decision does not delineate a formula for choosing among program alternatives but only suggests parameters for consideration of policy alternatives.

Still another consideration derived from judicial decision-making involves the constitutional implications of discriminatory treatment. Fertility-limitation programs must not be arbitrarily imposed on segments of the population merely because of race, alienage, or wealth.[105] To visit burdens on public-assistance recipients in their procreative choice in

---

[104] Davis, "Population Policy," 158. See Bernard Berelson, "Beyond Family Planning," *Science*, CLXIII (Feb. 7, 1969), 533, 535; Miles, "Whose Baby," 24–33. Zero Population Growth, Inc., 1158 Lisa Lane, Los Altos, Calif. 94022, is an organization devoted to public education and legislative activity on behalf of a zero population growth policy. See Ehrlich, *The Population Bomb*, 224. On the meaning of optimum population see U.S. Congress, House, *Environment Hearings*, 4.

[105] Dienes, "To Feed the Hungry," 613–14.

order to achieve population goals, for example, would not only seem to violate the vague commands of justice, but would also impair the constitutional guarantees of equal protection, privacy, freedom of religion, and substantive due process generally. As this indicates, the future promises an active role for the judiciary in the interactive process of fashioning population policy.

Before turning to the extant and potential programs for implementing a fertility-limitation policy, it is important to confront again the impediments to meaningful action. It would be quite easy to attribute the reluctance of political authorities to accept and effectuate a population policy solely to the fears born of Catholic intransigence. Indeed, the Church's negative reaction to the movement for abortion reform is indicative of its response to proposals generally which involve intervention of government toward increased fertility control. *Humanae Vitae* provides a clear condemnation of governmental intrusion into the inviolable family life, and the 1969 message of the Catholic bishops similarly castigated government interference with the free decision to procreate.

> We continue to believe that the proper answer to population problems is development—development of natural resources and of technological means, and development also of human beings themselves. Given educational opportunity and the economic means that go with it, we believe couples will make judgments about family size that will be in harmony with the common good. We affirm that parents themselves, and no governmental official, should make that judgment.... In the name of the priceless dignity of the right to life, we the Catholic Bishops of the United States protest the continuing and ever expanding role both at home and abroad of the government in the matter of population control through the limitation of births. We hope that our fellow Americans will appreciate the soundness of our stand.[106]

[106] "Statement of the Bishops of the United States in Protest of U.S. Government Programs against the Right to Life." See Appendix H. Pope Paul VI, *Humanae Vitae*, 11, poses the question: "Who will stop rulers from favoring, from even imposing upon their peoples, if they were to consider it necessary, the method of contraception which they judge to be most efficacious?" This is then used to attack governmental intrusion: "In such a way men, wishing to avoid individual, family, or social difficulties encountered in the observance of the divine law, would reach the point of placing at the mercy of the intervention of public authorities the most personal and most reserved sector of conjugal intimacy."

Even the strain of liberal Catholicism emphasizing "responsible parenthood" places emphasis of freedom of choice on the *right of parents* to determine family size.

But to attribute hesitancy to the fear of negative Catholic reaction would be simplistic. Far more important is the absence of any articulate public recognition or support for a comprehensive fertility-control policy and appropriate action programs. In fact, most Americans do not really seem to appreciate the severity of the problem of domestic population growth and their own part in it. When asked to rank domestic problems in the order of importance, population tends to bring up the rear position of the spectrum. Those who seek to educate regarding the dimensions of the problem and the need for prompt action are often castigated as prophets of doom, alarmists, or simply overly dramatic. Even the new-found interest in our environment is only grudgingly being related to the problem of excessive fertility. And just as in meeting the problems of our environment, Americans seem unable to comprehend their own personal responsibility for the population crisis. In our affluence we have lost the ability to project to the larger social implications of our own personal behavior. The very tendency to identify subsidized family planning for the poor as a population policy bespeaks this indifference or ignorance of a personal involvement. It is not the poor alone that must bear the burden of controlling population growth, but citizens generally appear unwilling to accept their own responsibility.

In the 1920s and 1930s Americans desired a family of approximately two children, and contraception provided the means to limit fertility accordingly. But in the 1950s and 1960s women have tended to want three or four children. The announcement of an impending birth is greeted with joy and enthusiasm by relatives and friends; the parents find deep psychological and perhaps biological fulfillment in reproduction; baby showers and gifts at birth limit the economic severity of the new addition; the childless couple and the unmarried are still held in some disrepute (although this may be changing), especially in the family-oriented suburbs. Not that Americans have opted for the return to the large family of the past (although even today many tend to look with some nostalgia on the "cheaper by the dozen" family and react with a sort of "isn't that wonderful" attitude). But we have chosen the moderate-size family as our objective.

Slowly, however, organized articulate interest groups promoting fertility control are beginning to appear and garner strength. While there are a number of ad hoc groups pursuing particularized objectives (e.g., abortion-law reform, conservation, family planning), the recognition of common interests and acceptance of a common action program is a definite possibility.[107] Again the slow maturation process which characterized the evolution of public acceptance and politio-legal change in birth-control norms can be perceived. But until such an organized force emerges, or crisis impends, meaningful political action is likely to be minimal and haphazard.

The problem arises, however, that delay in effective action tends to foreclose possible alternatives for response. Potential programs for fertility control can be conceptualized as lying along a continuum from most to least voluntary, from programs maximizing free choice to those emphasizing governmental compulsion (e.g., government licensing for pregnancies, compulsory mass sterilization, compulsory abortion). As time passes and the situation becomes more critical, the efficacy of voluntary responses in avoiding the negative consequences of excess population constantly diminishes; the tendency to employ coercive measures becomes increasingly compelling. There is a real need, then, for prompt response if we are to pursue nondiscriminatory fertility limitation consistent with a maximization of individual freedom and human dignity.

However, there does not appear to be anything approaching a governmental action program directed at general fertility limitation. Congress has implemented President Nixon's request for the formation of a Commission on Population Growth and the American Future to study and provide information concerning "the broad range of problems associated with population growth and their implications for America's future,"[108] and the Family Planning Services and Population Research

[107] In June, 1970, a Congress on Optimum Population and Environment was held in Chicago. Groups interested in population and those stressing protection of the environment explored their common interests and the possibility of united action. *Population Bulletin*, XXVI (Dec., 1970), 18-19.

[108] Section 4 of Public Law 91-213 set forth the duties of the new commission: "The Commission shall conduct an inquiry into the following aspects of population growth in the United States and its foreseeable social consequences: (1) The probable course of population growth, internal migration, and related demographic developments between now and the year 2000; (2) The resources and the public sector of the public economy that will be required to deal with the anticipated growth and population; (3) The ways in which population growth may affect the activity of Federal, State, and local governments; (4) The impact of population on environmental pollution and the depletion of natural resources; and (5) The various

Act does promise increased funding for facilities, manpower, and research regarding fertility control. There is an increased emphasis on the need for greater understanding of population dynamics, factors affecting fertility, and development of safer, cheaper, more effective, easier-to-use fertility-control devices. At the state and national level, courts and legislatures are interacting to make abortion more readily available—although this is more often based on the rights of the woman than on social (population) considerations.[109] And increased interest is also being generated in sterilization.

The value of all of these, however, is dependent on the desire or willingness of parents to limit their family size. As long as Americans want three, four, or more children, voluntary programs cannot affect population growth. The need is to change the very attitude and values of Americans regarding desirable family size. And this, in turn, demands recognition and alteration of the social, economic, psychological, moral, and legal factors affecting fertility patterns.

> There appears, then, to be only one viable approach to the population problem in the United States. This is the long, uphill route of encouraging the American people to modify their basic attitudes and behavior so that instead of idealizing large families in the abstract and creating them in flesh and blood, we will prefer small ones and act upon our preferences; so that instead of promoting forms of economic growth which will increasingly pollute our living space, we will insist that we clean up as we go, no matter what the cost; so that instead of measuring our welfare by the amount of our consumption, we will become deeply concerned about enhancing the quality and preserving the variety of life in its numerous forms. These goals require a change in the momentum of our society.[110]

---

means appropriate to the ethical values and principles of this society by which our nation can achieve a population level properly suited for its environmental, natural resources, and other needs."

While this book was in press, the commission issued its report detailing the dangers of future population growth and recommending a number of measures designed to permit individuals to control their fertility.

[109] Judicial activity revising the abortion laws is exemplified by Doe v. Scott, 321 F. Supp. 1385 (N.D. Ill. 1971); Roe v. Wade, 314 F. Supp. 1217 (N.D. Tex. 1970); Babbitz v. McCann, 310 F. Supp. 293 (E.D. Wis. 1970); United States v. Vuitch, 305 F. Supp. 1032 (D.D.C. 1969), rev'd 91 S. Ct. 1294 (1971) (on the issue of vagueness); People v. Belous, 80 Cal. Rptr. 354, 458 P.2d 194 (1969). See *Population Bulletin*, XXVI (Dec., 1970), 15–16, on legislative revision.

[110] Davis, "Population Policy," 733.

Perhaps the least odious approach toward influencing motivations regarding fertility is to initiate a broad program of public education. Having identified the factors that induce parents to produce larger-than-desired families, it is necessary to convince them that the rewards are outweighed by negative penalties in limiting birth or that greater rewards can be obtained from limiting fertility.[111] Such an educational program could seek to make Americans realize the dimensions of the domestic population problem, the relationship of excess fertility to the life-styles of themselves and their children, the personal economic costs of fertility excess, the scope of parental duties for already-born children, the advantages of delayed marriage and the values of the single life.

While the communications media bear a vital responsibility in sustaining such a program, given their access to, and influence on, the public, the dimensions of the task of altering deeply ingrained values demand the involvement of the resources of government. Further, as already indicated, development of better contraceptives, revision of the abortion laws, and improvement of sterilization techniques must be pursued to assure individuals desiring to control birth easy access to the requisite means. Again, a partnership of public and private resources would appear essential.

Realistically, however, it is questionable that this message would be heeded by most Americans. Inducements and disincentives may well be necessary to bring about the desired behavior. At the minimum, this involves an elimination of pro-natalist influences which are presently rampant in our legal and social policy.

> If it were admitted that the creation and care of new human beings is socially motivated like other forms of behavior, by being a part of the system of rewards and punishments that is built into human relationships, and thus is bound up with the individual's economic personal interest, it would be apparent that the social structure and economy must be changed before a deliberate reduction in the birth rate can be achieved.[112]

> The existence of . . . pronatalist policies becomes apparent when we recall that, among human beings, population replacement would not occur at all were it not for the complex social organization and system of incentives that encourage mating, pregnancy, and the care, support, and rearing of children. These institutional

[111] *Ibid.*, 733. See Roger O. Egeberg, "Defusing the Population Bomb: New Role for Government," *Trial*, Aug.–Sept., 1970, p. 11.
[112] Davis, "Population Policy," 733.

mechanisms are the pronatalist policies evolved unconsciously over millenia to give societies a fertility sufficient to offset high mortality. The formation and implementation of antinatalist policies must be based, therefore, on an analysis and modification of the existing pronatalist policies. It follows, as well, that antinatalist policies will not necessarily involve the introduction of coercive measures. In fact, just the opposite is the case. Many of these new policies will entail a *lifting* of pressures to reproduce, rather than an *imposition* of pressures not to do so.[113]

While a full inquiry into the myriad of proposals advanced is beyond the scope of the present study,[114] a few of the more realistic suggestions (in terms of potential acceptance and conformity to policy guidelines regarding voluntarism and nondiscrimination) might be noted.

The fertility behavior of Americans might be influenced by making it financially less attractive to overproduce. Tax benefits for having children, for example, might be reduced or eliminated after the birth of the second child and the heavy taxes presently imposed on single individuals vis-à-vis their married counterparts could be reduced. Utilizing affirmative sanctions, tax incentives could be afforded to those who voluntarily limit their family size. More subtle potential influences in fertility in our laws might also be considered. Instead of, or in addition to, promoting home ownership (especially in family-oriented suburbia) through home-mortgage guarantees and tax advantages, perhaps there might be gains realized, using similar techniques, to encourage renting. Inducements could also be used to encourage delay in marriage (e.g., raising the age of consent, offering enhanced opportunities for creative and meaningful, but time-consuming, work following graduation), to prompt women to embark on careers other than motherhood (e.g., financial assistance for continued education, legal action against sex discrimination), to offer alternatives to the psychological rewards perceived to result from childbearing (e.g., promotion of creative job and social opportunities).

These are only indicative of the panoply of the action programs that have been offered. All seek to influence values and behavior through social and legal inducements and disincentives. Most can be expected to generate political hostility and controversy. The line between persuasion and coercion is exceedingly fine and it is likely that many Americans will see any attempt to interfere with their free decision to produce

[113] Blake, "Population Policy for Americans," 528.
[114] See Berelson, "Beyond Family Planning"; Davis, "Population Policy."

children as a mode of coercion. It will take a brave or naive politician to recommend measures which are likely to impinge on individual choice. The potential for status quo challenge to such measures in the judicial forum charging excessive coercion, violative of constitutional guarantees of privacy, freedom of religion, and substantive due process generally is also a potential impediment. But as in most constitution adjudication, countervailing interests could be offered to support the reasonableness of the particular governmental action. Given the frightening implications of the population-pollution problems for future life-styles, none of the above proposals appears to be excessively coercive. But whether the political policy-makers will overcome motivational impediments to respond to the need for legal action in time to avoid more coercive measures and whether the courts can and will participate in fashioning creative population policy remains speculative. In any case, the threatening crisis augurs provision of still another measure of the role of the law and the legal system in responding to social change.

Conclusion

In the past half-century, a major revolution has taken place in American legal theory. Increasingly, the approach to law as a set of fixed norms contained in a statute or court decision to be applied in a mechanical fashion is rejected. Rather, law is perceived as a social institution, a device for satisfying societal wants and needs. Receiving its impetus in the writings of the sociological school and the realists, the new jurisprudence seeks to achieve a more efficacious "social engineering" through law.[1]

> I am content to think of law as a social institution to satisfy social wants—the claims and demands and expectations involved in the existence of civilized society—by giving effect to as much as we may with the least sacrifice, so far as such wants may be satisfied or such claims given effect by an ordering of human conduct through politically organized society. For present purposes I am content to see in legal history the record of a continually wider recognizing and satisfying of human wants or claims or desires through social control; a more embracing and more effective securing of social interests, a continually more complete and effective elimination of waste and precluding of friction in human

---

[1] See generally Edgar Bodenheimer, *Jurisprudence* (New York, 1940), 292–324; Wolfgang Friedmann, *Legal Theory* (4th ed., Toronto, 1960), 292–99; Edwin W. Patterson, *Jurisprudence: Men and Ideas of the Law* (Brooklyn, 1953), 509–58.

Roscoe Pound summarized the achievements of this approach in his summary on the changes which have occurred in jurisprudence since the turn of the century: (1) a concern with the functions of precepts rather than with their content; (2) an emphasis on social wants rather than social wills; (3) an attempt to avoid subjectivity in favor of objective analysis; (4) an emphasis on the concrete claims of concrete human beings rather than on abstractions; (5) a recognition of the need to work with the social sciences; (6) an emphasis on the fact that the task of measuring values belongs to all the social sciences and not merely jurisprudence. *Social Control through Law*, 123–26.

enjoyment of the goods of existence—in short, a continually more efficacious social engineering.[2]

This does not mean that men are to be treated as automatons to be manipulated by platonic guardians, but that law is to be understood as a vehicle for giving recognition to competing desires and needs. To understand the functioning of law and legal institutions, therefore, it is necessary to include in our inquiry the social environment that occasions their response. There is a recognition that the study of law and legal policy-making cannot be divorced from the study of society, that law finds its purpose, its reason for existence, in the adjustment of the conflicting interests of society, that any attempt to limit legal analysis to the precepts of law contained in statutes and case books ignores the real essence of law.

The concept of social engineering is highly dynamic. It postulates that change is a continual ongoing process that can be managed through mechanisms of social control with law perceived as a primary device. It demands that law serve the function of both maintenance and change. In part, law serves a *maintenance* function in that it must be the "instrument through which men seek to secure order against the threats and inroads of disorder";[3] there must be some sense of stability, an acceptance of "the rules of the game," a belief that in some way "justice will be done." But there must also be some mode through which society can respond to change and seek a more ideal order, a *creative* element. A breakdown in social relations is frequently productive of a better order. Conflict engendered by disintegration of existing relationships is frequently functional to order, especially in a highly pluralistic democratic society. New elements in society seek recognition; technological innova-

---

[2] Roscoe Pound, *An Introduction to the Philosophy of Law* (New Haven, 1954), 47. The concept of "social engineering" is premised on the belief that "conflict and competition and overlapping of man's desires and demands and claims, in the formulation and assertion of what they take to be their reasonable expectations, require a systematic adjustment of relations, a reasoned ordering of conduct, if a politically organized society is to endure." Pound, *New Paths of the Law* (Lincoln, Neb., 1950), 3. There are six facets to the approach: (1) the study of the actual social effects of legal institutions and legal doctrines; (2) the study of the means of making legal rules effective; (3) sociological study as a preliminary to law-making; (4) an emphasis on the juridical method; (5) a sociological legal history; (6) a stress on the importance of reasonable and just solution of individual cases. Pound, *Interpretations of Legal History* (London, 1923), 153. See Pound, *Social Control through Law*, 68; Pound, *Contemporary Juristic Thinking* (Claremont, Calif., 1940), 37; Pound, *The Task of Law*, 23.

[3] Iredell Jenkins, "Justice and Ideology," *Nomos VI: Justice*, ed. Carl J. Friedrich (New York, 1963).

tions create new hardships; economic or power relationships between groups change; in all cases, new norms must be fashioned, adjustments must be made, the conflict must be managed.

Rather than the resultant of the behavior of a single institution (myopic concern with the behavior of courts *or* legislatures *or* administrators has tended to dominate legal studies), however, the present study has approached this control process as the consequence of the interactions of the myriad of legal institutions. An attempt has been made to assess the relative contributions primarily of two of these varied elements, the courts and legislatures, the conflicts and cooperation existing among them, and generally the process alternatives and pressures influencing them as they interact in social engineering.[4] This required an effort to relate the behavior of the institutions in such a way as to clarify the process through which each element in the legal system behaves in responding to the demands made by a changing society. An appreciation of the actual relation of the legal order to our dynamic society would seem impossible if we are unable to define the strengths and weaknesses and the respective roles of the various legal forums as they engage in the process of legal change. Understood in these terms, the legal actors truly constitute a system—"a coordinated, functioning whole made up of a set of interrelated, interacting parts."[5]

> The solution of specific legal problems constantly requires an understanding of the functions and interrelationships of more than one institutional process and frequently of several. Problems arising in a court call for a perceptive awareness not only of what courts are for but of what a legislature is for . . . and of what matters can best be left to private decisions. . . . The development of awarenesses calls for study which comes to grips with the questions of what each of these various processes of decision *is* good for and how each interrelates and interacts with the others.[6]

[4] Wolfgang Friedmann, *Law in a Changing Society* (abr. ed., Baltimore, 1964), 20, notes: "It is now increasingly recognized by contemporary jurists that borderlines are fluid, and that cooperation rather than separation, in a constant interchange of give and take between legislature . . . and judiciary reflects the reality of the legal process." See Wolfgang Friedmann, *Law and Social Change in Contemporary Britain* (London, 1951); Charles D. Breitel, *The Lawmakers* (New York, 1965).

[5] Hart and Sacks, *The Legal Process*, iii. See Auerbach et al., *The Legal Process*, which manifests the "system" and interactive process approach in its analysis of the handling of industrial accidents.

[6] Hart and Sacks, *The Legal Process*, 111. The authors recognize the vital necessity of fashioning institutions capable of adjusting to their myriad of problems arising from the social order: "An organized society is one which has an interconnected system of procedures adequate, or claiming to be adequate, to deal with

Conclusion : 307

The framework employed in this book, however, seeks to go beyond even this perspective of a legal system composed of interacting institutions responding to social needs and wants. An attempt has been made to achieve an increased understanding of the actual workings of the system in terms of time and change. The behavior of one institution has an effect on the subsequent moves of other institutions. Response of the interacting institutions must be approached in terms of the point in the process at which they are asked to intervene. The legal system thus emerges as a dynamic process of recommending, intelligence, and prescribing functions by each legal actor, and the interaction between them and social forces in fashioning legal policy. The management of problems generates new issues; technological innovation produces additional demands for legal action.

LAW AND LAG

It has been approximately 100 years since Anthony Comstock stalked the halls of Congress and the state legislatures calling for a legal retooling in the struggle against evil. The social system which provided the impetus for his passionate pleadings has given way to a society with a far different orientation to sexual matters and questions of individual conscience. And his legal legacy has also been and continues to be abandoned or revised. But if one seeks to find support in the fashioning of birth-control policy for the creativity of law, he is likely to experience disappointment. The legal system did respond but only through a slow process of compromise and adjustment. For some, such a mode of legal action is grossly inadequate.

> Until recently, the pace of social, political, technological and industrial change was such that the law's solutions could lag a respectable distance behind the emergence of the problems newly

---

every kind of question affecting the group's internal relations, and every kind of question affecting its external relations which the group can establish competence to deal with. At least in its combination of procedures, therefore, every society's system is more or less distinctive and in some respects unique. Yet each system, whatever it may be, provides the indispensable framework of living within the society in question. Short of a violent reconstitution of the system, it provides the means, and the only means, by which the problems of that society can be resolved. It follows that no social question can be intelligently studied without a sensitive regard to the distinctive character of the institutional system within which the particular question arises."

created by such change. The law's digestive process—the much-vaunted adaptability of the common law—was almost as imperceptible as the changes themselves. We circled around the unseasoned and unestablished. One of the dividends of the slow march of the law has been that en route the seasonal problems arising from short-lived public impulses tend to die off to decide themselves. ... I suspect that this marking of time has not been altogether unprecedented.... Today and tomorrow, however, the slow pace of the past would be intolerable. The swift and radical changes already here and around the corner can no longer be digested by the law without acute distress on the day of reckoning.[7]

The "lag" in law, however, is not a unitary phenomenon. To the extent that such delay is born of a careful attempt to delineate the problem area, collect requisite data, and consider policy alternatives in an effort to maximize the realization of social wants and needs as effectively as possible, the lag appears necessary and desirable. To rush forward blindly with hastily drawn legal solutions to all social problems without considering whether legal action is presently desirable and what form that action should take is self-defeating.[8] Once on the books, the legal norm has a natural claim to continuation—perpetuation of the status quo produces its own motivational impediment to further change. As Margaret Sanger and her followers learned, it is often more difficult to change a law that has achieved a status of legitimacy than to fashion a legal norm in the first instance. Whether this is born of the desire of vested interests to perpetuate at least a symbolic claim to dominance for their values, or the influence of other motivational impediments within the legal system, especially apathy, the need for careful policy consideration before "legalizing" the problem deserves recognition. Indeed, the compromise of interests rather than a winner-take-all resolution of disputes, especially on hotly contested issues, is not only conducive to social order but also recognizes that there is seldom a panacea for social problems. Effective management, rather than final resolution of social problems, appears a far more realistic goal for defining the relationship of legal and social change.

There is, however, a different source of lag which emerges from this study: the delay generated by the legal institution itself. Blind adherence

[7] Bernard Botein, "The Future of the Judicial Process: Challenge and Response," *The Record of the Association of the Bar of the City of New York*, XV (Apr., 1960), 173.

[8] See Lawrence M. Friedman and Jack Ladinsky, "Social Change and the Law of Industrial Accidents," *Columbia Law Review*, LXVII (Jan., 1967), 50–82.

to precedent even after its reason for being has passed, imposition of overly technical rules unnecessarily barring access to particular legal policy-makers and reception of vitally needed data for effective fashioning of policy, and motivational impediments impairing realization of necessary policy revisions far beyond that necessary for more rational policy-making—these are too often characteristic of the legal process. It is this type of institutional conservatism that impairs a creative role for law in managing social change and produces the disillusion voiced by so many with the capacity and/or willingness of the legal system to respond to the challenges of rapid social change.

It is hoped that at least a partial answer has been suggested in the present analysis. Policy formation is an interactive process; effective cooperation between the legal actors can go far in producing increased creativity. The judiciary can place problems on the legislative agenda by communicating, whether formally or informally, policy problems and possible actions. It can provide at least partial solutions, thus easing social stress, when vested interests make legislative action impossible. The legislature can use its superior fact-gathering facilities in fashioning policies and can clarify its purposes in legislating through the statutory language. Sufficient leeway can be left in the statute to permit the judicial actor to adapt the policy to the social situation. But such interdependence demands effective channels of communication within the legal system.

Creative response also requires effective communications between the social and legal systems. Adequate modes of access to the legal system for the myriad of social interests must be provided; unnecessary technical impediments, especially in the judicial arena, on which minority interests so heavily rely, must be eliminated. The legal actors must be informed concerning social needs and demands, the consequences of past policy on society, and the probable effects of suggested policy alternatives. This demand for information in turn intensifies the need for greater collaboration between the social and natural sciences and the policy-makers. While scientists cannot and should not determine the ultimate value choices for society, they can assist in making those choices more informed. On the other hand, the present limitations of these disciplines must always be considered and preclude excessive reliance on their competence. But the aforementioned weaknesses in the intelligence function demand special attention to strengthening this facet of the legal-change process. Law can hardly be expected to lead if it doesn't know what it's leading, where it's been, or where it's going.

Nor should we ignore the fact that the formal legal system and the formal law on the books are only a facet of the total legal response. Even as exceptions are fashioned to what appear to be all-encompassing rules, the *informal* legal processes may be even further along in redefining the legal response to social change. As was indicated above: "The efficacy of a legal norm can be evaluated only after the law in the books is transformed into the law in action. In the implementation of the law, the legal norm attains meaning; it becomes socially relevant."

Administrative nonenforcement of the birth-control prohibitions had transformed the law in action even as the law on the books in the various jurisdictions appeared firm and unassailable. While the continued existence of the formal norms had symbolic implications and effectively inhibited some forms of social behavior (e.g., the opening of birth-control clinics in Massachusetts and Connecticut), the real "law" was substantially different from that which one might conclude if he looked solely to the law books. In assessing the capacity of law to respond to social change, then, care must be taken in defining what is meant by *law*. There is frequently a far greater correspondence between the informal law in action and social behavior than between the formal law on the books and social behavior. And a proper understanding of the relation of the legal and social systems demands a proper understanding of both spheres.

The present study has sought to probe these problems in analyzing the relationship of the legislature and the judiciary as they interact in the process of responding to social change. In doing so, the framework set forth in the Introduction has provided a functional tool for identifying, organizing, and analyzing the essential factors involved in the legal response to the changed place of birth control in American society, the gradual formation of a policy of public support for family planning, and the emerging problem of population control. It must now be applied to other areas and expanded to encompass the behavior of other legal institutions. But this is the very essence of scientific inquiry. One study gives birth to another, each yielding relevant items of knowledge, constantly increasing our understanding and appreciation of the legal process and its ability to respond creatively to and guide social change.

Appendixes

APPENDIX A

Federal Legislation Relating to Birth Control
(for 1971 changes see pp. 188–93 supra)

18 U.S.C. 1461–62

Tit. 18. Crimes and Criminal Procedure
Ch. 71. Obscenity

SECTION 1461. Mailing obscene or crime inciting matter.

Every obscene, lewd, lascivious, indecent, filthy or vile article, matter, thing, device or substance; and

Every article or thing designed, adapted, or intended for preventing conception or producing abortion, or for any indecent or immoral use; and

Every article, instrument, substance, drug, medicine, or thing which is advertised or described in a manner calculated to lead another to use or apply it for preventing conception or producing abortion, or for any indecent or immoral purpose; and

Every written or printed card, letter, circular, book, pamphlet, advertisement, or notice of any kind giving information, directly or indirectly, where, or how, or from whom, or by what means any of such mentioned matters, articles, or things may be obtained or made, or where or by whom any act or operation of any kind for the procuring or producing of abortion will be done or performed, or how or by what means conception may be prevented or abortion produced, whether sealed or unsealed; and

Every paper, writing, advertisement, or representation what any article, instrument, substance, drug, medicine, or thing may, or can, be used or applied for preventing conception or producing abortion, or for any indecent or immoral purpose; and

Every description calculated to induce or incite a person to so use or apply any such article, instrument, substance, drug, medicine, or thing—

Is declared to be nonmailable matter and shall not be conveyed in the mails or delivered from any post office or by any letter carrier.

Whoever knowingly uses the mail for the mailing, carriage in the mails, or delivery of anything declared by this section to be nonmailable, or knowingly causes to be delivered by mail according to the direction thereon, or at the place at which it is directed to be delivered by the person to whom it is addressed, or knowingly takes any such thing from the mails for the purpose of circulating or disposing thereof, or of aiding in the circulation or disposition thereof, shall be fined not more than $5,000 or imprisoned not more than five years, or both, for the first such offense, and shall be fined not more than $10,000 or imprisoned not more than ten years, or both, for each such offense thereafter.

The term "indecent" as used in this section includes matter of a character tending to incite arson, murder, or assassination.

SECTION 1462. Importation or transportation of obscene matters.

Whoever brings into the United States, or any place subject to the jurisdiction thereof, or knowingly uses any express company or other common carrier, for carriage in interstate or foreign commerce—

(a) any obscene, lewd, lascivious, or filthy book, pamphlet, picture, motion-picture film, paper, letter, writing, print, or other matter of indecent character; or

(b) any obscene, lewd, lascivious, or filthy phonograph recording, electrical transcription, or other article or thing capable of producing sound; or

(c) any drug, medicine, article, or thing designed, adapted, or intended for preventing conception, or producing abortion, or for any indecent or immoral use; or any written or printed card, letter, circular, book, pamphlet, advertisement, or notice of any kind giving information, directly or indirectly, where, how, or of whom, or by what means any of such mentioned articles, matters, or things may be obtained or made; or

Whoever knowingly takes from such express company or other common carrier any matter or thing the carriage of which is herein made unlawful—

Shall be fined not more than $5,000 or imprisoned not more than five years, or both, for the first such offense and shall be fined not more than $10,000, or imprisoned not more than ten years, or both, for each such offense thereafter.

19 U.S.C. 1305

Tit. 19. Customs Duties
Ch. 4. Tariff Act of 1930

SECTION 1305. Immoral articles; importation prohibited—prohibition of importation.

All persons are prohibited from importing into the United States from any foreign country any book, pamphlet, paper, writing, advertisement, circular, print, picture, or drawing containing any matter advocating or urging treason or insurrection against the United States or forcible resistance to any law of the United States, or containing any threat to take the life or inflict bodily harm upon any person in the United States, or any obscene book, pamphlet, paper, writing, advertisement, circular, print, picture, drawing, or other representation, figure, or image on or of paper or other material, or any cast, instrument, or other article which is obscene or immoral, or any drug or medicine or any article whatever for the prevention of conception or for causing unlawful abortion, or any lottery ticket, or any printed paper that may be used as a lottery ticket, or any advertisement of any lottery. No such articles, whether imported separately or contained in packages with other goods entitled to entry, shall be admitted to entry; and all such articles and, unless it appears to the satisfaction of the collector that the obscene or other prohibited articles contained in the package were inclosed therein without the knowledge or consent of the importer, owner, agent, or consignee, the entire contents of the package in which such articles are contained, shall be subject to seizure and forfeiture as hereinafter provided:

Provided, That the drugs hereinbefore mentioned, when imported in bulk and not put up for any of the purposes hereinbefore specified, are excepted from the operation of this subdivision: Provided further, That the Secretary of the Treasury may, in his discretion, admit the so-called classics or books of recognized and established literary or scientific merit, but may, in his discretion, admit such classics or books only when imported for non-commercial purposes.

Upon the appearance of any such book or matter at any customs office, the same shall be seized and held by the collector to await the judgment of the district court as hereinafter provided; and no protest shall be taken to the United States Customs Court from the decision of the collector. Upon the seizure of such book or matter the collector shall transmit information thereof to the district attorney of the district in which is situated the office at which such seizure has taken place, who shall institute proceedings in the district court for the forfeiture, confiscation, and destruction of the book or matter seized. Upon the adjudication that such book or matter thus seized is of the character the entry of which is by this section prohibited, it shall be ordered destroyed and shall be destroyed. Upon adjudication that such book or matter thus seized is not of the character the entry of which is by this section prohibited, it shall not be excluded from entry under the provisions of this section.

In any such proceeding any party in interest may upon demand have the facts at issue determined by a jury and any party may have an appeal or the right of review as in the case of ordinary actions or suits.

APPENDIX B

Compilation of State Statutes Relating to Birth Control, 1960

(alphabetic footnotes indicate post-1960 developments)

States	No Laws	Sales Prohibited	Allowed to Doctors	Allowed to Pharmacists	Special License	Advertisement Prohibited	Exemptions for Medical Schools, Textbooks, Professional Journals	Citation
Alabama	X							1
Alaska	X							2
Arizona						X		3
Arkansas		X	X		X	X		4[a]
California			X	X		X	X	5[b]
Colorado		X		X		X	X	6
Connecticut		X				X		
Delaware		X	X	X		X		
D. of Columbia	X							
Florida	X							
Georgia	X							
Hawaii						X*		7[c]
Idaho		X	X		X	X	X	8
Illinois	X							
Indiana		X	X	X		X	X	9[d]
Iowa		X	X			X	X	10
Kansas		X				X	X	11[e]
Kentucky		X	X		X	X	X	12
Louisiana						X	X	13

States	No Laws	Sales Prohibited	Allowed to Doctors	Allowed to Pharmacists	Special License	Advertisement Prohibited	Exemptions for Medical Schools, Textbooks, Professional Journals	Citation
Maine						X		14
Maryland	X							
Massachusetts		X				X		15[f]
Michigan			X			X		16
Minnesota		X				X		17[g]
Mississippi		X	X			X		18
Missouri		X	X	X		X		19[h]
Montana		X				X	X	20
Nebraska		X				X	X	21
Nevada		X	X			X		22
New Hampshire	X							
New Jersey		X[†]				X		23
New Mexico	X							
New York		X	X	X		X	X	24[i]
North Carolina	X							
North Dakota	X							
Ohio		X	X	X		X	X	25[j]
Oklahoma	X							
Oregon		X	X		X	X	X	26
Pennsylvania						X	X	27
Rhode Island	X							
South Carolina	X							
South Dakota	X							
Tennessee	X							
Texas	X							

Utah	X		
Vermont	X		
Virginia	X		
Washington	X	X	28
West Virginia			
Wisconsin	X‡	X	29
Wyoming	X	X	30

* Outside only.
† Without just cause.
‡ Sales to unmarried persons and from slot machines forbidden.

SOURCE: St. John-Stevas, *Birth Control and Public Policy*, 82–83.

CITATIONS: 1. Ariz. Rev. Stat. Ann. §13–213 (1956); 2. Ark. Stat. Ann. §§82-944 to 82-954 (1947); 3. Cal. Bus. & Prof. Code §§601, 4301–25; 4. Colo. Rev. Stat. Ann. §§40–9–17, 66-10-3 to 66-10-12 (1953); 5. Conn. Gen. Stat. Rev. §53-32 (1958); 6. Del. Code Ann. tit. 16, §2501–04 (1953); 7. Hawaii Rev. Laws §§155–73, 302A–1 to 302A-3 (1955); 8. Idaho Code Ann. §§18-603, 39-801 to 39–810 (Supp. 1959); 9. Ind. Ann. Stat. §§9–601, 10–2803 to 10–2806 (Supp. 1960); 10. Iowa Code Ann. §§725.5 to 725.10 (1950); 11. Kan. Gen. Stat. Ann. §21–1101 (1949); 12. Ky. Rev. Stat. Ann. §§14.190 to 214.270 (1953); 13. La. Rev. Stat. Ann. §14.88 (1951); 14. Me. Rev. Stat. Ann. ch. 134, §11, ch. 25, §114 (1954); 15. Md. Ann. Code art. 27, §41 (1957); Mass. Ann. Laws chap. 272, §§20, 21 (1956); 16. Mich. Stat. Ann. §28.229; 17. Minn. Stat. Ann. §§617-25 to 617-27 (1947); 18. Miss. Code Ann. §2289 (1957); 19. Mo. Rev. Stat. §563;300 (1949); 20. Mont. Rev. Codes Ann. §§94–3609, 94–3616 to 94–3619 (1949); 21. Neb. Rev. Stat. Ann. §§28-423, 71–1104 to 71–1114 (1958); 22. Nev. Rev. Stat. §§1142 to 1145; 25. N.C. Gen. Stat. §14-194 (1953); Ohio Rev. Code Ann. §§2A:170–76 (1953); 24. New York Pen. Law §§1142 to 1145; 25. N.C. Gen. Stat. §14-194 (1953); 27. Pa. Stat. Ann. tit. 18, §4525 (1945); §§2905.32 to 2905.37 (p. 1953); 26. Ore. Rev. Stat. §§435.010 to 435.130, 435.990 (1959); 27. Pa. Stat. Ann. tit. 36, §7323 (1947); 28. S.D. Code §13.1726 (1952); Utah Code Ann. §§58-19-1 (f), 58–19–2 to 58–19–11 (1953); Vt. Stat. Ann. §151.15 (1957). 30. [Wyo. Stat. Ann. tit. 6, Wash. Rev. Code §§9.68.030, 18.81.010 to 18.81.080 (1951); 29. Wisc. Stat. Ann. §315, tit. 24, §§201–03, tit. 33, §§1051–52 (1954). chap. 5, §§6–103 to 6–105 (1957)]. See also P.R. Laws Ann. tit. 10,

SOURCE: Comment, "Connecticut's Birth Control Law: Reviewing a State Statute under the Fourteenth Amendment," *Yale Law Journal*, LXX (Dec., 1960), 333–34

a. Repealed, Colorado, Laws of 1961, p. 327. b. Declared unconstitutional, Griswold v. Connecticut, 381 U.S. 479 (1965). c. Repealed, Hawaii, Laws of 1965, chap. 233, sec. 2. Hawaii, Revised Laws, title 21, chap. 155, sec. 128 (1965), providing that "no person shall display any outdoor advertising device giving or purporting to give information from whom or where ... may be obtained ... articles or means of preventing conception ..." enacted. d. Repealed, Indiana, Laws of 1963, chap. 12, sec. 9. e. Repealed, Kansas, Laws of 1963, chap. 222, sec. 1. f. Revised (1966); declared unconstitutional, Baird v. Eisenstadt. g. Amended to delete reference to the "prevention of conception." Minnesota, Laws of 1965, chap. 395, sec. 1. h. Amended to delete reference to "preventing conception." Missouri, Laws of 1967, S.B. no. 241, sec. 1. i. Amended, deleting references to contraception in Penal Laws and providing for regulation of contraception in Education Law, tit. 8, Art. 137, §§6804-b, 6816(1) (1967 Supp). j. Amended deleting all reference to contraception. Ohio, Laws of 1965, vol. 131, p. 672.

APPENDIX C

New York Legislation Relating to Birth Control

N. Y. Penal Law
(prior to 1965 revision)

Art. 106. Indecency

SECTION 1142. Indecent articles.

A person who sells, lends, gives away, or in any manner exhibits or offers to sell, lend or give away, or has in his possession with intent to sell, lend or give away, or advertises, or offers for sale, loan or distribution, any instrument or article, or any recipe, drug or medicine for the prevention of conception, or for causing unlawful abortion or purporting to be for the prevention of conception, or for causing unlawful abortion, or advertises, or holds out representations that it can be so used or applied, or any such description as will be calculated to lend another to so use or apply any such article, recipe, drug, medicine or instrument, or who writes or prints, causes to be written or printed, a card, circular, pamphlet, advertisement or notice of any kind, or gives information orally, stating when, where, how, of whom, or by what means such an instrument, article, recipe, drug or medicine can be purchased or obtained, or who manufactures any such instrument, article, recipe, drug or medicine, is guilty of a misdemeanor, and shall be liable to the same penalties as provided in section eleven hundred and forty-one of this chapter.

SECTION 1143. Mailing or carrying obscene prints and articles.

A person who deposits, or causes to be deposited, in any post office, within the state, or places in charge of an express company, or of a common carrier, or other person, for transportation, or for any purpose save the destruction thereof, any of the articles or things specified in section . . . eleven hundred forty-two of this article, or any circular, book, pamphlet, advertisement, or notice relating thereto, or any circular, pamphlet or notice offering to sell or provide any book, magazine, pamphlet, writing, still or motion picture purported or represented by said circular, pamphlet, advertisement or notice as being of an obscene, lewd, lascivious or indecent character or devoted to the presentation or description of acts of sexual immorality or sexual perversion, with the intent of having the same conveyed by mail or express, or in any other manner, or who knowingly or wilfully receives the same, with intent to carry or convey, or knowingly or wilfully carries or conveys the same, by express, or in any other manner, except in the United States mail is guilty of a misdemeanor.

SECTION 1145. Physicians' instruments.

An article or instrument, used or applied by physicians lawfully practicing, or by their direction or prescription, for the cure or prevention of disease, is not an article of indecent or immoral nature or use, within this article. The supplying of such articles to such physicians or by their direction or prescription, is not an offense under this article.

The 1965 revision removed the above penal-law provisions. Contraception is now dealt with under Title VIII (Professional Practice), article 137 (Pharmacy) of the New York Education Law, which provides:

SECTION 6804-b. Sale of articles for prevention of conception.

The sale or distribution of any instrument or article, or any recipe, drug or medicine for the prevention of conception, is authorized only by a duly licensed pharmacy and such sale or distribution to a minor under the age of sixteen years is prohibited. An advertisement or display of said articles, within or without the premises of such pharmacy, is hereby prohibited.

SECTION 6816. Construction of article.

1. This article shall not apply to the practice of a physician who is not the proprietor of a pharmacy, drug store or registered store, or who is not in the employ of such a proprietor. Except as to the quality of drugs dispensed, it shall not prevent physicians from supplying their patients with such drugs as the physician deems proper; provided, however, that all such drugs be dispensed in a container the label of which bears the name and address of the dispenser, the name and address of the patient, directions for use and date of delivery.

APPENDIX D

Massachusetts Legislation Relating to Birth Control

Mass. Ann. Laws (1956)
(prior to 1966 revision)

Tit. 1. Crimes and Punishments
Ch. 272. Crimes against Chastity, Morality, Decency and Good Order

SECTION 20. Penalty for advertising, etc., notices, etc., of means to procure abortion.

Whoever knowingly advertises, prints, publishes, distributes or circulates, or knowingly causes to be advertised, printed, published, distributed or circulated, any pamphlet, printed paper, book, newspaper, notice, advertisement or reference, containing words or language giving or conveying any notice, hint or reference to any person, or to the name of any person, real or fictitious, from whom, or to any place, house, shop or office where, any poison, drug, mixture, preparation, medicine or noxious thing, or any instrument or means whatever, or any advice, direction, information or knowledge, may be obtained for the purpose of causing or procuring a miscarriage of a woman pregnant with child or of preventing, or which is represented as intended to prevent, pregnancy, shall be punished by imprisonment in the state prison for not more than three years or in jail for not more than two and one half years or by a fine of not more than one thousand dollars.

SECTION 21. Other offences against decency.

Whoever sells, lends, gives away, exhibits, or offers to sell, lend or give away any instrument or other article intended to be used for self-abuse, or any drug, medicine, instrument or article whatever for the prevention of conception or for causing unlawful abortion, or advertises the same, or writes, prints or causes to be written or printed a card, circular, book, pamphlet, advertisement or notice of any kind stating when, where, how, of whom or by what means such article can be purchased or obtained, or manufactures or makes any such article, shall be punished by imprisonment in the state prison for not more than five years or in jail or the house of correction for not more than two and one-half years or by a fine of not less than one hundred nor more than one thousand dollars.

Legislative revision in 1966 added section 21A:

A registered physician may administer to or prescribe for any married person drugs or articles intended for the prevention of pregnancy or conception. A registered pharmacist actually engaged in the business of pharmacy may furnish such drugs or articles to any married person presenting a prescription from a registered physician.

A public health agency, a registered nurse, or a maternity health clinic operated by or in an accredited hospital may furnish information to any married person as to where professional advice regarding such drugs or articles may be lawfully obtained.

This section shall not be construed as affecting the provisions of sections twenty and twenty-one relative to prohibition of advertising of drugs or articles intended for the prevention of pregnancy or conception; nor shall this section be construed so as to permit the sale or dispensing of such drugs or articles by means of any vending machine or similar device.

APPENDIX E

Connecticut Legislation Relating to Birth Control
(prior to *Griswold*)

Conn. Gen. Stat. (1958 revision)

Tit. 53. Crimes
Ch. 939. Offenses against the Person

SECTION 53-32. Use of drugs or instruments to prevent conception.

Any person who uses any drug, medicinal article or instrument for the purpose of preventing conception shall be fined not less than fifty dollars or imprisoned not less than sixty days nor more than one year or be both fined and imprisoned.

Tit. 54. Criminal Procedure
Ch. 959. Jurisdiction and Powers of Courts

SECTION 54-196. Accessories.

Any person who assists, abets, counsels, causes, hires, or commands another to commit any offense may be prosecuted and punished as if he were the principal offender.

APPENDIX F

Complaint Leading to Introduction of Scheuer Bills; Letter of Reply by Customs Officials to ACLU Inquiry

Civil Liberties Union:
 The following occurred at the Immigrant and Customs Building in New York City on the 15th of October, 1962.
 I arrived as a passenger on board M/S *Kungsholm*, Swedish American Line, with an immigrant status. My fiance, an American citizen, was there to meet me and was present at the customs' check up. The official asked me to open a suitcase that he pointed out, which I did unhesitatingly. He caught sight of a box, wherein I kept my diaphram—fitted out and given to me by a Swedish M.D., prior to my departure. The official immediately took out the box, although I assured him it contained my highly personal property. He seemed to know right away, however, what was in the box for he told me I could not import "medical equipment" according to New York state law. After some discussion he brought the box with him to an office nearby and returned in the company of another official and with a paper he wanted me to sign.
 They both told me I would have lots of difficulties should I not agree to sign the paper and insist on having my diaphram. They would not listen to my argument that every married woman must be carrying her own diaphram, so how could they enforce such a law, saying that you could not "import" your own diaphram. Seeing however that there was nothing else I could do, but sign, I did so. The paper said that I agreed to have property confiscated and destroyed by U.S. official. Then the official told me to come with him and we walked to the end of the pier, where he told me to throw the box containing the diaphram into the water. Thereafter he let me leave without any further checking of my baggage.
 I swear that the above is told by me as truthfully as I know how.

ELLY FOOTE

Mr. John de J. Pemberton, Jr.
Executive Director
American Civil Liberties Union
156 Fifth Avenue
New York 10, New York

Dear Mr. Pemberton:

This is in further reference to your letter of September 18, 1963, enclosing a letter from Mrs. Elly Foote concerning the seizure of a contraceptive article from her upon her arrival at New York from abroad on October 15, 1962.

Mrs. Foote states that she arrived at New York as an immigrant on the MS *Kungsholm* on October 15, 1962, and that upon opening her suitcase the customs inspector caught sight of the article in question and informed her that she could not import it. She further states that she signed a paper and was told to throw the article into the river.

We have received a report from the collector of customs at New York in the matter. Mrs. Foote arrived at the port of New York as a passenger on the MS *Gripsholm* and executed a baggage declaration in her maiden name of Elly J. De Broen. When the customs inspector observed the contraceptive article, he seized it under section 305 of the Tariff Act of 1930 (19 U.S.C. 1305), which prohibits the importation of articles for the prevention of conception. The passenger assented to the destruction of the article.

Attention is invited to section 12.40(i) and (j), Customs Regulations (19 CFR 12.40(i) and (j)), pertaining to the importation of contraceptive devices by or for a physician to protect the health of his patients, etc. Such devices are also released to individuals in appropriate cases. It is the duty of the customs inspector to examine the baggage of incoming passengers with a view toward preventing smuggling and the entrance of prohibited articles into the United States.

When a prohibited article is observed by an inspector, he is required to seize it, unless, of course, a claim is made that it is otherwise admissible under an exception to the law, in which event the article would be detained in lieu of being seized.

Seizure of articles under section 305 of the tariff act requires their submission to the United States attorney for institution of libel action seeking condemnation thereof, unless the person assents to the forfeiture or destruction of the material. It would appear from the foregoing that the inspector's proceedings were in some respects irregular and on the other hand, the passenger's case, had she been informed of her rights, might have been found to come under an exception to section 305. Steps are being taken to obtain more seemly proceedings in future cases. Thank you for advising me of this occurrence. Sincerely yours,

LESTER D. JOHNSON
Acting Commissioner of Customs

APPENDIX G

On the Government and Birth Control: Statement of the Administrative Board of the National Catholic Welfare Conference

November 14, 1966

The good of the individual person and that of human society are intimately bound up with the stability of the family. Basic to the well-being of the family is freedom from external coercion in order that it may determine its own destiny.

This freedom involves inherent personal and family rights, including the freedom and responsibility of spouses to make conscientious decisions in terms of nuptial love, determination of family size and the rearing of children. The Church and the State must play supportive roles, fostering conditions in modern society which will help the family achieve the fullness of its life and mission as the means ordained by God for bringing the person into being and maturity.

We address ourselves here to certain questions of concern to the family, with special reference to public policies related to social conditions and the problems of our times.

In so doing, we speak in the light of the Pastoral Constitution on the Church in the Modern World adopted by Vatican Council II. Faced with our Government's stepped-up intervention in family planning, including the subsidizing of contraceptive programs at home and abroad, we feel bound in conscience to recall particularly the solemn warning expressed in these words:

". . . [There] are many today who maintain that the increase in world population, or at least the population increase in some countries, must be radically curbed by every means possible and by any kind of intervention on the part of public authority. In view of this contention, the Council urges everyone to guard against solutions, whether publicly or privately supported, or at times even imposed, which are contrary to the moral law. For in keeping with man's inalienable right to marry and generate children, the decision concerning the number of children they will have depends on the correct judgment of the parents and it can in no way be left to the judgment of public authority" (Constitution on the Church in the Modern World, sec. 2, n. 87).

Therefore, a major pre-occupation in our present statement must be with the freedom of spouses to determine the size of their families. It is necessary to underscore this freedom because in some current efforts of government—federal and state—to reduce poverty, we see welfare programs increasingly proposed which include threats to the free choice of spouses. Just as freedom is undermined when poverty and disease are present, so too is freedom endangered when persons or agencies outside the family unit, particularly persons who control welfare benefits or represent public authority, presume to influence the decision as to the number of children or the frequency of births in a family.

Free decision is curtailed when spouses feel constrained to choose birth limitation because of poverty, inadequate and inhuman housing, or lack of proper medical services. Here we insist that it is the positive duty of government to help bring about those conditions of family freedom which will relieve spouses from such material and physical pressure to limit family size.

Government promotion of family planning programs as part of tax-supported relief projects may easily result in the temptation and finally the tragic decision to reduce efforts to foster the economic, social and indeed moral reforms needed to build the free, enlightened society.

In connection with present and proposed governmental family limitation programs, there is frequently the implication that freedom is assured so long as spouses are left at liberty to choose among different methods of birth control. This we reject as a narrow concept of freedom. Birth control is not a universal obligation, as is often implied; moreover, true freedom of choice must provide even for those who wish to raise a larger family without being subject to criticism and without forfeiting for themselves the benefits or for their children the educational opportunities which have become part of the value system of a truly free society. We reject, most emphatically, the suggestion that any family should be adjudged too poor to have the children it conscientiously desires.

The freedom of spouses to determine the size of their families must not be inhibited by any conditions upon which relief or welfare assistance is provided. Health and welfare assistance should not be linked, even indirectly, to conformity with a public agency's views on family limitation or birth control; nor may the right to found a large family be brought properly into question because it contradicts current standards arbitrarily deduced from general population statistics. No government social worker or other representative of public power should in any way be permitted to impose his judgment, in a matter so close to personal values and to the very sources of life, upon the family seeking assistance; neither should he be permitted to initiate suggestions placing, even by implication, public authority behind the recommendation that new life in a family should be prevented.

For these reasons, we have consistently urged and we continue to urge, as a matter of sound public policy, a clear and unqualified separation of welfare assistance from birth control considerations—whatever the legality or morality of contraception in general or in specific forms—in order to safeguard the freedom of the person and the autonomy of the family.

On previous occasions we have warned of dangers to the right of privacy posed by governmental birth control programs; we have urged upon government a role of neutrality whereby it neither penalizes nor promotes birth control. Recent developments, however, show government rapidly abandoning any such role. Far from merely seeking to provide information in response to requests from the needy, Government activities increasingly seek aggressively to persuade and even coerce the underprivileged to practice birth control. In this, government far exceeds its proper role. The citizen's right to decide without pressure is now threatened. Intimate details of personal, marital and family life are suddenly becoming the province of government officials in programs of assistance to the poor. We decry this overreaching by government and assert again the inviolability of the right of human privacy.

We support all needed research toward medically and morally acceptable methods which can assist spouses to make responsible and generous decisions in seeking to cooperate with the will of God in what pertains to family size and well-being. A responsible decision will always be one which is open to life rather than intent upon the prevention of life; among religious people, it includes a strong sense of dependence upon God's Providence.

It should be obvious that a full understanding of human worth, personal and social, will not permit the nation to put the public power behind the pressures for a contraceptive way of life. We urge government, at all levels, to resist pressures toward any merely mathematical and negative effort to solve health or population problems. We call upon all—and especially Catholics—to oppose, vigorously and by every democratic means, those campaigns already under way in some states and at the national level toward the active promotion, by tax-supported agencies, of birth prevention as a public policy, above all in connection with welfare benefit programs. History has shown that as people lose respect for any life and a positive and generous attitude toward new life, they move fatally to inhuman infanticide, abortion, sterilization and euthanasia; we fear that history is, in fact, repeating itself on this point within our own land at the moment.

Our government has a laudable history of dedication to the cause of freedom. In the service of this cause it is currently embarked upon a massive, unprecedented program of aid to underdeveloped nations. Through imaginative and constructive efforts, it shows itself willing to do battle with the enemies of freedom, notably poverty and ignorance. We gladly encourage our government to press this struggle with all the resources at its disposal and pledge our cooperation in all the ways in which we or those responsive to our leadership can be of assistance. Our nation's duty to assist underdeveloped countries flows from the Divine Law that the goods of the earth are destined for the well-being of all the human race.

In the international field, as in the domestic field, financial assistance must not be linked to policies which pressure for birth limitation. We applaud food supply programs of foreign aid which condition our cooperation on evidence that the nations benefited pledge themselves to develop their own resources; we deplore any linking of aid by food or money to conditions, overt or oblique, involving prevention of new life. Our country is not at liberty to impose its judgment upon another, either as to the growth of the latter or as to the size of its families.

Insofar as it does so, our country is being cast in the role of a foreign power using its instrumentalities to transgress intimate *mores* and alter the moral cultures of other nations rather than in the historic American role of offering constructive, unselfish assistance to peoples in need. Indeed, we are aware of existing apprehension in the minds of many of the peoples of the world that the United States, in its own great affluence, is attempting, by seeking to limit their populations, to avoid its moral responsibility to help other peoples help themselves precisely that they may grow in healthy life, generous love and in all the goods which presuppose and enrich both life and love.

Programs inhibiting new life, above all when linked to offers of desperately needed aid, are bound to create eventual resentment in any upon whom we even seem to impose them and will ultimately be gravely detrimental to the image, the moral prestige and the basic interests of the United States.

Obviously, therefore, international programs of aid should not be conditioned upon acceptance of birth control programs by beneficiary nations. Equally obvious, however, should be the fact that, in the practical administration of overseas assistance, neither direct nor indirect pressure should be exerted by our personnel to affect the choice of spouses as to the number of children in their family. In the international field, as in the domestic field, both our government in its policy and our American representatives in their work, should strive above all to bring about those economic and social advances which will make possible for spouses conscientious family planning without resort to contraceptive procedures fostered among them by controversial policies backed by American political power and financial aid.

Sobering lessons of history clearly teach that only those nations remain stable and vigorous whose citizens have and are encouraged to keep high regard for the sanctity and autonomy of family life among themselves and among the peoples who depend in any way upon them. Let our political leaders be on guard that the common good suffer no evil from public policies which tamper with the instincts of love and the sources of life.

APPENDIX H

Statement of the Bishops of the United States in Protest of U.S. Government Programs against the Right to Life, 1969

Every human person is made in the image of God and is called to share in eternal life with God. No price can be set on human life.

In 1959, the Bishops of the United States warned against the involvement by the U.S. Government in programs of population control by immoral means. In 1966, we reiterated our serious concern. We now speak out again because of the ever increasing and ever expanding programs against the right to life in many areas. We cautioned in 1966 that programs of birth control related to public welfare could hardly fail to be coercive. Today that element of coercion is being openly advocated by some of the leading exponents of population control.

Government sponsored programs of birth control have already made use of methods, such as the intra-uterine devices, which informed scientists tell us may produce harmful effects after conception. Projected research programs, sponsored by the National Institute of Child Health and Human Development, include the quest for effective methods of inducing abortion early in an established pregnancy. In effect, the government is supporting birth control by early abortion.[1] Besides some private organizations[2] that receive government funding are considering seriously means of population limitation that go beyond family planning; these will involve coercion and abortion as well as other objectionable elements.

In the present situation, we reaffirm our stand in defense of the right to life and we affirm that there is a role for government sponsored scientific research for the preservation of life. Commendable work has been done, for example, in the development of a vaccine which would prevent German measles, and thus eliminate this source of harm to unborn children, a source of harm often mentioned by advocates of relaxed criminal laws against abortion.

We continue to believe that the proper answer to population problems is development—development of natural resources and of technological means, and development also of human beings themselves. Given educational opportunity and the economic means that go with it, we believe couples will

[1] A new Contract Research Program for the Development of new contraceptives (Research and Development Resources sought).

[2] E.g., Federation of Planned Parenthood; Population Council "Studies in Family Planning" (February, 1969).

make judgments about family size that will be in harmony with the common good. We affirm that parents themselves, and no government official, should make that judgment.

We also continue to believe that the common welfare requires government not only to avoid but also to forbid and prevent methods of population limitation that attack human life from conception onward. The equal protection of the laws, guaranteed by the Fourteenth Amendment of the U.S. Constitution to all persons, should not be withheld from the unborn. Anglo-American law has recognized the rights of the unborn.

Certainly no one should be deprived of life merely because it is more convenient for some that he should die.

In the name of the priceless dignity of the right to life, we the Catholic Bishops of the United States, protest the continuing and ever expanding role both at home and abroad of the government in the matter of population control through the limitation of births. We hope that our fellow Americans will appreciate the soundness of our stand.

APPENDIX I

Report of the Illinois Commission on Birth Control

RECOMMENDATIONS

Based upon the recommendations submitted by the Subcommittee appointed by the Chairman of the Commission, and based upon the testimony and evidence submitted to the Commission, the Commission did on February 24, 1965 adopt a Resolution setting forth, in the preamble thereof, the attitude and feelings of the Commission, and setting forth therein the specific recommendations of the Commission, said Resolution being as follows, to-wit:

RESOLUTION

WHEREAS, Justice, opportunity and material help for the poor and culturally deprived of our State are important goals urgently and immediately challenging us all; and

WHEREAS, As we take up the complex problem of birth prevention among the poor, we do so in the context of our common failure to deal effectively with racial discrimination and its ugly consequences; we do so with a common re-dedication and commitment of our resources—public and private—to remedy the serious evils of inadequate housing, to provide full and free employment, to establish programs of education and social rehabilitation, and to attack the problem of poverty on every level; and

WHEREAS, To make such a program effectual it is mandatory that the general health and well-being of persons on public aid be improved to a level sufficient to make them capable of functioning to their best ability; and

WHEREAS, Health, as herein used, is defined as "A state of complete physical, mental and social well-being, and not merely the absence of diseases and infirmity"; and

WHEREAS, The needs of the poor in the midst of our affluence demand response from the hearts and from the substance of every citizen; and

WHEREAS, They require the finest efforts that can be put forth by private, civic, religious, and governmental institutions and agencies; and

WHEREAS, It is the position of the Commission that sexuality is one of mankind's greatest gifts, and that it should be exercised with proper judgment and responsibility; and

WHEREAS, All efforts should be made to improve the general economic situation and education of those on public aid; and

WHEREAS, In conjunction with these efforts, when it is felt that the situation warrants it, the Department of Public Aid should be free to suggest means of birth prevention, it being recognized that promiscuity and fornication are against public welfare, and programs designed to ameliorate the problem of illegitimacy are not to be construed as encouraging immorality but rather to preventing the compounding of immorality by inflicting added burdens on the State and the persons involved; therefore, be it

RESOLVED, by the Commission on Birth Control of the State of Illinois, under and in accordance with the provisions of Senate Bill No. 66 as enacted by the 73rd General Assembly of the State of Illinois, as follows:

A. That the Commission recommends that the Department of Public Aid be allowed to extend its policy of dissemination of birth control information and services to all mothers on the public aid rolls, including, but not limited thereto, those mothers who are not married or are married but are not living with their spouses, subject as follows, to-wit:
   1. That any such information and services be given to a relief mother only upon request of the relief mother. This shall not be construed so as to prohibit personnel of the Department of Public Aid from discussing responsible parenthood with a mother on public aid.
   2. That no such information and services be given to any relief mother who has not as yet reached her fifteenth birthday.
   3. That the rights of Department of Public Aid personnel and of the relief mother who do not wish to participate in any such birth control program, because of religious or other convictions, be fully and completely respected.
   4. That the dissemination of birth control information and services by the Department of Public Aid shall, at all times, be under the supervision and control of a physician duly licensed in Illinois to practice medicine in all its branches.

BE IT FURTHER RESOLVED, That no recommendation for legislation be made to the Illinois General Assembly, either making mandatory or prohibiting, partially or fully, the dissemination of birth control information and services by the Department of Public Aid. However, it is the recommendation of the Commission that the Illinois General Assembly, as soon as possible, pass appropriate legislation and/or proper resolutions, expressing, or having the effect of expressing, that the dissemination of birth control information and services, as recommended heretofore in this Resolution, is not contrary to the public policy and/or statutory law of the State of Illinois.

Bibliography

BOOKS

Abbott, Edith. *Women in Industry*. New York: Appleton, 1910.
Addams, Jane. *Forty Years at Hull House*. New York: Macmillan, 1910.
Ad Hoc Committee on Family Planning and Public Assistance in Pennsylvania. *What about Pennsylvania's Family Planning Program?* Harrisburg, 1966.
Auerbach, Carl A., et al. *The Legal Process: An Introduction to the Decision-Making by Judicial, Legislative, Executive and Administrative Agencies*. San Francisco: Chandler, 1961.
Bacon, Leonard W. *A History of American Christianity*, vol. XIII. New York: Christian Literature, 1893.
Bailey, S. K. *Congress Makes A Law*. New York: Vintage Books, 1950.
Bay, Christian. *The Structure of Freedom*. New York: Atheneum, 1964.
Bayles, G. J. *Women and the Law*. New York: Century, 1907.
Becker, Theodore. *Political Behavioralism and Modern Jurisprudence*. Chicago: Rand McNally, 1964.
―――, ed. *The Impact of Supreme Court Decisions*. New York: Oxford University Press, 1969.
Bentley, Arthur F. *The Process of Government*. Cambridge: Harvard University Press, 1967.
Besant, Annie. *Autobiography*. London: Theosophical Press, 1893.
Birth Control League of Massachusetts. *Contraceptive Advice and the Massachusetts Law*. Boston, 1930.
Black, Charles L., Jr. *The People and the Court*. New York: Macmillan, 1960.
Bodenheimer, Edgar. *Jurisprudence*. New York: McGraw-Hill, 1940.
Bonner, Hypatia B. *Charles Bradlaugh*. 2 vols. London: Unwin, 1894.
Botein, Bernard, and Murray A. Gordon. *The Trial of the Future*. New York: Cornerstone Library, 1963.
Boulding, Kenneth E. *The Image*. Ann Arbor: University of Michigan Press, 1956.
Bowlby, J. *Maternal Deprivation*. New York: Schocken Books, 1966.
Boyer, Paul S. *Purity in Print: The Vice-Society Movement and Book Censorship in America*. New York: Scribner's, 1968.

Bradford, Gamaliel. *D. L. Moody: A Worker in Souls.* Garden City: Doubleday, 1928.
Braybrooke, David, and Charles E. Lindblom. *A Strategy of Decision.* New York: Free Press, 1963.
Breitel, Charles D. *The Lawmakers.* New York: The Association of the Bar of the City of New York, 1965.
Briggs, Charles A. *Whither?* New York: Scribner, 1889.
Bromley, Dorothy. *Catholics and Birth Control: Contemporary Views on Doctrine.* New York: Devin-Adair, 1965.
Bross, Irwin D. J. *Design for Decision.* New York: Free Press, 1953.
Broun, Heywood, and Margaret Leech. *Anthony Comstock: Roundsman of the Lord.* New York: Albert and Charles Boni, 1927.
Bryce, James. *The American Commonwealth.* 2 vols. Rev. ed. New York: Macmillan, 1927.
Cahill, Fred V. *Judicial Legislation.* New York: Ronald Press, 1952.
Calhoun, A. W. *A Social History of the American Family.* 3 vols. Cleveland: Arthur H. Clark, 1919.
Callahan, Daniel, ed. *The Catholic Case for Contraception.* New York: Macmillan, 1969.
Cardozo, Benjamin N. *The Growth of the Law.* New Haven: Yale University Press, 1924.
———. *The Nature of the Judicial Process.* New Haven: Yale University Press, 1921.
———. *The Paradoxes of Legal Science.* New York: Columbia University Press, 1928.
Carlston, Kenneth S. *Law and Structures of Social Action.* New York: Columbia University Press, 1966.
Carroll, H. K. *The Religious Forces of the United States.* Rev. ed. New York: Scribner's, 1912.
Center for Family Planning Program Development. *Family Planning Programs in the United States*, pub. 7. New York, 1969.
Cherryholmes, Cleo, and Michael Shapiro. *Representatives and Roll Calls.* Indianapolis: Bobbs-Merrill, 1969.
Chilman, C. S. *Growing Up Poor.* Washington: U.S. Department of Health, Education and Welfare, 1966.
Churchman, C. West. *Prediction and Optimal Decision.* Englewood Cliffs: Prentice-Hall, 1961.
Citizens's Board of Inquiry into Hunger and Malnutrition in the United States (Citizens' Crusade against Poverty). *Hunger, U.S.A.* Washington: New Community Press, 1968.
Cochran, T. C., and William Miller. *The Age of Enterprise.* New York: Macmillan, 1942.
Cohen, Morris. *American Thought: A Critical Sketch.* Glencoe, Ill.: Free Press, 1954.
———. *Law and the Social Order.* New York: Harcourt, Brace, 1933.
Cole, S. G. *The History of Fundamentalism.* New York: R. R. Smith, 1931.
Commager, Henry S. *The American Mind.* New Haven: Yale University Press, 1950.

Comstock, Anthony. *Frauds Exposed*. Montclair, N.J.: Patterson Smith, 1969.
―――. *Traps for the Young*. New York: Funk and Wagnalls, 1884.
Cook, Robert C. *The Population Awakening*. Victor Fund for the International Planned Parenthood Fund, rpt. 4. New York, 1966.
Corwin, Edward S. *The Constitution of the United States of America: Analysis and Interpretation*. Washington: U.S. Government Printing Office, 1964.
Craig, Alec. *Suppressed Books*. New York: World, 1963.
Crawford, J. B. *The Credit Mobilier in America*. Boston: Calkins, 1880.
Croly, Herbert. *The Promise of American Life*. New York: Macmillan, 1909.
Curti, Merle. *The Growth of American Thought*. 2nd ed. New York: Harper and Bros., 1951.
Davis, James F., et al. *Society and the Law*. New York: Free Press, 1962.
De Forest, R. W., and Lawrence Veiller. *The Tenament House Problem*. 2 vols. New York: Macmillan, 1903.
DeGuchteneere, R. *Judgment on Birth Control*. New York: Macmillan, 1931.
Dennet, Mary Ware. *Birth Control Laws*. New York: Frederich H. Hitchcock, 1926.
Devlin, Sir Patrick. *The Enforcement of Morals*. Oxford: Oxford University Press, 1959.
Dewitt, B. P. *The Progressive Movement*. New York: Macmillan, 1915.
Ditzion, Sidney. *Marriage, Morals and Sex in America: A History of Ideas*. New York: Bookman Associates, 1953.
Dorfman, Joseph. *The Economic Mind in American Civilization*. 3 vols. New York: Viking Press, 1946–49.
Douglas, William O. *A Living Bill of Rights*. Garden City: Doubleday, 1961.
―――. *The Right of the People*. Garden City: Doubleday, 1958.
Dror, Yehezkel. *Public Policymaking Reexamined*. San Francisco: Chandler, 1968.
Dupre, Louis. *Contraception and Catholics: A New Appraisal*. Baltimore: Helicon, 1964.
Easton, David. *A Framework for Political Analysis*. Englewood Cliffs: Prentice-Hall, 1964.
―――. *A Systems Analysis of Political Life*. New York: Wiley, 1965.
Edelman, Murray. *The Symbolic Uses of Politics*. Urbana: University of Illinois Press, 1964.
Edwards, G. W. *The Evolution of Finance Capitalism*. New York: Longmans, Green, 1938.
Egner, G. *Contraception vs. Tradition: A Catholic Critique*. New York: Herder and Herder, 1967.
Ehrlich, Paul. *The Population Bomb*. New York: Ballantine Books, 1968.
Elderton, Ethel M. *Report on the English Birthrate: Part I. England, North of Humber*. London: University of London, 1914.
Emerson, Thomas I. *Towards a General Theory of the First Amendment*. New York: Random House, 1967.
Ernst, Morris L., and William Seagle. *To the Pure . . . : A Study of Obscenity and the Censor*. New York: Viking Press, 1928.

Faulkner, Harold V. *The Quest for Social Justice, 1898-1914*. History of American Life Series, vol. XI. Ed. Arthur M. Schlesinger and Dixon R. Fox. New York: Macmillan, 1931.
Ferman, L. A., J. L. Kornbluh, and A. Haber, eds. *Poverty in America*. Rev. ed. Ann Arbor: University of Michigan Press, 1968.
Fine, Nathan. *Labor and Farmer Parties in the United States, 1828-1928*. New York: Rand School of Social Sciences, 1928.
Frank, Jerome. *Courts on Trial*. New York: Atheneum, 1963.
———. *Law and the Modern Mind*. New York: Brentano's, 1949.
Freedman, R., P. K. Whelpton, and A. A. Campbell. *Family Planning, Sterility and Population Growth*. New York: McGraw-Hill, 1959.
Friedman, Lawrence M., and Stewart Macaulay, eds. *Law and the Behavioral Sciences*. Indianapolis: Bobbs-Merrill, 1969.
Friedmann, Wolfgang. *Law and Social Change in Contemporary Britain*. London: Stevens and Sons, 1951.
———. *Law in a Changing Society*. Abr. ed. Baltimore: Penguin Books, 1964.
———. *Legal Theory*. 4th ed. Toronto: Carswell Company, 1960.
Friedrich, Carl J., ed. *Rational Decision*. New York: Atherton Press, 1964.
Fryer, Peter. *The Birth Controllers*. New York: Stein and Day, 1966.
Garrison, Winfred E. *The March of Faith: The Story of Religion in America since 1865*. New York: Harper and Bros., 1933.
Gladden, Washington. *Who Wrote the Bible?* Boston: Houghton Mifflin, 1891.
Gorden, Mitchell. *Sick Cities*. Baltimore: Penguin Books, 1965.
Greer, Thomas H. *American Social Reform Movements*. New York: Prentice-Hall, 1949.
Grossman, Joel, and Joseph Tanenhaus, eds. *Frontiers of Judicial Research*. New York: Wiley, 1969.
Group for the Advancement of Psychiatry. *The Right to Abortion: A Psychiatric View*. New York: by the authors, 1969.
Gurvich, George. *Sociology of Law*. New York: Philosophical Library, 1942.
Guttmacher, Alan F. *Babies by Choice or by Chance*. Garden City: Doubleday, 1959.
Hacker, Louis. *The Shaping of the American Tradition*, vol. II. New York: Columbia University Press, 1947.
Hall, Jerome. *Living Law of a Democratic Society*. Indianapolis: Bobbs-Merrill, 1949.
Hand, Learned. *The Bill of Rights*. Cambridge: Harvard University Press, 1958.
Hardin, Garrett, ed. *Population, Evolution and Birth Control*. San Francisco: W. H. Freeman, n.d.
Harkavy, Oscar, Frederick S. Jaffe, and Samuel M. Wishik. *Implementing DHEW Policy on Family Planning and Population*. New York: Columbia University, 1967.
Harrington, Michael. *The Other America*. Baltimore: Penguin Books, 1962.
Harris, George. *A Century's Change in Religion*. Boston: Houghton Mifflin, 1914.

Hart, H. L. A. *Law, Liberty and Morality*. New York: Vintage Books, 1966.
Hart, Henry M., Jr., and Albert M. Sacks. *The Legal Process: Basic Problems in the Making and Application of Law*. Cambridge, 1958 (mimeo.).
Haynes, Frederick. *Social Politics in the United States*. Boston: Houghton Mifflin, 1924.
Hendrick, B. J. *The Age of Big Business*. Chronicles of America Series, vol. XXXIX. New Haven: Yale University Press, 1919.
Hicks, John D. *The American Nation*. 3rd ed. Cambridge, Mass.: Riverside Press, 1955.
Himes, Norman E. *Medical History of Contraception*. Baltimore: Williams and Wilkins, 1936.
Hodge, Charles. *What Is Darwinism?* New York: Scribner, Armstrong, 1874.
Holmes, Oliver Wendell. *The Common Law*. Boston: Little, Brown, 1963.
Hopkins, C. H. *The Rise of the Social Gospel in American Protestantism*. Yale Studies in Religious Education, vol. XIV. New Haven: Yale University Press, 1940.
Hotchkiss, Rev. B. B. *Infidelity against Itself*. Philadelphia: Presbyterian Board of Publication, 1850.
Howard, Charles G., and Robert S. Summers. *Law: Its Nature, Function and Limits*. Englewood Cliffs: Prentice-Hall, 1965.
Hurst, James W. *The Growth of American Law*. Boston: Little, Brown, 1950.
Information Center on Population Problems. *Public Health and Birth Control*. New York, 1965.
In the High Court of Justice: Queen's Bench Division, June 18th, 1877: The Queen v. Charles Bradlaugh and Annie Besant. London, 1878.
Ireven, Inez H. *Angels and Amazons*. Garden City: Doubleday, 1933.
Jackson, Robert H. *The Supreme Court in American Society*. New York: Harper and Row, 1955.
Jacob, Herbert. *Justice in America*. Boston: Little, Brown, 1965.
Jewell, Malcolm E., and Samuel C. Patterson. *The Legislative Process in the United States*. New York: Random House, 1966.
Josephson, Matthew. *The Politicos, 1865–1900*. New York: Harcourt, Brace, 1938.
———. *The Robber Barons*. New York: Harcourt, Brace, 1935.
Kenedy, Thomas B. *Official Catholic Directory*. New York: P. J. Kenedy, 1967.
Knowlton, Charles. *Fruits of Philosophy, or The Private Companion of Adult People*. Ed. Norman E. Himes. New York: Peter Pauper, 1937.
———. *A History of the Recent Excitement in Ashfield Part I*. Ashfield, Mass., 1834.
Konovitz, Milton R., ed. *Law and Social Action: Selected Essays of Alexander H. Pekeles*. Ithaca: Cornell University Press, 1950.
Krislov, Samuel. *The Supreme Court in the Political Process*. New York: Macmillan, 1965.
Lader, Lawrence. *The Margaret Sanger Story*. Garden City: Doubleday, 1955.

La Follette, Robert M. *Autobiography*. Madison: Robert M. La Follette Co., 1913.
Larson, Orvin. *American Infidel: Robert G. Ingersoll*. New York: Citadel Press, 1962.
Laws Relating to Birth Control. New York: Birth Control Clinical Research Bureau, 1939.
Levi, Edward H. *An Introduction to Legal Reasoning*. Chicago: University of Chicago Press, 1948.
Levitan, Sar A. *The Great Society's Poor Law*. Baltimore: Johns Hopkins Press, 1969.
———. *Programs in Aid of the Poor for the 1970's*. Baltimore: Johns Hopkins Press, 1969.
Llewellyn, Karl N. *The Bramble Bush*. New York: Columbia University Press, 1930.
———. *The Common Law Tradition: Deciding Appeals*. Boston: Little, Brown, 1960.
———. *Jurisprudence: Realism in Theory and Practice*. Chicago: University of Chicago Press, 1962.
Lockhart, William, Yale Kamisar, and Jesse Choper. *Constitutional Law*. 3rd ed. St. Paul: West, 1970.
Loud, B. D. *Evangelized America*. New York: L. MacVeegh, 1923.
Lynch, Dennis T. *"Boss" Tweed: The Story of a Grim Generation*. New York: Boni and Liveright, 1927.
———. *The Wild Seventies*. New York: Appleton, 1941.
McCloskey, Robert A. *The American Supreme Court*. Chicago: University of Chicago Press, 1960.
McLuhan, Marshall. *Understanding Media: The Extensions of Man*. New York: New American Library (Signet Books), 1964.
Matthews, Donald R. *U.S. Senators and Their World*. New York: Vintage Books, 1960.
Matthews, Shailer. *The Church and the Changing Order*. New York: Macmillan, 1909.
Meiklejohn, Alexander. *Political Freedom*. New York: Oxford University Press, 1965.
Mendelson, Wallace, ed. *The Supreme Court: Law and Discretion*. Indianapolis: Bobbs-Merrill, 1967.
Moody, Dwight L. *Gospel Awakening*. 16th ed. Chicago: Fairbanks, Palmer, 1883.
———. *Short Talks*. Chicago: Moody Press, 1900.
Moody, John. *Masters of Capital*. Chronicles of America Series, vol. XLI. New Haven: Yale University Press, 1919.
Moody, W. R. *D. L. Moody*. New York: Revell, 1930.
Moore, Edward R. *The Case against Birth Control*. New York: Century, 1931.
Morison, Samuel E., and Henry S. Commager. *The Growth of the American Republic*. 2 vols. 4th ed. New York: Oxford University Press, 1950.
Mowry, E. *Theodore Roosevelt and the Progressive Movement*. Madison: University of Wisconsin Press, 1946.

Murphy, Walter. *Congress and the Court.* Chicago: University of Chicago Press, 1962.
———. *The Elements of Judicial Strategy.* Chicago: University of Chicago Press, 1964.
———, and Herman C. Pritchett. *Courts, Judges and Politics.* New York: Random House, 1961.
Murray, John C., Father. *We Hold These Truths: Catholic Reflection on the American Proposition.* New York: Sheed and Ward, 1960.
Myers, Gustavus. *History of Great American Fortunes.* Rev. ed. New York: Modern Library, 1937.
———. *The History of Tammany Hall.* New York: Ben Franklin, 1917.
Nagel, Stuart S. *The Legal Process from a Behavioral Perspective.* Homewood, Ill.: Dorsey Press, 1969.
National Academy of Sciences. *The Growth of U.S. Population.* Washington, 1965.
National Committee on Federal Legislation for Birth Control. *A New Day Dawns for Birth Control.* New York, 1937.
National Council of Churches. *Responsible Parenthood.* New York, 1961.
National Defense Association. *Words of Warning to Those Who Aid and Abet in the Suppression of Free Speech and Free Press.* New York, 1879.
Nethercot, Arthur E. *The First Five Lives of Annie Besant.* Chicago: University of Chicago Press, 1960.
Nevins, Allan. *The Emergence of Modern America, 1865-1878.* New York: Macmillan, 1927.
New England Watch and Ward Society. *Annual Report, 1887–88.* Boston, 1888.
New York Society for the Suppression of Vice. *Sixth Annual Report.* New York, 1880.
Noonan, John T. *Contraception: A History of Its Treatment by the Catholic Theologians and Canonists.* Cambridge: Harvard University Press, 1965.
Oberholtzer, E. P. *The Referendum in America.* New York: Scribner's, 1915.
Ogburn, William F. *Social Change.* New York: Dell, 1966.
———, and M. Nimkoff. *Technology and the Changing Family.* Boston: Houghton Mifflin, 1955.
Osborn, Fairfield. *Our Crowded Planet: Essays on the Pressures of Population.* Garden City: Doubleday, 1962.
Parrington, Vernon L. *The Beginnings of Critical Realism in America, 1860–1920.* New York: Harcourt, Brace, 1930.
Parsons, Talcott. *The Social System.* New York: Free Press, 1964.
———. *The Structure of Social Action.* Glencoe, Ill.: Free Press, 1951.
———, and Edward Shils, eds. *Toward a General Theory of Action.* Cambridge: Harvard University Press, 1951.
Patterson, Bennett B. *The Forgotten Ninth Amendment.* Indianapolis: Bobbs-Merrill, 1955.
Patterson, Edwin W. *Jurisprudence: Men and Ideas of the Law.* Brooklyn: Foundation Press, 1953.
———. *Law in a Scientific Age.* New York: Columbia University Press, 1963.

Patton, C. W. *The Battle for Municipal Reform*. Washington: American Council on Public Affairs, 1940.
Paul, James C., and Murray L. Schwartz. *Federal Censorship: Obscenity in the Mail*. New York: Free Press, 1961.
Paul VI, Pope. *Humanae Vitae* (On the Regulation of Birth). Washington: U.S. Catholic Conference, 1968.
Peltason, Jack W. *Fifty-eight Lonely Men*. New York: Harcourt, Brace, 1961.
Pennsylvania Catholic Conference. *Betty and Jack Talk about Government Birth Control*. Harrisburg, n.d.
Perry, Ralph B. *Puritanism and Democracy*. New York: Vanguard Press, 1944.
Persons, Stow. *Free Religion: An American Faith*. New Haven: Yale University Press, 1947.
Pius XI, Pope. *Casti Connubi* (On Christian Marriage). New York: Paulist Press, 1941.
Planned Parenthood Association, Chicago Area. *Chronological History of the Birth Control Controversy in Chicago*, Chicago, 1964.
Planned Parenthood Federation of America–World Population Emergency Campaign. *Birth Control and Public Policy*. New York, 1962.
Planned Parenthood League of Connecticut, Inc. *History of Planned Parenthood League of Connecticut, Inc.: Legislation and Legal Action*. New Haven, n.d.
Planned Parenthood League of Massachusetts. *Birth Control and the Massachusetts Law*. Boston, 1959.
Planned Parenthood–World Population. *Five Million Women*. New York, 1969.
———. *Just Delete Six Words and a Comma....* New York, 1965.
———. *Laws Relating to Birth Control and Family Planning in the U.S.* New York, 1968.
———. *The Morality of Birth Control: What the Major Faiths Say*. New York, 1965.
———. *The Poverty of Abundance*. New York, 1966.
———. *When More Is Less*. New York, 1968.
Pound, Roscoe. *Contemporary Juristic Thinking*. Claremont, Calif.: Pomona, Scripps and Claremont colleges, 1940.
———. *Interpretations of Legal History*. London: Macmillan, 1923.
———. *An Introduction to the Philosophy of Law*. New Haven: Yale University Press, 1954.
———. *New Paths of the Law*. Lincoln: University of Nebraska Press, 1950.
———. *Social Control through Law*. New Haven: Yale University Press, 1942.
———. *The Task of Law*. Lancaster, Pa.: Franklin and Marshall College, 1944.
Powell, Aaron M., ed. *The National Purity Congress*. New York: American Purity Alliance, 1896.
President's Committee on Population and Family Planning. *Population and Family Planning: The Transition from Concern to Action*. Washington, 1968.

Pritchett, C. Herman. *Congress versus the Supreme Court, 1957–1960.* Minneapolis: University of Minnesota Press, 1961.
Radcliffe, Lord. *The Law and Its Compass.* Evanston: Northwestern University Press, 1960.
Regler, C. C. *The Era of the Muckrakers.* Chapel Hill: University of North Carolina Press, 1932.
Rembaugh, Bertha A. *The Political Status of Women in the United States.* New York: Putnam's, 1911.
Riis, Jacob A. *The Battle with the Slum.* New York: Macmillan, 1902.
———. *The Children of the Poor.* New York: Scribner's, 1892.
———. *How the Other Half Lives.* New York: Scribner's, 1932.
Robinson, Caroline H. *Seventy Birth Control Clinics.* Baltimore: Williams and Wilkins, 1930.
Robinson, William J. *Fewer and Better Babies; or The Limitation of Offspring by the Prevention of Conception.* 11th ed. New York: Robinson, 1915.
Rosenblum, Victor G. *Law as a Political Instrument.* New York: Random House, 1955.
Ross, E. A. *Sin and Society.* Boston: Houghton Mifflin, 1907.
Rossiter, Clinton. *Parties and Politics in America.* New York: New American Library, 1960.
St. John–Stevas, Norman. *Birth Control and Public Policy.* Washington: Family Life Bureau, NCWC, 1964.
———. *Life, Death and the Law.* Bloomington: Indiana University Press, 1961.
———. *Obscenity and the Law.* London: Secker and Warburg, 1956.
Sanger, Margaret. *An Autobiography.* New York: W. W. Norton, 1938.
———. *Birth Control: The Proceedings of the First American Birth Control Conference, New York, Nov. 11, 12, 1921.* New York: Birth Control Review, 1921.
———. *My Fight for Birth Control.* New York: Farrar and Rinehart, 1931.
———. *Women and the New Race.* New York: Brentano's, 1920.
Schlesinger, Arthur M. *The Rise of Modern America, 1865–1951.* 4th ed. New York: Macmillan, 1951.
———. *The Rise of the City, 1878–1898.* New York: Macmillan, 1933.
Schubert, Glendon. *Judicial Policy-Making.* Chicago: Scott, Foresman, 1965.
———. *Quantitative Analysis of Judicial Behavior.* New York: Free Press, 1960.
———, ed. *Constitutional Politics: The Political Behavior of Supreme Court Justices and the Constitutional Policies That They Make.* New York: Holt, Rinehart and Winston, 1960.
———, ed. *Judicial Behavior.* Chicago: Rand McNally, 1964.
Schwartz, Richard, and Jerome Skolnick, eds. *Society and the Legal Order.* New York: Basic Books, 1970.
Seitz, Don C. *The Dreadful Decade, 1869–1879.* Indianapolis: Bobbs-Merrill, 1926.

Shapiro, Martin. *Freedom of Speech: The Supreme Court and Judicial Review.* Englewood Cliffs: Prentice-Hall, 1966.
Sheppard, Harold L. *Effects of Family Planning on Poverty in the United States.* Kalamazoo: W. E. Upjohn Institute for Employment Research, 1967.
Sigler, Jay A. *An Introduction to the Legal System.* Homewood, Ill.: Dorsey Press, 1968.
Smith, G. B., ed. *Religious Thought in the Last Quarter Century.* Chicago: University of Chicago Press, 1927.
Spahr, C. B. *The Present Distribution of Wealth in the United States.* New York: Crowell, 1896.
Stanton, Elizabeth C., et al. *History of Woman Suffrage.* 6 vols. New York: Fowler and Wells, 1881–1922.
Stephen, James Fitzjames. *Liberty, Equality, Fraternity.* London: Smith, Elder, 1873.
Suenans, Leon J. *Love and Control.* Westminster, Md.: Newman Press, 1961.
Sulloway, Alvah. *Birth Control and Catholic Doctrine.* Boston: Beacon Press, 1959.
Tarbell, Ida M. *The History of the Standard Oil Company.* 2 vols. New York: McClure, Phillips, 1904.
Truman, David. *The Governmental Process.* New York: Knopf, 1951.
Turner, Julius. *Party and Constituency: Pressures on Congress.* Baltimore: Johns Hopkins Press, 1941.
Ussher, R. *Neo-Malthusianism: An Enquiry into That System with Regard to Its Economy and Morality.* London: Gibbings, 1898.
Vines, Kenneth N., and Herbert Jacob. *Studies on Judicial Politics.* New Orleans: Tulane University Studies in Political Science, 1962.
Vose, Clement. *Caucasians Only: The Supreme Court, the NAACP, and the Restrictive Covenant Cases.* Berkeley: University of California Press, 1959.
Wahlke, John C., and Heinz Eulau, eds. *Legislative Behavior.* New York: Free Press, 1959.
——— et al. *The Legislative System.* New York: Wiley, 1962.
Wallas, Graham. *The Life of Frances Place.* London: Longman, 1898.
Warren, Sidney. *American Freethought, 1860–1914.* New York: Columbia University Press, 1943.
Wasby, Stephen L. *The Impact of the United States Supreme Court: Some Perspectives.* Homewood, Ill.: Dorsey Press, 1970.
Wasserstrom, Richard. *The Judicial Decision.* Stanford: Stanford University Press, 1961.
Westin, Alan F. *Privacy and Freedom.* New York: Atheneum, 1967.
Weyl, W. E. *The New Democracy.* New York: Macmillan, 1912.
Whelpton, P. K., A. A. Campbell, and J. E. Patterson. *Fertility and Family Planning in the United States.* Princeton: Princeton University Press, 1966.
White, Andrew D. *A History of the Warfare of Science with Theology.* New York: Appleton, 1941.
Wilson, Jeanie L. *The Legal and Political Status of Women in the United States.* Cedar Rapids: Torch Press, 1912.

Bibliography : 345

The Works of Robert G. Ingersoll, vol. XII. New York: Dresden, 1908.
Young, Louise B., ed. *Population in Perspective*. New York: Oxford University Press, 1968.
Zink, H. *City Bosses in the United States*. Durham: Duke University Press, 1930.

ARTICLES AND PERIODICALS

"Abortion Laws, under Challenge, Are Being Liberalized," *Congressional Quarterly*, July 24, 1970, pp. 1913-16.
"Ahead: Acid Test of a Law," *Connecticut Life*, July 27, 1961, pp. 8-10.
Alfange, Dean, Jr. "Free Speech and Symbolic Conduct: The Draft-Card Burning Case," *Supreme Court Review: 1968*, ed. Philip Kurland (Chicago: University of Chicago Press, 1968), 1-52.
American Medical Association, Committee on Human Reproduction, "The Control of Fertility," *Journal of the American Medical Association*, CXCIV (Oct. 25, 1965), 462-70.
Anderson, V., et al. "The Medical, Social, and Educational Implications of the Increase of Out-of-Wedlock Births," *American Journal of Public Health*, LVI (Nov., 1966), 1866-73.
Annotation, "The Supreme Court and the Right of Free Speech and Press," 21 L.Ed.2d 976 (1969).
"Anti-Pollution Funds Are Short, Time Lags Are Long," *Congressional Quarterly*, May 23, 1969, pp. 817-22.
Anton, Thomas J. "The Legislature, Politics and Public Policy: 1959," *Rutgers Law Review*, XIV (Winter, 1960), 269-89.
Auerbach, Carl A. "Law and Social Change in the United States," *University of California at Los Angeles Law Review*, VI (July, 1959), 516-32.
Ball, William B. "Government Birth Control: Reply to George M. Sirilla, S.J.," *Catholic Lawyer*, XII (Summer, 1966), 216-24.
Balter, Harry G. "Some Observations Concerning the Federal Obscenity Statutes," *Southern California Law Review*, VIII (June, 1935), 267-87.
Beany, William M. "The Constitutional Right to Privacy in the Supreme Court," *Supreme Court Review*, ed. Philip Kurland (Chicago: University of Chicago Press, 1962), 212-51.
Berelson, Bernard. "Beyond Family Planning," *Science*, CLXIII (Feb. 7, 1969), 533-43.
Bickel, Alexander M. "Forward: The Passive Virtues," *Harvard Law Review*, LXXV (Nov., 1961), 60.
Birth Control Federation of America, "Birth Control Education in Public Health Services Favored," *Information Service*, Apr., 1940, p. 3.
"Bitter Pill," *Greater Philadelphia Magazine*, Sept., 1966 (PP-WP reprint).
Blackshield, Anthony R. "Constitutionalism and Comstockery," *Kansas Law Review*, XIV (Mar., 1966), 403-52.
Blake, Judith. "Population Policy for Americans: Is the Government Misled?," *Science*, CLXIV (May 2, 1969), 522-29.

Blossom, Frederick A. "Growth of the Birth Control Movement in the U.S.," *Birth Control Review,* I (Mar., 1917), 4.
Bloustein, Edward J. "Privacy as an Aspect of Human Dignity: An Answer to Dean Prosser," *New York University Law Review,* XXXIX (Dec., 1964), 962–1007.
Botein, Bernard. "The Future of the Judicial Process: Challenge and Response," *The Record of the Association of the Bar of the City of New York,* XV (Apr., 1960), 152–73.
Brandeis, Louis, and Simon Warren. "The Right to Privacy," *Harvard Law Review,* IV (Dec., 1890), 193–220.
"Brief Submitted in Behalf of Paul D. Cravath and Others," *Birth Control Review,* VI (Apr., 1922), 54–55.
Brimhall, D. R., and A. D. Otis. "Consistency of Voting of Our Congressmen," *Journal of Applied Psychology,* XXXII (Feb., 1948), 1–14.
Brooks, Carol F. "The Early History of the Anti-Contraceptive Laws in Massachusetts and Connecticut," *American Quarterly,* XVIII (Spring, 1966), 3–23.
Bruno, H. L. "Birth Control Welfare Funds and the Politics of Illinois," *The Reporter,* June 20, 1963, pp. 32–35.
Buckman, Rilma. "Social Engineering: A Study of the Birth Control Movement," *Social Forces,* XXII (May, 1944), 420–28.
Buetel, Frederick K. "Pressure of Organized Interests in Shaping Legislation," *University of Southern California Law Review,* III (Oct., 1929), 10–37.
Campbell, Arthur A. "The Role of Family Planning in the Reduction of Poverty," *Journal of Marriage and the Family,* XXX (May, 1968), 236–45.
Carter, Luther J. "The Population Crisis: Rising Concern at Home," *Science,* CLXVI (Nov. 7, 1969), 722–26.
"The Catholic Church and Birth Control," *U.S. News and World Report,* Aug. 12, 1968, pp. 38–39.
"Catholic Church Moves toward Biggest Crisis in 400 Years," *U.S. News and World Report,* Sept. 30, 1968, pp. 66–67.
Clark, Tom C. "Religion, Morality and Abortion: A Constitutional Appraisal," *Loyola University Law Review,* II (Apr., 1969), 1–11.
Cohen, Felix. "Transcendental Nonsense and the Functional Approach," *Columbia Law Review,* XXXV (June, 1935), 809–49.
Cohen, Julius. "Hearings on a Bill: Legislative Folklore?," *Minnesota Law Review,* XXXVII (Dec., 1952), 34–45.
Commander, Lydia. "Has the Small Family Become an American Ideal?," *Independent,* LVI (Apr. 14, 1904), 836–40.
———. "Why Do Americans Prefer Small Families?," *Independent,* LVII (Oct. 13, 1904), 847–50.
Comment, "Connecticut's Birth Control Law: Reviewing a State Statute under the Fourteenth Amendment," *Yale Law Journal,* LXX (Dec., 1960), 322–34.
Comment, "Constitutional Law—Connecticut Contraceptive Ban v. Right of Privacy," *University of Missouri at Kansas City Law Review,* XXXIV (Winter, 1966), 95–120.

Comment, "Developments in the Law—Equal Protection," *Harvard Law Review*, LXXXII (Mar., 1969), 1067–1192.
Comment, "The History and Future of the Legal Battle over Birth Control," *Cornell Law Quarterly*, XLII (Winter, 1964), 275–303.
Comment, "Legislative Purpose and Federal Constitutional Adjudication," *Harvard Law Review*, LXXXIII (June, 1970), 1887–1903.
Comments, "Constitutional Law: Supreme Court Finds Marital Privacy Immunized from State Intrusion as a Bill of Rights Periphery," *Duke Law Journal*, MCMLXVI (Spring, 1966), 562–77.
Comments, "Privacy after Griswold: Constitutional or Natural Law Rights," *Northwestern University Law Review*, LX (Jan.–Feb., 1966), 828–33.
Comments, "Private Consensual Adult Behavior: The Requirement of Harm to Others in the Enforcement of Morality," *University of California at Los Angeles Law Review*, XIV (Aug., 1967), 581–603.
Comstock, Anthony. "Lotteries and Gambling," *North American Review*, CLIV (Feb., 1892), 217–24.
———. "Pool Rooms and Pool Selling," *North American Review*, CLVII (Nov., 1893), 601–10.
———. "Vampire Literature," *North American Review*, CLIII (Aug., 1891), 160–71.
"Contraceptive Advice and the Massachusetts Law," *New England Journal of Medicine*, Jan. 23, 1930, pp. 187–89.
Crane, Wilder, Jr. "A Caveat on Roll-Call Studies on Party Voting," *Midwest Journal of Political Science*, IV (Aug., 1960), 237–49.
Curtis, Charles P. "A Modern Supreme Court in a Modern World," *Vanderbilt Law Review*, IV (Apr., 1951), 427–45.
Dahl, Robert A. "Decision-Making in a Democracy: The Supreme Court as a National Policy-Maker," *Journal of Public Law*, VI (Fall, 1957), 279–95.
Davis, Kingsley. "Population Policy: Will Current Programs Succeed?," *Science*, CLVIII (Nov. 10, 1967), 730–39.
Denison, Lindsay. "The Rev. Billy Sunday and His War on the Devil," *American Mercury*, LXIV (Sept., 1907), 451–68.
Dennett, Mary Ware. "Legislators, Six-Hour Weeks and Birth Control," *Birth Control Review*, III (Mar., 1919), 4–5.
Dewey, John. "Logical Method and the Law," *Cornell Law Quarterly*, X (Dec., 1924), 17–27.
Dexter, Lewis A. "The Job of the Congressman," *Readings in American Political Behavior*, ed. Raymond E. Folfinger (Englewood Cliffs: Prentice-Hall, 1966), 5–26.
Dickinson, John. "The Problem of the Unprovided Case," *University of Pennsylvania Law Review*, LXXXI (Dec., 1932), 115–29.
Dienes, C. Thomas. "Moral Beliefs and Legal Norms: Perspectives on Birth Control," *St. Louis Law Journal*, XI (Summer, 1967), 536–69.
———. "The Progeny of Comstockery–Birth Control Laws Return to Court," *American University Law Review*, XXI (Sept., 1971), 1–129.
———. "To Feed the Hungry: Judicial Retrenchment in Welfare Adjudication," *California Law Review*, LVIII (May, 1970), 555–627.
Dixon, Robert G. "The Griswold Penumbra: Constitutional Charter for an

Expanded Law of Privacy," *Michigan Law Review*, LXIV (Dec., 1965), 197–218.
"The Doctors and Birth Control," *Birth Control Review*, VII (June, 1923), 144–45.
Dorsey, Joseph L. "Changing Attitudes toward the Massachusetts Birth Control Law," *New England Journal of Medicine*, CCLXXI (Oct. 15, 1964), 823–27.
———. "Massachusetts Liberalizes Birth Control Law," *Dartmouth Medical School Quarterly*, III (Summer, 1966), 8–12.
Douglas, William O. "Stare Decises," *The Record of the Association of the Bar of the City of New York*, IV (May, 1949), 152–79.
Drinan, Robert P. "Catholics, Birth Control and Public Policy," *U.S. Catholic*, XXXI (May, 1965), 6–18.
Dror, Yehezkel. "Law and Social Change," *Tulane Law Review*, XXXIII (June, 1959), 787–802.
Editorial, "Birth Control Martyrs," *Medico-Legal Journal*, XXXIX (Jan.–Feb., 1922), 1–2.
Editorial, "Medical Indications for Contraception: Changing Viewpoints," *Obstetrics and Gynecology*, XXV (Feb., 1965), 285.
Editorial, "New York Physicians and Birth Control," *America*, VI (Jan. 6, 1917), 304–5.
Editorial, "What They Said–the Sanger Trial," *America*, XIII (Sept. 18, 1915), 568.
Egeberg, Roger O. "Defusing the Population Bomb: New Role for Government," *Trial*, Aug.–Sept., 1970, p. 11.
Ely, John H. "Legislative and Administrative Motivation in Constitutional Law," *Yale Law Journal*, LXXIX (June, 1970), 1205–1341.
Emerson, Thomas I. "Nine Justices in Search of a Doctrine," *Michigan Law Review*, LXIV (Dec., 1965), 219–34.
"Evolution and Theology," *Nation*, Jan. 15, 1874, pp. 44–46.
"The Exposure of Vice," *Nation*, Feb. 21, 1907, pp. 169–70.
"Family Planning Services in the U.S.: A National Overview," *Family Planning Perspectives*, I (Oct., 1969), 4–12.
Fenno, Richard R., Jr. "The House Appropriations Committee as a Political System: The Problem of Integration," *American Political Science Review*, LVI (June, 1962), 310–24.
Flemming, Robert B. "Contraception and a Working Public Policy," *The Pharos of Alpha Omega Alpha*, XXVIII (July, 1965), 95–98.
Frank, Jerome. "Words and Music: Some Remarks on Statutory Interpretation," *Columbia Law Review*, XLVII (Dec., 1946), 1259–78.
Frankfurter, Felix. "Some Reflections on the Reading of Statutes," *The Record of the Association of the Bar of the City of New York*, II (June, 1947), 213–37.
Franklin, Mitchell. "The Ninth Amendment as Civil Law Method and Its Implications for Republican Form of Government: Griswold v. Connecticut; South Carolina v. Katzenbach," *Tulane Law Review*, XL (Apr., 1966), 487–522.

Freund, Paul A. "The Supreme Court and Civil Liberties," *Vanderbilt Law Review*, IV (Apr., 1951), 533–54.
Friedman, Lawrence M., and Jack Ladinsky. "Social Change and the Law of Industrial Accidents," *Columbia Law Review*, LXVII (Jan., 1967), 50–82.
Friendly, Henry J. "The Gap in Lawmaking—Judges Who Can't and Legislatures Who Won't," *Columbia Law Review*, LXIII (May, 1963), 787–807.
Garceau, Oliver, and Corrine Silverman. "A Pressure Group and the Pressured," *American Political Science Review*, XLVIII (Sept., 1954), 672–92.
Gelhorn, Walter. "The Legislative and Administrative Response," *Vanderbilt Law Review*, XVII (Dec., 1963), 91–107.
Gibbs, Robert W. "Certiorari: Its Diagnoses and Cure," *Hastings Law Journal*, VI (Nov., 1955), 133–70.
Gilman, Charlotte P. "The Passing of the Home in Great American Cities," *Cosmopolitan*, XXXVIII (Dec., 1904), 137–47.
Goldberg, A. "Perils of the Pill," *Ramparts Magazine*, VII (May, 1969), 45–46.
"Government Seeks Way to Limit Population Growth," *Congressional Quarterly*, June 12, 1970, pp. 1554–58.
Green, Leon. "The Study and Teaching of Tort Law," *Texas Law Review*, XXXIV (Nov., 1956), 7–33.
Greenberg, Jack. "Social Scientists Take the Stand," *Michigan Law Review*, LIX (May, 1956), 953–70.
Greenwalt, Kent. "The Right of Privacy," *The Rights of Americans*, ed. Norman Dorsen (New York: Random House, 1970), 299–325.
Griswold, Erwin N. "The Right to Be Let Alone," *Northwestern University Law Review*, LV (May–June, 1960), 216–26.
Gunther, Gerald. "The Subtle Vices of the 'Passive Virtues'—a Comment on Principle and Expediency in Judicial Review," *Columbia Law Review*, LXIV (Jan., 1964), 1–25.
Gusfield, Joseph R. "Moral Passage: The Symbolic Process in Public Designations of Deviance," *Social Problems*, XV (Fall, 1967), 175–88.
Hanks, Eva H. and John L. "The Right to a Habitable Environment," *The Rights of Americans*, ed. Norman Dorsen (New York: Random House, 1970), 146–71.
Harkavy, Oscar, Frederick S. Jaffe, and Samuel M. Wishik. "Family Planning and Public Policy: Who Is Misleading Whom?," *Science*, CLXV (July 25, 1969), 367–73.
Harper, Fowler V., and Edwin D. Etherington. "Lobbyists before the Court," *University of Pennsylvania Law Review*, CI (June, 1953), 1172–77.
Hauser, Philip M. "The Population of the United States, Retrospect and Prospect," *The Population Dilemma*, ed. Hauser (2nd ed., Englewood Cliffs: Prentice-Hall, 1969), 85–105.
"The Hearings at Hartford," *Birth Control Review*, VII (Mar., 1923), 63–64.
Henkin, Louis. "Forward: On Drawing Lines," *Harvard Law Review*, LXXXII (Nov., 1968), 63–92.
Hill, Adelaide C., and Frederick S. Jaffe. "Negro Fertility and Family Size Preference: Implications for Programming of Health and Social Services,"

The Negro American, ed. Talcott Parsons and Kenneth B. Clark (Boston: Houghton Mifflin, 1966), 205-24.
Himes, Norman E. "Note on the Early History of Contraception in America," *New England Journal of Medicine*, CCV (Aug. 27, 1931), 438-40.
Hopkins, Mary A. "Birth Control and Public Morals," *Harpers*, May 22, 1915, pp. 489-90.
Horack, Frank E., Jr. "The Common Law of Legislation," *Readings in Jurisprudence and Legal Philosophy*, ed. Morris R. and Felix S. Cohen (New York: Prentice-Hall, 1951), 491-96.
Horstman, Peter M. "Problem Areas in the Federal Provision of Family Planning Services," *Clearinghouse Review*, IV (Feb., 1971), 463-64, 483-95.
"How Came 'Comstockery,'" *Literary Digest*, XCIII (Apr. 2, 1927), 32-33.
"The Intimidation of Congress," *Nation*, Feb. 12, 1874, pp. 103-4.
Jack, Cerise C. "The Fight from Coast to Coast, Massachusetts," *Birth Control Review*, II (Apr., 1918), 7.
Jacobi, Abraham. "The Best Means of Combatting Infant Mortality," *Journal of the American Medical Association*, LVIII (June 8, 1912), 1735-44.
Jaffe, Frederick S., and Allan F. Guttmacher. "Family Planning Programs in the United States," *Demography*, V, no. 2 (1968).
Jaffe, Louis L. "Law Making by Private Groups," *Harvard Law Review*, LI (Dec., 1937), 201-53.
Jenkins, Iredell. "Justice and Ideology," *Nomos VI: Justice*, ed. Carl J. Friedrich (New York: Prentice-Hall, 1963), 191-228.
Jewell, Malcolm E. "Party Voting in American State Legislatures," *American Political Science Review*, XLIX (Sept., 1955), 773-79.
Kauper, Paul G. "Penumbras, Peripheries, Emanations, Things Fundamental and Things Forgotten: The *Griswold* Case," *Michigan Law Review*, LXIV (Dec., 1965), 235-58.
Keefe, William J. "Parties, Partisanship, and Public Policy in the Pennsylvania Legislature," *American Political Science Review*, XXXVIII (June, 1954), 450-64.
―――. "Party Government and Lawmaking in the Illinois General Assembly," *Northwestern University Law Review*, XLVII (Mar., 1952), 55-71.
Kelsey, Knowlton H. "The Ninth Amendment of the Federal Constitution," *Indiana Law Journal*, XI (Apr., 1936), 309-23.
Kleegman, S. "Planned Parenthood: Its Influence on Public Health and Family Welfare," *Abortion in America*, ed. H. Rosen (Boston: Beacon Press, 1967), 254-65.
Lasswell, Harold. "The Decision-Process: Seven Categories of Functional Analysis," *Politics and Social Life*, ed. Nelson W. Polsby, Robert A. Dentler, and Paul A. Smith (Boston: Houghton Mifflin, 1963), 93-105.
―――, and Myres McDougall. "Legal Education and Public Policy: Professional Training in the Public Interest," *Yale Law Journal*, LII (Mar., 1943), 203-95.
"Lay Organization," *Catholic Action*, XIV (Jan., 1932), 27-28.
Lees, Hannah. "The Negro Response to Birth Control," *The Reporter*, May 19, 1966, pp. 46-48.

Lenhoff, Arthur. "Extra-Legislational Process of Law—the Place of the Judiciary in Shaping New Law," *Nebraska Law Review*, XXVIII (May, 1949), 542–74.
Lerner, Max. "Constitution and Court as Symbols," *Yale Law Journal*, XLVI (June, 1937), 1290–1319.
Lincoln, Richard. "S. 2108: Capitol Hill Debates the Future of Population and Family Planning," *Family Planning Perspectives*, II (Jan., 1970), 6–12.
Lindblom, Charles E. "The Science of Muddling Through," *Public Administration Review*, XIX (Spring, 1959), 79–88.
Lister, Charles. "The Right to Control the Use of One's Body," *The Rights of Americans*, ed. Norman Dorsen (New York: Random House, 1970), 348–64.
Llewellyn, Karl N. "The Constitution as an Institution," *Columbia Law Review*, XXXIV (Jan., 1934), 1–40.
Loewenberg, Bert J. "Darwinism Comes to America, 1858–1900," *Mississippi Valley Historical Review*, XXVIII (Dec., 1941), 339–68.
McConaughy, John. "Certain Personality Factors of State Legislators in South Carolina," *Introductory Readings in Political Behavior*, ed. S. Sidney Ulmer (Chicago: Rand McNally, 1961), 45–52.
McDonough, Thomas. "Distribution of Contraceptives by the Welfare Department: A Catholic Response," *The Problem of Population: Practical Catholic Applications*, Conference on Population Problems (South Bend: University of Notre Dame Press, 1964), 94–118.
McDougall, Myres S. "Law as a Process of Decision: A Policy-Oriented Approach to Legal Study," *Natural Law Forum*, I, no. 1 (1956), 53–72.
McElroy, William D. "A Special Report on Birth Control," *Johns Hopkins Magazine*, May, 1963, pp. 6, 11.
McKay, Robert B. "The Preference for Freedom," *New York University Law Review*, XXXIV (Nov., 1959), 1182–1227.
McMahon, Charles A. "The Meaning of Catholic Action," *Catholic Action*, XIV (Jan., 1932), 7–8.
McWilliams, William J. "Laws of New York and Birth Control: A Survey," *Birth Control Review*, XIV (Feb., 1930), 46–47, 61–63.
Miles, Rufus E., Jr. "Whose Baby Is the Population Problem," *Population Bulletin*, XVI (Feb., 1970), 3–36.
Mill, John Stuart. "On Liberty," *Essential Works of John Stuart Mill*, ed. Max Lerner (New York: Bantam Books, 1971), 255–360.
Miller, Arthur S., and Ronald F. Howell. "The Myth of Neutrality in Constitutional Adjudication," *University of Chicago Law Review*, XXVII (Summer, 1960), 661–95.
Morton, James F., Jr. "Shall We Have a Limited Birth Control," *Birth Control Review*, III (Oct., 1919), 12–14.
Murphy, Walter F. "Lower Court Checks on Supreme Court Power," *American Political Science Review*, LIII (Dec., 1959), 1017–31.
"N.C.C.M. Active in Fight against Birth Control," *Catholic Action*, XV (Mar., 1933), 27.
"N.C.W.C. Executives Again Protest Passage of Contraceptive Legislation by Congress," *Catholic Action*, XVI (May, 1935), 12.

"New Field for Fanatics," *Nation*, May 14, 1868, p. 386.
Note, "Congressional Reversal of Supreme Court Decision, 1945–1957," *Harvard Law Review*, LXXI (May, 1958), 1324–37.
Note, "Evasion of Supreme Court Mandates in Cases Remanded to State Courts since 1941," *Harvard Law Review*, LXVII (May, 1954), 1251–59.
Note, "Judicial Regulation of Birth Control under Obscenity Laws," *Yale Law Journal*, L (Feb., 1941), 682–89.
Note, "Symbolic Content," *Columbia Law Review*, LXVIII (June, 1968), 1091–1126.
Note, "The Void-for-Vagueness Doctrine in the Supreme Court," *University of Pennsylvania Law Review*, CIX (Nov., 1970), 67–116.
Notes, "Contraceptives and the Law," *University of Chicago Law Review*, VI (Feb., 1939), 260–69.
Notes and Comments, "Connecticut's Birth Control Law: Reviewing a State Statute under the Fourteenth Amendment," *Yale Law Journal*, LXX (Dec., 1960), 322–34.
Notes and Comments, "Constitutional Law—Statutes Regulating Use of Contraceptives," *Boston University Law Review*, XX (June, 1940), 551–54.
O'Brien, John A. "Family Planning in an Exploding Population," *Ave Maria*, Aug. 24, 1963, pp. 5–7.
———. "Let's End the War on Birth Control," *Ave Maria*, Nov. 2, 1963, pp. 5–8.
"Opposition to Birth Control Bills Registered at Congressional Hearings," *Catholic Action*, XVII (June, 1932), 17.
Orshansky, Mollie. "The Shape of Poverty in 1966," *Social Security Bulletin*, Mar., 1968, pp. 3–32.
———. "Who's Who among the Poor: A Demographic View of Poverty," *Social Security Bulletin*, July, 1965, pp. 2, 14–15.
"Our Better Politicians," *Nation*, July 10, 1873, pp. 21–22.
"Past, Present, Future: An Interview with Gary D. London," *Family Planning Perspectives*, I (Oct., 1969), 18–22.
"Pastoral Constitution on the Church in the Modern World," *The Documents of Vatican II*, ed. Walter M. Abbott and Joseph Gallagher (New York: Guild Press, 1966), 249–58.
Peck, Cornelius J. "The Role of Courts and Legislatures in the Reform of Tort Law," *Minnesota Law Review*, XLVIII (Dec., 1963), 265–312.
"The Pill on Trial," *Time*, Jan. 26, 1970, pp. 60–62.
Pilpel, Harriet F. "Birth Control and a New Birth of Freedom," *Ohio State Law Journal*, XXVII (Fall, 1966), 679–90.
Planned Parenthood League of Massachusetts. "Bill H-1401: Before and After the Hearing," *Planned Parenthood News*, Spring, 1965, p. 4.
———. "Massachusetts Tries Again!!," *Planned Parenthood News*, Winter, 1966, p. 1.
———. "The Time Has Come—a Bill Is Filed in Mass.," *Planned Parenthood News*, Winter, 1965, p. 1.
Pollack, Louis H. "Racial Discrimination and Judicial Integrity: A Reply to Professor Wechsler," *University of Pennsylvania Law Review*, CVIII (Nov., 1959), 1–34.

"Pollution: Will Man Succeed in Destroying Himself," *Congressional Quarterly*, Jan. 30, 1970, pp. 279-85.
"Pope's Birth-Control Stand: How U.S. Reacts," *U.S. News and World Report*, Sept. 9, 1968, p. 11.
"Population Activities in the United States," *Population Bulletin*, XXVI (Dec., 1970), 7-25.
Population Council. "United States: Methods of Fertility Control, 1955, 1960 and 1965," *Studies in Family Planning*, no. 17, Feb., 1967.
———. "The United States: The Pill and the Birth Rate, 1960-1965," *Studies in Family Planning*, no. 20, June, 1967.
Porritt, Annie G. "Publicity in the Birth Control Movement," *Birth Control Review*, VII (Apr., 1923), 88-89, 99.
Pound, Roscoe. "A Ministry of Justice," *Harvard Law Review*, XXXV (Dec., 1921), 113-26.
"President Nixon's Message on the Environment," *Congressional Quarterly*, Feb. 13, 1970, pp. 435-40.
Price, Derek J. D. "Diseases of Science," *Readings on Social Change*, ed. Wilbert E. Moore and Robert M. Cook (Englewood Cliffs: Prentice-Hall, 1967), 49-68.
"The Pros and Cons of the Pill," *Time*, May 2, 1969, pp. 58-59.
Recent Criminal Cases, "Contraceptives—Prescription by a Physician as a Health Measure (Connecticut)," *Journal of the American Institute of Criminal Law and Criminology*, XXXI (Sept.-Oct., 1940), 312-14.
Recent Decisions, "Constitutional Law—Connecticut Birth Control Act—Validity Contested by Physician," *St. John's Law Review*, XVII (Apr., 1943), 122-23.
Redlich, Norman. "Are There Certain Rights... Retained by the People?," *New York University Law Review*, XXXVII (Nov., 1962), 787-812.
Reese, Thomas J. "Catholic Charities and Family Welfare," *The Problem of Population: Practical Catholic Applications*, Conference on Population Problems (South Bend: University of Notre Dame Press, 1964), 1-27.
Reich, Charles A. "Mr. Justice Black and the Living Constitution," *Harvard Law Review*, LXXVI (Feb., 1963), 673-754.
Riegel, Robert E. "The American Father of Birth Control," *New England Quarterly*, VI (Sept., 1933), 470-90.
Rosenblum, Victor G. "Justiciability and Justice: Elements of Restraint and Indifference," *Catholic University of America Law Review*, XV (May, 1966), 141-55.
Routt, Garland C. "Interpersonal Relationship and the Legislative Process," *Annals*, CXCV (Jan., 1939), 129-36.
Ryder, N. B., and C. F. Westoff. "Relationships among Intended, Expected, Desired and Ideal Family Size: United States, 1965," *Population Resources*, Mar., 1969, pp. 1-7 (available from the Center for Population Research, National Institute of Child Health and Human Development).
Sabine, William T. "Social Vice and National Decay," *The National Purity Congress*, ed. Aaron M. Powell (New York: American Purity Alliance, 1896).

Sanger, Margaret. "Birth Control—Past, Present and Future," *Birth Control Review*, V (June, 1921), 11–13.
———. "Church Control," *Birth Control Review*, V (Dec., 1921), 3–5.
———. "Editorial," *Birth Control Review*, V (Mar., 1921), 3–4.
———. "Editorial Comment," *Birth Control Review*, III (Jan., 1919), 2.
———. "How Shall We Change the Law," *Birth Control Review*, III (July, 1919), 8–9.
———. "Intelligence Tests for Legislators," *Birth Control Review*, VII (May, 1923), 107–8.
———. "Outlines of Legislative Work at Albany," *Birth Control Review*, V (May, 1923), 107–8.
———. "Politicians vs. Birth Control," *Birth Control Review*, V (May, 1921), 3–4.
Schields, C. W. "Does the Bible Contain Scientific Errors?," *Century*, XLV (1892–93), 126–34.
Schubert, Glendon. "Policy without Law: An Extension of the Certiorari Game," *Stanford Law Review*, XIV (Mar., 1962), 284–327.
Sedler, Robert A. "Standing to Assert Constitutional Jus Tertii in the Supreme Court," *Yale Law Journal*, LXXI (Mar., 1962), 599–660.
Selznick, Philip. "Legal Institutions and Social Controls," *Vanderbilt Law Review*, XVII (Dec., 1963), 79–90.
Shils, Edward A. "Resentments and Hostilities of Legislators: Sources, Objects, Consequences," *Legislative Behavior*, ed. John D. Wahlke and Heinz Eulau (New York: Free Press, 1959), 347–54.
Silverman, Corrine. "The Legislator's View of the Legislative Process," *Legislative Behavior*, ed. John D. Wahlke and Heinz Eulau (New York: Free Press, 1959), 298–304.
Sirilla, George M. "Government Policy and Family Planning," *Catholic Lawyer*, XII (Summer, 1966), 203–15.
Smith, Mary. "Birth Control and the Negro Woman," *Ebony*, 1968 (PP-WP reprint).
Snyder, Richard C. "A Decision-Making Approach to the Study of Political Phenomena," *Approaches to the Study of Politics*, ed. Roland Young (Evanston: Northwestern University Press, 1958), 3–38.
Sorokin, Pitirim A. "Reasons for Sociocultural Change and Variably Recurrent Processes," *Readings on Social Change*, ed. Wilbert E. Moore and Robert M. Cook (Englewood Cliffs: Prentice-Hall, 1967), 68–80.
Stone, Abraham, and Harriet F. Pilpel. "The Social and Legal Status of Contraception," *North Carolina Law Review*, XXII (Feb., 1944), 212–25.
Stone, Harlan F. "The Common Law in the United States," *Harvard Law Review*, L (Nov., 1936), 4–26.
Stumpf, Harry. "Congressional Response to Supreme Court Rulings," *Journal of Public Law*, XIV, no. 2 (1965), 377–95.
Sulloway, Alvah. "The Legal and Political Aspects of Population Control in the United States," *Law and Contemporary Problems*, XXV (Summer, 1960), 593–629.
Symposium, "The Griswold Case and the Right of Privacy," *Michigan Law Review*, LXIV (Dec., 1965), 197–288.

Symposium (Stuart S. Nagel, ed.), "Law and Social Change," *American Behavioral Scientist*, XIII (Mar.–April, 1970), 483–593.
Symposium, "Social Science Approaches to the Judicial Process," *Harvard Law Review*, LXXIX (June, 1966), 1551–1628.
Symposium, "What Should Be the Relation of Morals to Law?," *Journal of Public Law*, I (Fall, 1952), 259–322.
Tanenhaus, Joseph, et al. "The Supreme Court's Certiorari Jurisdiction: Cue Theory," *Judicial Decision-Making*, ed. Glendon Schubert (New York: Free Press, 1963), 111–32.
Thayer, James B. "The Origin and Scope of the American Doctrine of Constitutional Law," *Harvard Law Review*, VII (Oct., 1893), 129–56.
Thomas, John. "Problems of the Future; Sterilization, Abortion and Other Issues," *The Problem of Population: Practical Catholic Applications*, Conference on Population Problems (South Bend: University of Notre Dame Press, 1964), 28–61.
Tussman, Joseph, and Jacobus Tenbroek. "The Equal Protection of the Laws," *California Law Review*, XXXVII (Sept., 1949), 341–81.
Von der Ahe, Clyde. "The Unwed Teen-age Mother," *American Journal of Obstetrics and Gynecology*, CIV (May 15, 1969), 279–87.
Wagner, N. "Sexual Behavior of Adolescents," *Postgraduate Medicine*, XLVI (Oct., 1969), 68–71.
"The Way Congress Does Business," *Nation*, Feb. 27, 1873, pp. 145–46.
Wechsler, Herbert. "Toward Neutral Principles of Constitutional Law," *Harvard Law Review*, LXXIII (Nov., 1959), 1–35.
Wells, Richard S., and Joel B. Grossman. "The Concept of Judicial Policy-Making: A Critique," *Journal of Public Law*, XV, no. 2 (1966), 286–310.
"What Is Darwinism?," *Nation*, May 28, 1874, pp. 348–50.
"What the Birth Control Leagues Are Doing," *Birth Control Review*, I (Feb., 1917), 10.
Zimmermann, Gereon. "Contraception and Commotion in Connecticut," *Look*, Jan. 30, 1962, pp. 78–83c.

PUBLIC DOCUMENTS

Connecticut. *Journal of the House*. Hartford, 1879, 1941.
———. *Journal of the Senate*. Hartford, 1879, 1941.
———. *Public Acts Passed by the General Assembly of the State of Connecticut*. Hartford, 1879.
———. *Register and Manual*. Hartford, 1941.
Great Britain. *Hansard's Parliamentary Debates*, vols. CXLV–CXLIX.
Massachusetts. *Journal of the House*. Boston, 1879, 1941, 1948, 1965, 1966.
———. *Journal of the Senate*. Boston, 1879, 1941, 1948, 1966.
———. *Manual of the General Court*. Boston, 1941, 1948, 1965, 1966.
New York. *The New York Red Book, 1965–66*. Albany: Williams Press, 1965.
Pennsylvania, Office of Public Assistance. *Policy of the Department of Public Welfare Concerning Family Planning, Memorandum No. 870*. Dec. 17, 1965.

United Nations. "Statement by Secretary-General U Thant on Population." U.N. Press Release S6/SM/620, Dec. 9, 1966.
U.S. *Congressional Globe.* 42nd Cong., 3rd Sess., 1873.
———. *Congressional Record.* 73rd Cong., 2nd Sess., 1934, vol. LXXVIII, pts. 7, 10.
———. *Economic Report of the President.* 1964.
———. Nixon, President Richard M. "Message on Population Growth," *House Doc. 91–139,* July 21, 1969.
U.S. Bureau of Labor Statistics. "3 Standards of Living for an Urban Family of Four Persons," bull. 1570–5, Mar., 1969.
U.S. Bureau of the Census. *Religious Bodies: 1936.*
———. *Sixteenth Census of the United States: 1940.*
———. *Statistical Abstract of the United States: 1967* and *1970.*
U.S. Congress, House. *Misc. Doc. 243.* 88th Cong., 2nd Sess., 1967.
———, House, Ad Hoc Subcommittee on Urban Growth of the Committee on Banking and Currency. *Hearings on Population Trends.* 91st Cong., 1st Sess., 1969.
———, House, Subcommittee of the Committee on Government Operations. *Hearings on the Effects of Population Growth on Natural Resources and the Environment.* 91st Cong., 1st Sess., 1969.
———, House, Subcommittee of the Judiciary Committee. *Cummins-Vaile Bill, Hearings on H.R. 6542 and S. 2290.* 68th Cong., 1st Sess., 1924.
———, House, Subcommittee on Public Health and Welfare of the Committee on Interstate and Foreign Commerce. *Hearings on Family Planning Services.* 91st Cong., 2nd Sess., 1970.
———, House, Ways and Means Committee. *Hearings on H.R. 11082.* 72nd Cong., 1st Sess., 1932.
———, Senate, Committee on Government Operations. *Hearings on S. 2701 to Establish a Commission on Population Growth and the American Future.* 91st Cong., 1st Sess., 1969.
———, Senate, Small Business Subcommittee on Monopoly of the Committee on Banking and Currency. *Hearings* [on Oral Contraceptives]. 91st Cong., 2nd Sess., 1970.
———, Senate, Subcommittee of the Judiciary Committee. *Hearings on S. 4436, Birth Control.* 72nd Cong., 1st Sess., 1932.
———, Senate, Subcommittee of the Judiciary Committee. *Hearings on S. 1842, Birth Control.* 73rd Cong., 2nd Sess., 1934.
———, Senate, Subcommittee on Employment, Manpower, and Poverty of the Committee on Labor and Public Welfare. *Hearings on Hunger and Malnutrition in America.* 90th Cong., 1st Sess., 1967.
———, Senate, Subcommittee on Employment, Manpower, and Poverty of the Committee on Labor and Public Welfare. *Hearings on S. 2993, Family Planning Program.* 89th Cong., 2nd Sess., 1966.
———, Senate, Subcommittee on Health of the Committee on Labor and Public Welfare. *Hearings on Family Planning and Population Research, 1970.* 91st Cong., 1st Sess., 1970.
———, Senate, Subcommittee on Foreign Aid Expenditures of the Committee on Government Operations. *Hearings on S. 1676, Population Crisis.*

89th Cong., 1st Sess., 1965, 2nd Sess., 1966; 90th Cong., 1st Sess., 1967.
U.S. Department of Agriculture. *Household Food Consumption Survey, 1955 and 1965, Food Consumption of Households in the United States.* Rpt. 1.
U.S. Department of Health, Education and Welfare. *Report on Family Planning.* Sept., 1966.
―――. *The Role of Public Welfare in Family Planning.* N.d.
U.S. Office of Economic Opportunity. *Community Action for Health: Family Planning.* Oct., 1967.
―――. *Conference Report on Family Planning.* 1969.
―――. *Family Planning Program Fact Sheet.* N.d.
―――. *Need for Subsidized Family Planning Services: United States, Each State and County, 1968* (prepared by PP–WP, Center for Family Planning Program Development).
―――. *The Office of Economic Opportunity Family Planning Program.* Oct. 6, 1969.

ADDRESSES, INTERVIEWS, LETTERS

Addresses

R. Browning and L. L. Parks. "Child Bearing Aspirations of Public Health Maternity Patients." American Public Health Association, 1963.
Robert C. Cook. "U.S. Population Prospects." National Conference on Family Planning, Planned Parenthood–World Population, May 5–6, 1966.
Dexter L. Hanley, S.J. Family Law Section, American Bar Association, Aug. 9, 1965.
―――. "Religious and Political Values in Population Policies." National Conference on Family Planning, Planned Parenthood–World Population, May 6, 1966.
Arnold H. Maremont. "Birth Control and Public Responsibility." Planned Parenthood–World Population, Oct. 16, 1963.
Representative William H. Robinson. Planned Parenthood Conference, Minneapolis, May 16, 1961 (from the files of the Planned Parenthood Association, Chicago Area).

Interviews

Mrs. Carita Bersohn, consultant for Public Programs, Planned Parenthood–World Population. New York, May 15, 1967.
Representative George Bush. Houston, May 22, 1970.
Dr. Lee Buxton. New Haven, May 23, 1967.
Mrs. Lorraine Campbell, former president of the Planned Parenthood League of Massachusetts. Cambridge, May 24, 1967.
Representative Paul J. Cavenaugh. Boston, May 25, 1967.
Joseph Clark, prosecutor. New Haven, May 22, 1962.
Edward J. Collins, former legislative coordinator of the Massachusetts Public Health Association. Chicago, Apr. 7, 1967.

Joseph Cooney, legal representative of the Archdiocese of Hartford. Hartford, May 24, 1967.
Municipal Judge Joseph Corso, former chairman of the New York State Assembly Codes Committee. Brooklyn, May 17, 1967.
Dr. Joseph L. Dorsey. New Haven, May 22, 1967.
Thomas Duffy, former chairman of the New York State Senate Codes Committee. Queens, May 17, 1967.
Representative Paul Elward. Chicago, Mar., 1963.
Thomas I. Emerson, Yale law faculty. New Haven, May 23, 1967.
Frederick Jaffe, vice-president of Planned Parenthood–World Population. New York, May 15, 1967.
Representative Kathrine Kane. Boston, May 25, 1967.
Gordon Kerr, legislative assistant to Representative Scheuer. Feb. 15, 1971 (telephone).
Jerome Koenig, legislative assistant to Representative Scheuer. May 19, 1970 (telephone).
Representative Theodore Mann. Boston, May 25, 1967.
Representative Donald Manning. Boston, May 25, 1967.
Julius Martz, former chief prosecutor. New Haven, May 23, 1967.
Dr. Lonnie Meyers, former chairman of Citizens for the Extension of Birth Control Services. Chicago, Feb., 1967.
Miss Catherine G. Roraback, attorney. New Haven, May 2, 1967.
Mrs. Maurice Sagoff, president of Planned Parenthood League of Massachusetts. Boston, May 25, 1967.
Mrs. Mary Jane Snyder, coordinator of Public Relations, Planned Parenthood Association, Chicago Area. Chicago, Feb. 20, 1967.
Charles Tobin, representative of the New York State Catholic Welfare Committee. Albany, May 19, 1967.
Mrs. Nancy Wechsler, attorney. New York, May 17, 1967.

Letters

Representative Joseph E. Brett to Mr. and Mrs. Harry A. Sweetes, Aug. 10, 1965 (from the files of PPLM).
Harriet F. Pilpel to Frederick Jaffe, Nov. 9, 1964 (from the files of PP–WP).
Beekman H. Pool, director of the Legislative Information Service, State Communities Aid Association, to the author, July 18, 1967.
Representative James H. Scheuer to the author, Jan. 30, 1967.
Senator Joseph D. Tydings to the author, Apr. 22, 1970.

SELECTED NEWSPAPER ARTICLES; UNPUBLISHED AND MISCELLANEOUS MATERIALS

"Abstract of Mr. Ernst's Remarks," Oct. 19, 1938, p. 2 (from the files of PPLM).
"Albany Kills Bill to Repeal Law against Birth Control," *New York Times*, May 6, 1965, p. 1, col. 2.
"Annual Meeting of Society for the Suppression of Vice," *New York Herald Tribune*, Jan. 28, 1876, p. 5, col. 4.

"Anthony Comstock's Work," *New York Times*, Jan. 19, 1887, p. 8, col. 4.
"Anti-Criminal Societies," *New York Times*, Jan. 30, 1881, p. 6, col. 4.
"Birth Control Aid Assailed Up State," *New York Times*, Feb. 27, 1965, p. 26, col. 5.
"Birth Control Law Opponents Dominate Hearing," *Hartford Times*, Apr. 21, 1963.
Birth Control League of Connecticut. "An Analysis of the Vote in the House of Representatives, May 20, 1941," May 24, 1941.
"Birth Control Plan Set Up for State's Relief Recipients," *Evening Bulletin*, Dec., 17, 1965, p. 1.
"Birth Control under Fire in 24th Assembly Repeal Try," *New Haven Register*, Apr. 12, 1963.
Brief for Appellant, United States v. One Package, 86 F.2d 737 (2d Cir. 1936).
Brief for Appellants, Griswold v. Connecticut, 381 U.S. 479 (1965).
Brief for Appellants, Poe v. Ullman, 367 U.S. 497 (1960).
Brief for Appellants, State v. Nelson, 126 Conn. 412, 11 A.2d 856 (1940).
Brief for Appellants in Support of Motion for Stay of Proceedings, People v. Sanger, 222 N.Y. 193, 118 N.E. 637 (1918).
Brief for Appellee, Griswold v. Connecticut, 381 U.S. 479 (1965).
Brief for Commonwealth, Commonwealth v. Baird, 247 N.E.2d 574 (1969).
Brief for Defendant, Commonwealth v. Baird, 247 N.E.2d 574 (1969).
Brief for Defendant, Commonwealth v. Corbett, 307 Mass. 7, 29 N.E.2d 151 (1940).
Brief for Defendants, Commonwealth v. Gardner, 300 Mass. 372, 15 N.E.2d 222 (1938).
Brief for Defendants–Appellants, State v. Griswold, 200 A.2d 479 (1964).
Brief for State-Appellee, State v. Griswold, 151 Conn. 544, 200 A.2d 479 (1964).
Brief for Massachusetts Civil Liberties Union as Amicus Curiae, Commonwealth v. Baird, 242 N.E.2d 574 (1969).
Brief for the Planned Parenthood Federation of America, Inc., as Amicus Curiae, Griswold v. Connecticut, 381 U.S. 479 (1965).
Brown, Gordon E., executive director of the State Charter Aid Association. "Report on Meeting with Mayor Wagner, Concerning Repeal of Sections 1142 and 1145 of the Penal Law," May 3, 1965 (from the files of the State Communities Aid Association, formerly State Charities Aid Association).
Bureau of Social Science Research, Inc. *Living Costs and Welfare Payments*. Washington, 1969.
Canons of Judicial Ethics 2 and 14.
Casey, Rt. Rev. George W. "Implications of the Death of the Massachusetts Birth Control Bill," *Boston Sunday Herald*, Aug. 8, 1965, sec. 4, p. 3.
"Catholics Urged to Oppose Birth Control Referendum," *Stanford-Times*, Nov. 2, 1942.
Comstock, Anthony. "The Reign of Vice," *New York Times*, July 16, 1873, p. 4, col. 6.
Cowan, F. C. "Memorandum Concerning the Case of Commonwealth v. Allison," Mar. 14, 1950, p. 4 (from the files of PPLM).

Editorial, "Our 1881 Legislature in 1965," *New York Times*, May 11, 1965, p. 38, col. 1.

Editorial, "The Prelate's Accusation," *New York Times*, Nov. 17, 1966, p. 46, col. 1.

"Editorial on Anthony Comstock," *New York Herald Tribune*, June 24, 1878, p. 4, col. 3.

"House Unit Backs Ban on Birth Control," *Philadelphia Inquirer*, May 24, 1966.

Howard, Stephen D. "The Birth Control Law Conflict in Massachusetts." Unpublished B.A. thesis, Harvard College, 1959 (from the files of PPLM).

Kilborn, Peter W. "Birth Control Statutes: Constitutionality and Other Aspects." Unpublished manuscript, 1960 (from the files of PPLM).

Knowlton, Charles. Letter in *Boston Investigator*, Sept. 25, 1835, p. 1, cols. 2, 3.

"Krol Says Birth Control Is Not State's Business," *Evening Bulletin*, Dec. 17, 1965, p. 1.

"Legislature Voids Birth Control Ban in Effect 84 Years," *New York Times*, June 17, 1965, p. 1, col. 4.

"Letters in Rebuttal," *New York Herald Tribune*, June 29, 1878, p. 2, col. 2; July 13, 1878, p. 2, col. 3.

Littlewood, Thomas B. "The Politics of Birth Control." Unpublished mimeo, Eagleton Institute Case Studies Program, 1965.

McGlincy, James. "A New Challenge Is Sounded against Birth Control Law," *Boston Sunday Herald*, Mar. 6, 1966, sec. 4, p. 3.

McHugh, James T. "The Government's Baby Limit," NC Feature, Mar. 9, 1970 (available from the National Catholic Welfare Conference).

Memorandum for Plaintiff, Robinson v. Hackney, Civ. No. 68-4-294 (S.D. Tex., filed Apr. 2, 1968).

"Memorandum from Beekman H. Pool to Messrs. Brown, Ibery, McMahon," Jan. 12, 1965 (from the files of PP-WP).

"Memorandum in Support of Senate Intro. 3980 by Senator Thompson and Senator Metcalf" (from the files of PP-WP).

National Catholic Welfare Conference, Administrative Board. "On the Government and Birth Control," Nov. 14, 1966 (available from the National Catholic Welfare Conference).

"Old Law Imperils Birth Control Aid," *New York Times*, Feb. 21, 1965, p. 1, col. 5.

Paul VI, Pope. "Populorum Progressio" (On the Development of Peoples), *New York Times*, Mar. 27, 1967, p. 34, col. 1 (city ed.).

Pilpel, Harriet F. Testimony before the Commission on Penal Law Revision, Nov. 24, 1964 (from the files of PP-WP).

———, and Nancy Wechsler. "Memorandum of Law on Constitutional Liberties and Publicly Supported Family Planning Programs Presented to the Subcommittee on Foreign Aid Expenditures of the Senate Committee on Government Operations on Behalf of Planned Parenthood–World Population," Mar. 1, 1966.

Planned Parenthood League of Connecticut. "Report of the Legislative Committee," 1957 (from the files of PPLM).

Planned Parenthood League of Massachusetts. "An Evaluation of H. 1401 and the Hearing," Mar. 10, 1965 (from the files of PPLM).
Planned Parenthood–World Population. *Ending Comstockery in America*, I–V, Sept., 1966.
"Preliminary Memorandum of Law re Unconstitutionality of Massachusetts Birth Control Statutes," Oct. 18, 1965 (from the files of PPLM).
"Public Opinion Counts," *World Telegram*, Jan. 4, 1937.
"Public Policy, Birth Control and Freedom of Choice," statement by George N. Lindsey in response to the bishops' declaration, Planned Parenthood–World Population, Nov. 16, 1966.
Record, Griswold v. Connecticut, 381 U.S. 479 (1965).
Rodman, John R. "Trying to Reform the Birth Control Law: A Study in Massachusetts Politics." Unpublished thesis, Government 225, Harvard University, 1955.
"Rosen Defends Aid to Unwed Mothers, Cites Child's Needs," *Philadelphia Inquirer*, June 19, 1966.
Saint, Irene. "How and Why Mass. Birth Control Law Is Likely to Be Amended," *Boston Sunday Herald*, Jan. 31, 1965, p. 5.
"State Bill Gains in Birth Control," *New York Times*, June 15, 1965, p. 32, col. 3.
"State Discloses Birth Control Aid to Unwed Mothers," *Philadelphia Inquirer*, June 9, 1966.
"Statement of the Bishops of the United States in Protest of U.S. Government Programs against the Right to Life" (1969) (available from the National Catholic Welfare Conference).
"A Study Is Urged of Birth Control," *New York Times*, Jan. 24, 1965, p. 55, col 1.
"The Suppression of Vice," *New York Times*, Jan. 1, 1876, p. 2, col. 3.
"The Suppression of Vice," *New York Times*, Jan. 28, 1876, p. 8, col. 3.
Transcript of Hearings before the Joint Committee on Public Health of the Massachusetts Legislature on H. 2035, Apr. 3, 1941 (from the files of PPLM).
Transcript of Hearings before the Joint Committee on Public Health of the Massachusetts Legislature on H. 1748, Apr. 6, 1948 (from the files of PPLM).
Transcript of Proceedings, I, 93, Commonwealth v. Gardner, First District Court of Essex, Salem, Mass., July 20, 1937.
Transcript of the Hearing on House Bill No. 1401 before the Public Health Committee, Boston, Mar. 2, 1965 (from the files of PPLM).
Tydings, Joseph D. "Family Planning: A Basic Human Right," reprint of a speech delivered before the U.S. Senate, May 8, 1969, p. 2.
"Work of the Society for the Suppression of Vice Reviewed by A. Comstock," *New York Times*, Jan. 23, 1884, p. 3, col. 3.

CASES

Ackley v. United States, 200 Fed. 217 (8th Cir. 1912).
Adler v. Board of Education, 342 U.S. 485 (1952).

Aero Spark Plug Co. v. B. G. Corp., 130 F.2d 290 (2d Cir. 1942).
Ashwander v. TVA, 297 U.S. 288 (1936).
Babbitz v. McCann, 310 F. Supp. 293 (E.D. Wis. 1970).
Baretta v. Baretta, 182 Misc. 852, 46 N.Y.S.2d 261 (1944).
Bates v. City of Little Rock, 361 U.S. 516 (1960).
Bates v. United States, 10 Fed. 92 (N.D. Ill. 1881).
Beard v. Alexandria, 341 U.S. 622 (1951).
A Book Named John Cleland's Memoirs of a Woman of Pleasure v. Attorney General, 383 U.S. 413 (1966).
Bouie v. City of Columbia, 378 U.S. 347 (1964).
Bours v. United States, 229 Fed. 960 (7th Cir. 1915).
Bridges v. California, 314 U.S. 252 (1941).
Brown v. Board of Education, 347 U.S. 483 (1954).
Browne v. Louisiana, 383 U.S. 131 (1966).
Buxton v. Ullman, 147 Conn. 48, 156 A.2d 508 (1959).
Cameron v. Johnson, 390 U.S. 611 (1968).
Cheney Bros. v. Doris Silk Corp., 35 F.2d 279 (2d Cir. 1929).
Coleman v. Miller, 307 U.S. 433 (1939).
Commonwealth v. Allison, 227 Mass. 57, 116 N.E. 265 (1917).
Commonwealth v. Baird, 355 Mass. 746, 247 N.E.2d 574 (1969), cert. denied 396 U.S. 1029 (1970).
Commonwealth v. Corbett, 307 Mass. 7, 29 N.E.2d 151 (1940).
Commonwealth v. Gardner, 300 Mass. 372, 15 N.E.2d 222 (1938), appeal dismissed 305 U.S. 559 (1938).
Commonwealth v. Goldberg, 316 Mass. 563, 55 N.E.2d 951 (1944).
Commonwealth v. Holmes, 17 Mass. 336 (1821).
Commonwealth v. Sharpless, 2 S. & R. (Pa.) 91 (1815).
Commonwealth v. Werlinsky, 307 Mass. 608, 29 N.E.2d 150 (1940).
Compton et al. v. State Ballot Law Commission, 311 Mass. 643 (1942).
Connally v. General Constr. Co., 269 U.S. 385 (1926).
Connecticut Mut. Life Ins. Co. v. Moore, 333 U.S. 541 (1948).
Consumers Union of United States v. Walker, 145 F.2d 33 (D.C. Cir. 1944).
Cowgill v. California, 396 U.S. 371 (1970).
Cox v. Louisiana, 379 U.S. 536 (1965).
Dandridge v. Williams, 397 U.S. 471 (1970).
Davis v. United States, 62 F.2d 473 (6th Cir. 1933).
Dillon v. Legg, 69 Cal. Rptr. 72, 441 P.2d 912 (1968).
District of Columbia v. Thompson Co., 346 U.S. 100 (1953).
Doe v. Scott, 321 F. Supp. 1385 (N.D. Ill. 1971).
Dombrowski v. Pfister, 380 U.S. 479 (1965).
Eisenstadt v. Baird, 92 S.Ct. 1029 (1972), aff'g 429 F.2d 1398 (1st Cir. 1970), rev'g 310 F. Supp. 951 (D. Mass. 1970).
Evers v. Dwyer, 358 U.S. 202 (1958).
Ex parte Jackson, 96 U.S. 727 (1877).
Fay Productions v. Graves, 253 App. Div. 475, 3 N.Y.S.2d 573, aff'd 278 N.Y. 498, 15 N.E.2d 435 (1938).
Gardner v. Massachusetts, 305 U.S. 559 (1938).
Giboney v. Empire Storage Co., 366 U.S. 490 (1949).

Bibliography : 363

Gibson v. Florida Legislative Investigation Committee, 372 U.S. 539 (1963).
Gideon v. Wainwright, 372 U.S. 335 (1963).
Goesaert v. Cleary, 335 U.S. 464 (1948).
Graves v. Minnesota, 272 U.S. 425 (1926).
Griswold v. Connecticut, 381 U.S. 479 (1965).
Halstead v. Nelson, 36 Hun. (N.Y.) 147 (1885).
Hipolite Egg Co. v. United States, 220 U.S. 45 (1911).
Hobson v. Hansen, 269 F. Supp. 401 (D.D.C. 1967).
Hoke v. United States, 227 U.S. 308 (1913).
In re Cavitt, 182 Neb. 712, 157 N.W.2d 171 (1968).
International News Services v. Associated Press, 248 U.S. 214 (1918).
Interstate Circuit, Inc. v. Dallas, 390 U.S. 676 (1968).
Jacobson v. Massachusetts, 197 U.S. 11 (1905).
Joint Anti-Fascist Refugee Committee v. McGrath, 341 U.S. 123 (1951).
Katz v. United States, 389 U.S. 347 (1967).
Keyeshian v. Bd. of Regents, 385 U.S. 589 (1967).
Knowles v. State, 3 Day (Conn.) 103 (1808).
Korematsu v. United States, 323 U.S. 214 (1944).
Kotch v. Board of River Port Pilot Commission, 330 U.S. 552 (1947).
Labine v. Vincent, 91 S. Ct. 1017 (1971).
Lambert v. Yellowley, 272 U.S. 581 (1926).
Lanteen Laboratories, Inc. v. Clark, 294 Ill. App. 81, 13 N.E.2d 678 (1938).
Lanza v. New York, 370 U.S. 139 (1962).
Levy v. Louisiana, 391 U.S. 68 (1968).
Lincoln Union v. Northwestern Co., 335 U.S. 525 (1949).
Lindsley v. Natural Carbonic Gas Co., 220 U.S. 61 (1911).
Lottery Case, 188 U.S. 321 (1903).
Loving v. Virginia, 388 U.S. 1 (1966).
McGowan v. Maryland, 366 U.S. 420 (1961).
McLaughlin v. Florida, 379 U.S. 184 (1964).
Martin v. Struthers, 319 U.S. 141 (1943).
Maryland v. Baltimore Radio Show, 338 U.S. 912 (1950).
Message Photo-Play v. Bell, 100 Misc. 267, 167 N.Y.S. 129, rev'd 179 App. Div. 13, 166 N.Y.S. 338 (1917).
Meyer v. Nebraska, 262 U.S. 390 (1923).
Molitor v. Kaneland Community Unit Dist., 18 Ill.2d 11, 163 N.E.2d 89 (1959).
Monroe v. Pape, 365 U.S. 167 (1961).
Morey v. Dowd, 354 U.S. 457 (1957).
NAACP v. Alabama, 357 U.S. 449 (1958).
NAACP v. Button, 371 U.S. 415 (1963).
Nat'l Labor Relations Bd. v. Int'l Longshoremen's Assn., 332 F.2d 992 (4th Cir. 1964).
Near v. Minnesota, 283 U.S. 697 (1931).
New York Times v. Sullivan, 376 U.S. 254 (1964).
Olmstead v. United States, 277 U.S. 438 (1928).
Olsen v. Nebraska, 313 U.S. 236 (1941).
Opinion of the Justices, 309 Mass. 555 (1941).

Osborn v. Bank of the United States, 9 Wheaton 738 (1824).
Pavesich v. New England Life Ins. Co., 122 Ga. 190, 50 S.E. 68 (1905).
People v. Belous, 80 Cal. Rptr. 354, 458 P.2d 194 (1969).
People v. Byrne, 99 Misc. 1, 163 N.Y.S. 682 (1917).
People v. Hagen, 181 App. Div. 153 (1917).
People v. Sanger, 222 N.Y. 193, 118 N.E. 637 (1918), appeal dismissed 251 U.S. 537 (1919).
People v. Sideri (Magistrates Court, 2d District, Manhattan, May 14, 1929, unreported).
Pierce v. Society of Sisters, 268 U.S. 510 (1925).
Pilson v. United States, 249 Fed. 328 (2d Cir. 1918).
Planned Parenthood Committee of Phoenix, Inc. v. Maricopa County, 92 Ariz. 231, 375 P.2d 719 (1962).
Poe v. Ullman, 29 U.S.L.W. 3257–60 (U.S. Mar. 7, 1961) (oral argument).
Poe v. Ullman, 367 U.S. 497 (1961).
Pointer v. Texas, 380 U.S. 400 (1965).
Powell v. Alabama, 287 U.S. 45 (1932).
Powell v. Pennsylvania, 127 U.S. 678 (1888).
Prince v. Massachusetts, 321 U.S. 158 (1964).
Queen v. Hicklin, L.R. 3 Q.B. 360, 11 Cox C.C. 19 (1868).
Queen v. Read, 11 Mod. 142, 88 Eng. Rep. 953 (1708).
Reed v. Reed, 92 S. Ct. 251 (1971).
Reisman v. Monmouth Consolidated Water Co., 9 N.J. 134, 87 A.2d 325 (1952).
Rex v. Curl, 2 Str. 788, 93 Eng. Rep. 849 (1727).
Rochester Tel. Co. v. United States, 307 U.S. 125 (1939).
Roe v. Wade, 314 F. Supp. 1217 (N.D. Tex. 1970).
Rothstein v. Wyman, 303 F. Supp. 339 (S.D. N.Y. 1969).
Rowan v. United States Post Office Department, 90 S. Ct. 1484 (1970).
Shapiro v. Thompson, 394 U.S. 618 (1969).
Shuttlesworth v. City of Birmingham, 394 U.S. 147 (1968).
Skinner v. Oklahoma, 315 U.S. 535 (1942).
Snyder v. Massachusetts, 291 U.S. 97 (1933).
South Carolina State Highway Dep't v. Barnwell Bros., 303 U.S. 177 (1938).
Southern Pacific Co. v. Jensen, 244 U.S. 205 (1917).
Stanley v. Georgia, 394 U.S. 557 (1969).
State v. Arnold, 217 Wis. 340, 258 N.W. 843 (1935).
State v. Baird, 50 N.J. 376, 235 A.2d 673 (1967).
State v. Certain Contraceptive Materials, 126 Conn. 428, 11 A.2d 863 (1940).
State v. Nelson, 126 Conn. 412, 11 A.2d 856 (1940).
Stephans and Co. v. Albers, 81 Colo. 488, 256 Pac. 15 (1927).
Street v. New York, 394 U.S. 576 (1969).
Sturgis v. Attorney General, ——— Mass. ———, 260 N.E.2d 687 (1970).
Thomas v. Collins, 323 U.S. 516 (1945).
Thornhill v. Alabama, 310 U.S. 88 (1940).
Tileston v. Ullman, 129 Conn. 84, 26 A.2d 582 (1942), appeal dismissed 318 U.S. 44 (1943).
Tinker v. Des Moines Community School Dist., 393 U.S. 503 (1969).

Tresca v. United States, 3 F.2d 556 (2d Cir. 1918).
Trubek v. Ullman, 147 Conn. 633, 165 A.2d 158 (1960), appeal dismissed 367 U.S. 907 (1961).
Two Guys from Harrison–Allentown, Inc. v. McGinley, 366 U.S. 582 (1961).
United Pub. Workers v. Mitchell, 330 U.S. 75 (1947).
United States v. Adams, 58 Fed. 674 (D. Ore. 1894).
United States v. Beleval (District Court of Puerto Rico, Jan. 19, 1939, unreported).
United States v. Bott, 24 Fed. Cas. 1204 (no. 14, 626) (S.D. N.Y. 1873).
United States v. Carolene Products Co., 304 U.S. 144 (1938).
United States v. Currey, 206 Fed. 322 (D. Ore. 1913).
United States v. Darby, 312 U.S. 100 (1941).
United States v. Dennett, 39 F.2d 564 (2d Cir. 1930).
United States v. Foote, 25 Fed. Cas. 1140 (no. 15, 128) (S.D. N.Y. 1876).
United States v. H. L. Blake Co., Inc., 189 F. Supp. 930 (W.D. Ark. 1960).
United States v. Himes, 97 F.2d 510 (2d Cir. 1938).
United States v. Kaltmeyer, 16 Fed. 760 (E.D. Mo. 1883).
United States v. Kelly, 26 Fed. Cas. 695 (no. 15,514) (D. Nev. 1876).
United States v. Miller, 367 F.2d 72 (2d Cir. 1966).
United States v. Nickolas, 97 F.2d 510 (2d Cir. 1938).
United States v. O'Brien, 391 U.S. 367 (1968).
United States v. One Book Entitled "Contraception," 51 F.2d 525 (S.D. N.Y. 1931).
United States v. One Obscene Book Entitled "Married Love," 48 F.2d 821 (S.D. N.Y. 1931).
United States v. One Package, 13 F. Supp. 334 (E.D. N.Y. 1936), aff'd 86 F.2d 737 (2d Cir. 1936).
United States v. Popper, 98 Fed. 423 (N.D. Cal. 1899).
United States v. Pupke, 133 Fed. 243 (E.D. Mo. 1900).
United States v. Robel, 389 U.S. 258 (1967).
United States v. Standard Oil Co., 332 U.S. 301 (1947).
United States v. 31 Photographs, 165 F. Supp. 350 (S.D. N.Y. 1957).
United States v. Vuitch, 305 F. Supp. 1032 (D.D.C. 1969), rev'd 91 S. Ct. 1294 (1971).
United States v. Whitehead, 24 Fed. Cas. 1204 (no. 14, 626) (S.D. N.Y. 1873).
United States v. Whittier, 28 Fed. Cas. 591 (no. 16, 688) (E.D. Mo. 1878).
Universal Film Co. v. Bell, 100 Misc. 281, 167 N.Y.S. 124, aff'd 179 App. Div. 928, 166 N.Y.S. 344 (1917).
Vegelahn v. Gutner, 169 Mass. 92 (1896).
Wieman v. Updegraff, 344 U.S. 183 (1952).
West Virginia Bd. of Educ. v. Barnette, 319 U.S. 624 (1943).
Williamson v. Lee Optical Co., 348 U.S. 483 (1955).
Winters v. United States, 201 Fed. 845 (8th Cir. 1912).
Young's Rubber Co. v. C. I. Lee and Co., 45 F.2d 103 (2d Cir. 1930).

Index

Abortion, 235, 240, 258, 300
Abstention, judicial. *See* Judicial behavior—in abstaining from decision
Act for the Suppression of Trade in, and Circulation of Obscene Literature and Articles of Immoral Use of 1873: passage, 26-42; judicial action relating to, 55-66, 79-80, 83, 108-15; legislative action relating to, 68-73, 90-96, 104-8, 188-93. *See also* Comstock laws
Advisory Committee on Population and Family Planning: study of government-supported family planning, 284
Aid to Families with Dependent Children (AFDC), 241, 259, 275, 276
Aldrich, Chief Judge, 235, 237. *See also Eisenstadt v. Baird*
Allison, Van Kech, 97. *See also Commonwealth v. Allison*
American Birth Control League, 90, 104
Amicus brief: in *Commonwealth v. Gardner*, 117; in *Poe v. Ullman*, 153-54; in *Griswold v. Connecticut*, 163-65, 241; in *Eisenstadt v. Baird*, 214-15, 222
Attorney: as policy-maker, 84

Baird, William R., 211-12. *See also Eisenstadt v. Baird*
Baird v. Eisenstadt. See Eisenstadt v. Baird
Baldwin, Raymond, 142
Ball, William, 278
Barnum, Phineas T., 46
Bartlett Commission: and revision of New York Penal Code, 194
Bennett, DeRobigne M., 42, 68, 71
Besant, Annie, 81
Bickel, Alexander M., 160-61
Birth control: linked to obscenity, 21, 25, 37, 109; and poor, 80, 92, 103, 107, 116, 193, 235, 240, 255-59, 264, 284, 286; nature of subject inhibits articulate demands, 92, 95, 150, 265; restrictions as symbol of negative public policy, 107-8; as private moral question, 150, 282; abstinence, 156; and race, 240, 264; opposition to government support for, 269-71; aid to unmarried mothers, 274-80. *See also* Birth rate; Catholic Church; Contraceptives; Family planning; Fertility control; Medical policy; Population; Poverty; Public opinion
Birth-control clinics: in New York, 84; and poor, 103, 116, 193; in Massachusetts, 117; in Connecticut, 137
Birth-control movement: national, 26-27, 40-41, 78-88, 90-96, 104-5, 108-9, 114; in New York, 84-88, 88-96, 194-95; early organizational deficiencies, 89, 104, 131; in Massachusetts, 97-100, 117, 121, 123-24, 131-37, 200-201, 203, 204-5; in Connecticut, 100-102, 137, 140, 142-43, 146-47, 162, 186. *See also* Interest groups; Judicial behavior; Legislative behavior; Sanger, Margaret
Birth rate: influences by socioeconomic class, 255, 257-59; and population growth, 260-61

Black, Justice Hugo, 175, 177–81, 182
Blackmun, Justice Harry A., 248
Bours v. United States, 109
Bradlaugh, Charles, 80–83
Brandeis, Justice Louis D., 229, 230
Brennan, Justice William J., Jr., 175, 229–30, 245–50
Burger, Chief Justice Warren E., 250–52
Bush, George, 190
Butler, General Ben, 71
Buxton, Dr. Lee, 152, 162, 166
Buxton v. Ullman, 152–56

Case of first impression, 12, 22–26
Casti Connubi (On Christian Marriage), 106. See also Catholic Church
Catholic Church: opposition to birth control, 5, 84, 106, 117, 123–35, 137, 186, 195, 202, 268–73, 281–82; as legislative pressure group, 92–93, 106, 127, 130–32, 134, 144–47, 150, 187, 268; early support for Comstock laws, 92–93; National Catholic Welfare Council, 106; changes in Catholic position, 149, 151, 197, 200–201, 206–7, 282–84; opposition to government-supported birth control, 265, 266, 268–84, 292, 297–98
Celler, Emanuel, 190
Center for Population Research, 285, 289
Child Health Act: on family planning, 286
Christianity: nineteenth-century changes in, 77–78
Citizens Advisory Council on the Status of Women, 231
Civil disobedience, 80–83, 84, 89, 108–9, 162, 211–12
Clark, Justice Tom C., 228–29
Cockburn, Lord Chief Justice, 81
Coercion from tax-supported birth control: fears of Catholic bishops, 269–70, 278; sources of, 269–70; prevention of, 270–71; in population control, 299–303
Colgate, Samuel, 71
Collins, Edward J., 204–6
Commission on Population Growth and the American Future, 299–300

Committee of Seven, 68–71, 74
Commonwealth v. Allison, 97–100, 116–19
Commonwealth v. Baird. See *Eisenstadt v. Baird*
Commonwealth v. Corbett, 121–22, 232, 243
Commonwealth v. Gardner, 117–22, 134, 135
Commonwealth v. Sharpless, 21
Comstock, Anthony: Comstockery, 32–35, 37–38, 41–42; and passage of Comstock Act, 34, 37–38, 40, 42, 307; as postal department agent, 40, 50–54; in New York, 43–44; in Massachusetts, 44, 45, 46; in Connecticut, 46; and liberals, 67–73. See also Comstock laws; Society for the Suppression of Vice
Comstock laws: nineteenth-century passage, 26–48; nineteenth-century enforcement, 49–55; effect on medical practice, 53, 54, 58, 79–80, 103; nineteenth-century judicial response, 55–66; nineteenth-century liberal opposition, 68–73; desuetude, 103, 157–58. See also Act for the Suppression of Trade in, and Circulation of Obscene Literature and Articles of Immoral Use of 1873; Comstock, Anthony; Connecticut; Massachusetts; New York
Connecticut birth-control laws: passage, 46–47; legislative action relating to, 100–102, 142–47, 186–87; origins of repeal movement, 100–102; judicial activity relating to, 137–40, 140–42, 152–86
Constitutional decision-making. See Judicial behavior—in constitutional decision-making; see also Due process; Equal protection; Freedom of speech; Police power
Contraceptives: in nineteenth century, 26; alleged dangers of, 38, 148n, 233–34, 235–36, 246–47, 248–49, 251; health interest in, 85, 98, 112, 113, 122–23, 125, 133–34, 138, 183, 230–31, 235–36, 239–

41, 245–46, 246–47, 248–49; modern advances, 148. *See also* Birth control; Family planning
Cooney, Joseph, 144, 147, 187
Corruption, public: in mid-nineteenth century, 29, 30
Crane, Judge, 86–88
Cropsey, Judge, 86–88
Cultural lag, 3–4. *See also* Legal lag
Cummins-Vaile bill, 91–92, 96
Cushing, Richard Cardinal, 149–50, 201, 207

Davis v. United States, 111
Day, Mrs. George H., Sr., 101
Dennett, Mary Ware, 89, 105
Desuetude, 103, 107, 116, 156–57
Dodge, Robert, 124
Donahue, Justice, 122
Dorsey, Joseph L., 200
Douglas, Justice William O.: on standing, 158, 167; approach to due process, 173–74, 175–76, 179; on privacy, 173–74; on vagueness, 225–26; on freedom of speech, 249–50
Draper Committee, 266
DuBridge, Lee, 294
Due process, 118, 214; decisional approaches to, 173–82, 229, 250–51, 252; and right to privacy, 173–82, 228–42, 247, 248–49, 250; sentencing disparities as violation of, 238; and Ninth Amendment, 175–76; statutory vagueness as violation of, 242–45; right to practice medicine, 152, 153, 212, 243. *See also* Equal protection; Judicial behavior—in constitutional decision-making; Police power
Dukakis, Rep. Raymond, 200

Economic Opportunity Act: and family planning, 290–91
Education: effect of Comstock laws on, 53, 89–90; as tool for legal change, 82, 84, 301
Egebert, Robert, 294
Eisenhower, Dwight D., 266
Eisenstadt v. Baird: recommendation for change, 211–14; issues raised in, 214–20, 228–33, 242; state court decision in *Commonwealth v. Baird*, 220–26, 233, 237, 238, 242, 243; federal district court decision in *Baird v. Eisenstadt*, 226–27, 233–34, 237; Court of Appeals decision in *Baird v. Eisenstadt*, 227–28, 234–42, 242–45; Supreme Court decision in, 245–52. *See also* Due process; Equal protection; Freedom of Speech; Vagueness
Ellis, Judge, 140
Entrapment, 50–53, 59–60, 88
Environment. *See* Pollution
Equal protection, 177n, 214; married-unmarried classification, 233, 234–37, 240, 246–48, 249, 250, 251, 252; poverty classifications, 240

Family: institutional changes in, 76–77, 148; desired family size, 76, 257–59, 264, 294, 297–98, 300
Family planning: among poor, 5, 254–60, 264, 286, 290–91, 293; public opinion and use of, 76, 148, 151, 152–53, 257–58, 259–60, 286; medical opinion of, 117, 150, 153–54; psychological considerations, 151, 153; as medical treatment, 152, 153; government support for, 194, 265–68, 284–92, 293–94; and freedom of choice, 258, 264–65, 270, 290; effect of race, 259, 260, 264; cost-benefit advantages of, 259–60; distinguished from fertility or population control, 264–65, 293–94; meaning of, 265; Catholic Church opposes tax-supported, 265–74, 281–82. *See also* Birth control; Catholic Church; Coercion; Contraceptives; Fertility control; Population
Family Planning Services and Population Research Act of 1970, 291–92, 299–300
Federal Council of Churches, 105, 106
Fertility control: distinguished from family planning, 264–65; present status, 293–94, 299–300; toward public acceptance of, 294–95, 298–99, 302; potential threat to personal liberties, 296, 299, 303; nondiscriminatory, 296, 299;

Catholic Church's reaction to, 297–98; alternative policies for promoting, 301–3
Finch, Robert, 294
Foote, Edward Bliss, 58. *See also United States v. Foote*
Fornication laws: and birth-control laws, 236–39, 246
Frankfurter, Justice Felix, 157, 170, 171, 182
Freedom of speech: early challenges to Comstockery based on, 62, 68–73, 215; in *Griswold v. Connecticut*, 164; speech and conduct, 215–20, 221–22, 222–23, 226–27, 249–50; clear and present danger test, 217, 262; balancing test, 217, 218–20, 221–23, 227, 250; vagueness and overbreadth, 222–26, 243–44, 250. *See also* Obscenity
Fruits of philosophy, 22, 81–82

Goldberg, Arthur, 174–76
Griffiths, Martha W., 190
Griswold, Estelle, 162, 166
Griswold v. Connecticut, 162–83; recommendation of legal change, 162; intelligence function in, 163–66, 182–83; state court decision, 165–66; standing and ripeness in, 166–67; Supreme Court decision-making in, 173–83; implications of decision, 183, 188–89, 210, 228–29, 236–37, 242, 244, 246, 248, 251; and legislature, 186, 188–89, 199, 207–9, 210, 246
Gruening, Ernest, 189, 267

Hadley, Rev. Dexter L., 283
Hand, Judge Augustus, 112–13
Hand, Judge Learned, 113
Harkavy Report, 287–88
Harlan, Justice John: on standing and ripeness, 157–58; on due process and privacy, 173, 176, 182; on conduct and freedom of expression, 216, 217
Harper, Fowler, 164
Harrington, Michael, 180
Health, Education and Welfare, Department of, 267, 285, 286; National Center for Family Planning Services, 104, 114, 289; National Institute for Population Research, 285; criticism of family-planning activities of, 287–88; reorganizing family planning in, 288–89, 292; funding, 289–90, 292
Heffron, Edward, 107
Hepburn, Mrs. Thomas, 101
Heywood, Ezra H., 27, 45, 53
Hinman, Judge, 138–39, 239
Hoar, Samuel, 124
Humanae Vitae, 281–82, 297

Illegitimacy, 233, 239–41
Illinois and publicly supported birth control, 274–77, 278, 280
Intelligence function, 8–10, 16–17, 18, 19; in passage of Comstock laws, 35–39; in courts, 54–55, 85–86, 98, 109–12, 117–18, 137–38, 140, 153–54, 163–65, 214; in legislature, 69–72, 91–92, 101–2, 105–6, 124–25, 132–34, 143–44, 187, 189, 201–2, 204–5. *See also* Judicial behavior; Legislative behavior
Interest groups: legislative role of, 7, 33, 39–42, 44–46, 48, 67, 72–73, 89–94, 99, 100, 101, 105–6, 130, 135, 147, 195, 196–97, 201, 203, 204–5, 268–71, 299; and courts, 7–8, 11, 66–67, 114; lobbying, 20, 40, 89; liberal forces, 27, 45, 68–73; anti-vice forces, 32, 33–34, 36, 37, 40–42, 67–68, 73; activity explained by Sanger, 82, 104–5; new pro-change interests, 201; and family planning, 265; and fertility control, 298–99. *See also Amicus* brief; Birth-control movement; Catholic Church
Interstate commerce, 63

Johnson, Lyndon B., 267, 284
Judicial behavior, 7–8, 9–10, 11–12, 14–15, 15–16, 17–18, 63–65, 84–85, 86–87, 112–15; weakness of court as policymaker, 9–10, 85, 119–20, 160–61, 184–85; judicial deference (restraint), 10, 16, 57, 63, 120, 138–39, 177–82, 184–85; communicating need for legislative action, 13, 15, 24, 119–20, 122, 139, 142,

158–59; social impact of, 13–14, 15–16, 18–19, 115, 183; legislative deference to judiciary, 15, 107, 118–19, 165; social influences effecting, 63–64, 113–14, 152, 169, 310; personal values effecting, 64–65, 87–88, 99, 120; fact-finding by, 85
—in cases of first instance, 12, 22–26
—in abstaining from decision, 16, 24, 140–42, 156–62, 166–67, 228, 245–46, 250
—in statutory interpretation, 16–17; purposive approach, 16, 17, 24–25, 57–58, 86–87, 112–15; literalist approach, 16, 55–58, 118–19, 154–55
—in constitutional decision-making, 16, 167–73, 178–80, 181–82, 214–15, 246; legitimization, 60–62, 119, 163, 166, 168
See also Due process; Equal protection; Freedom of speech; Police power
Jurisprudence: social engineering, 19, 304–7; purposive or teleological, 170; mechanistic, 172; of civil rights, 181
Jury, 84

Kane, Kathrine, 205
Kennedy, John F., 266–67
Knowlton, Dr. Charles, 22, 25–26, 38
Konekow, Dr. Antoinette, 99, 100, 117

Lally, Rt. Rev. Msgr. Francis J., 200, 202
Law: as social institution, 19, 304–7; in action and law on books, 49, 103; maintenance function of, 155, 305; creative function of, 155, 156, 305. See also Comstock laws; Desuetude; Judicial behavior; Jurisprudence; Legal system; Legislative behavior
Leen, Henry, 201
Legal change: and social change, 4, 10, 18–19, 20–21, 253–54, 304–10. See also Cultural lag; Legal lag; Social change
Legal lag, 3, 7, 154–55, 307–10. See also Cultural lag
Legal system: description of, 4–19, 48, 305–7, 310; interaction of legislature and judiciary, 13–19, 49, 103, 167, 253–54, 300, 306–7, 309, 310

Legislative behavior, 6–7, 9, 11, 13, 14–15, 17–18, 66, 184–86; effect of interest groups on, 7, 11, 33, 39–42, 44–46, 48, 67, 72–73, 89–94, 99, 100, 101, 105–6, 130, 135, 147, 195, 196–97, 201, 203, 204–5, 268–71, 299; legislative non-action, 9, 17–18, 96, 107, 108, 122–23, 139, 147, 154, 158, 186, 187–88, 267–68, 303; effect of personal values (ideology) on, 11, 42, 48, 93–94, 135, 146–47, 196–98, 203, 206–7; effect of perception of need on, 11, 15, 33, 67, 95, 125–26, 134–35, 192, 198–99, 206–7; effect of constituency on, 11, 127–30, 135, 144–46, 198; effect of societal values and attitudes on, 33, 41–42, 46, 67, 73, 94–95, 142, 298, 310; effect of party affiliation on, 90, 93, 94, 126–27, 135, 144, 147, 202–3, 207; effect of institutional variables on, 95–96, 146, 190–91, 191–92, 204; influence of *Griswold* on revision of Comstock laws, 186, 188–89, 199, 207–9, 210, 246; effect of personal relationships on, 190, 204, 205–6. See also Intelligence function; Interest groups; Legislative hearings; Prescriptive function; Recommendation function
Legislative hearings, 9, 35–36, 71, 91, 101, 105–6, 124–25, 133–34, 143–44, 184, 187, 189, 201–2, 205, 267–68, 287–88; as fact-finding process, 9, 35–36, 38, 91–92, 101, 124–25, 133–34, 143–44, 201–2; other functions of, 9, 36, 71, 144, 186
Legitimacy crisis, 60
Liberalism, 27, 45, 68–73
Llewellyn, Karl N., 168–70
Lobbying. *See* Interest groups
Lord Campbell's Act of 1857, 21

McInery, Judge, 88
McKeon, Msgr. John F., 131
McLuhan, Marshall, 216
Mann, Theodore, 205
Mansfield, Fredrick, 123, 125, 134
Massachusetts birth-control laws: passage, 44–46; origins of movement, 97–100; judicial action relating to, 97–99, 117–21, 121–22, 123–24, 210–52; legis-

lative action relating to, 99, 100, 123–30, 133–35, 136, 200–207; Massachusetts Birth Control League, 117; 1941–42 referendum, 123, 131–32; Massachusetts Mothers' Health Council (MMHC), 123, 124; Medical Society supports birth control, 125; 1948 referendum, 132–33, 135, 137; Planned Parenthood League of Massachusetts, 132, 214; Massachusetts Public Health Association leads 1966 reform effort, 204–5

Medicaid (Title XIX), 286

Medical policy regarding birth control: negative impact of Comstock laws, 53, 54, 58, 103, 120; expanded by judiciary, 86, 87, 108, 109, 110, 112, 113, 114, 115, 188, 193; freer use favored by physicians, 117, 142, 147, 150; considered by legislature, 117, 125, 143; limited by judiciary, 118, 119; services to public, 120; right to practice medicine, 152, 153, 212, 243; related to married and unmarried classification, 210, 243, 246–47. *See also* Contraceptives

Merriam, Representative, 34, 41, 42–43

Mills, Wilbur, 191

Morality: of nineteenth century, 20–22, 26–35; legal support of, 21–22, 41, 52, 53, 59, 60, 153, 186, 197–98, 203, 205, 238; modern changes in morality, 148–49. *See also* Catholic Church; Comstock, Anthony

Moscowitz, Judge Grover, 112

Muckrackers, 75. *See also* Progressive era

National Birth Control League, 89. *See also* Birth-control movement

National Council of Churches of Christ, 149

National Defense Association, 55

National Liberal League, 68–72, 74

New England Free Love League, 45

New York birth-control laws: passage, 43–44; judicial action relating to, 84–88; origins of birth-control movement, 84–88, 88–96; legislative action relating to, 88–90, 93, 96, 193–99

Nixon, Richard M., 285, 291, 295, 299–300

Obscenity: birth control as, 21–22, 25–26, 36–37, 49, 65, 68, 74, 109, 113, 153, 220–21

Office of Economic Opportunity, 267, 285–86, 290–92

Paul VI, Pope, 273–74, 280–81

Pennsylvania: and publicly supported birth control, 277–80

People v. Byrne, 85–86, 87–88, 99, 236

People v. Sanger, 85–87, 88, 89–90, 116, 193

Place, Francis, 26

Planned Parenthood Federation of America, 153–54, 163–64, 194–95, 241–42, 276

Poe v. Ullman, 152–62

Police power, 38, 62–63, 98–99, 117, 119, 120, 121, 163–66, 177, 212, 233, 251. *See also* Contraceptives; Due process; Judicial behavior—in constitutional decision-making

Political parties, 90, 126, 127, 128, 135, 144, 146, 147, 202, 207. *See also* Legislative behavior, effect of party affiliation on

Pollution, 261–65

Population: control of, 5, 265, 293–303; zero growth, 148, 295–96; growth, 254, 260–61, 263–64, 298; concentration in urban areas, 260–61; accommodation policy, 295; danger to personal freedom, 296–97. *See also* Family planning; Fertility control; Pollution

Populorum Progressio, 274, 281

Poverty: access to family-planning services, 80, 92, 107, 116, 193, 235, 239–40, 257–58, 284, 286; extent of, 254–55; fertility rates, 255, 257–58; effects of, 255–57, 293; correlated with race, 259. *See also* Birth control; Equal protection; Family planning

Prescriptive function, 11, 19, 184–86,

284–92, 309; in passage of Comstock laws, 39–42, 44, 45–46, 46–47, 48; in courts, 11–12, 13, 16–17, 55–66, 83–84, 86–88, 98–99, 100, 112–15, 118–20, 121–23, 138–40, 140–42, 154–62, 165–83, 220–28, 233–42, 242–45, 245–52; in legislature, 11, 13, 15, 17–18, 71–73, 92–96, 100, 102–3, 106–8, 125–30, 134–35, 144–47, 187–88, 190, 191–93, 195, 196–99, 202–4, 205–9. *See also* Judicial behavior; Legislative behavior
President's Committee on Population and Family Planning, 290
Privacy, right of: in *Griswold v. Connecticut*, 164, 173–74, 176–77, 181; in *Baird* litigation, 214, 228–31, 247–48, 248–49, 250, 251, 252; and population, 260, 295; threatened by government intervention, 269, 270–72, 277–78, 296, 299
Progressive era, 74–78
Prosecutor, discretion of, 83–84
Public opinion, 84, 104, 113, 117, 121, 151, 265–66
Puritanism, 30–35, 77, 82, 100, 200

Queen v. Hicklin, 98

Race, 240, 259, 264
Reardon, Justice, 212–13, 236–37
Reasonable construction rule, 109, 112–13
Recommendation function, 5–6, 15, 19, 265–68, 309; in legislature, 6–7, 17, 66–71, 88–91, 99, 100, 101, 104–5, 121, 123–24, 132–33, 140, 142–43, 186, 189, 190–91, 193, 195–96, 200, 202, 204; in courts, 7–8, 15–16, 49–55, 82–83, 84–85, 97–98, 99, 108–9, 116–17, 121, 137, 140, 152–53, 162, 211–14; in passage of Comstock laws, 26–35, 43–44, 44–45, 46, 47. *See also* Judicial behavior; Legislative behavior; Test cases
Referendum. *See* Massachusetts
Religion: of nineteenth century, 30–32; changing values, 148–50. *See also* Catholic Church; Christianity; Morality
Responsible parenthood, 280

Restell, Ann Lohman, 50
Robber barons, 28
Roosevelt, Theodore, 72
Roraback, Catherine, 163
Rosenblum, Victor G., 161
Ruggs, Chief Justice, 120

Saltonstall, Leverett, 126
Sanger, Margaret, 5; background, 78–79; philosophy, 79–80, 82–83, 212, 241; prosecuted under Comstock laws, 80, 83–84, 84–88, 150; advocacy of legislative change, 89, 90, 97, 101, 104–6, 114, 308
Sanger, William, 88
Scheuer, James H., 189–91
Smith, Carlos, 46
Social change, 3, 26–32, 74–78, 103, 148–51, 254–65; influence of legal system on, 3, 14–15, 17, 18–19, 33, 49, 53, 66, 67, 81–82, 88–89, 103, 107–8, 115, 171, 253–54, 301–3, 304–7; in birth-control attitudes and practices, 4, 92, 104–5, 116, 118, 132, 142, 148–51, 164–65, 265–66; influences on legal system of, 4, 5–13, 15–16, 17, 18, 19, 22–25, 47, 56–57, 64, 67, 83, 88–89, 103, 107, 113–14, 142, 148–49, 152, 160–61, 165–66, 172–73, 177, 183, 192, 253–54, 266, 277, 304–7, 307–10. *See also* Cultural lag; Legal change; Legal lag
Social Security Act, 286
Society for the Suppression of Vice, 33, 40, 42, 50, 52; New England, 44, 45–46; English, 81
Spiegel, Judge, 223, 242–43
Standing, 152, 166–67, 229, 245–46, 250. *See also* Judicial behavior—in abstaining from decision
Stare decisis, 154–56, 165
State v. Nelson, 137–40, 142, 158
Sterilization, 300
Stewart, Justice Potter, 177–78
Stone, Dr. Hannah, 108–9
Strong, Justice William, 34
Sturgis v. Attorney General, 212, 234–35, 236–37
Swan, Judge Thomas, 110–11

Taft, William H., 75
Test cases, 97–98, 108–9, 132–33, 141, 162, 211–12. *See also* Recommendation function
Thompson-Metcalf bill, 194
Tilston v. Ullman, 140–42, 152, 166
Tinker v. Des Moines Independent Community School Dist., 219–20, 222
Tobin, Charles, 195
Tydings, Joseph, 190, 192, 267, 287, 288

United States v. Foote, 58–61
United States v. O'Brien, 218–19, 227
United States v. One Package, 109–15, 116, 188
United States v. Popper, 62–63

Vagueness and overbreadth, 214, 225–26, 242–45, 247. *See also* Judicial behavior—in constitutional decision-making
Volpe, John, 202, 206
Voluntary Parenthood League, 90. *See also* Birth-control movement

Wagner, Mayor, 195–96
Wallis, Frank B., 133–34
Wechsler, Herbert, 171–72
White, Justice Byron, 177, 179, 248–49, 251
Wilkins, Chief Justice, 221, 233–34
Wilson, Henry, 34
Windham, Senator, 34
The Woman Rebel, 80

YMCA, 33–34, 40, 50
Yarborough, Ralph, 287
Young's Rubber Co. v. C. I. Lee and Co., 110

DATE DUE